OPERATION WRATH OF GOD

In this unprecedented history of intelligence cooperation during the Cold War, Aviva Guttmann uncovers the key role of European intelligence agencies in facilitating Mossad's Operation Wrath of God. She reveals how, in the aftermath of the 1972 Munich Olympics massacre, Palestinians suspected of involvement in terrorism were hunted and killed by Mossad with active European cooperation. Through unique access to unredacted documents in the Club de Berne archive, she shows how a secret coalition of intelligence agencies supplied Mossad with information about Palestinians on a colossal scale and tacitly supported Israeli covert actions on European soil. These agencies helped to anticipate and thwart a number of Palestinian terrorist plots, including some revealed here for the first time. This extraordinary book reconstructs the hidden world of international intelligence, showing how this parallel order enabled state relations to be pursued independently of official foreign policy constraints or public scrutiny.

Dr Aviva Guttmann is a lecturer in strategy and intelligence at Aberystwyth University and author of *The Origins of International Counterterrorism* (2018).

OPERATION WRATH OF GOD

*The Secret History of European Intelligence and
Mossad's Assassination Campaign*

Aviva Guttmann

CAMBRIDGE
UNIVERSITY PRESS

CAMBRIDGE
UNIVERSITY PRESS

Shaftesbury Road, Cambridge CB2 8EA, United Kingdom

One Liberty Plaza, 20th Floor, New York, NY 10006, USA

477 Williamstown Road, Port Melbourne, VIC 3207, Australia

314–321, 3rd Floor, Plot 3, Splendor Forum, Jasola District Centre,
New Delhi – 110025, India

103 Penang Road, #05–06/07, Visioncrest Commercial, Singapore 238467

Cambridge University Press is part of Cambridge University Press & Assessment,
a department of the University of Cambridge.

We share the University's mission to contribute to society through the pursuit of
education, learning and research at the highest international levels of excellence.

www.cambridge.org
Information on this title: www.cambridge.org/9781009503075

DOI: 10.1017/9781009503068

First published 2025

Printed in the United Kingdom by CPI Group Ltd, Croydon CR0 4YY

A catalogue record for this publication is available from the British Library

A Cataloging-in-Publication data record for this book is available from the Library of Congress

ISBN 978-1-009-50307-5 Hardback

To Zenobia and Emrys

Contents

Timeline of Main Events

1969	creation of the Club de Berne
21 February 1970	Würenlingen attack
September 1970	Skyjack Sunday
October 1971	start of Kilowatt intelligence exchanges
8 May 1972	Sabena hijacking
30 May 1972	Lod Tel Aviv Airport massacre
5 August 1972	pipeline attack in Trieste
16 August 1972	aircraft sabotage attempt in Rome
5 September 1972	Munich Olympics massacre
October 1972	first letter bomb campaign
16 October 1972	assassination of Wael Zwaiter
29 October 1972	Lufthansa Kiel hijacking
8 December 1972	assassination of Mahmoud al-Hamshari
28 December 1972	attack against the Israeli embassy in Bangkok
15 January 1973	thwarted attack in Rome using surface-to-air missiles
22 January 1973	assassination of Hussein Abu-Khair
26 January 1973	killing of Baruch Cohen
early February 1973	thwarted attack against the transit camp Schönau near Vienna
mid February 1973	thwarted attack against King Hussein of Jordan
1 March 1973	attack against the Saudi embassy in Khartoum
mid March 1973	thwarted attack against Jordanian or Israeli embassy in Paris
5 April 1973	assassination of Dr Basil al-Kubaisi
9 April 1973	Operation Spring of Youth in Lebanon
11 April 1973	assassination of Zaid Muchassi
27 April 1973	killing of Vittorio Olivares
17 June 1973	assassination of Abdel Hadi Nakaa and Abdel Hamid Shibli

TIMELINE OF MAIN EVENTS

28 June 1973	assassination of Mohamed Boudia
1 July 1973	killing of Colonel Yosef Alon
20 July 1973	JAL404 hijacking over Amsterdam
21 July 1973	assassination of Ahmed Bouchiki
August 1973	second letter bomb campaign

Acronyms

ANYOLP	Arab National Youth Organisation for the Liberation of Palestine
BfV	Bundesamt für Verfassungsschutz
BND	Bundesnachrichtendienst
BOAC	British Overseas Airways Corporation
BuPo	Bundespolizei
BVD	Binnenlandse Veiligheids Dienst
CESID	Centro Superior de Information de la Defensa
CIA	Central Intelligence Agency
DDS	Diplomatic Documents of Switzerland
DFLP	Democratic Front for the Liberation of Palestine
DST	Direction de la Surveillance du Territoire
EC	European Community
ETA	Euskadi Ta Askatasuna
EU	European Union
FBI	Federal Bureau of Investigation
FRG	Federal Republic of Germany
GCHQ	Government Communications Headquarters
GDR	German Democratic Republic
GUPS	General Union of Palestinian Students
IDF	Israeli Defense Forces
INTERPOL	International Criminal Police Organisation
IRA	Irish Republican Army
JRA	Japanese Red Army
KGB	Komitet Gosudarstvennoy Bezopasnosti [Committee for State Security]
MANPADS or MPADS	man-portable air-defence systems
MI5	Military Intelligence, Section 5 [UK domestic counterintelligence]
MI6 or SIS	Military Intelligence, Section 6 [UK foreign counterintelligence] or Secret Intelligence Service

PET	Politiets Efterretningstjeneste
PFLP	Popular Front for the Liberation of Palestine
PFLP-GC	Popular Front for the Liberation of Palestine – General Command
PLO	Palestine Liberation Organisation
RAF	Red Army Faction
Rasd	Fatah intelligence special operations
RG	Renseignements Généraux
RPS/Säk	Rikspolisstyrelsens Säkerhetsavdelning
SFA	Swiss Federal Archives
SISDE	Servizio Informationi e Sicurezza Democratica
SISM	Servizio Informationi e Sicurezza Militare
SREL	Service de Renseignement de l'État
TWA	Trans World Airlines

INTRODUCTION: INTELLIGENCE THAT KILLS

One evening, in the autumn of 1972, a young Palestinian man took a last sip of his drink, left the neighbourhood bar, and walked towards his apartment. His name was Wael Zwaiter and he freelanced as a translator at the Libyan embassy in Rome. He also translated classics and had just finished the Italian translation of *One Thousand and One Nights*.[1] That October night, Mossad, the Israeli foreign intelligence service, decided it would be Zwaiter's last: as he entered the stairway that led up to his apartment, two men with handguns appeared and shot eleven bullets into his body – eleven bullets for the eleven Israeli athletes killed in the Munich Olympics massacre, which had happened just a month earlier.[2]

According to Mossad, Wael Zwaiter not only was a poet and translator, but also actively supported Palestinian terrorism in Europe, including the Munich attack. How did Mossad select Zwaiter as a target, how did they know about his alleged terrorism involvement, and what help did they receive to organise this killing operation? As this book reveals for the first time, it was with the help of European intelligence agencies.

The murder of Wael Zwaiter was the first of ten assassination missions in Europe and the Middle East undertaken by Mossad after the 1972 Munich Olympics attack. This assassination campaign is known today as Operation Wrath of God (Hebrew: מבצע זעם האל *Mivtza Za'am Ha'el*) and is one of Mossad's most spectacular targeted killing operations.[3] The operation consisted of ten missions to kill Palestinians who were directly or loosely associated with Palestinian terrorism. The purpose of this covert action was to avenge past terrorist victims, to disrupt current terrorist plans, and to deter anyone from perpetrating future terrorist actions.

This volume examines the role of European intelligence agencies in Operation Wrath of God and in countering Palestinian terrorist attacks. Its central argument is that European intelligence played a vital role in the organisation and execution of Operation Wrath of God. The book demonstrates this by analysing the intelligence that was shared within a multilateral intelligence liaison.[4] It is shown that intelligence agencies

1

kept each other updated about Palestinian terrorism and thus maintained direct links with one other. This led to a shared mindset among intelligence officers across national boundaries. Officers generally assumed that Palestinians were potential terrorist suspects who needed to be stopped. In doing so, European intelligence agencies helped to prevent Palestinian terrorists from organising attacks, but they also helped Mossad in assassinating terrorist suspects. Altogether, the book thus reveals a covert European struggle against the Palestinians. This active role of European intelligence agencies has until today not been known and will be revealed here for the first time.

This research is innovative because of its perspective of linking a country that carries out a covert action and the one that hosts it. The volume reveals European complicity in a controversial Israeli covert action, explains the methods that Mossad used to organise the operation, and recounts the story as a back-and-forth between Palestinian terrorist actions and intelligence agencies' reactions. It is unique because an intelligence service's sources, methods, and foreign connections are among the most carefully guarded secrets in the world. This book analyses all three based on large-scale documentary evidence.

Israel was able to (ab)use European intelligence through a secret liaison called the Club de Berne. This multilateral liaison was founded in 1969 by eight intelligence agencies from Western European countries and was linked to ten additional European and extra-European partners (including Mossad, Shin Bet, and the FBI).[5] In October 1971, Israel suggested that a separate encrypted communications channel be opened to share warnings and intelligence about Palestinian terrorist activities in Europe. This channel sent cables under the code word 'Kilowatt'. From there developed a fruitful cooperation mechanism.

Kilowatt was used daily by the agencies to track Palestinian organisations and share intelligence about terrorist operational methods, planned attacks, weapon acquisitions, and innovations in terrorist techniques. All agencies provided timely replies to requests, especially when it was believed that a terrorist suspect was in their country. The information on suspects (mostly in Europe) included, for instance, which hotel a Palestinian terrorist suspect had stayed at, what phone numbers they called, flight routes if applicable, address, passport, and anything else of relevance that could be found.

In terms of the historical importance of the Club de Berne, this secret group hosted the first multilateral counterterrorism warning channel.[6] Cooperation continued over decades and has developed into a cross-country near-institutionalised intelligence apparatus.[7] Today, the Club de Berne is the most important informal counterterrorism intelligence channel in Europe and among its partners.[8]

By the time the Israeli government decided to approve Operation Wrath of God, the Club de Berne exchanges had already developed into a widely used counterterrorism intelligence-sharing tool. With the existence of such a mechanism, it was logical for Israel to use it to operationalise Operation Wrath of God. Thus, without prior knowledge or approval, European intelligence agencies had become a central component of the operation. Their intelligence was useful in three main ways.

First, through the Club de Berne, Israel received help from European agencies in identifying the Palestinians responsible for or involved in the planning or execution of the Munich massacre. This was important for Mossad because every killing operation had to be justified to Prime Minister Golda Meir and a Palestinian's involvement in Munich was a clear reason to put someone on the kill list.

Second, Mossad received valuable intelligence on the whereabouts and movement of Palestinian suspects, some of whom had been on Mossad's kill list. European partners helped Mossad locate terrorist suspects, initially without knowing that they were going to be killed. Israel thus received help in the planning and organisation of their killing operations. In other words, the European intelligence agencies helped with the groundwork to trace the alleged terrorists on Israel's death list. The Israelis only enquired about some of the targets, as it would have raised suspicions if Palestinians were killed shortly after Israel informally asked about them.

Third, and most importantly, after every assassination in Europe, the respective intelligence agencies would report to the Club de Berne about the case, share detailed police reports, and regularly provide updates about the ongoing criminal investigations. This provided Mossad with very clear indications as to whether the European authorities had any suspicions that Israel might have been behind the murder.

Two examples are worth mentioning in this respect, which illustrate how this type of intelligence was useful for Israel. First, after the above-mentioned assassination of Wael Zwaiter in Rome on 16 October 1972, the Italian intelligence agency SISDE sent – in good faith – every detail about the killers that they could find. For instance, a witness at the murder scene had been able to write down the licence plate of the car that the killers had used to escape. Italy investigated this car further, found out that it was a rental car, and shared with its Club de Berne partners the alleged name of the driver. This was, of course, the cover name of the Mossad officer who had rented the car for this operation. Mossad thus knew that it needed to be more careful next time when organising the escape of its hit men.

Similarly, as a second example, after the assassination of Mohamed Boudia on 28 June 1973 in Paris, the French intelligence agency, DST, shared the results of its investigation. It informed its partners that the French police believed that the car explosion was an accident during the transport of weapons. In reality it was, of course, Mossad who had placed the explosives in Boudia's car and detonated them remotely.

This kind of intelligence was very helpful for Mossad because they could gauge whether their cover had been blown or where they might have to be more careful with the next killing. The European agencies thus sent very useful information on how to continuously improve Mossad's killing operations in Europe. In short, the murderers were kept updated about the investigations of their own murders.

A central question related to the European role is: how much did European intelligence know about Operation Wrath of God? If they did, at what point did they understand that they were being used for this operation? According to secondary literature and contemporary newspaper articles, some suspicions circulated that Mossad might have been behind the frequent murders of Palestinians. Arab circles already pointed to Mossad as early as the second kill (Mahmoud al-Hamshari), in early December 1972. After the fourth assassination (Basil al-Kubaisi) in April 1973, mainstream newspapers like *Le Monde* strongly suggested that Israeli intelligence was behind it. Nevertheless, Italy and France continued to share intelligence with the Kilowatt group, which included Mossad. These intelligence reports were about Palestinian terrorist activities more generally but also specifically about investigations concerning these murder cases. This means that countries on whose soil the assassinations happened shared intelligence with Mossad despite the rising suspicions that Mossad was the killer.

In July 1973 there was the so-called Lillehammer affair. In Lillehammer, a small Norwegian town, Mossad organised the execution of someone who it thought was a top terrorist. However, the Israeli intelligence agency in fact murdered a completely innocent man, a Moroccan waiter and father-to-be. In an amateurishly executed escape and cover-up attempt, some Mossad officers were caught by the Norwegian police. The subsequent trial exposed Operation Wrath of God and clearly linked Mossad to the assassination operations in France, Italy, Greece, and Cyprus that had occurred over the previous months.

This was the point when France and Italy officially realised the extent of Mossad's killing operation and that the lion's share happened on their territory. This infringed European countries' sovereignty and brought the Middle East conflict right to their doorsteps. It was also a form of intelligence abuse because Club de Berne intelligence exchanges were meant to collectively enhance knowledge about Palestinian terrorists in Europe, not to help kill them. European governments heavily criticised Israel for this covert action, which led to a Euro-Israeli diplomatic crisis.

However, amidst official condemnations and crises, the strong counterterrorism ties between the countries' intelligence communities remained entirely intact. Club de Berne and its counterterrorism intelligence channels continued uninterrupted on a daily basis. In essence, nothing changed in any way on the operational level, neither when rumours about Mossad involvement first appeared nor when European intelligence agencies unmistakably understood that their intelligence had supported Israel's killing operation.

One can thus describe the practice in the Club de Berne as a 'don't ask, don't tell' policy. Even at the height of the Lillehammer scandal, it was 'business as usual' in the intelligence world. Agencies continued to share warnings about Middle Eastern terrorists, reports based on past terrorist attacks, alerts about suspects, and explanations of terrorist groups' operational methods.

The preservation of close Euro-Israeli intelligence ties can be explained through the important benefits that Club de Berne cooperation yielded for all parties involved. European agencies entered this liaison in 1971 with a genuine concern about terrorism. Israeli intelligence also needed European help to counter the threat. The Club de Berne and Kilowatt pre-dated the Munich Olympics attack and the Israeli decision to avenge its victims.

In Israel's view, killing terrorists before they were able to perpetrate an attack was one of many ways to counter the threat. It is thus logical or understandable that Mossad used the already existing framework to obtain information for its operations. From an Israeli perspective, Club de Berne cooperation served as a force multiplier and was essential to successfully combat the terrorist threat. From the European perspective, similarly, cooperation with Israel was essential to thwart terrorist plots in Europe.

The mutual interests of all parties, even the ones who might not have agreed that their intelligence could be used for an assassination campaign, explain why Club de Berne cooperation also continued after the Lillehammer affair. It not only continued over the following decades, but also grew in scope and importance. It is today the most important informal counterterrorism intelligence liaison between Europe and its partners; only the cooperation code word changed from 'Kilowatt' to 'Phoenix' in the 1990s.

5

MOSSAD'S COVERT ACCOMPLICES

When Operation Wrath of God was launched, Mossad was directly connected to seventeen European intelligence agencies through the Club de Berne, a secret coalition of intelligence agencies. They shared information about Palestinians on a colossal scale. Because intelligence cooperation was so beneficial for all the parties, the Europeans let Mossad operate and tolerated the use of its shared intelligence to kill Palestinians. Hence, this volume's overall argument is that the extensive advantages European agencies gained through Club de Berne intelligence-sharing led them to turn a blind eye towards, or tacitly support, Israeli covert actions on their respective territories. In other words, European agencies, and, indirectly, the governments they served, implicitly condoned Israel's covert actions on their territories.

One can push this argument further and speculate that some European agencies even benefited from or agreed with Israel's practice of killing Palestinian terrorist suspects. Or, more provocatively, one can ask whether the Israelis did the 'dirty work' for the Europeans. This remains an open question, but it is clear that Euro-Israeli liaison in the Club de Berne was such an asset for European intelligence that they were willing to ignore any risks, possible downsides, or repercussions of this cooperation. European intelligence that was used for Operation Wrath of God thus highlights an extreme case of intelligence-sharing and shows how far counterterrorism intelligence cooperation could go.

This book consistently shows how Club de Berne intelligence was used for two purposes. First, it helped Mossad organise its killing mission. Second, it collectively enhanced European capacities to counter Palestinian terrorism. The book thus employs a dual focus. First, each chapter analyses a Mossad assassination and the role of European intelligence in conducting it. Second, each chapter recounts Black September attacks and explains how the Club de Berne tried to counter them. Some of the terrorist plots are revealed for the first time. Particularly interesting are the cases where agencies thwarted attacks through cooperation, uncovered new terrorist methods, and collectively increased their knowledge about Palestinian groups.

This demonstrates the centrality of intelligence-sharing to European security. The book highlights the hands-on experiences of intelligence practitioners in the 1970s and shows how intelligence officers managed to establish successful and effective counterterrorism cooperation early in the decade. By the same token, through the intelligence reports the book presents new insights into terrorist practices at the time and terrorism innovation. These include terrorist methods, how Black September and other Palestinian groups were working, and the role of women in terrorist plots.

The book further illustrates the international relations of the secret state – a secret security order that was enabled because intelligence agencies were able to have direct connections with one another. Since intelligence agencies could keep their actions secret, their policies did not have to be justified publicly. This meant that intelligence services did not need to respect the same normative considerations as official foreign policy lines. In this way, Club de Berne cooperation created a covert space where Europeans (even neutral states) could facilitate an Israeli assassination operation. It also created space for state relations to be pursued independently of official foreign policy constraints. This was the case, for instance, between the UK's MI5 and Mossad, both Club de Berne members. These agencies cooperated closely in security matters, even though in the early 1970s the UK had a very critical foreign policy towards Israel. Relatedly, direct communication channels among intelligence officials enabled an additional layer of state diplomacy, one that could follow different rules to official state relations. Through the analysis of intelligence-sharing about Black September terrorism, new aspects of this secret security order become apparent.

The story of Europe's covert struggle against Palestinian terrorism is recounted chronologically 'kill by kill' and 'attack by attack' in three main parts. Part I focuses on the preparation of Operation Wrath of God and how the Europeans were instrumental to it. Part II analyses how Operation Wrath of God was carried out, details how European intelligence contributed to it, and examines how agencies tried to prevent Black September attacks via intelligence cooperation. Part III analyses the continuation of cooperation after Operation Wrath of God was exposed by the Lillehammer affair.

The above-mentioned dual-focus structure allows the story of Operation Wrath of God to be told as back-and-forth actions and reactions between Mossad assassinations, Black September attacks, and the role of European intelligence agencies in relation to both.

Some themes run across the volume, including questions relating to the effectiveness of covert actions, Mossad's logic and rationale for selecting the Palestinians who were killed, terrorism innovation techniques, European leniency towards terrorist offenders, and the day-to-day workings of intelligence practitioners and how they moulded a parallel secret security order.

SECRET RECORDS

This volume uses archival records from the above-mentioned secret intelligence-sharing group called the Club de Berne. The goal of the Club de Berne was to ensure an effective exchange of information and knowledge about terrorism and espionage. When the above-mentioned Kilowatt alerting system was introduced, the intelligence agencies had a direct link to one another and could send information straight from one operative to another. All eight Western European Club de Berne founding members and ten partner agencies participated in the Kilowatt encrypted telex system. In alphabetical order, the countries that were part of the Kilowatt system were Australia, Austria, Belgium, Canada, Denmark, the Federal Republic of Germany (West Germany), France, Ireland, Israel, Italy, Luxemburg, Netherlands, Norway, Spain, Sweden, Switzerland, the United Kingdom, and the United States.

The agencies shared warnings, threat assessments, updates about ongoing police investigations, intelligence about suspects, and detailed insights into the inner workings of terrorist groups. In short, Kilowatt members and their partners shared intelligence if it was deemed timely, relevant, and helpful for another agency to counter the common terrorist threat.[9]

The author was the first historian to obtain completely unredacted access to all cables that were sent under the Club de Berne alerting system from October 1971 onwards.[10] This amounts to more than forty thousand cables that were sent from eighteen different intelligence agencies.[11] The source material for this volume includes the daily correspondence among Kilowatt members before, during, and after Operation Wrath of God (1972–1979).[12] The core of the operation lasted from September 1972 until July 1973 and these dates form the main timeframe of the book.

The policy in this book is to identify a person's name only if they were mentioned in the press, were convicted, have since passed away, were well-known at the time, or are mentioned in publicly available records. Otherwise, their names have been changed or only anonymised initials are given. All intelligence reports, warnings, and assessments are compared with what we currently know about the Operation Wrath of God assassinations and Palestinian terrorism through journalistic accounts and secondary literature. This provides important context to the book's storyline. Furthermore, use of the term 'terrorism' or 'terrorist' is not a moral or political judgement but refers to the strategy employed by the Palestinian armed groups at this time.

Despite its importance, or precisely because of it, to this day the Club de Berne remains an extremely secretive liaison and very little is known about its operations. It is very rare for researchers to obtain access to the documentary evidence of a multilateral intelligence liaison, especially where one can see exactly what was shared by which agency.

Through the uniqueness of the source base, the rare insights into the operational work of intelligence agencies, and the novel questions that it raises about the international relations of the secret state, this volume makes a significant contribution to existing scholarship.

NEW REVELATIONS

This book embarks on entirely new research territory as it is the first study of a Mossad covert operation based on documentary evidence. Furthermore, there are at present very few publications that look at covert action and intelligence cooperation.[13] The source body for this book is exceptional as it reveals intelligence agencies' methods and interactions among a secret group of partner services. By using currently available publications about every aspect of Operation Wrath of God in conjunction with more than forty thousand intelligence records from eighteen agencies, this book offers the most authoritative account of this covert action to date.

The first accounts of the operation, published in 1976 and 1984, focused on its spectacular nature and included the stories of how the individuals were killed by Mossad's assassination teams.[14] In 1993, Operation Wrath of God was acknowledged for the first time by a former Israeli intelligence official. In a BBC interview on 23 November 1993, General Aharon Yariv confirmed that a covert operation to kill Palestinian terrorists in Europe did indeed happen.[15] In 1972, Yariv was the core counterterrorism adviser to Prime Minister Golda Meir and part of the decision-making team that authorised the operation. More recent studies have analysed the operation through the lens of Israeli intelligence, based on interviews with Mossad officials.[16] Other studies covered Operation Wrath of God as part of a broader history of Israeli intelligence.[17]

This volume builds on these works and adds two crucial elements. First, it demonstrates that European intelligence cooperation was a key element for Mossad to plan, organise, and carry out Operation Wrath of God. European involvement in Operation Wrath of God has until now been unknown, and it has not been addressed in either academic writing or journalistic accounts.[18] Second, this book explains how Mossad selected the Palestinian targets who were to be killed. It is currently not well understood why certain Palestinians were on Mossad's kill list. Mossad is often accused of having arbitrarily selected its victims because some of them were believed to have no relation to terrorist activities.[19] With the Club de Berne files it becomes clear that for each Operation Wrath of God victim, Mossad held intelligence that showed they were directly involved in the planning and execution of terrorist operations, either as an active operative or in a supporting role. This explains the logic behind this covert operation. Altogether, this book tells the story of a major Mossad covert operation and the role of European intelligence in its execution. It is the first study to discuss in such detail an agency's methods when organising a covert action and its reliance on foreign intelligence.

Given that we currently know very little about the international relations of the secret state, this volume has the potential to revise the way we see these relations. It opens up new ways of thinking of these secret relations as parallel ties to official diplomatic relations that can at times both reflect and also defy official state policies. In the case of the intelligence exchanges surrounding Operation Wrath of God, we see official condemnation but secret collaboration. We see European complicity with Israel's ruthless killing measures, which brings to light a rather dark aspect of the history of European counterterrorism policy. Altogether, this story reveals entirely new facets of European and Middle Eastern history. It is a history that stakeholders perhaps would have preferred to keep secret forever. However, the story is important in understanding past and future international relations of intelligence agencies and their wider political cross-regional implications.

This book makes a significant contribution to existing scholarship in various fields. Its contribution is strongest in four major debates in international and intelligence history. First, the book contributes to the field of international history by recounting hitherto entirely unknown aspects of the history of Euro-Middle Eastern relations, the Arab–Israeli conflict, and the global Cold War. During that time an international secret struggle raged, in which Soviet intelligence supported liberation movements in Africa and the Middle East, including Palestinian movements. Recent historiography has provided a more nuanced picture of the logistical support and the level of influence that Eastern bloc countries were able to exert over resistance movements.[20] By researching the support of European intelligence for Israel in its fight against Palestinians, this book reveals that European countries were secretly supporting the other side, Israel, while upholding very critical foreign political stances towards Israel. It thus reveals an important component of the secret global Cold War.

Second, this volume contributes to intelligence studies by revealing for the first time the sources and methods of Mossad's covert action and by exposing the extent to which it relied on foreign intelligence. This debunks a common myth about Mossad, as it shows that the Israeli agency was not as omnipotent or omniscient as often portrayed in secondary literature. The book further addresses the dilemmas of countries on the receiving end of covert operations, a perspective rarely considered. With its focus on Mossad's covert actions in Europe, it also contributes to scholarship that moves away from the dominant analysis of US or UK covert actions.[21]

Third, this book makes an important contribution to international relations (IR), as it shows how nations secretly worked together to counter a common threat. The chapters about intelligence cooperation especially reveal new insights into the politics and mechanisms of intelligence-sharing. Research on intelligence cooperation is growing, albeit slowly, and it is still a research area with very few works that use primary sources or archival data.[22]

There is a dominant view among IR scholars that there is no or only minimal intelligence cooperation between states. These works argue that intelligence touches on the very core of national security and sovereignty and assume therefore that there are no or only very limited intelligence exchanges and only in selected cases where there is a specific shared interest.[23]

Using the Club de Berne's decade-long exchanges of intelligence reports that were based on extremely vulnerable sources and sensitive national security information, this volume contributes to the growing understanding that, on the contrary, intelligence agencies do work together intensely on numerous aspects. In doing so, they create their own dynamic and foster strategic links between themselves, independent of official foreign political interests.[24]

The third part of this book in particular shows a discrepancy between official European political condemnations of Israel and a continued secret support for its counterterrorism policy. Essentially, European capitals walked a tightrope between keeping good official relations with Arab states, publicly taking a very critical stance towards Israeli settlement policies, and all the while secretly helping Israel in its fight against the Palestinian armed struggle. The analysis of these secret Euro-Israeli ties advances our understanding of covert diplomacy and strengthens the view of intelligence agencies as actors in their own right, who pursue their own foreign policies that can be independent of official diplomatic relations.[25]

Fourth, another core focus of this volume is Palestinian terrorist activities and how intelligence agencies attempted to counter these terrorist plans through cooperation. Several terrorist plots as described in this book have until today remained entirely unknown. The book recounts new aspects of the Palestinian armed struggle. Some terrorist events have only been mentioned by contemporary journalistic accounts and this book substantiates some of these claims with documentary evidence from the intelligence agencies and contextualises them in the wider Arab–Israeli conflict.[26] The analysis of these terrorist events and the intelligence agencies' reactions offers important insights into and contributes to the study of terrorism and international security.[27] Through the eyes of intelligence reports, the volume advances knowledge about terrorist practices at the time and terrorism innovation.[28]

Altogether, this book is of interest to people in various fields, including international relations scholars, intelligence scholars, historians, and students of war and conflict studies. Given its proximity and relevance to current events, it will also be of great interest to a non-academic audience.

REFLECTIONS ON CURRENT EVENTS

The massacre that happened in Israel on 7 October 2023 is sometimes referred to as 'Israel's 9/11'. But, arguably, Israel already had a watershed terrorist moment deeply ingrained in its national consciousness: the Munich Olympics massacre in 1972. Both terrorist attacks, 7 October and 5 September, have indelibly changed Israel. Neither event was foreseen by its security and intelligence forces. Both events were broadcast globally, the Olympics via television and the 7 October attack via social media. Both terrorist groups took hostages and demanded the release of Palestinian prisoners in exchange. Lastly, albeit the scale of events was different, both attacks triggered strong Israeli demands for revenge: the perpetrators needed to be punished and wiped out.

Echoing Operation Wrath of God, Israeli intelligence formed a special unit as a reaction to the 7 October massacre. This unit, called 'Nili' (an acronym in Hebrew which translates to 'the Eternal One of Israel will not Lie'), is tasked with hunting down and eliminating any person involved in the attacks. Israeli intelligence thus not only launched military operations against Hamas in the Gaza Strip, but also sought to assassinate its leadership abroad.

As this book demonstrates, the success of Operation Wrath of God depended heavily on intelligence cooperation with Europe. The Nili unit, with targets spread around mainly Muslim countries, is confronted with a rather more hostile environment. This makes Nili's operations a lot riskier than those of its precursor in Europe. This raises the question of whether European or Middle Eastern powers will again support Israel's extrajudicial killings. If they do, they may face serious political risks if it ever becomes known that they provided intelligence for Mossad's assassinations. Informal intelligence-sharing arrangements with regional powers, which are kept entirely secret, plausibly denied, and minimally documented, might again prove useful for Israel's operation. Perhaps in fifty years' time we will see another book that reveals how Nili operated and whether Israeli intelligence received help from the 'hosts' of the covert action. Altogether, recent events have shown that assassinating Palestinian terrorist leaders abroad has remained a core element in Israel's counterterrorism policy.

PART I

PREPARING FOR GOD'S WRATH

1

SETTING THE SCENE

BLACK SEPTEMBER ORGANISATION

The Black September organisation was founded in 1971 as a reaction to a Palestinian leadership crisis that ensued after Palestinians were evicted from Jordan in late 1970. Frustrated with the new situation, many Palestinians lost confidence in Yasser Arafat as their leader. Disgruntled members of the Palestinian cause assumed that Arafat's tactic of waging a local guerrilla war from the West Bank had failed. When Black September was created, international terrorism gave a new sense of purpose to Palestinians, particularly the younger generation.[1]

Originally, Black September directed its attacks towards Jordan, as revenge for the Jordanian military's raid that had killed several thousand Palestinians and banished them from the country. This brutal military campaign started in September 1970, which is what gave the group its name 'Black September'.[2]

Black September first came to prominence in Cairo on 28 November 1971. Members of the group assassinated the Jordanian prime minister, Wasfi Tal (also called Wasfi al-Tel). Four operatives shot him in the lobby of the Sheraton Hotel when he was about to attend an Arab League summit. Already Jordanian prime minister in 1970, Tal was also an important military general who led the war against the Palestinians late in that year.[3] Black September killed him to avenge their peers who had died and were expelled under his command. Witness accounts reported that one of his assassins bent down on the marble floor and licked Tal's blood.[4] A month later, Black September shot (but did not kill) Zeid al Rifai, the Jordanian ambassador to the United Kingdom.[5]

From early 1972 onwards, the group expanded its targets and directed its terrorist operations towards Israeli interests abroad.[6] Following a letter bomb campaign and other attacks, on 8 May 1972 Black September hijacked a Sabena flight from Brussels to Tel Aviv and landed the plane at Lod Airport (now Ben Gurion Airport, Israel's main air hub situated between Tel Aviv and Jerusalem). The hijackers demanded the release of 317 prisoners in Israel. Negotiations between Israeli representatives and the hijackers ensued via wireless communications. This lasted for twenty-three hours until, on 9 May, the Israeli Defense Forces (IDF) carried out a rescue operation. The IDF operatives, disguised as aircraft mechanics, burst on to the plane, killed two of the hijackers and arrested the other two, and released the passengers.[7]

While this attack was clearly directed against Israel, Mossad analysts were still convinced that Black September primarily targeted the Jordanian kingdom, not Israel.[8] This, and an important gap in human intelligence sources among Palestinians in Europe, explains why Israeli security was taken by surprise by the attack at the Munich Olympics.[9]

The Munich Olympics massacre was Black September's most notorious assault. It is widely considered one of the most dramatic international terrorist events of the Cold War. It was the first terrorist hostage-taking on German soil, and it marked the escalation of the terrorist threat in Europe.[10] With journalists present on site covering the Olympics, the terrorist event received global media attention. (See Figure 1.)

The attack was perpetrated on 5 September 1972 by members of Black September. The terrorists entered the Olympic campus in Munich, broke

Figure 1 Police car with three Munich Olympics terrorists. Source: EPU/AFP/Getty Images.

Figure 2 Munich Olympics 1972 hostage crisis. Source: Russell McPhedran/The Sydney Morning Herald/Fairfax Media/Getty Images.

into the Israeli male team's quarters, killed two Israeli athletes and took nine as hostages. (See Figure 2.) Intense negotiations ensued between Black September and the West German authorities, in consultation with the Israeli government.[11]

Black September finally agreed to be transported to the nearby airport, Fürstenfeldbruck, where they believed a plane was waiting for them that would take them to Egypt. The head of Mossad, Zvi Zamir, had meanwhile arrived in Munich and suggested that Israeli security forces undertake a rescue operation. Allowing Israeli special forces to act on German soil would have been a major embarrassment with the entire world watching. The West German authorities thus disregarded Zamir's suggestion and attempted a rescue operation at the airport themselves, which failed miserably. All the Israeli hostages were killed, one West German police officer died, four terrorists were killed, and three others were taken into custody.

What for Israel was a shocking tragedy and disaster was a success for Black September, especially in terms of the publicity and media attention that their cause received. Journalists who were covering the Olympics suddenly also covered the terrorist crisis. An estimated 900 million people in more than a hundred countries watched the events on their television screens.[12] Even though the use of violence was condemned by many countries, it was precisely the group's relentlessness and brutality that showed the world that the Palestinian armed struggle had become an entity to be reckoned with.

The Munich massacre was also a success for Black September in the context of internal Palestinian rivalries and competition among the various factions. After the attack, thousands of new recruits poured in, keen to join the group's international terrorist efforts.[13] In the Arab world, the attack was celebrated and, in many cities, people chanted in the streets that 'We are all Black September!'[14] Western European states and Israel realised that more terrorist attacks in Europe were looming.

In the historiography of Black September, there is a degree of uncertainty as to whether the group was part of Fatah (the dominant faction of the multi-party Palestine Liberation Organisation) and controlled by it, or whether it was independent.[15] Most authors see Black September as the unofficial violent branch of Fatah and believe that the Fatah leadership only distanced itself from terrorism or other Black September actions on the official level.[16] This, the argument goes, allowed Arafat to peacefully foster diplomatic efforts and international recognition, all the while covertly maintaining terrorist pressure on Israel and European states.

However, other authors challenge the degree of control that Fatah was able to exert over Black September. These authors argue that the roots of Black September lay in Fatah, but that Black September grew out of various Palestinian activists' frustration with clashes between Jordanians and Palestinians in September 1970, independently of Fatah.[17] According to this view, once the group developed its own organisational structures, Fatah had less and less influence over its decisions and Black September became a separate entity.

Arafat himself further added to this confusion by sending different messages to different audiences. When he spoke to Arab media, he claimed that 'Palestine Resistance is one body and fights for one aim: to regain Palestine,' which indicated that the Palestine Liberation Organisation (PLO) and Black September were part of the same organisation, directed by Arafat. In contrast, he told Western media that the PLO included some extremist organisations over which he had no control or influence.[18]

Overall, the Fatah leadership had an ambiguous relationship with Black September. While it might not have been able to exert direct and full control over Black September, it certainly condoned it and approved its actions, including terrorist operations in Europe.[19] It also helped organise some terrorist attacks, including through the provision of logistical support.[20]

However, after several months of Black September terrorist actions, Israeli reprisals (including Operation Wrath of God and Israeli bombardments in Lebanon), and international condemnations, the Fatah leadership increasingly understood the political and diplomatic costs of maintaining terrorism abroad. Furthermore, Arafat did not appreciate that a faction had slipped out of his control. By the spring of 1973, Fatah made efforts to rein Black September back in.[21] While it approved a few final terrorist operations such as an attack in Khartoum in March 1973, by the summer of that year Black September had mostly ceased to exist.

This book, using sources based on Western intelligence and not Palestinian organisations, cannot take a stand on this controversy. But it is worth adding that Mossad and Western European agencies, including MI5 in the UK and West Germany's BfV, along with US intelligence, saw Black September as Fatah's special operations service and believed Fatah had a high level of control over and support for its operations.[22]

ISSUING A LICENCE TO KILL

Days after the Munich Olympics massacre, the attack was discussed in the Israeli parliament. To express their anger, some Israeli politicians quoted the following passage from the ancient 'Olympic Truce' agreement:

> Olympia is a sacred place.
> Anyone who dares to enter it
> by force of arms commits an
> offence against the gods.
> Equally guilty is he who has
> it in his power to avenge a
> misdeed and fails to do so.[23]

There was widespread anger among the Israeli population, and newspapers were full of heated articles demanding retaliation.[24] The eleven athletes were Israel's pride and were the *crème de la crème*. The fact that they were all wiped out at one dash was an outrage as much as it was a humiliation. (See Figure 3.)

While the government was devising counteractions, it appeared impotent. Anger and the desire for revenge was so strong that some

Figure 3 Funeral of the killed Munich Olympics hostages. Source: AFP/Getty Images.

citizens took it upon themselves to organise reprisal attacks. At the end of September 1972, Amihai Paglin, a former chief of operations at the Irgun, the Zionist paramilitary organisation, attempted to smuggle arms and explosives to Europe to organise attacks against Palestinians.[25] He was arrested before he could strike, but this initiative illustrates the strong sentiments that swept through the country.

Golda Meir answered the calls for revenge against Black September in both words and deeds. (See Figure 4.) On 12 September 1972, she addressed the Israeli parliament and solemnly promised to avenge the killers of the Jews in Munich. In her speech, she declared 'a war of revenge' in which Israel would fight 'with assiduity and skill', operating on a 'far-flung, dangerous and vital front line'.[26]

Turning rhetoric into action, Meir initiated the first steps in organising reprisals and bringing the terrorists to (self-administered) justice. Shortly after the Munich massacre, she created the new post of 'prime minister's special adviser for terrorism'. She appointed to this role recently retired general Aharon Yariv, who had just finished an eight-year tenure as the head of Aman, Israel's military intelligence service. Meir, Yariv, and the director of Mossad, Zwi Zamir, pushed the Israeli parliament

Figure 4 Israeli prime minister, Golda Meir. Source: Hulton-Deutsch Collection/ Corbis/Getty Images.

to create a top secret committee tasked with devising a response to the Munich massacre. (See Figure 5.)

This was called 'Committee X' and it was chaired by Meir and the defence minister, Moshe Dayan. (See Figure 6.) The committee's name was chosen specifically so that other cabinet members or civil servants would not know what it was about.[27] In a top secret act, Committee X decided that the covert action in response to the Munich massacre was to assassinate any Black September operatives who were directly or indirectly involved in the planning and execution of the Olympics attack. A name would go on the kill list whether the individual held a leading or supportive role in the preparation of the attack, and especially if they were known to be preparing further attacks.[28]

Given that breaking the Olympic truce was an 'offence against the gods', it may have been this that inspired the operation's name, Operation Wrath of God. In addition to the phrase also being a biblical reference, the way that Mossad killed, as will be shown in this book, was also comparable to 'God's hand'. Mossad struck suddenly, unexpectedly, and with near divine precise force. Like God, Mossad decided exactly when, where, and how its victims were going to meet their maker.

Figure 5 The head of Mossad, Zwi Zamir. Source: IDF Spokesperson's Unit, public domain.

Figure 6 Israeli defence minister, Moshe Dayan. Source: History/Universal Images Group/Getty Images.

The goal of Operation Wrath of God can be summarised in three words: vengeance, deterrence, and prevention. *Vengeance*, or, as the architects of the covert action phrased it more dramatically, 'to kill those that killed', corresponded to the nation's demands. Israeli officials believed that only a government's pledge to avenge the dead athletes could placate the Israeli public's anger, shock, and frustration over Palestinian terrorism.

The strategic logic of *deterrence* was to kill Black September leaders so that nobody would be willing to risk their lives as replacement leaders. Furthermore, finding a replacement terrorist leader took time and disrupted operational structures. The idea was to disrupt more Black September organisational structures than they could rebuild. This is how this covert action was meant to wipe out Black September step-by-step.[29] This also explains why the operation gradually extended the range of targets. It was not only directed against those responsible for the Olympics massacre; Mossad also eliminated political or military activists of Fatah and Black September who did not have a specific link to the Munich attack.[30]

For deterrence to work, and indeed to instil fear and trembling among Palestinian armed groups, the Israelis needed to make sure that the deterrence 'message' of the killings would be understood. The deniability of the mission was thus chosen to be in a grey zone between plausible and implausible deniability.[31] Namely, while Israel officially denied having anything to do with the killings, Mossad unofficially made it crystal clear that an Israeli finger had pulled the trigger. Mike Harari, the Mossad officer in charge of Operation Wrath of God, later explained the intended degree of traceability as follows: 'We looked for the selective strike, one that the terrorists would know was Israeli but would not leave any fingerprints.'[32]

Adding another element of fear, Mossad sometimes directly phoned Palestinians living in Europe and threatened them. A Mossad operative would start the conversation in Arabic and, once it became clear that the operative was very familiar with most aspects of the listener's life (including details about their family), Mossad warned the Palestinian to immediately disassociate themself from any armed branches of the PLO or risk being killed.[33] This was often accompanied by a brick being thrown through their window or their front door being battered. Without actually killing them, Mossad made it clear that the agency could do so anytime, anywhere. Similarly, sometimes Mossad published obituaries in Arabic newspapers, eulogising the deeds of Palestinians who were still alive and perfectly healthy.[34]

The mission also had a clear *preventive* purpose. The Talmud, the Jewish guide to life, gives the following advice: 'He who rises up to slay you, rise up and slay him first.'[35] In this vein, Mossad intended to 'slay' Black September terrorists before they could come and slay Jews. As this

Figure 7 Mossad officer Mike Harari in Vienna. Source: IDF, public domain.

book will show, most targets of Operation Wrath of God were deeply involved in terrorist activities and most of them were indeed actively planning future operations.

Soon after the mandate of Operation Wrath of God was defined, Meir designated Mike Harari to take charge of the assassination squads.[36] (See Figure 7.) Harari was a senior officer in the operations department of Mossad. At the start of the mission, he spent several weeks in Europe undertaking reconnaissance. He eventually decided to run the covert action from Paris, where he rented several safe houses. Paris was also well suited as an operational base because the Israeli embassy there had the capacity to support the hit teams.[37]

Given the top secret nature of the operation, not much is currently known about the organisation of the covert action and the hit teams. According to journalist David B. Tinnin, one of the first authors to publish about the operation, the hit team for each killing mission consisted of fifteen people, divided into five squads. The teams were named according to the Hebrew alphabet.

Team *aleph* (א the first letter) consisted of two killers who were trained in silent and close-range assassinations. They could be selected either from Mossad, such as from its targeted killing unit, Kidon, or from elite military units.[38] Team *beth* (ב the second letter) were two guards, who would protect getaway routes while team aleph was killing the target. If team aleph were to get into trouble, team beth would come to the rescue. These two teams were forbidden to meet beforehand, so that if one was caught, they could not identify the other. This minimised the risk of compromising the whole operation if one team was caught (a policy that was not adhered to during the Lillehammer blunder).

Team *heth* (ח the eighth letter) were two people in charge of organising the cover that allowed all teams to work undetected. These two were the 'front people' who would rent apartments, arrange hotel reservations and rental cars, and organise logistical support. Team heth was usually a man and a woman because a couple aroused less suspicion.

Team *ayin* (ע the sixteenth letter) consisted of six to eight people in charge of gathering operational intelligence before the hit. They would survey their targets to find out about their habits and movements. Based on this, Mossad then determined the best place and time to organise the hit and decided on the best escape routes.

Team *qoph* (ק the nineteenth letter) were two people in charge of internal communications. One of the two stayed at a secret location near the theatre of operation and was in contact with the hit team and the second communications operative. This second person was temporarily stationed at an Israeli embassy and was in contact with the Mossad base in Paris. The Paris base, in turn, was connected to Mossad headquarters in Tel Aviv.[39]

Looking at the initial phase of Operation Wrath of God, the most extraordinary part is not the fact that Mossad organised a targeted killing operation, but that it was initiated and backed up at the highest level. In this context, the question arises as to why the Israeli government opted for this violent option, as opposed to tracking and requesting extradition of Black September members, and then holding a trial in Israel.

One can find two reasons for the Israeli government's course of action. First, several Palestinian terrorists received sanctuary in Arab states, with which Israel was at war at the time and which would not have honoured an Israeli extradition request for fellow Arab citizens. This was similar for European countries, as most terrorists were set free after a short amount of time without being tried or extradited. Israel simply had no hope that extradition requests would yield any results. Second, if Black September members were put on trial in Israel, the government feared that they would be turned into Palestinian national heroes. It was likely that terrorist campaigns inside and outside Israel would have increased dramatically in order to achieve the release of the defendants.[40] Hence, Israeli decision-makers chose a secret (and violent) response. But despite the secrecy, the Israeli government aimed to give each killing operation an official sense of justice. Before approving a killing mission, the above-mentioned Committee X convened and listened to a presentation by Mossad about the selected target. Mossad had to lay out the evidence that clearly showed the Palestinian suspect had a terrorist past, present, and likely future.[41]

This is where intelligence-sharing with European agencies in the Club de Berne turned out to be extremely useful. As will be shown, European agencies gave as many details as possible about Black September operatives. This helped Mossad select a target and present the received intelligence as evidence to Committee X to get the mission approved. Once Committee X secretly sanctioned the mission, Golda Meir signed the so-called 'Red Page', the kill order that was usually typed on red paper.[42]

COOPERATION WITHIN THE CLUB DE BERNE

The Club de Berne, sometimes also called the 'Berne Club', is an association of the heads of domestic intelligence services primarily of Western European countries. Sources from Swiss archives suggest that the Club de Berne was established in 1969.[43] The Club's eight founding members were the intelligence agencies of (in alphabetical order) Belgium, France, Great Britain, Italy, Luxembourg, the Netherlands, Switzerland, and West Germany.[44]

The goal of the Club de Berne was to facilitate effective exchanges of information and knowledge about counterterrorism and counterespionage. The heads of the member services met twice a year for a threat evaluation, to set priorities in their operational work, and to determine where cooperation could be improved. Occasionally, specialised officers from the member countries also participated in workshops or training courses on relevant themes. The members of the Club de Berne deemed this personal contact among the leadership and the operational staff as extremely valuable and helpful to foster international counterterrorism cooperation.[45]

Even though the Club included a relatively large group of intelligence agencies, its existence was kept entirely secret. In the case of Switzerland, where the Club was founded, only a handful of high government officials knew about it. In the early 1970s, these were the minister of interior, the head of Swiss intelligence, the attorney general, and the operational staff directly involved in the information exchanges. Other countries kept a similarly opaque veil of secrecy.

The most important element of this liaison was the establishment of a common encrypted telex system. In order to prevent terrorist attacks, the countries alerted one another about imminent threats, and shared new insights into terrorist strategies and the tracing of terrorist movements. Furthermore, they distributed general threat assessments or lessons learned after a successful attack.

In addition to the Club de Berne members, ten further countries were also included in the encrypted telex system. From 1971 onward, Israel and the US were included, and gradually over the course of the decade Denmark, Canada, Australia, Ireland, Sweden, Norway, Austria, and Spain (after Franco's death) joined too.[46] This warning system was installed to prepare and protect against Palestinian terrorism. Information regarding terrorist activities was given under the code name 'Kilowatt'.

More specifically, the different security agencies of the main Kilowatt countries and their code names were as follows:

- for Belgium, the Sureté d'Etat, code name jusbrb;
- for Denmark, the Politiets Efterretningstjeneste (PET), no code name: it was addressed as pet;
- for France, the Renseignements Généraux (RG) and the Direction de la surveillance du territoire (DST), code name suretat;
- for Great Britain, the Military Intelligence, Section 5 (MI5), code name snuffbox;
- for Italy, the Servizio Informationi e Sicurezza Militare (SISMI) and the Servizio Informationi e Sicurezza Democratica (SISDE), code name arm rome;
- for Israel, the HaMossad leModi'in uleTafkidim Meyuḥadim (Mossad) and the Israel Security Agency (ISA, also known as Shabak or Shin Bet), code names orbis for Mossad and spedis for Shin Bet;
- for Luxembourg, the Service de Renseignement de l'État (SREL), code name sereta or reselux;
- for the Netherlands, the Binnenlandse Veiligheids Dienst (BVD), code name syth or sytha nl;
- for Spain, the Centro Superior de Information de la Defensa (CESID), code name cesid;
- For Sweden, the Rikspolisstyrelsens säkerhetsavdelning (RPS/Säk), code name pot;
- for Switzerland, the Bundespolizei (BuPo), code names bupo and tell;
- for the USA, the Federal Bureau of Investigation (FBI), no code name: it was addressed as fbi;
- for West Germany, the Bundesamt für Verfassungsschutz (BfV), code name arminius.[47]

While Austria, Australia, Canada, Ireland, and Norway were regularly included in Kilowatt correspondence if it concerned them, it is not currently known which agency was part of Kilowatt.

In terms of the relative contributions of individual intelligence agencies, generally the various countries' inputs to the Club de Berne communication network were even. A country's contribution varied on a case-by-case basis and depended mostly on the availability of information and the degree to which they had been affected by an event. For instance, if an event happened in Rome, the Italian intelligence agency usually sent more cables about the case than did the others.

Comparing the first year of Kilowatt cooperation (1971–1972) with the following years, the intelligence-sharing became much better organised and the cable exchanges increasingly resembled a conversation among the members. Agencies sent replies to specific requests and helped piece together different elements of the puzzle. From 1973 onwards, one can also see substantially more back-and-forth on specific topics. Agencies were much more able to build on and cross-reference previous cases. An example that will be discussed below includes the discovery via Kilowatt that car companies served as a cover for terrorists to smuggle weapons.[48] Similarly, if an agency identified a specific person as a potential terrorist suspect, most Kilowatt members replied and shared the records they had on that person in their respective countries or from partner services.

There are two possible reasons for the intensification of cooperation. First, by late 1972 cooperation was much more established and trusted, and its usefulness had been tested and proved on numerous occasions. For instance, in April 1973, the head of Swiss intelligence spoke in very high terms of the Club de Berne and was convinced that several planned attacks had been thwarted through Kilowatt cooperation.[49] Second, the intensification of the terrorist threat was met with an increased professionalisation of counterterrorist efforts by intelligence agencies. After the Munich Olympics attack, several countries, including the US, UK, Canada, and Australia, set up counterterrorism units within their domestic intelligence agencies.[50] Agencies had thus more resources and more intelligence to share than the year before, as they had become more sensitised to the terrorist threat.

An aspect of this increased professionalisation of counterterrorist efforts is the creation by Kilowatt agencies of a so-called 'terrorist album',[51] sometimes called a 'register of terrorist identity cards'.[52] This was a shared database with known personal details and pictures of Palestinian terrorist suspects. Each agency used the same reference for each terrorist suspect. For instance, a suspect called Ahmad Misbah Omrin, from the Jibril terror organisation, was mentioned to have picture number c.72 in the terrorist album.[53] This register was continuously updated by all members of the Club de Berne and Kilowatt. All Kilowatt agencies were able to access and retrieve this database and it served as a common reference point for known terrorists and to facilitate the search for these suspects.

Looking at the role of Mossad in the Club de Berne, an interesting technical aspect is worth mentioning about its office in Paris. Some Kilowatt cables to Mossad were addressed 'Bonjour Paris' or the cables from Mossad were signed with 'Orbis Paris'.[54] Orbis was the Kilowatt code word for Mossad. This means that Kilowatt agencies knew that Mossad was based in Paris and that the agency sent its cables from there.

In terms of languages that were acceptable within Kilowatt, each agency was free to write in English, German, French, or Italian. Sometimes the same content circulated in different languages, but English was used most frequently. The categorisations of secrecy were comparable to what agencies usually use; frequent examples are 'routine, confidential', 'secret' or 'top secret', or it was mentioned that under no circumstances could the contents be forwarded to third parties, which usually was specified in a phrase like 'transmission strictly prohibited'. Some cables mentioned a sense of urgency and either added 'flash' or 'urgent' in the header.

Most cables included a rating or assessment of the credibility of the source. The credibility of the source and plausibility of content was either described in a paragraph or explained in a number-letter system where the quality of the source was rated in letters and the likely veracity of the content rated in numbers.

Every cable further specified the origin of the source. For instance, most frequently a cable included the specification 'source reliable, has access to terrorist circles' or 'source has access to subject'. Sometimes agencies mentioned that the information came from 'a friendly agency in the region'. Occasionally an agency would send intelligence from a source that was 'unreliable' or 'untested', but in these cases typically the intelligence itself was deemed likely to be true.

Specifically in the Swiss context, Club de Berne records allow us to see the drafting process of the cables that were to be sent to the Kilowatt partners. If Swiss intelligence officers had enough time (if it was not an urgent matter), they carefully drafted the text and weighed every word. A cable could go through many drafts and revisions until the final version was sent to the Kilowatt group. Swiss intelligence officials were very careful and aimed to provide information as accurately as possible in the most comprehensible language.[55]

Lastly, the cables reveal a typical and somewhat funny Swiss habit. Swiss intelligence observed strict business hours and explained to its partners that it could only receive cables during their opening times (7:30–11:45 and 13:30–18:00).[56] The other Kilowatt agencies were aware of this, and MI5, for instance, apologised for sending a cable so close to the end of the business day.[57] One can only consider oneself lucky that no terrorist attacks happened during lunchtime in Switzerland!

2

PREPARING THE KILL LIST

In the Israeli security and intelligence community, the Munich Olympics massacre was assessed as a serious security lapse. It was seen as a major intelligence failure because the Israeli intelligence community had insufficiently anticipated the terrorist threat in Europe and was taken by complete surprise by the events in Munich.[1]

The main reason for the failure was that, in 1972, Israeli agencies had almost no intelligence on Palestinian terrorism in Europe.[2] Mossad's spy network in Palestinian circles in Europe was still in its infancy and it had thus not been able to draw an accurate picture of Palestinian conspiratorial activities there. All the while Palestinians were striking hard and with increased frequency at Israeli people and interests. Under these circumstances, European intelligence was desperately needed. The Club de Berne had proved extremely useful in this matter, for all parties but especially for Israel.

The question arises whether there had been any warnings in the Kilowatt channel about the Munich attack. Interestingly, six days previously, on 1 September 1972, MI5 sent out a cable about a suspect, Yousef Issa (or Elisa) el-Bandak. He was a representative of the Arab League in Buenos Aires and MI5 stated that he had come to Europe to prepare and support a large Fatah operation.[3] He allegedly oversaw the management of caches for arms and safe houses for this imminent attack.

As will be described below, Bandak indeed turned out to have helped with the logistics of the Munich massacre. This cable can thus be seen as a pre-warning of Munich, although arguably MI5 was rather vague and only mentioned an impending 'large Fatah operation in Europe'. Mossad and other agencies could not have known that Bandak was preparing to attack the Munich Olympics and that the attack would happen so soon after the message was sent.

After the Munich massacre, Mossad identified the first names for the kill list and needed to justify its selection of targets for its internal approval process. As mentioned above (see Chapter 1), the Israeli government aimed to give an aura of justice to each killing operation and each assassination had to be approved individually. In each case, Mossad was required to show Prime Minister Meir and senior government officials that the person on the kill list either had been directly involved in preparation of the Munich massacre or was actively preparing more Palestinian terrorist operations.[4] Mossad received exactly this type of information from the Kilowatt channel.

After the Munich massacre, the Club de Berne was used intensively by its members to share information about the latest police and intelligence investigations and what they revealed about Black September's planning and execution of the attack. The agencies that were most active were the West German Bundesamt für Verfassungsschutz (BfV), Italy's Servizio per le Informazioni e la Sicurezza Democratica (SISDE), the Dutch Binnenlandse Veiligheids Dienst (BVD), MI5, and both Israeli agencies, Mossad and Shin Bet. Hence, as a force multiplier these agencies contributed to collectively enhance their understanding of this relatively new Palestinian group that took the world by surprise with the Munich attack.

Thus, the Club de Berne unwittingly proved most useful for Mossad's Operation Wrath of God in two crucial ways. First, European intelligence provided information that allowed the Israelis to determine who exactly organised and materially supported the Munich massacre. Second, through Kilowatt, Mossad was able to understand Black September's terrorist activities and who its major players were in Europe.

This chapter details what Club de Berne members shared about the Munich attack perpetrators, accomplices, and support networks in Europe, and what they knew about how the attack was organised. The chapter further discusses what Kilowatt agencies knew about Black September operational methods and their anticipation of or warnings about next attacks. All this, as will become clear, was useful for anyone who wanted to counter terrorism, but also for anyone who wanted to kill terrorists.

IDENTIFYING THE MUNICH PERPETRATORS

Immediately after the Munich Olympics attack, a priority for the Kilowatt agencies was to collect and share intelligence about the perpetrators of the attack. If prior records on them were available, they were shared as well.

The very first cable was sent the day after the Munich crisis had been resolved, on 6 September 1972, and came from the Dutch intelligence agency BVD. The BVD held intelligence from a 'vulnerable source' that the Munich attack was prepared by Arab circles in Paris and Lyon.[5] Their informant reported that these circles had been very active in the days right before the Munich attack. The informant added that a considerable number of Arabs from Paris and Lyon were at the time still in Munich to help with the escape of the terrorists involved and to prepare more attacks.[6]

Also on 6 September 1972, the West German BfV sent a summary of the situation after the shooting.[7] It specified that eight terrorists carried out the attack, five had been killed, two were lightly wounded, and one remained unharmed. West German intelligence provided the names and all available known details of the surviving Munich perpetrators. Their names were given as Ibrahim Badran (or Bedran) Masoud, Mohammed Abdulah Samer (or Semir), and Abdelkadir el-Danawy.[8] Lastly, the cable asked whether any of the terrorists were known to other agencies in the Kilowatt group. MI5 replied instantly that Ibrahim Badran Masoud was the name used by one of the Black September assassins who had killed Wasfi Tal in Cairo in 1971. Masoud had been released on bail in March 1972.[9]

A week later, the BfV relayed intelligence that the West German foreign intelligence agency, the Bundesnachrichtendienst (BND), had received from a 'friendly service'.[10] The BND believed that the leader of the Munich attack was still in the area. The BfV's sister agency believed that it had also found the real names of the three surviving perpetrators: the real name of Ibrahim Badran was allegedly Ahmed el-Ceysi, Mohammed Abdulah Samer was allegedly Husseyn al-Ceysi, and Abdelkadir El-Danawy was in reality Mohammed Safady. Today we know that, of these, only Mohammed Safady was the correct name, while the other two, while indeed sharing the same surname (they were uncle and nephew), were Adnan al-Gashey and Jamal al-Gashey. (See Figure 8.)

The BND further reported that the Munich attack perpetrators had in fact been Fatah members and had only shortly before the attack been recruited by Black September in the Shatila refugee camp in Lebanon.[11] From secondary literature it is known that several of the perpetrators had indeed been recruited from among Fatah members. However, most accounts say the location of the camp where the terrorists were recruited was in Libya.[12]

A week later, Italian intelligence replied and gave the names of two suspects who had allegedly been in contact with one of the perpetrators.[13] However, a few months later the BfV corrected Italian intelligence and specified that the Italians had confused two very similar-sounding first and

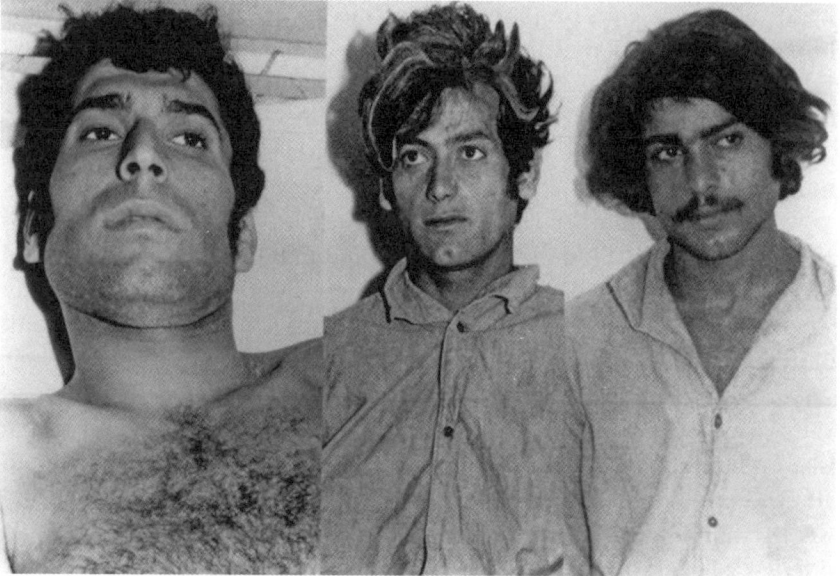

Figure 8 Surviving perpetrators of the Munich Olympics attack. Source: EPU/AFP/ Getty Images.

last names and that their intelligence was not about one of the Munich perpetrators.[14] This indicates, as happened a few times within Kilowatt, that Western intelligence agencies struggled with Arab names and often confused a person's first and last name.

In its efforts to follow the Munich perpetrators' trails before the attack, West German intelligence meticulously consulted its records and compared the names in hotel registers to check whether it could find any traces of the perpetrators prior to the attack. Indeed, BfV shared that three of the Munich perpetrators, all of them killed at Füstenfeldbruck, had stayed in the Hotel Salzburg in the city right before the attack.[15] Their handlers, local helpers, and another accomplice could be ascertained by tracking the phone numbers that they called from the hotel or by checking who paid their bills. Importantly, as will be mentioned below, in this cable Wael Zwaiter was mentioned as one of their handlers. Zwaiter was killed in Rome as Operation Wrath of God's first victim. His potential role in the Munich attack preparations will be discussed further below.[16]

The BfV extended its search internationally and enquired among West German diplomatic representations. The West German consulate in Tripoli (Libya) replied to the BfV that it had found the visa application of one of the killed Munich perpetrators. In July 1972, Jesa Fouad al-Khouri had applied for a tourist visa for September 1972, as he said, 'to attend the Olympic Games in Munich'.[17] Part of the application was written in German, so the BfV inferred that he spoke some basic German. The consulate denied him entry and he likely entered West Germany illegally.

This was the first indication that the Libyan state supported the organisation of the Munich Olympics attack. Mossad and other agencies found evidence of its involvement, including the use of Libyan diplomatic pouches for weapons transfer and facilitating escape routes for Black September operatives after the attack.[18] As will be described below, Libya also helped later with the organisation of the hijacking that freed the three surviving Munich perpetrators.[19]

The search for traces of the Munich perpetrators continued for several months. In 1973, Mossad noted that a group of three Black September operatives had left Damascus for Madrid on 2 March.[20] It said that one of them had been involved in the Munich attack and was deported from West Germany after the massacre. This new terrorist squad was allegedly tasked with an attack against a Western aircraft or diplomatic representation. Spain was believed to be only a stopover on the way to another European country.[21]

A year after the attack, in September 1973, the West German BfV shared a record about another terrorist suspect. It claimed that he was part of the preparations for the Munich massacre.[22] He and two others were seen travelling from Paris to Stuttgart in late August 1973 and the BfV believed that they had come to organise terrorist attacks in the Stuttgart area.

IDENTIFYING THE ORGANISERS AND ACCOMPLICES OF THE MUNICH MASSACRE

In September 1972, a large amount of Kilowatt intelligence-sharing centred around understanding how the Munich attack had been prepared. Similar to the search for the perpetrators, the agencies aimed to identify the organisers of the attack, who their likely accomplices were, what support mechanisms they enjoyed in Europe, and the methods that they used to plan and execute the attack. They were also trying to find out if some of the organisers were still present in Europe, especially whether the so-called 'masterminds' behind the Munich attack were still there.

A week after the attack, a 'friendly service', as the BfV called it, claimed to have had access to leaders of Palestinian terrorist groups in Beirut and Athens. This service alerted the BfV, which shared the information through

Kilowatt, that the terrorist commanders who organised the Munich attack were apparently still in West Germany and could not leave the country.[23]

This was also believed by Mossad, which claimed that Abu Daoud (real name Mohamed d'Aud Awadh) and three Black September gunmen had remained in Europe to plan more major terrorist operations.[24] From secondary sources it is known that Abu Daoud was the principal planner and organiser of the Munich attack.[25]

Relatedly, the BfV received intelligence that the Iraqi embassies in Paris and Brussels were helping Black September operatives escape from Europe after they had organised the Munich attack.[26] The BfV knew of at least one such case, where the Iraqi embassy in Brussels brought a Black September operative to Paris and from there smuggled him out aboard an Iraqi Airways flight to Baghdad.[27]

In its attempt to understand the Black September network and its accomplices, the BfV further investigated the hotel where the perpetrators had stayed and shared the numbers they had dialled in the days right before the Munich attack. The terrorists called a phone line in Tunis and requested to speak to three people in Tunisia. The names of these three were also included in the cable, and West German intelligence asked if any of them was known to another Kilowatt service.[28] Distributing more intelligence on the perpetrators' network, the BfV shared two names found in the notebook of one of the deceased Munich perpetrators. One of the named people was known to be an Iraqi lawyer who was believed to have stayed at a hotel in Munich at the same time as the perpetrators.[29]

Aiming to detect covert Palestinian communication methods, Mossad sent an interesting cable a week after the attack. Israeli intelligence listened to the 'Voice of Palestine' radio station broadcasting from Cairo and the 'Radio Fatah' station based in Daraa in Syria. On the night of 4–5 September (the eve of the Munich attack), both stations broadcast the following message: 'Ali to Samir. Attention.' Mossad suspected that this was a concealed Black September message and that it may have given the order to proceed with the Munich attack. In other words, Mossad believed this broadcast to have been a 'go ahead' signal from headquarters to the men in the field to start executing an attack.[30]

In the agencies' search for accomplices of the Munich perpetrators, the above-mentioned pre-warning sent by MI5 a week before the attack was met with several follow-ups after the attack. This eventually confirmed MI5's suspicion that Bandak had helped with the logistical aspects of Black September terrorism. Cooperation revealed direct connections between him and people in Italy who supported the perpetrators of the Munich massacre.

As mentioned above, on 1 September 1972 (a few days before the massacre), MI5 enquired about a terrorist suspect called Yousef Issa (or Elisa) el-Bandak.[31] MI5 specified that he was the Arab League delegate in Argentina and the British agency alerted that he had travelled to Europe tasked to help prepare a large Fatah terrorist attack. He was allegedly supervising the finding of caches for arms and safe houses. MI5 requested to be informed should Bandak enter a Kilowatt country and was particularly interested to hear about what contacts he might have made.[32]

On 6 September 1972, a day after the Munich massacre, MI5 referred to the cable sent on 1 September and added that Bandak had been in Europe with Saleh Khalaf, alias Abu Iyad, and Ali Hassan Salameh – two top Black September leaders and main organisers of the Olympics attack. MI5 believed that Bandak organised the Munich massacre together with Abu Iyad and Salameh.[33] This directly linked the suspect Bandak with the preparations for the massacre.

Two days later, Italian intelligence replied and mentioned that Bandak had been in Italy a few months before the Munich attack.[34] He stayed in a hotel, showing a diplomatic passport in June 1972, and had lived in Rome for a few months in 1959. At immigration in 1959 he declared that he was a former member of parliament in Bethlehem and that he had to leave Jordan clandestinely in 1957 because he was considered a 'philo-Communist' by the local authorities. While he was living in Rome in 1959, he was accredited to the Libyan embassy as a journalist for *El Kifah* and lived with a younger woman, also from Jordan, who he said was his niece. Italian intelligence did not know when he had left Italy, but he returned briefly in 1969 and said he was travelling to West Germany.[35]

Based on the suspicion that Bandak was likely connected to the Munich massacre, Swiss intelligence, together with Genevan local authorities, opened an investigation about him. A couple of weeks later, in early October 1972, the BuPo communicated the results of the case.[36] It had discovered that Bandak had stayed in Geneva in the Hotel du Rhône from 8 to 20 August 1972 (two weeks before the massacre). While the Genevan authorities could not trace whom he had met in person, they reported the landlines that Bandak called during his stay: in Stockholm, various places in West Germany, London, and Rome. Interestingly, two weeks before the Munich massacre, he called Munich several times. Switzerland asked that the different countries try to find out to whom these numbers belonged.

Two countries, the UK and Italy, undertook investigations about these landlines and replied to the Swiss cable. MI5 reported that the line Bandak called in London belonged to Clarkes Employment Agency, located at New Bond Street. MI5 was going to enquire further about this firm.[37] Several months later, in June 1973, it did indeed follow up.[38] According to British intelligence, the firm was an accommodation address for individuals and firms with connections to the Middle East. MI5 knew that some of them had very shady backgrounds and were known to the British police to be connected to illegal arms deals in the region. Another person hiding behind Clarkes Employment Agency had a 'distinguished war record' and was involved in business with Arab and African governments as a consultant on security. MI5, however, had no evidence that any of them had been in contact with Bandak and it did not know whether they were in London on the day of the call (10 August 1972).[39]

Similarly, Italy followed up on the landline in Rome that Bandak had called numerous times while he was in Geneva in August 1972. In February 1973, Italian intelligence reported that the landline belonged to an Italian woman who was known to them as a 'professional illegal terrorist host', and her name and personal details were shared among the group.[40] The Italian police cross-checked these revelations with other known information about the Munich perpetrators and concluded that the woman must have hosted some of them in August 1972 before they left for West Germany.[41]

In this vein, according to Western intelligence, a few weeks before the attack Bandak had called the Munich perpetrators, who stayed in Rome with their host. Based on the cables, it seems that Bandak likely held an important coordinating role and supported Black September with some of the logistics of the Munich attack. The question arises whether Mossad might have added him to the Operation Wrath of God target list. As will be shown below, Wael Zwaiter held a similar logistical support role and was killed as Operation Wrath of God's first victim. Presumably, the fact that Bandak resided in Buenos Aires and only sporadically visited Europe made him a so-called 'hard target'. A hard target was a person who was difficult to kill because Mossad could not determine a routine or fixed point that could be exploited for the assassination.

Club de Berne records show that Bandak indeed survived at least until after Operation Wrath of God came to a temporary halt in July 1973. Namely, in July and August 1973 he reappeared on the intelligence radar when MI5 reported it had found traces of him in Spain.[42] An intense back-and-forth between the agencies that were tracking him ensued, and they shared information about the people he met and the phone numbers he dialled. Since this correspondence is an example of the continuation of

Club de Berne cooperation before and after the Lillehammer affair, this exchange of cables in July and August 1973 will be discussed further below.[43]

Besides Bandak, the agencies were able to identify further accomplices and co-organisers of the Munich attack and investigated their links to the Munich perpetrators. For instance, the Italian intelligence agency, SISDE, sent a cable with the names and personal details of people who were said to have been part of Black September networks in Italy and who allegedly also helped with the logistics of the Munich attack.[44] Italy explained that these suspects had been expelled to the Middle East, with the exception of one person who was sent back to Yugoslavia. In this context, Italian intelligence mentioned a worry that Black September operated a cell in Yugoslavia, which interestingly was confirmed in later cables.[45]

While Yugoslavia may have harboured a nascent terrorist cell, West Germany was nevertheless believed to have been housing the largest Palestinian terrorist network. Mossad believed that Black September had built a strong permanent terrorist base particularly in West Berlin.[46] With a view to entering West Germany undetected, the terrorists were said to have forged Turkish and Iranian passports because nationals from these countries could enter West Germany without visas.[47]

The search for Black September terrorist operatives in Europe, however, turned into a general mistrust of all Arab travellers to the region. Several cables asked for intelligence about specific people simply owing to their Arab nationalities. Such was the case with Luxembourg's Service de Renseignement de l'État (SREL), which in late September 1972 enquired about a Tunisian traveller whose only 'link' to terrorism was that he came from an Arab country.[48] Another example concerns a West German enquiry about an Iraqi national. The BfV had no indication of any terrorist connection, but because of the person's nationality, they treated him with suspicion.[49]

Similarly, a week after the Munich attack, Italian intelligence informed its partners that the sixtieth conference of the Inter-Parliamentary Union, an international organisation of national parliaments, was going to be held in Rome. Because Arab delegations were scheduled to attend, SISDE worried that there could be terrorists or sympathisers of terrorist organisations among the attendees.[50] Italian intelligence shared the list of names of the Arab delegations and asked if anyone had been identified as a member of Black September. While it is understandable that after the Munich massacre security agencies were on high alert, it seems that agencies often indiscriminately lumped all Arabs together as potential terrorists or terrorist sympathisers.

UNDERSTANDING BLACK SEPTEMBER

Besides the tactical questions of how the Munich attack was organised and who in Europe supported it, agencies devoted considerable time and effort to gaining a better understanding of Black September itself, its operational methods, and its relationship to Fatah and other Palestinian groups.

The first cable attempting to clarify Black September's relationship with Fatah was sent by MI5 on 6 September. The British agency stated that: 'Black September is not separate from Fatah, but the cover name used for non-attributable Fatah terrorist operations.'[51]

Two weeks later, the BfV sent a long and detailed Kilowatt message that explained Black September's operational methods and their tactics for planning a terrorist attack.[52] In a similar assessment to MI5's, the BfV believed that Black September was 'Fatah's violent branch'.[53] It claimed that a known Palestinian figure, Faruk Kaddumi (who was said to work under the cover name Lutuf), was the alleged real leader of Black September in charge of all the group's terrorist operations. But he apparently kept his identity entirely secret. He was believed to have lived in Amman until the Jordanian army attacked the Palestinians in September 1970 (whence the term 'Black September' was coined). Since then, an informant told the BfV, he had been living in a secret apartment in Damascus and 'remained in hiding at all times'.[54]

Adding more details about Black September's organisational structures, the BfV noted that the group was divided into two main operational bodies: one was in charge of sabotage operations and the other was tasked with gathering intelligence to determine appropriate targets. Both operational divisions were based in Sabra, in Lebanon, and the BfV cable included the landline phone numbers of these Black September bases.

Ali Hassan Salameh was mentioned as a Black September intelligence officer in Europe.[55] His intelligence gathering division allegedly helped select targets by investigating people and institutions in Europe that worked with Israel. A middleman named Abu Jihad would then bring the information to Kaddumi. On this basis, Kaddumi would then decide the next target and task the sabotage unit with the planning of the operation. The sabotage unit, as the BfV specified, drew from its own resources and personnel, and assembled its own team to execute the attack. The team members were first brought to rental apartments in Beirut and then flown to hotels in the destination country.[56]

An important component of the operational method, as the cable stressed, was a very strict need-to-know policy. The team members would not meet each other beforehand and would only receive their instructions at the very last minute, sometimes as late as three hours before the attack. This also made it very difficult for the police to thwart it. During the attack, there was usually one additional team member who did not take part in the action and whose role was solely to update headquarters in Beirut about the course of the operation.

This cable from West German intelligence was not only one of the most extensive descriptions of Black September's operational methods at the time, but also corresponds most closely with what is currently known about the group's tactics. This 'need-to-know' policy is mentioned in other Kilowatt cables and in the secondary literature.[57] Works that describe how the Munich attack was planned also mention that the terrorists had not known each other and had not met until a day before the attack, when they received their instructions for the first time.[58] This complete separation of operatives was also mentioned in an interview by Jamal al-Gashey, one of the surviving Munich terrorists.[59]

WARNINGS AFTER MUNICH

Once the agencies obtained a better sense of what Black September and its members were, a large proportion of Kilowatt correspondence centred on estimative intelligence, where agencies anticipated the terrorists' next operations. While most cables about Black September as a terrorist organisation were precise, carefully drafted, and cross-referenced with other sources, warning cables or predictions about the group's next move were often hastily written and based on sketchy intelligence. Most of the alerts after the Munich attack were not thoroughly assessed in terms of their likelihood or the accuracy of their content.

In September 1972, the warnings and alerts were pouring in from all sides, and most of them were sent from the West German BfV. These alerts can be grouped according to the different types of terrorist attacks that were allegedly being planned by Black September: cables warned about sabotage missions, hijackings, and embassy attacks, and some, while not mentioning a specific target, sent alerts about terrorist suspects who were tasked with (as yet unspecified) operations.

Two days after the Munich attack, the BfV gave details about three terrorist suspects affiliated with the Popular Front for the Liberation of Palestine (PFLP) who had apparently been sent to Europe to perpetrate sabotage attacks.[60] A similar warning was sent through the Kilowatt channel two weeks later, on 26 September 1972, again by the BfV. In this cable,

West German intelligence alerted its partners that Black September had been able to recruit eleven new terrorist operatives. The cable gave all known details about these eleven recruits, including their names, last known addresses, and professions. West Germany flagged that they had all received training in sabotage missions and were now ready to be deployed for terrorist operations. Originally, as the BfV claimed, these Palestinians were members of Fatah but had now been allocated to Black September for their operations in Europe.[61] Three more warnings about sabotage missions being prepared were also sent by BfV in mid and late September.[62]

Before the Munich Olympics attack, many terrorist operations involved hostage-takings through hijackings. Unsurprisingly, many cables warned that Palestinian terrorists were going to attack planes. Such an example was Italy's warning that a jumbo jet travelling from Munich to the United States would be attacked.[63] The Italian agency exceptionally provided the source for this alert: Italian police received an anonymous letter, allegedly from a Black September member who disagreed with his peers and thus provided the warning. He wrote: 'please do not publish this announce [sic] in newspaper otherwise I will be killed. Please.'[64] The cable was also shared with the FBI.

Over the course of three days, starting on 11 September, the BfV warned about terror threats against Lufthansa planes every day.[65] The predicted goal of the hijacking was to free the three Munich perpetrators who were awaiting their trial in the city.[66] Shin Bet confirmed and assessed that it was indeed very likely that Black September was planning to hijack a plane to liberate fellow travellers in West German or Israeli prisons.[67]

In late September, the BfV warned once more that Lufthansa and El Al were at high risk of suffering a Black September attack.[68] On 10 October 1972, the BfV sent a very detailed warning about a Lufthansa hijacking. As will be discussed in Chapter 3, the cable was remarkably accurate in relation to the way the hijacking to free the Munich perpetrators indeed unfolded a few weeks after this warning.[69]

Another target was believed to be Israeli embassies in Europe. Mossad was worried that Black September was going to hit the embassy personnel at a most vulnerable spot: terrorists were allegedly planning to kidnap the children of embassy staff.[70] Israeli security estimated that this was a serious risk, and one Israeli embassy in Europe reported that an Arab man had made suspicious enquiries at a school that was attended by Israeli children.[71]

Around the same time, Mossad sent another very detailed warning that Palestinian terrorist groups were going to attack Israeli embassies in Europe, with particular attention drawn to London and Paris.[72] MI5 concurred with this assessment and warned that the threat of Black September attacks in London was very high. It reassured Mossad, though, that the UK government had taken 'stringent precautions' to check all Arabs arriving in the UK.[73]

A target that was mentioned numerous times concerned the American military presence in Europe. The West German BfV obtained intelligence that Palestinian terrorists were going to attack American or NATO institutions. A cable alerted its partners that Lelah Khaled, at the time a well-known PFLP terrorist, was in Western Europe for these operations.[74] A BfV cable the next day gave the names of four Black September operatives who planned attacks against American military and civilian targets.[75] The cable claimed that Black September had obtained anti-tank weapons and handguns for this mission.

When looking at Kilowatt after the Munich attack, it is noticeable that the West German BfV sent the most warnings about Black September operations. This disproportionally strong effort on the part of West German intelligence in the Club de Berne is particularly interesting given that Israel and West Germany experienced a deep diplomatic crisis after the Munich attack. The Israeli government was horrified at how the West German authorities handled the incident. Mossad's head, Zvi Zamir, witnessed in person the failed rescue operation at Füstenfeldbruck and had been outraged. The BfV's very active contribution to Kilowatt can be seen as an attempt to compensate for West Germany's security failures and mistakes during the Munich Olympics. It was a way for West German intelligence to prove its worth to Mossad and Shin Bet and to rehabilitate its image as a 'good counterterrorism citizen', despite the disastrous resolution of the Munich Olympics terrorist crisis.[76]

THE FIRST WAVE OF LETTER BOMB ATTACKS

Even before Mossad struck back with the first targeted killing, Black September organised a series of letter bombs a few weeks after the Munich massacre.[77] For Black September this was a very effective method of hitting Israeli and Jordanian targets: relatively few technical means were needed – envelopes, explosives, and a mechanism that triggered the explosion upon opening – but the damage could be substantial.

The Kilowatt channel was used extensively to alert partner agencies about the detection of letter bombs. Most were sent in batches of ten to twenty identical letters from the same sender. Once a bomb was detected, the likelihood was high that other letter bombs had also been posted with the same origin and that they were similar in design. Through Kilowatt, agencies were often made aware of a specific batch in circulation. Individual countries could then advise their post offices or the letters' addressees. Kilowatt was an effective means to minimise the damage of explosive letters.[78]

The first series of explosive letters was dispatched from Amsterdam, and one of them, addressed to the Israeli embassy in London, killed its target. When it arrived on 19 September, the agricultural attaché opened it. This detonated the explosion and injured him so badly that he died on the way to hospital.[79]

Immediately after the explosion, around noon of the same day, MI5 sent out a warning.[80] This prevented other embassies from opening letters sent from Amsterdam and part of the same dispatch. One of them was directed against the Israeli mission to the United Nations in Geneva. Alerted by the explosion in the morning at the Israeli embassy in London, the staff in Geneva understood the potential danger of the letter and called the Genevan police.[81] The next day, Swiss intelligence shared the details of the bomb and included pictures of the detonation mechanism.[82] Further letters from Amsterdam were intercepted and neutralised before they reached Israeli representations in New York, Montreal, Brussels, and Paris.[83]

In early October 1972, Mossad ascertained that Black September was behind this wave of letter bombs. It further alerted Kilowatt agencies that Black September had recently trained an operative in Damascus in how to build booby-trapped letters or parcels. He was allegedly sent to Europe to train others and send more explosive letters from different countries and in various disguises.[84] Dutch intelligence led an investigation and a week later informed the Kilowatt members that it suspected two Arabs to have sent the letter bomb from Amsterdam that killed the Israeli embassy staff member.[85] The BVD shared the names of the two suspects and asked for help in tracing them.

Generally, the main addressees of the letter bombs were Israeli embassies around the world and Jewish institutions in Europe. Especially after the death of the staff member of the Israeli embassy in London, these targets were soon made aware of the danger. People became suspicious when a particularly thick letter arrived from an unfamiliar sender. In November 1972, a letter was indeed intercepted thanks to the receiver's vigilance: a very thick letter from an unknown sender in Malaysia reached an elderly lady at a Jewish old age home in Düsseldorf, West Germany.

The nursing home manager called the police, who defused the bomb. The BfV alerted the Kilowatt agencies and advised them to watch out for such letters with Malaysian stamps.[86] Shortly afterwards, another letter from the same series of explosive letters from Malaysia reached a Jewish nursing home in the UK. Like in Düsseldorf, a letter from an unknown Jewish-sounding sender in Malaysia raised suspicion and the letter was intercepted before it hurt anyone.[87] Besides the UK and West Germany, letter bombs originating in Malaysia were also found in Italy, Australia, and South Africa.[88]

Dutch intelligence led an investigation into the letter bomb series that was dispatched from Malaysia and found that in some of these letters, the explosives were mixed with a poison called curare.[89] This was a plant-derived poison traditionally used by indigenous people in Central and South America as arrow poison. If the letter bomb detonated, the poison would have burned up in the explosion. However, anyone trying to disarm the bomb could have come into skin contact with the poison.[90] Similarly, a poisonous letter was also sent to the Israeli embassy in Bonn.[91] This letter contained cyanide, a rapidly acting and potentially deadly chemical.[92]

Besides adding poison, Black September devised further techniques to increase the danger of letter bombs. It used flatter and more delicate detonators, which allowed the use of thinner envelopes and increased the sensitivity when opening the letter.[93] This made the bombs harder to both detect and defuse.

In early October 1972, an Algerian diplomat was arrested at Schiphol Airport, and it later turned out that he had with him a list of addresses to which letter bombs had been posted.[94] Later that month, Mossad also obtained a list of addresses to which letter bombs were allegedly going to be sent; the addressees were Israeli citizens in Israel or Jewish people living in Europe.[95]

An important aspect of these letter bomb attacks is the range of targets. Black September not only geographically extended it to include targets outside Israel such as its embassies, but also hit people who were only loosely affiliated with Israel, working together with Israeli companies, or who were Jewish. Black September found the addresses of Jewish people through the *Jewish Year Book*, a yearly directory and guide for Jewish people that listed various Jewish institutions and notable Jewish people, or published updates about Jewish life in and outside Israel.[96]

Starting on 24 October 1972, Mossad retaliated with its own series of letter bombs to Palestinian leaders in Algiers, Tripoli (Libya), and Cairo.[97]

A parcel exploded when a senior Palestinian leader in Tripoli, Mustafa Awadh Abu Zeid, opened it. He sustained serious facial injuries. A few days later, a PLO representative in Algeria, Abu Khalil, was badly hurt when he opened a parcel. Farouk Kadumi and Hail Abed el-Hamid were also sent a booby-trapped parcel in Cairo, but the bomb did not explode.[98]

While Black September continued to send explosive letters throughout November and December 1972, including poisonous and increasingly thinner ones, all the letters were defused before they reached their targets. After the initial shock of the letter that killed the agricultural attaché at the Israeli embassy in London, personnel at Israeli embassies, Jewish people in Europe, and security agencies became a lot more sensitised to the threat and were able to defuse the letter bombs before they could do any harm.

In late December 1972, Black September used the increased parcel posts around Christmas to send another round of booby-trapped letters and parcels, which were all intercepted.[99] At the beginning of 1973, there were a few more explosive letters that were caught before they could reach Jordanian high government officials.[100]

Gradually, this first wave of letter bombs faded out by late January 1973.[101] In March 1973, a letter bomb injured a staff member at a shipping company in Singapore.[102] After this incident, a second wave flared up again in August 1973.[103]

CONCLUSIONS

After the Munich massacre, the Club de Berne was *the* means by which intelligence about the attack was shared. The cooperation served four main purposes. First, cooperation helped to collect *ex post facto* information about the massacre. The goal was to understand how the terrorists managed to perpetrate the attack. For this, concerned agencies carefully reconstructed how it was organised, and who exactly was involved, in either an active or a supporting role. The Club de Berne thus served as a collective force multiplier to retrospectively understand how such a terrorist tragedy could have happened.

Second, Mossad received information about the perpetrators of the Munich massacre and was able to use this information for the planning of Operation Wrath of God. Kilowatt also helped gather evidence against specific suspects in order to justify the targeted killing operation. As mentioned above, Prime Minister Meir wanted to know exactly what the charges were against any person who was going to be killed. With the information from the Club de Berne, Mossad received incriminating material on various suspects.

Third, since Black September was a relatively new entity for most concerned parties, intelligence agencies were also keen to gather and share intelligence about the group itself. Numerous cables outlined its organisational structure, terrorist methods, membership, and local support networks. Many cables thus included the names of alleged Munich perpetrators, but also further background information about Black September as a group.

Fourth, during the Black September explosive letters campaign, Kilowatt served as an effective way for the partners to alert one another about a batch of letters that had been posted. Knowing the origin and design of a booby-trapped letter made it a lot easier to detect and intercept before it could reach its target. Constant alerts also helped to sensitise security agencies to the threat, and in turn they could inform the targeted addressees. With raised awareness and increased vigilance among the addressees, more letters were detected before they were opened.

The Club de Berne cables also provided numerous new tactical details about the organisation of the Munich Olympics attack. Intelligence reports suggested that Black September was able to draw on a large network of supporters in various European countries, ranging across Yugoslavia, Italy, Switzerland, France, and West Germany. Preparations seemed to have taken place months in advance, while the actual hit squad only met shortly before the attack. After the attack, the perpetrators allegedly benefited from Libyan and Iraqi help in organising their escape from Europe.

PART II

EUROPE'S COVERT WAR AGAINST THE PALESTINIAN ARMED STRUGGLE

3

A FIRING SQUAD IN ROME AND FOUR
BLACK SEPTEMBER ATTACKS

UPDATING THE MURDERERS: THE ASSASSINATION
OF WAEL ZWAITER

After a lavish dinner at a friend's place on 16 October 1972, Wael Zwaiter took a bus back to his neighbourhood. After a last drink at a bar, he walked towards his apartment at 4 Piazza Annibaliano in Rome. 'The beautiful Sarah has left the building and is making her way to her house' was the message that was transmitted to Mike Harari over a radio network.[1] Harari subsequently gave the order to kill. Two Mossad officers were waiting for Zwaiter behind the stairway next to the elevator. As Zwaiter pressed the button, the killers approached and shot eleven bullets into his body. He collapsed on the floor and died in a pool of blood. Within hours, the four-man hit team and all seventeen team members of Operation Wrath of God were out of Italy and on their way back to Israel.

THE CHARGES AGAINST ZWAITER

Secondary literature and journalistic reports about Operation Wrath of God's first killing mission question Mossad's decision to assassinate Zwaiter. He was generally considered to have led a peaceful life as a poet and part-time translator at the Libyan embassy.[2] Some mention Italian and Israeli suspicions that Zwaiter had been the mastermind behind the attempted sabotage of an El Al plane on 16 August 1972 (discussed below).[3] However, most authors believe that he was no more than the PLO representative in Rome. While he was Arafat's cousin, he only expressed general support for the Palestinian cause, allegedly without any involvement in terrorist actions.[4]

Investigative journalist Ronen Bergman cites a top Mossad official who confessed that Zwaiter's death was a 'terrible mistake'. In his view, Zwaiter had not had anything to do with the killing of the athletes at the Munich Olympics.[5] The Club de Berne files, however, suggest there were reasons behind Israeli thinking. Correspondence between the Kilowatt agencies explains why Mossad thought that Zwaiter was much more heavily involved in terrorism than simply paying lip service to the Palestinian armed struggle.

Two months before the Munich Olympics massacre, on 7 July 1972, Wael Zwaiter was mentioned in a Club de Berne cable for the first time. It was sent by Mossad and warned about an imminent suicide attack in Europe.[6] Mossad described the terrorist plan in detail and gave the names of the three-man suicide squad and their handlers. The three terrorists were said to have met for the first time in Rome to rendezvous with their controller. He gave them exact instructions, provided them with weapons, and introduced them to a German named Wolf, who was going to help them with logistics.[7] Their handler in Rome, the cable specified, was Wael Zwaiter. He was described as Fatah's local representative and an employee at the Libyan embassy. The cable specified that Zwaiter used the cover name Wail Saadani.[8]

Mossad thought that, in addition to providing weapons, Zwaiter was also going to supply the terrorists with the money and documentation they needed for the attack. He was said to have been able to recruit an Air France captain, who collaborated with Fatah in exchange for money and hashish. The cable added that the organisers of this operation further aimed to recruit a plane technician, who would bring the weapons onboard via one of his toolboxes. Mossad considered this intelligence to be of high quality and mentioned that it came from a source who had good access to Fatah.[9] For Operation Wrath of God, this means that already in July 1972, Mossad had attributed a key role to Zwaiter in the organisation of Fatah terrorist operations in Europe. Zwaiter was thus believed to help with the practicalities and logistics of attacks.

The next time that Zwaiter appeared in the Club de Berne records was in a cable sent by West Germany on 13 September 1972, a week after the Munich Olympics massacre.[10] The West German domestic intelligence agency, the BfV, reported that three of the Munich perpetrators had stayed at Hotel Salzburg in Munich before the attack. They stayed there for two weeks in early August 1972, and then again at the end of August until 4 September 1972, which was the day before the Munich attack. From the hotel, BfV acquired the phone numbers that they had dialled during their stay. They were landlines in Libya, Tunisia, and Lebanon.[11]

Importantly, the cable stressed that Wael Zwaiter, using his cover name Wail Saadani, had allegedly been in constant contact with the three men. The cable reported that Zwaiter had stayed at a different hotel in Munich, Hotel Eden-Wolf, from 15 August to 5 September. The BfV reported that he had paid the hotel bills for the Munich attack perpetrators at the Salzburg

Hotel. He had also paid the bill of a fourth person at Hotel Eden-Wolf, who was believed to be another accomplice. Further, a physical description of Zwaiter was provided.[12]

This cable, sent from West Germany to all Kilowatt partners including Israel, directly connected Wael Zwaiter with the Munich perpetrators. It implicated him as having provided logistical and financial support for the attack. Given the lack of other incriminating material on Zwaiter, it is conceivable that the West German BfV provided the Israelis with the 'smoking gun' they needed to make a case to Israeli Prime Minister Golda Meir to select him as the first Operation Wrath of God target. Since German intelligence linked him to the Munich perpetrators only a week after the Munich massacre, it may have been no coincidence that Zwaiter was Mossad's first victim.

Altogether, intelligence correspondence reveals that Mossad already had intelligence in July 1972 that identified Zwaiter as an active terrorist organiser. Furthermore, through the Club de Berne the Israelis received European intelligence that directly linked him to the Munich massacre.

THE ZWAITER MURDER INVESTIGATION

After Wael Zwaiter's murder in Rome, the Club de Berne members (particularly Italy) were determined to understand who the murderers were and what their motives may have been. A day after the assassination, on 17 October 1972, the Italian intelligence agency, SISDE, sent a first report detailing the circumstances of the killing and shared clues it had gathered based on eyewitness accounts.[13] SISDE genuinely tried to be as helpful as possible and hoped to collectively uncover the identities of the murderers. The cable explained that there had been two killers and that they had waited for Zwaiter next to the elevator in the lobby of his building. When Zwaiter came home at around 22:30, they shot him with several bullets. Afterwards, as the cable reported, the two killers ran outside and got into their car, a Fiat 124 with an Italian licence plate. A witness was able to write down the licence plate number, which was shared with the Kilowatt group.[14] The Italian police further investigated the car and found out that it was a rental from the Avis rental car agency and had been rented by a person named Anthony Hudon. Italy shared the Canadian driver's licence and passport details that Hudon had showed Avis, which were both presumed to be fake.[15]

The Italian cable specified that Zwaiter had been living in Rome for years and that he worked at the Libyan embassy there. However, according to the cable, his exact role at the embassy was unclear. The cable also mentioned that he was part of a solidarity committee for the Palestinian cause and a member of 'the terrorist group Fatah'.[16] It ended with a request for any information on the matter and especially any clues about Anthony Hudon. Altogether, the Italian authorities were eager to solve this murder and SISDE was hoping the Club de Berne would be able to help.

Looking at the recipients of the cable on the other side of the Mediterranean, the Club de Berne provided Israel with a thorough report about how well their killers had fared. Obviously, the fact that a bystander was able to take down the licence plate number was a blunder. Mossad's hit team needed to either kill and escape faster next time or use a different method. Mossad chose the latter. The only time that Mossad chose to kill someone again in such a manner (a point-blank shooting near someone's home) was in Lillehammer, which also resulted in a blunder – and as will be shown, the blunder was on a much larger scale.

On 24 October 1972, in its continued effort to be helpful and keep its partners updated on the course of the murder investigation, Italian intelligence sent three copies of a description and sketch of Anthony Hudon. The Italian authorities had followed up with Avis and had Hudon's face drawn based on the memories of its staff members.[17] Further, to facilitate Hudon's arrest, the Italian police informed their partners that they had issued an international search warrant and sent his likeness to Interpol, the global crime prevention agency, which at the time consisted of more than a hundred police agencies. Italian intelligence also gave a detailed description of Hudon, including his appearance (slim, greying hair, corrective glasses), age (forty-five years), and linguistic abilities (he spoke Italian reasonably well, but had a 'meridional inflexion').[18]

For Mossad, being updated on the police investigation was very useful. It was important to them to know that an international arrest warrant had been issued based on the description of one of their operatives. This meant that this Mossad officer ran the risk of being recognised or apprehended if he travelled or came into contact with the police abroad. Mossad likely refrained from using this officer for a while, at least for any international missions.

Hudon was mentioned only one more time by the Club de Berne network: West German intelligence informed its partners that he was not in their intelligence records.[19] That Hudon was not known to the West German authorities makes sense, since it was the Mossad killer's cover name and not an actual person. The German reply is indicative that at this early stage of Operation Wrath of God, nobody had the slightest idea that Mossad was behind this assassination. After this, Hudon was not mentioned by the Club de Berne again.

The next time that the murder of Wael Zwaiter came up in Kilowatt correspondence was months later, in March 1973. The Italian intelligence agency informed its partners that on 12 March, two Palestinians with Jordanian passports, whose names were shared, had been arrested in Como for theft.[20] When the men were searched, the police found nine colour pictures of important buildings in Milan, such as the central station and the Hilton Hotel. These, the police suspected, could be possible targets for a terrorist attack.[21] The Italian intelligence agency requested any available information about these two suspects.

A few days later, the French DST replied, informing its partners that its services only had a few records on the two Jordanians arrested in Como and that it had linked one of the suspects to Zwaiter's death. Namely, French intelligence shared that, since October 1972, the Iraqi embassy in Paris had discreetly been conducting a search for one of the Como arrestees. The embassy apparently suspected that this Jordanian had been responsible for the assassination of Wael Zwaiter.[22] The cable further mentioned that he was married to an Italian and that he was known to be fighting in a pro-Palestinian revolutionary organisation. The DST did not, however, know what his link to Zwaiter's case might be. For Mossad, it may have been useful to know that Iraqi diplomats were discreetly investigating Zwaiter's assassination and that they suspected this person was connected to the murder.[23]

BLACK SEPTEMBER ATTACKS: AIRCRAFT SABOTAGE, LETTER BOMBS, AND A HIJACKING

Soon after Zwaiter was killed, the Club de Berne shared intelligence about four Black September terrorist operations, some of which we only know about today through these records. Of the four, one failed, one was thwarted, one was aborted, and one was successful. The successful one was the hijacking of a Lufthansa plane from Frankfurt to Zagreb in October 1972 to demand the release of the three surviving terrorists who carried out the Munich Olympics attack. All four operations are discussed below and illustrate both Black September's terrorist actions and the Club de Berne's cooperation to counter them.

The cooperation in these four cases further reveals a certain degree of interdependency. Each agency added a piece of the puzzle, which the others would not have been able to provide. This meant that all of them were needed in order for the threat as a whole to be understood. It also meant that no single agency could counter Palestinian terrorism on its own. This again highlights the value of Club de Berne cooperation for all members.

This perceived value of the Kilowatt exchanges explains why European agencies preferred to continue intelligence-sharing with Israel even when it became evident that Mossad had been organising killing missions in Europe.

TWO ATTEMPTS AT AIRCRAFT SABOTAGE IN ROME

On 16 August 1972, Black September attempted to sabotage an aircraft at Rome Fiumicino Airport. Secondary literature suggests that Italian and Israeli intelligence believed that Zwaiter organised this attack.[24] Zwaiter, along with other Palestinians living in Italy, was interrogated by the police about his possible involvement.[25] However, according to the Club de Berne cables, a link between Zwaiter and this attack could not be confirmed. Instead, correspondence shows that Mossad thought the PFLP-General Command or 'Jibril Organisation' was the mastermind behind the attempted attack. The Club de Berne files about this operation are interesting because they bring to light more details, including the likely perpetrator, and reveal that a similar attack had been attempted a year before by the same terrorist group. The links between the two attacks were uncovered by Dutch intelligence and shared within the Club de Berne.

It is important to know that, more than two years before this attempted sabotage incident in August 1972, there had been two other attacks against aircraft. On 21 February 1970, terrorists placed altitude-activated bombs on Swissair and Austrian Airlines flights, both headed for Tel Aviv. The Austrian airliner was able to land near Vienna unharmed, while the Swissair plane crashed in Würenlingen (Switzerland), killing forty-seven passengers and crew.[26] To counter the threat of further air attacks, the Israeli airline reinforced its cargo holds.[27]

The attack that the Italians suspected Zwaiter of committing happened on the evening of 16 August 1972, when an El Al Boeing 707 carrying 140 passengers departed from Rome Fiumicino Airport for Tel Aviv. At around 1,500 metres above the Mediterranean, there was an explosion in the luggage hold, which blew a 30 × 50 centimetre hole in the ceiling.[28] Luckily, the plane had departed half an hour behind schedule, at 19:35 local time, and the bomb exploded ten minutes after takeoff. Had the flight left on time, the bomb would have denotated when the plane was at a much higher altitude. With greater cabin pressurisation, it might have caused much more serious damage.[29] The lower altitude and the reinforced cargo hold (in reaction to the earlier attacks in February 1970) were the reasons why the explosion was contained and only injured four passengers with light burns.[30] It also helped that the pilot was a seasoned aviator who had worked in the Israeli Air Force. He immediately alerted the Rome control tower and landed the plane in less than six minutes.[31]

Immediately, on the day after the attack, Italian investigations revealed that the explosion was caused by a time bomb hidden in a record player, which had been taken on board by two eighteen-year-old British women.[32] Italian intelligence sent the women's names and passport details to all Kilowatt members. SISDE believed that the kindness (and/or naiveté) of the two British tourists had been abused for a terrorist plot. A few days before, the two women had met two Middle Eastern men in Rome. The men claimed that they were Iranians and gave them the record player as a farewell gift.[33] According to the women, the men had shown them tickets to Tel Aviv and promised to join them later.[34]

During their interrogation after the attempted attack, the two young women burst into tears when they heard that their gramophone had caused the explosion. They readily provided the police with information and gave the names of the two men. One of the men was known to the Italian police and both had addresses in Rome. The police planned to search their apartments later that evening.[35] The young women also possessed two photographs of the men, which SISDE also shared with their Kilowatt partners.[36]

Three days later, Italian police arrested the two men – Said Ahmed and Adnan Ali Hashem – as prime suspects in the aircraft bombing and shared their photos, fingerprints, and passport details, including all visas and entry stamps.[37] They also confiscated all the men's documents and letters, and on 23 August found the first indication of the group responsible for the attack: a slip of paper bearing the symbol of the PFLP-GC.[38]

On the same day, the police were further able to ascertain the two most direct accomplices of the perpetrators and shared their personal details through Kilowatt.[39] Other cables centred on the bomb itself, explaining how it was concealed inside the gramophone and the detonation mechanism.[40] Interestingly, the type of detonator and altimeter were exactly the same as the ones used in previous acts of aircraft sabotage, such as those in Würenlingen and Vienna on 21 February 1970.[41]

After a further search of Ahmed's and Hashem's flats in Rome, on 25 August 1972, SISDE informed its partners that the landline in one had received two calls from Yugoslavia on 17 August, a day after the attack.[42] One of the calls was made by an Arab, Issawi Ahmed, and came from a hotel in Belgrade.[43] The next day, it became clear from a search of the documents found that Issawi Ahmed was a Libyan contact of the two terrorist suspects. He too had stayed in Rome from 12 to 16 August (the day of the attack), on which day he then flew to Belgrade.[44] This is important because the second attempt at aircraft sabotage, as will be shown below, was also planned and coordinated from Belgrade.

After numerous updates, mainly provided by Italy, no cables were sent about the case for a month. In September 1972, the Club de Berne became more active on this subject, with further hints about the involvement of the PFLP-GC and its leader, Ahmed Jibril. In mid September, Mossad informed its partners about the movement of Ahmed Jibril to Europe. Mossad claimed that Jibril had personally been present in Rome on 16 August 1972, the day of the attempted attack against the El Al plane. Mossad believed that Jibril was currently planning more attacks, especially because this attempt had been unsuccessful, like the previous ones.[45]

A month later, on 30 October 1972, Mossad followed up and shared that a Jibril operative, Dia Aly Khan, was said to have been staying in Europe since July of that year. Khan was believed to be the brother of one of the perpetrators of the 16 August aircraft sabotage in Rome.[46] Khan, as another Mossad cable specified, had been given full discretion to decide whether to go forward with the operation and to work out the details of the attack himself.[47]

After the aircraft sabotage attack of August 1972, intelligence agencies became very suspicious of Arab men befriending or courting young European women. On 20 October 1972, Italian intelligence informed Kilowatt members that Arab national Sami Abrahim Adham, potentially a terrorist, had come to Italy and shortly after had become engaged to a young Italian woman.[48] The Italian authorities were worried that this was a fake engagement, aimed at getting the woman to travel with pieces of luggage in which a bomb could be hidden.[49]

France confirmed after a week that Adham was known to the DST. He was believed to be preparing a terrorist operation, ongoing since July 1972, to assassinate the Israeli ambassador to France or Israelis in France more generally.[50] France also gave the names of other group members who had allegedly been working on this same terrorist plot. It further specified that a person with nearly the same name was mentioned as a weapons smuggler for another terrorist operation.[51] The DST thus agreed that partner agencies should put Adham under very tight surveillance and asked to be informed if it was discovered that he was coming to France.[52]

A month later, on 20 November 1972, the Dutch intelligence agency, BVD, sent a very long report with further details of how the 16 August 1972 air attack in Rome was carried out and how a second attack had been organised (but failed as well) a year before.[53] It explained how the two attacks were linked and how the terrorists used similar methods of abusing the good faith of young women. The report is particularly interesting because it provides a glimpse into the workings of both sides of the law. On the one hand, it shows the operational methods of a terrorist group, and on the other hand, it shows the workings of the Dutch intelligence agency in its efforts to uncover the organisation of the attacks. Both attempted attacks were coordinated from Yugoslavia and organised by a Jordanian, called George Farah, who lived in Belgrade.

The terrorist plot of the first attack began when, in 1971, Farah met a young Dutch woman, Antje (her name was changed in the BVD report), on a train in Yugoslavia.[54] She was with Yugoslav friends and Farah joined the group. When they heard that he had been to Beirut, they asked him if he could provide them with hashish. They spent a few days together and Farah supplied large quantities of the drug. Antje mentioned how much she liked travelling, and so Farah asked her if she would be willing to fly to Israel for him and bring a bag of presents to his mother in Bethlehem. He insisted that she not tell anyone about the gift, otherwise she might get into trouble with the Israeli authorities. She agreed and they both flew to Rome on 26 August 1971. Farah brought a brown leather suitcase intended for his mother.

In Rome, he gave her some money to buy a one-way ticket to Tel Aviv, affirming that his mother in Israel would give her the money for the return ticket. He specified that he wanted her to book a flight on a Boeing 747 Jumbo Jet, but because these planes did not fly this route, she settled for a Boeing 707. She bought the ticket and on 28 August 1971 she flew from Rome to Tel Aviv with the suitcase. The suitcase contained presents, a blanket, and – without her knowledge – a bomb hidden underneath the blanket. But because it was a Boeing 707, which did not fly as high as a Boeing 747 Jumbo Jet, the altimeter in the bomb did not detonate. The young woman arrived safely in Israel and tried to find Farah's mother in Bethlehem. When she realised that the address did not exist, she went to the police, but they could not help her. She then finally opened the suitcase and discovered a false bottom under the blanket and explosives in the space under it. She took the suitcase to the police, where they determined that the weapon included four detonators with barometrically adjusted batteries and two sticks of THT of 0.25 kg each.

A few months later, in February 1972, Antje received a visit in the Netherlands from a Yugoslav friend. He stayed at her place and, unannounced, brought with him another friend, who introduced himself as Ljubomir Miljkovic. Antje introduced them to a Dutch friend of hers called Birgit (her name was changed in the BVD report). In one of their conversations, Antje was asked and readily talked about her experience with Farah and his suitcase packed with explosives.

After Miljkovic's unexpected visit to Holland, he and Birgit kept in contact and became pen pals. He invited her to come to Belgrade and to his surprise, she accepted. In April 1972, she left the Netherlands, but on her trip her rucksack was stolen in Munich and she returned. She notified Miljkovic but received no answer. Nevertheless, in June 1972, she called him at his apartment in Belgrade, and on 23 June she travelled there. She promptly took up quarters in his two-room apartment in Belgrade, where he lived alone. Miljkovic was upset by her sudden arrival and forbade her to contact other people. She disobeyed and met up with the Yugoslav friend who had come to visit her in February 1972. He told her that Miljkovic was a 'shady individual' who financed his trip to the Netherlands through drug dealings. She still stayed at Miljkovic's place until, one night, he 'offered' her to a Sudanese friend, who spent the night alone with her at his apartment. Birgit refused, was asked to leave, and flew back to the Netherlands on 28 June 1972. During her stay, Miljkovic told her that he was going to Italy soon with his friend Vladimir, a fair-haired Yugoslav who was going to drive him there.

On 16 August 1972, the air attack happened, when the two eighteen-year-old British women carried the bomb in their luggage. As mentioned above, the women had spent some time with the terrorists before their flight and took snapshots of them in their apartments. Through these pictures, the perpetrators were identified and arrested. These same pictures were now shown to the two young Dutch women and both, independently, identified Miljkovic as Said Ahmed, one of the perpetrators of the Rome aircraft sabotage attack.[55]

Dutch intelligence commented on the report and believed that Said Ahmed (alias Miljkovic) had gone to the Netherlands unannounced to learn from Antje what she did when she found the explosives in the suitcase. They thought he had been attempting damage control and wanted to assess which of his terrorist conspirators might have been blown to the Israeli police. Furthermore, the BVD suspected that Said Ahmed invited Birgit to Belgrade for a similar job but abandoned the idea for his own security. Based on this, the Dutch report alerted the Kilowatt group to the fact that there was a relatively large centre of Palestinian terrorist activities in Yugoslavia, maybe even several centres or cells. The report concluded with a list of recent terrorist events or plots that had links to Yugoslavia.[56]

The account of these air attacks is interesting for the detailed insights into terrorist operations that it offers. It is also somewhat disturbing to see how young women were unwittingly lured into becoming part of the attacks. This method seems particularly unscrupulous because it not only abused the kindness of unsuspecting people, but if the terrorist plan had worked, these people would have lost their lives. The assumption that the women would be dead might explain why the terrorists agreed to have their pictures taken with the British tourists. If the plan had worked and the women had died, they obviously would not have been able to identify the terrorists to the police.

Unlike today, in the 1970s airport screenings were very limited. This explains the large number of hijackings in the 1960s and 1970s but also the ease of taking a bomb on board a passenger plane. Furthermore, as became clear a few months later, the Italian authorities showed remarkable clemency towards the perpetrators of the Rome attack. Namely, in February 1973, Italian intelligence informed its partners about the court ruling related to the 16 August 1972 attempted attack.[57] The Italian court had temporarily released the two main suspects, Ahmed and Hashem, under the condition that they present themselves to the police every week. Finally, several months after the attack, they were freed completely without charges.[58] It is possible that this legal decision was so lenient because nobody was physically harmed in the attempted attacks. Politically, the reason may have been that incarcerating them risked making Italy a target of Palestinian terrorism to release the prisoners. Overall, when perpetrators could expect near impunity and airport security checks were kept at a minimum, it is not surprising that the threat of terrorism was so intense.

A TERRORIST CELL IN LATIN AMERICA
AND EXPLOSIVE LETTERS

About two weeks after Zwaiter was killed, Black September was preparing further attacks. On 23 October 1972, Dutch police at Amsterdam's busy international airport, Schiphol, arrested a man, Rubhi Halloum, with a suitcase full of weapons, including hand grenades, 8 kg of explosives, detonators, letter bombs, pistols, ammunition, notes, and address books.[59] Aaron Klein discusses this arrest in his book, *Striking Back*, but uses a different name for the detainee, believing he was called Kamal Al-Khatib.[60] This name does not appear in Kilowatt correspondence, where the arrested man was consistently referred to as Rubhi Halloum. Mossad specifically mentioned his full name as Rubhi Halloum abd al-Rahim Hejaz.[61]

Halloum was in transit in Amsterdam on his way to Rio de Janeiro and hid the weapons in his checked-in luggage, which was labelled straight for Rio. Most likely, he had not planned to collect the suitcase in Amsterdam. When Dutch security screened the suitcase in transit, they found the weapons.[62]

The day after his arrest, on 24 October, he was expelled from the Netherlands and allowed to take a plane to Rio.[63] In the cables, there was no explanation for why he was released. Klein claims that the authorisation to free him was granted by the highest levels of the Dutch government, while security personnel at the airport were allegedly perplexed by the decision.[64]

After Halloum was released, the Dutch intelligence service did a thorough investigation of the confiscated material, trying to infer what his plans may have been and sharing every detail with the Club de Berne and with Brazilian intelligence. These Dutch cables reveal how the BVD worked and how it tried to reconstruct terrorist plots and actions based on these documents.

Most useful for the agency were Halloum's passport and visas. He held an Algerian diplomatic passport and claimed to work for the Algerian embassy in Rio in charge of Palestinian matters.[65] The BVD found, based on his travel documents, that he was in Europe during the Munich massacre, and right before this attack he travelled a lot between Europe, the Middle East, and Latin America.

Dutch intelligence connected Halloum to the Palestinian armed struggle and believed that he was in close contact with various armed groups. He had the names and addresses of PLO and Fatah members, which the BVD shared with the Kilowatt channel.[66] He also possessed a list of locations of Israeli or Jewish people. These, the agency presumed, were the places where he was going to send the letter bombs that were found on him. For instance, one letter bomb was addressed to the general manager of a Swiss-Israeli bank in Geneva.[67]

A week later, Dutch intelligence found a crucial document in Halloum's possession, namely a 'terrorism to-do list'.[68] The list was written in Arabic and the BVD translated it into English and shared it with its Kilowatt partners. It included items to be acquired, such as different firearms, silencers, bullets, smoke grenades, high-explosive grenades, and plastic explosives. There were also tasks or pending action items on the list, some of which had check marks next to them. The list was as follows:

Acquiring different passports, ✓
training one or two local residents, ✓
Pinhas Lapir (Finance Minister Israel), ✓ [likely referring to Pinhas
    Sapir]
the proposed plane, ✓
reserve-money 5,000 dollars,
new people to get in touch with, ✓
new way to get in touch by telegram or by postal correspondence, ✓
the address is wrong: another more precise address, ✓
reaction of the German ambassador, ✓
the Israeli tourist-ship, ✓
the warning, ✓
the lease of a reserve house, ✓
travel ticket expenses,
the brothers in Paraguay, ✓
last letters.[69]

Because most of the items had been ticked off, the BVD believed that Halloum was very close to completing the preparations for a terrorist attack.[70] It assumed that the 'brothers in Paraguay' was a reference to two Palestinians who were being held in a prison in Paraguay. Halloum, who resided in Brazil, was believed to have planned a terrorist attack to obtain their release.[71]

Among the Kilowatt agencies, Mossad had intelligence about Halloum in its records and provided some complementary information about his family.[72] It knew that his parents were dead, he had a brother in Brazil, and a sister in the United States. Israeli intelligence further notified its partners that he was briefly arrested in Jordan in 1967 for subversive activities against the state.[73]

A week after his release and departure for Brazil, MI5 informed its partners that Halloum had been arrested in Rio.[74] The Kilowatt members were advised to warn their local offices of the Brazilian airline Varig that the airline was at high risk of being a target for Palestinian terrorist attacks. The cable specified that MI5's 'sister service', namely the SIS, was going to notify other European countries that were not covered by the Kilowatt distribution system but were part of Varig's air route network.[75]

Three weeks after Halloum's initial arrest at Schiphol, the Dutch BVD sent a detailed report about him, which was a comprehensive summary of what the agency had been able to ascertain after his arrest.[76] Annexed to the summary was an inventory of the arms found on Halloum, the original Arabic documents that were in his suitcases, and their translation. Additionally, the BVD created a very detailed curriculum vitae of Halloum's professional and personal path. This CV was collated through various bits of intelligence pieced together from different sources. The document was divided into three columns: the first column was based on 'his own story'; the second was drawn from information found in 'his own documents'; and the third was called 'traces received'. The last column was pieces of information from partner agencies that complemented Halloum's own account.[77] This terrorist CV (it was indeed called a CV) included every detail that was known about Halloum, his whereabouts since his birth and positions that he had held.

The analysis of Halloum's possessions allowed Dutch intelligence to better understand Palestinian efforts to expand terrorism to Latin America. The Kilowatt agencies had relatively little intelligence about Palestinian terrorist structures in South America and the BVD thus shared every detail about Halloum with the Kilowatt group. For instance, some of Halloum's documents were letters sent by Palestinians criticising Brazil's policy towards Israel.[78] Several letters complained about the 'pro-Israeli' disposition of the Brazilian government and that Israel and Brazil had close military cooperation.[79] Another letter advised Palestinians in Brazil on how to use propaganda as a mobilisation strategy to persuade more Arabs living in Brazil to join the Palestinian armed struggle.[80] An expense claim was also shared with Kilowatt, which showed that Halloum was conducting transactions involving large sums.[81]

Lastly, the BVD forwarded the list of Jewish and Israeli addressees to which Halloum was going to send the explosive letters.[82] This last document was very important with regard to immediate actions and thwarting the letter bombs.[83] A few days later, on 9 November 1972, MI5 sent a 'flash' cable, marked 'very urgent', with the information that a letter bomb had exploded at the Bombay post office.[84] It had been sent to one of the addresses on Halloum's list.[85] The urgency stemmed from the worry that other letters may have already been dispatched and needed to be intercepted. The next day, 10 November 1972, MI5 sent an update that three more letter bombs with addressees in London had been intercepted.[86] Letters were being disarmed and examined forensically.[87] Over the next several days, in cables also marked urgent, the British intelligence agency informed its partners that more letter bombs with Jewish targets had been intercepted. The letters had been dispatched from India to the UK, for instance to a rabbi living in London.[88]

Halloum's arrest yielded two types of very useful counterterrorism intelligence. First, agencies obtained new insights into ongoing terrorist plans to build cells in Brazil and other Latin American counties. Second, the arrest led to actionable intelligence. For instance, the confiscated documents revealed that Halloum was preparing an attack against Brazilian interests to extort the liberation of Palestinian prisoners. Furthermore, the list with names and addresses where explosive letters were going to be sent was also very useful. This alerted the agencies to the likelihood that another batch of letter bombs was going to be, or had already been, dispatched. Knowing who the addressees were, however, was no guarantee of success. Letter bombs could still explode before they were intercepted, as was the case at the post office in Bombay.

SUITCASES CONTAINING ARMS IN ROME

After the air attack in August 1972, another Palestinian terrorist incident occurred at Rome Fiumicino Airport. At midnight on 26 November 1972, four small, abandoned suitcases were found in the waiting hall of one of the transit terminals. The luggage contained guns, pistols, chargers, grenades, and a large number of explosives.[89] The Italian authorities assumed that terrorists had planned an attack but had given up because the police maintained 'intense surveillance' at the airport.[90]

Another explanation could be that this was a failed weapons transfer. It is also possible that the terrorists changed their minds for other reasons. At the time, Rome was frequently selected as a target of Palestinian terrorism. The fact that SISDE highlighted the high level of security at the Rome airport was an opportunity for Italian intelligence to present its security forces as highly effective (and to counter the rumours that the Italian police were lax vis-à-vis terrorism). The cable thus included an element of self-praise in order for the agency to present itself in a better light to other Kilowatt agencies.[91]

A day later, on 28 November 1972, Italian intelligence gave more details about the suitcases and provided further information about the types of weapons.[92] Through the serial number of one of the weapons (a Beretta pistol), SISDE was able to identify its previous owner. A few years previously, a Libyan national, whose name was shared, had bought one of the pistols that was left in the suitcase.

A few hours before the suitcases were found, three Libyan nationals had arrived from Tripoli in the same terminal. These three men were originally booked for flight connections to London, Belgrade, and Paris respectively. All rebooked in a hurry and took the same flight to Cairo instead.[93] At the gate before departure, the three appeared hurried and nervous.

Italian intelligence inferred that it must have been these three men who abandoned the suitcases shortly before boarding their plane to Cairo. The cable shared their names and asked the Kilowatt partners for any intelligence they might have on them.[94]

After the cables were sent from SISDE, MI5 followed up and asked about the exact series numbers of the British Sterling submachine guns that were found in the suitcases.[95] MI5 knew that a specific set of exported weapons had landed in the hands of Black September. Namely, three Sterling MK5s that were part of a larger batch of weapons exported to the Middle East had been used in Fatah operations. MI5 needed to know the exact specifications to find out whether other weapons of that same batch had also ended up in the hands of terrorists. This seemed to be of great concern for MI5 and the agency wanted to make sure that the Italians understood this request. The cable specified that they should 'understand that weapons number can be retrieved if subjected to fluoroscope examination'.[96] While it was sensible to specify, given that the terrorists would likely have tried to rub the number off, one would expect that a police agency knew how to retrieve a gun series number (even after an attempt at blurring it). MI5 wanted to make sure that the Italians would be able to get the information and urged them to send the numbers as soon as possible.

On 22 December 1972 – nearly a month after the 'urgent' MI5 request – Italian intelligence replied.[97] SISDE sent pictures of the weapons found in the suitcases and informed MI5 that it had undertaken the technical examination as suggested to decipher the registration numbers of the Sterling guns. However, this test only revealed the registration number of one submachine gun. The high quality of the metal of the other guns prevented the numbers from being deciphered.[98] As an explanation for the delay in SISDE's reply, it is likely that this test took some time, and that the Italian service was embarrassed that it could not find more details.

A few agencies followed up on the names of the three suspects Italy mentioned. Several intelligence services checked the names against airline ticket reservations. MI5 found that one of the suspects appeared on the reservation list of a British Overseas Airline Company (BOAC) flight scheduled from Cairo to London and another flight from London to Paris. Another suspect had a reservation for a BOAC flight from Bombay to Abu Dhabi. The cables were sent shortly before the flight dates, which were all scheduled for early December.[99] MI5 enquired further about this reservation and specified that the booking from London to Paris had been made in Paris by Tourisme moderne on 30 November 1972 at 13:20 hrs GMT. The names of other travel companions were also shared via Kilowatt.[100]

Finally, MI5 informed its partners that shortly before departure, all the reservations had been cancelled again.[101] MI5 mentioned that Reuters had recently reported a 'hijack scare' in Europe. The British agency speculated that this might have prompted the terrorist suspects to abandon their travel plans. With increased European awareness of the terrorist threat, tighter security measures, and closer observation of terrorist suspects, hijacking operations had indeed become more difficult to carry out.

LUFTHANSA KIEL HIJACKING AND GERMAN–ISRAELI COVERT DIPLOMACY

Seven weeks after the Munich Olympics attack and less than two weeks after Zwaiter's assassination, on 29 October 1972, Black September hijacked a Lufthansa plane, the Kiel, which was scheduled to fly Damascus–Beirut–Ankara–Munich–Frankfurt.[102] The aircraft's name gave the hijacking its name in the literature: the Lufthansa Kiel hijacking. The plane left Damascus without any passengers, but thirteen male travellers boarded in Beirut, including two Black September terrorists. Shortly after takeoff from Beirut, the hijackers took control and forced the pilot to steer the plane towards Munich, where they demanded the release of the 'heroes of Munich'.

Immediately, the Bavarian Ministry of Justice established a crisis management committee. The Bavarian authorities, not the federal government, had the formal judicial power to decide what to do about the prisoners. The Bavarian justice minister, Philipp Held, and the Bavarian interior minister, Bruno Merk, nevertheless coordinated with the federal interior minister, Hans-Dietrich Genscher. Very quickly, Bonn and Munich agreed that the Palestinian prisoners should be freed, despite Israel's embassy urging them not to give in to the terrorists' demands.[103]

In a matter of hours, the perpetrators of the Munich Olympics attack were brought to Munich-Riem airport, together with a high security presence. When the hijackers in the approaching Lufthansa Kiel plane saw the police cars, they feared that the West German authorities had planned an attack to free the hostages (which they had not) and decided to turn around. After a quick stopover to refuel in Nicosia (Cyprus), the plane headed to Zagreb (Yugoslavia). The hijackers demanded that the Black September prisoners be brought to Zagreb. For West Germany, this complicated the situation because the Yugoslav authorities would have to handle the negotiations on behalf of the Germans. Eventually, the three Black September prisoners, two police officers in civilian clothes, a pilot, and the head of Lufthansa, Herbert Culmann, boarded a Condor plane.[104]

The Condor plane had explicit instructions not to leave West German airspace unless the Lufthansa Kiel hijackers agreed to liberate the hostages in Zagreb in exchange for the Black September prisoners. The Condor plane got close enough to the Lufthansa Kiel plane to establish a plane-to-plane communication line and began negotiations. The hijackers in the Lufthansa Kiel plane were circling over Zagreb with less and less fuel. They threatened to let the plane run out of fuel and crash if the Condor plane with the Black September prisoners was not immediately landed in Zagreb and handed over to the Lufthansa Kiel plane.

At that moment, communication broke off between Munich-Riem airport and the Condor plane. Lufthansa chief Culmann, as he later explained, had to make an emergency decision. He believed that the hijackers' threat to let the plane crash was real and so he decided – against orders from Bonn and Munich – to land in Zagreb. The Lufthansa Kiel plane followed suit. A criminal proceeding later investigated Culmann's role and acknowledged that his decision was justified as he was acting in an 'extra-statutory emergency situation'.[105]

In Zagreb, the Black September prisoners were taken on to the Lufthansa Kiel plane. The West German Ministry of the Interior strongly requested that the Yugoslav authorities not let the plane depart with the hostages still onboard. Despite this request, the plane was refuelled and allowed to leave, mainly because the Yugoslav authorities wanted to avoid any further involvement in the crisis. The hijackers ordered the plane to Tripoli (Libya) where the hostages were finally released and the Black September members were welcomed and celebrated as national heroes.

Based on documents from the West German Foreign Ministry and what is known today from official records, one can identify two main reasons why West Germany immediately caved in to terrorist pressure. First, the Palestinian attack caused foreign political problems for the West German government because it brought negative publicity and involuntarily drew the government into the Arab–Israeli conflict. In particular, prosecuting the three Arab terrorists risked alienating Arab states and endangering West German trade interests in the Arab world. Therefore, it was believed that West Germany was eager to free the three jailed Munich attackers to avoid putting them on trial.[106]

Second, by keeping the three Palestinian terrorists in prison, West Germany assumed that it would remain a target of Black September. The West German authorities considered the Arab–Israeli dispute a Middle Eastern problem and preferred to stay aloof. They thus wanted to keep Middle Eastern-related terrorism as far away as possible.[107] With the terrorists liberated, Black September would have no fellow travellers in West German prisons and the West German government hoped that it could therefore avoid being a terrorist target in the future.[108] With these considerations in mind, it is clear that the West German government had a strong interest in setting the Munich attackers free.

In the media, the West German resolution of the crisis was dubbed a 'capitulation to terrorism' and was strongly criticised around the world, particularly in Israel.[109] West Germany was accused of applying a double standard: when Israeli lives were at stake, the country was willing to confront the terrorists and risk the hostages' lives. When German lives were at stake, it saw a need to 'avoid bloodshed' and agreed to the immediate release of prisoners.

Upon closer examination, this reproach is not entirely fair. At the Munich Olympics attack, West Germany did try to negotiate for an entire day, offered vast sums of money for the release of the Israeli hostages (which Black September refused), and its government had to coordinate its crisis management with Israel, since the terrorists demanded the release of prisoners in Israel. The Israeli government categorically refused to negotiate or release prisoners and thus the only way out of the Munich Olympics crisis was a rescue attempt. In the case of the Kiel hijacking, West Germany had full authority over the negotiations since it only concerned prisoners in its jails. It is likely that the West German authorities would have negotiated at the Olympics attack, but in that instance, it was not up to them. Hence, the German–Israeli crisis was also a dispute about how terrorist crises should be handled in general.

Intelligence cooperation before and after the Kiel hijacking is particularly interesting when considering the contribution made by the West German BfV. The West German government was heavily criticised for the resolution of both crises – the Munich massacre and the Kiel hijacking. Sharing intelligence, especially information that had come from sources inside Palestinian terrorist circles, was a means for the BfV to prove its value as a partner in the fight against terrorism.

After the Munich Olympics attack, alerts from West Germany could vary considerably regarding the amount of detail and precision. The first cables right after Munich were extremely vague (and rather unrealistic), like one that was sent two days later, on 8 September 1972. The BfV believed that Black September's military capabilities were very strong and warned that its members were going to attack US military and civilian targets in West Germany with anti-tank weapons and handguns.[110] It gave the names of the four alleged Black September operatives in charge of the operation.[111]

Other cables contained detailed and specific warnings about planned operations and their likely perpetrators. In late September 1972, the BfV told its Club de Berne partners that, 'based on a reliable source with access', Fatah had assigned some of its members to Black September operations.[112] It gave the names, places of origin, and presumed current locations of these eleven Fatah members, who would first be attending a training session in sabotage operations and then remain at Black September's disposal for three months as terrorist commandos in Europe.[113] This cable contained a remarkable amount of detail, which could only have come from a source inside Black September circles. In several other instances, West German intelligence gave the names of Black September terrorist suspects, their exact movements, and known whereabouts.[114]

West Germany's alerts about planned attacks centred most frequently on Lufthansa planes and the threat of hijackings. Ten days after Munich, on 15 September 1972, the BfV sent a general alert informing its partners that Black September was going to hijack a Lufthansa plane to free the incarcerated Palestinian terrorists of the Munich attack and bring them to an Arab country.[115] Almost every week, more cables followed with warnings that Black September wanted to 'avenge the murders' of their comrades and that they planned to liberate the Munich perpetrators by hijacking a Lufthansa plane.[116]

A month after the Munich massacre, on 10 October 1972, the BfV sent a highly detailed account based on information from the West German embassy in Beirut.[117] This cable will be referred to as Club de Berne cable no. 1039. The BfV explained that an attack was planned for the morning of 30 October 1972 to free the jailed terrorists, who were to be taken to Libya. Preparations for the attack were believed to have started before the Munich massacre and originally its goal was said to be twofold. First, the group wanted to show its strength and capacity to hit German and Israeli targets and, second, in doing so, Black September wanted to increase its standing in the Palestinian resistance. It was also believed that it wanted to impress its Palestinian counterparts in Syria and gain further independence from Libyan president Muammar Qaddafi.

The cable continued with a list of the names of the five Black September members assigned to the job, all of whom were believed to have come from the Palestinian refugee camp of Ain El Halweh bei Saida (Sidon), south of Beirut. The BfV further informed its partners that these Black September operatives had meanwhile illegally entered West Germany via the German Democratic Republic with false Lebanese passports.

What is most remarkable about cable no. 1039 is that the attack indeed happened almost exactly as described and almost exactly on the predicted day. The BfV forecast that the attack would occur on 30 October, when in fact it took place on 29 October. The perpetrators indeed flew with Lebanese passports and boarded the plane in Lebanon (but they had not already been in West Germany, unlike the assumption in the cable). The cable was correct in its view that the terrorists would be taken to Libya. This attack was the Kiel hijacking.

The West German intelligence service received this information from a member of Black September after it promised to pay him $5,000 should his information turn out to be true. The BfV considered the Black September informant's story to be plausible. He explained that the reason for his betrayal of the group was that he could only support Black September's actions while they were directed against Israeli targets. Now that other states were also being targeted, he was considering defecting. He was hoping that with this information he could establish trust and, in exchange for further information, be allowed to settle in West Germany with his closest friend, who had also been present when West German agents first met the informant. He asked for $50,000 for him and his friend to begin a new life and to pay four more Black September informants who would help him gather more intelligence.[118]

The West German government was not sure to what extent the warning about the Lufthansa hijacking was credible. After the Munich Olympics massacre, security measures were a lot tougher and the BfV had the impression that the Black September plan of attack had not taken these enhanced security measures into consideration.[119] With the credibility of the source unconfirmed, the West German government did not pursue relations with this informant. Had it continued to work with him, one could speculate, the hijacking of Lufthansa flight 615 on 29 October 1972 might have been prevented.

This last hypothesis is politically charged because the day after the Lufthansa Kiel hijacking, the international press, based on sources from Israeli intelligence, accused the West German government of connivance and insinuated that it had staged the attack in order to free the Black September members.[120] These accusations resonated strongly in Israel and the Israeli public was widely convinced that the Kiel attack was in fact a secret deal between the Palestinian terrorists and the West German government.[121]

An important argument was that the Lufthansa plane only carried eleven male hostages (no women or children) on a plane that could carry 149 to 189 passengers, and among them was only one West German national.[122] The assumption was that the West German government guaranteed a swift exchange of hostages in exchange for the Palestinians agreeing to limit German damage and to spare West Germany from future involvement in terrorist attacks.

According to senior officials in the West German government, agreeing to such a deal would have corresponded to the pragmatic approach to counterterrorism of Willy Brandt's administration.[123] For instance, two years before, in September 1970, during another Lufthansa hijacking known in the literature as Skyjack Sunday, the West German government released three Palestinian prisoners even though all the West German hostages had already been freed by the terrorists. This decision to release the Palestinians was explicitly connected to the hope that West Germany could avoid being a target of Palestinian terrorist attacks in the future.[124]

Israeli intelligence further intimated that the West German government had contacts with Black September and used these connections to forge a deal with the hijackers. Lastly, rumours circulated that the West German government paid $5 million for the Palestinians to simulate an attack.[125]

Most intriguing in this story is that Mossad leaked intelligence to the press that accused the West German government of connivance and complicity in the hijacking. Leaking such accusations to the press was an unusual step by Israeli intelligence. Even more unusual was that these accusations were based on, among others, West German intelligence that Shin Bet had received directly from the BfV through the Club de Berne. By publishing West German intelligence, Mossad essentially removed the basis of confidentiality. Mossad's leak thus shows how furious the Israeli government was that the Munich perpetrators had been allowed to escape unharmed and without a trial. The thought that West Germany could have prevented the escape made matters even worse.

Indeed, the Lufthansa Kiel hijacking, which happened so soon after the Munich massacre, engulfed the two countries in a deep diplomatic crisis. Golda Meir later wrote in her autobiography that she had been 'physically sickened' when she heard about the release of the perpetrators of the Munich Olympics massacre.[126] A report from the West German embassy in Tel Aviv characterised the diplomatic incident as 'The most severe crisis between the Federal Republic and Israel since the establishment of diplomatic relations in 1965.'[127] During this political crisis, Israel recalled its ambassador.[128] It issued strongly worded formal protests to West German diplomatic representations and the United Nations. Domestically, a wave of anti-German sentiment swept across Israel. This crisis erupted at a time when the West German and Israeli governments were still overcoming tensions that persisted well into the 1970s.[129]

Amidst this troubled relationship, it proved very useful for the two countries' intelligence agencies to have a direct link to one another via the Club de Berne. Despite strained relations on the official diplomatic level and despite Mossad's leak, on the secret level the intelligence communities could still count on each other. They quickly reverted to pre-established and trusted security ties with the Kilowatt group. This, over the long term, helped with the normalisation process between the two countries after the crisis.

Furthermore, for the BfV, Club de Berne intelligence-sharing after the Kiel hijacking provided an opportunity to rectify its image in the eyes of its partners. The agency could demonstrate its relevance and willingness to covertly help Israel in the fight against terrorism. West German intelligence was also able to send secret justifications for the way its government had resolved the crisis. Both allowed the West German authorities to be presented in a more positive light.

Three cables are worth highlighting in this respect, because they not only included intelligence about the hijacking, but also discussed the West German government's role during the Kiel crisis and presented it in a more favourable way. These BfV cables also showed that West Germany had access to relevant counterterrorism intelligence, which insinuated that the BfV remained an important partner in the struggle against terrorism, despite the current political difficulties.

The first cable in which West German intelligence demonstrated its relevance to its partners was sent two weeks after the hijacking. The BfV informed its partners about the course of the investigations into the methods that the terrorists used to organise the hijacking and mentioned that a 'friendly service' had notified West Germany that the two hijackers obtained their visas to travel through Turkey from the Turkish consulate in Beirut.[130] The cable provided the exact names, birth dates, birthplaces, professions, and passport numbers as they were written in the passports. The same service also gave the name of the Black September leader who was said to have finalised the hijacking plot and advised that the explosives were placed on board by a member of airport staff at Beirut Airport.[131] Black September had recruited this staff member, who hid the explosives in the plane.[132]

Considering the German–Israeli context and the two countries' strained relations after the crises, arguably this cable provided more than sheer technical intelligence about the planning of the hijacking. The fact that the BfV mentioned (as an unverifiable claim) that the explosives had been smuggled aboard in Beirut meant that the West German authorities could not have done anything to prevent the attack. It simply had no control over airport security in Beirut. Furthermore, by sending such detailed intelligence regarding Black September's operational plans and names, West German intelligence demonstrated to its partners its relevance and goodwill to continue the fight against Palestinian terrorism.

In another cable, West German intelligence further shared that the perpetrators of the hijacking were Libyans and belonged to a Libyan special operations force that perpetrated reprisal actions in the name of the Libyan government.[133] This same Libyan special operations force was said to be planning further attacks, specifically against the federal minister of the interior, Hans-Dietrich Genscher, the Bavarian interior minister, Bruno Merk, and the then president of the Munich police, Manfred Schreiber.[134] These three officials were accused of having broken their promise during the Munich Olympics attack, presumably when they promised the kidnappers safe passage via Fürstenfeldbruck but actually had a police rescue operation planned. Even though the Munich perpetrators were free, the German officials would still need to be punished through 'a spectacular terrorist action'.[135]

This cable too should be interpreted with the wider Israeli–German context in mind. Namely, as mentioned above, the West German government was accused of liberating the Munich perpetrators so that the country would no longer be targeted by Black September. With this cable, the BfV suggested that even if this was the government's reasoning, it would not have worked since German nationals remained a target even after the Munich perpetrators were set free.

A week later, the BfV sent a more substantial cable, which reconstructed the planning of the attack, allegedly based on intelligence from a Black September informant in Libya, whose name was shared.[136] According to this informant, alongside two prime Lebanese suspects, the leader of the hijacking was said to be a Libyan-Yemeni dual citizen. The cable included this suspect's name, Sei Shahid, and passport details, including age (twenty-three years old) and professional background (studies in architecture at the University of Michigan). This confirmed earlier cables which stated that the perpetrators of the Kiel hijacking were of Libyan nationality.

Furthermore, according to this informant, the hijackers were given two main instructions. First, they had to refuse any offer by the West German government to exchange hostages. Consequently, anyone who approached the plane to negotiate or to offer him- or herself as a replacement would have been taken hostage. This, as the cable pointed out, would have increased the number of hostages, and would have made the attack even more spectacular. Second, if the West German authorities did not release the Munich perpetrators, the hijackers had a strict order to destroy the plane and kill its passengers. The Black September informant allegedly insisted that he personally knew the Kiel hijackers and that he was convinced that they would have followed through had the West German government not agreed to free the prisoners.

Arguably, this cable too was more than just an update about recently acquired intelligence concerning the Kiel attack. It instead justified the West German government's management of the crisis and explained its reasons for the release. Namely, owing to the risks involved, the BfV suggested that West Germany had no other choice but to free the Palestinian prisoners and that negotiations would have been impossible. The content of this cable can be read in conjunction with the official justification given by Chancellor Willy Brandt: 'The passengers and crew were threatened with annihilation unless we released the three Palestinian survivors of the Fürstenfeldbruck massacre. Like the Bavarian government, I then saw no alternative but to yield to this ultimatum and avoid further senseless bloodshed.'[137] The cable can be interpreted as a secret reinforcement of Brandt's justification with evidence acquired through the West German domestic intelligence service. It is conceivable that the two cables were intended to calm the Club de Berne partners and to demonstrate the BfV's relevance to the group, since it could provide first-hand intelligence from Black September informants. It is likely that the BfV wanted to ensure that intelligence cooperation was not impeded by political differences or by the controversial resolution of the Kiel hijacking.

After the Kiel hijacking, the BfV and several other agencies were involved in identifying the security loopholes that allowed Black September to carry it out. The Club de Berne proved very useful, particularly for the identification of the perpetrators and organisers of this operation. On 29 October 1972, while it was still ongoing, the BfV informed its partners about the hijacking and explained that the terrorists had boarded in Beirut.[138] The West German agency provided the list of passengers who had boarded the plane in Beirut. This list proved very helpful, as it allowed the Kilowatt agencies to follow up on the names and gradually identify the perpetrators. Through a BfV–MI5 Kilowatt exchange of cables (into which all Kilowatt agencies were copied), it became apparent that two Lebanese businessmen were among the prime suspects for the attack.[139]

For several months, the Club de Berne had no further information on them, until they reappeared more than six months later. In June 1973, the two men tried to obtain visas at the UK and Dutch embassies in Beirut.[140]

Their applications were immediately rejected, their names formally put on a watchlist, and all Kilowatt partners informed immediately. However, remarkably, no country was interested in arresting them, even though they were the likely perpetrators of the Lufthansa Kiel hijacking. Dutch intelligence followed up on some of the claims that the suspects had made during their visa application interviews, finding that all were false. For instance, one claimed to be the CEO of a company that did not exist. The other gave a fictitious address in Beirut.[141] As far as is currently known, the perpetrators of the Lufthansa Kiel hijacking survived and were never brought to justice.

TERRORIST TACTICS AND INNOVATION

After Zwaiter's death, the Club de Berne continued to share operational intelligence about Black September's tactics and methods. Besides cables about the above-mentioned attacks, in the autumn of 1972, the agencies were concerned with understanding new terrorist methods and tactical innovations, and complementing each other's records about terrorist suspects. Generally, the agencies readily shared information if it was deemed to be relevant and timely enough for other Kilowatt members to combat the threat of terrorism. Correspondence shows how counterterrorism cooperation collectively increased knowledge about terrorist groups and thus provides insight into terrorists' innovation and tactics at the time.

In a warning about recent developments in terrorists' tactical innovation, Mossad alerted its partners on 16 October 1972 – incidentally, on the same day Zwaiter was killed – that Palestinian terrorists had obtained the uniforms of British and German police as well as those of Swissair and other European airlines.[142] Replying to this cable, MI5 confirmed that it would not be difficult for terrorists to obtain British police uniforms from surplus stocks on the open market, including theatrical agencies, nor would it be difficult to obtain appropriate badges and insignia. MI5 informed the relevant authorities about it.[143] The French DST confirmed that there had recently been a burglary at the home of an Air France flight attendant.[144] Most worrying were two issues. First, the thieves were able to steal the attendant's uniform, which would be the perfect disguise to use in the hijacking of a plane. Second, an aeroplane manual was also stolen, which was marked as 'confidential' and strictly meant to be read only by the flight crew. The missing manual also included a map of all Air France planes and flight security procedures.[145]

Another alleged tactical advance concerned an expansion of Palestinian groups' local support networks in Europe. In early November 1972, the

BfV informed its partners about a new terrorist ally of Black September. It had received reports that Black September was now cooperating with the 'National Liberation Organisation for Turkey', described as a 'socialist extremist' organisation consisting of Turkish expatriates based in West Germany.[146] The deal between the two organisations was described as follows: Black September offered training in one of the Fatah camps and the Turkish-German group provided unlimited logistical support for all Fatah terror attacks in Europe.[147] Two Turkish people, whose names were shared in the cable, were said to have travelled to Beirut to discuss this deal.[148]

Numerous cables in the autumn of 1972 concerned warnings about terrorist suspects. From late October 1972 onwards, West Germany regularly sent very long lists of people who had been deported from the country or were refused entry owing to being suspected of actively supporting the Palestinian armed struggle. The BfV called these suspects 'politically radicalised Arabs'.[149] This was in the context of West Germany's post-Munich tightening of aliens law and measures against Arabs living in the country.

The measures entailed five main changes to the law on aliens, including tightened security controls and stricter entry permissions for Arabs.[150] Law enforcement was further allowed to enhance surveillance of Arabs and use all available legal resources to expel anyone suspected of planning, supporting, or promoting terrorist violence.[151] This measure was expanded to Arab residents with an unsettled legal right to remain, who were deported from West Germany without legal procedures.[152] Most controversially, suspicious Palestinian associations were banned, including the General Union of Palestinian Students (GUPS) and the General Union of Palestinian Workers.[153]

On 24 October 1972, the BfV sent the first of many long lists of Arabs who were either being expelled from or refused entry to West Germany.[154] Most were members of the GUPS in Berlin, which had been outlawed as part of the post-Munich tightening of security measures.[155] In late January 1973, the BfV sent another long list with names of foreigners who had been either deported or refused entry.[156] This time, too, several Arabs on the list were part of the GUPS.

In these lists, West Germany provided as many details as possible about the expelled Arabs, including their names, birth dates, birthplaces, nationalities, professions, places of residence, addresses in West Germany before they were evicted, where they had been deported to (mostly Middle Eastern countries), and, most importantly, their alleged role within Palestinian terrorist organisations. For instance, one of the deportees was suspected of working as a courier for the PFLP. Another allegedly received donations for

Fatah and helped use the funds for terrorist operations, such as a planned bomb attack in Hamburg in February 1972. Another was said to be an activist of an Arab student association and in 1970 was seen at a protest rally in front of the American embassy in Bonn. Another Arab man was deported because he was heard to have glorified the Munich Olympics attack.[157]

In one instance in February 1973, a suspect was able to challenge his deportation before the court and won the case. The BfV thus sent an update that this person had not been deported and was instead still living in West Germany.[158] Similarly, in the spring of 1973, the BfV sent numerous updates specifying whether suspects had been deported or not, or the agency added new deportees to the list.[159] These cables show the extent to which the BfV and other Club de Berne agencies kept each other up to date about all known Palestinian terrorist suspects in Europe and collected as many records of them as possible.

After introducing the above-mentioned changes to its aliens law, West Germany was heavily criticised for the measures. Naturally, strong condemnation came from Arab countries, which reproached the West German authorities for using a discriminatory practice against Arab citizens and called these measures 'undeserving'.[160] Looking at the reasons that the BfV gave in the cables for deporting or expelling these people, one can understand this criticism. If the accusations were true, it made sense to expel some of the people on the list, such as the above-mentioned suspect who was believed to have actively prepared an attack in Hamburg.[161] However, other reasons appear to be purely arbitrary, and in several cases, Arabs were deported simply for expressing their political opinions. Deportations or entry bans happened immediately after they were issued. Thus, a core legal shortcoming was the near impossibility of the affected people being able to appeal against these decisions. This is especially problematic given that many of these people had been living in West Germany for years and were now suddenly forced to leave.

Besides the bulk lists of suspects sent by the BfV, agencies also sent regular updates about higher-placed terrorist suspects and advised that they be placed on the Kilowatt watchlist (also called register or terrorist album). In the autumn of 1972, the BfV suggested adding to the list a high-level Black September operative called Mahrouf Ghanem. He was allegedly in charge of terrorist missions across the European continent.[162] The French intelligence agency, Renseignements Généraux (RG), updated the Kilowatt records with further details about him, including his last known whereabouts and movement across Europe.[163]

Italy informed its partners about other high-placed Arab terrorist suspects who had stayed in Venice.[164] SISDE mentioned the hotel where they stayed, all their known activities during the day in Venice and Como, the phone number of a landline they called in Vienna, and also how long they were on the phone.[165] The Italian authorities considered these suspects high risk and urgently requested further intelligence on them from the other Kilowatt members.

In mid October, the BfV provided more details about a terrorist suspect with allegedly strong ties to Fatah terrorism in Cologne.[166] He was known to work as a ticket collector for a German sleeper train company. German intelligence was thus worried that this profession allowed him to travel in Western Europe unnoticed by border control.

On 10 November 1972, the Dutch intelligence agency, BVD, arrested Maan Ziadeh, a Lebanese national, on suspicion of being connected with Palestinian terrorism.[167] After having been thoroughly searched, Ziadeh was released and allowed to resume his travel to Beirut. He had a PLO identity card, which he tried to eat when the police arrested him, but he later denied that it was his ID.[168] His notebook included some addresses, which the BVD promised to send to the Kilowatt members. The BVD received intelligence from Canadian security agencies that Ziadeh was a member of the Democratic Front for the Liberation of Palestine (DFLP), and that he was linked to this group's leader, Nayef Hawatmeh.[169] A few days later, the BVD sent an update about him and said that it had indeed found a DFLP leave-pass on him.[170] Lastly, Mossad consulted its records and shared that Ziadeh was known to them as 'an Arab communist extremist in Montreal'.[171] It added that in September 1972, at a conference held at the University of Chicago,he was the representative, not of the DFLP, but of the PFLP.[172]

These examples of agencies tracking the whereabouts, activities, and affiliations of terrorist suspects show the agencies' eagerness to share extensive details on relevant subjects. Agencies complemented each other's records and included everything they could find, from conference attendance to phone lines that were dialled. Overall, on the collective task of keeping track of terrorist suspects, they were very thorough, specific, and readily contributed as much information as possible.

In autumn 1972, only two warnings were issued after Zwaiter's assassination. In late October, Mossad sent a broad warning about recent terrorist plans as follows: 'Black September is planning a spectacular operation involving explosions and murder. The attack will happen either in Paris or London and either in November or December, and the perpetrators will have false Iraqi passports (either forged Iraqi passports or genuine passports made out in false names).'[173] Except for the likely nationality of the perpetrators, this alert was uncharacteristically vague. The purpose of the cable is thus not clear. It was either a 'fearmongering' attempt to exaggerate the threat to keep the Europeans worried about terrorism and pressured to work with Mossad, or Mossad genuinely wanted to warn that Palestinian terrorists were attempting to carry out something spectacular, without knowing what it might be.

The second cable was sent by MI5 about PFLP plans to hijack a plane from Nigeria, from either Lagos or Kano.[174] The cable mentioned the European airlines that flew to these airports. The British agency insisted that the source of this intelligence was extremely vulnerable and thus asked that only the bare minimum of people be warned about this attack, ideally only local airline station managers. It emphasised in the cable that the local authorities should not talk about the matter among themselves.[175] A request for such a high amount of secrecy was rare and surprising given that the entire content of the intelligence was the likely location of where an attack might happen. The purpose of this cable may thus have been less about the warning itself than a way for MI5 to show that it had 'vulnerable' sources, human intelligence, in Palestinian terrorist circles.

CONCLUSIONS

Many authors who write about Mossad's Operation Wrath of God see the killing of Wael Zwaiter as a mistake.[176] In their view, Zwaiter was a poet and translator who had no connection whatsoever with Palestinian terrorism or with the Munich massacre. With the Club de Berne files, a different picture emerges. This chapter has shown that Mossad received intelligence from Italy and West Germany that identified Zwaiter as a logistical support officer for Black September operations and associated him directly with the logistical preparations for the Munich attack. Given that the West German BfV sent its intelligence just when Mossad was determining the first Operation Wrath of God targets, the Israeli agency's decision to kill Zwaiter was very likely influenced by the German message.

After the assassination, Club de Berne reporting about Zwaiter's death showed the efforts of Italian intelligence to enable a collective Kilowatt search for Zwaiter's murderer. This bore an element of absurdity, because among the partners who were supposed to help identify the murderer, was the murderer. For obvious reasons, being updated about the murder investigation was highly beneficial to Mossad. It showed Israeli intelligence exactly how much the police knew and what traces their hit men had left. This was probably useful for the planning of the next mission.

Analysing cooperation after Zwaiter's death, it is interesting to note that several cables included an 'additional' unspoken message. This concerns the cables sent by the West German BfV before and after the Lufthansa Kiel hijacking. Many of the BfV's cables were meant to signal to its partners that it was a 'good counterterrorist citizen' and an asset to the Kilowatt members. It showed the German agency's access to human sources in Palestinian networks and that its warnings were precise (in one case even prescient). Similarly, the cables that included long lists of deportees can be seen as a way for West Germany to show its resolve against Palestinian terrorists by enforcing such strict anti-Palestinian security and immigration measures.

Other BfV cables highlighted the dilemmas faced by the West German authorities, stressed their lack of alternatives in the face of terrorist pressure, and emphasised that there was nothing in their power that could have prevented the attack. These messages aimed at exculpating the West German authorities from any blame for the Kiel hijacking and the resolution of the crisis. In short, the BfV wanted to ensure that intelligence cooperation was not impeded by political differences or by the controversial resolution of the Kiel crisis. This is a form of covert diplomacy where one party tried to change its image through a secret communication channel. West Germany was able to send secret information via Kilowatt, which it otherwise would not have been able to send through official diplomatic routes.

Similarly, some updates about Palestinian tactical innovations and warnings also contained a hidden message that went beyond the straightforward technical reports. Namely, some agencies sent cables to boast about their own capabilities. These cables included, for instance, the long Dutch report about the Yugoslavian terrorist cell, or the MI5 warning that was based on a 'vulnerable' human source. Agencies wanted to appear as powerful, well-networked, and knowledgeable about Palestinian conspiratorial activities as a way of cultivating their image in the eyes of their partners.

Besides the many setbacks or attacks that were carried out, the agencies nevertheless saw some counterterrorism successes, not least through intelligence cooperation. The detection of a terrorist cell in Yugoslavia happened through, among other things, the persistence and diligence of Dutch intelligence. At the airport in Rome, a potentially very brutal attack did not happen, although whether or not Italian security indeed deterred the terrorists is anyone's guess.

Cooperation after Zwaiter's death further demonstrates that intelligence agencies and Black September were running a neck-and-neck race.

Intelligence agencies were putting substantial effort into understanding how an attack happened. If an attack was thwarted, agencies tried to understand how it had been planned. Cooperation was very valuable as it allowed them to collectively put together missing puzzle pieces. As this book argues, from the perspective of European intelligence, the benefits of cooperation outweighed the risks of potential abuse of intelligence, leaks, or an agency using the information for a killing mission.

4

A BOMB IN PARIS AND TWO ATTACKS IN BANGKOK AND ROME

UPDATING THE MURDERERS: THE ASSASSINATION OF MAHMOUD AL-HAMSHARI

On the morning of 8 December 1972, the phone rang in an elegant apartment at 175 Rue d'Alésia in the 14th arrondissement in Paris, the home of Dr Mahmoud al-Hamshari. He rushed to the little marble table where the phone was, picked up the receiver, and was greeted by an Italian journalist who had tried to meet him a few days before. Hamshari confirmed his identity and a moment later, Mossad transmitted a detonation signal for a bomb that was installed inside the table. This signal made a high-pitched whine and Hamshari immediately stepped back from the marble table.[1] A millisecond later, the bomb exploded. Because he stood back and because the bomb contained a relatively small amount of dynamite, Hamshari survived the explosion. Mossad chose to use a relatively small amount of explosives as they did not want to cause any physical damage to Hamshari's neighbours. Similarly, it wanted to spare his family and waited to set off the explosion until after his wife and daughter were seen to have left the building that morning. However, the blast badly injured Hamshari and destroyed parts of his apartment. He was taken to hospital and three weeks later, owing to substantial internal bleeding, he succumbed to his injuries.

THE CHARGES AGAINST HAMSHARI

Hamshari, who two months before was coincidentally in charge of organising Zwaiter's funeral in Rome, was the second victim of Mossad's Operation Wrath of God.[2] In intelligence parlance, he was a 'soft target': easy to reach and took few security precautions. He was the official PLO representative in France and was thus obliged to meet with anyone who might be interested in discussing the Palestinian cause. Furthermore, even though Zwaiter's assassination instilled great fear among the Palestinian leadership in Europe, Hamshari believed that his status as a quasi-diplomat would spare him from

85

Mossad's deadly hand.[3] As a result, he did not go into hiding and instead followed his normal routines. Mossad simply planned the assassination at the most convenient time in his daily schedule as a PLO official.

Hamshari was mentioned several times in the Club de Berne exchanges as the official Fatah representative in France. In June 1972, for instance, the Dutch intelligence agency, BVD, informed its partners about a Fatah representative in the Netherlands, Mahmud Salim al-Rabbani, who was allegedly in contact with his counterpart in France, Dr Hamshari.[4] Dutch intelligence described the following tasks of the Fatah representative: disseminating propaganda for the Palestinian cause, maintaining a close network of Arab diplomats, fundraising for Fatah among Arab expatriates, and maintaining regular contact with the Fatah leadership (including Arafat, Nabil Sharath, and Abu Omar) and other Fatah representatives in Europe. Further, the Fatah representative was in charge of recruiting Fatah members from among local Arab circles, organising free trips for them to the Middle East, and, most surprisingly, building cells for terrorist activities.

Regarding this last function, the BVD had received reports that the Fatah representative in the Netherlands had been involved in various terrorist operations. However, the cable specified that, other than publicly endorsing terrorist actions after they happened, the Fatah representative 'prefer[red] to remain entirely ignorant of intended subversive actions in view of his vulnerable position in the Netherlands'.[5] This assessment by the Dutch suggests that there was generally only a distant connection between official Fatah representatives in Europe and Palestinian terrorism, even if the representatives endorsed it. However, the secondary literature suggests that in Hamshari's case, Mossad assumed that he was a lot more directly involved in terrorist operations. Namely, it believed that Hamshari planned specific attacks and transferred money, mail, and weapons to Black September.[6]

According to the authors Aaron Klein and Ronen Bergman, Mossad thought that Hamshari was responsible for the bombing on 21 February 1970 of a Swissair flight from Zurich to Tel Aviv, which crashed in Würenlingen and caused the deaths of forty-seven passengers and crew.[7] The Israelis also thought he was an accomplice in a PFLP plan to murder David Ben-Gurion, Israel's first prime minister, during a trip to Denmark in May 1969. Furthermore, they believed that Hamshari's apartment in Paris was used as an arms cache for Black September.[8]

In terms of Hamshari's position within Fatah, some journalistic accounts suggest that he was the head of Black September in France.[9] Some suggest that Mossad thought he held an even higher position,

namely second-in-command of Black September for all its worldwide oper-
ations.[10] This could not be confirmed in the Kilowatt cables. After his death
Hamshari was generally referred to as the 'senior ex-representative of the
Fatah in France'.[11]

Lastly, documents in the French Foreign Ministry archives suggest that
Hamshari was in the process of negotiating a potential deal between the
PLO and the French state that would have shielded France from future
terrorist attacks.[12] If this is true and if Mossad was aware, assassinating him
would have sent a signal to France that Israel condemned such approaches
to terrorism and that it aimed to disrupt such deals.

Taken together, Hamshari's clear alleged links to Palestinian terrorism, outspoken support for it, prominent position within Fatah and Black
September, alleged direct involvement in attacks, and role as potential facilitator of a non-aggression deal led Mossad to consider him a legitimate
target for Operation Wrath of God. In keeping with this covert operation's
declared goal of 'intercept and prevent', Mossad officials later claimed that
they simply saw what Hamshari had done in the past and what damage he
could cause in the future. Mossad acted according to this assessment.[13]

THE HAMSHARI MURDER INVESTIGATION

Because Hamshari was not killed on the spot, police were able to interrogate him before he died. This explains how French security knew how the
murder was executed and were able to piece together how it was planned.

A few days after the explosion, the French domestic intelligence agency,
DST, shared details about the case among the Kilowatt group.[14] The cable
mentioned again that Hamshari had been the Fatah representative in France
and explained how the assassination had unfolded. It also shared that the
murderer used the cover of an Italian journalist. As the DST cable specified,
somebody pretending to be an Italian journalist had requested a meeting
with Hamshari on 6 December 1972 at the office of the Arab League in
Paris. Nobody showed up to the meeting. Then, on 8 December 1972 at 9
a.m., Hamshari received a phone call from this same ostensible 'Italian journalist'. At that moment the explosives, which had been concealed underneath the telephone table, were detonated. This severely injured Hamshari
and blew apart his apartment.[15] The French police believed that Hamshari
had been called so that he would be standing next to the phone table that
contained the explosives. Once he was on the line, the murderer knew that
he was standing next to the bomb. The French cable assumed that 'the killer
activated the explosion via remote control from a nearby phone booth'.[16] It

also mentioned that the investigation was still ongoing and that this was the latest information. It was, of course, very useful for Mossad to know that the French authorities (for the moment) did not suspect that it was behind the attack, or if they did, they decided to keep it quiet.

There are a few minor differences between the way this killing operation is described in the French cable and in the secondary literature. The first difference concerns the meeting between Hamshari and the Mossad officer. According to Klein, Reeve, and Bergman, the 'journalist' indeed came to an in-person meeting at a café near Hamshari's home on the Left Bank.[17] However, Hamshari's account to the police that there was no meeting, as shared among the Club de Berne, seems more plausible. An actual meeting would have carried more risk for Mossad. If the two had met, the Mossad operative could have made Hamshari suspicious. Additionally, if they had met, Hamshari would have been able to give a physical description of the 'journalist' to the police. The police report sent by the DST did not mention or include any description of the journalist's appearance.

Another small difference concerns the likely reason for the phone call. Mossad phoned Hamshari not only so that he would be standing close to the bomb, but also to confirm his identity so it knew it was killing the right target. The French police further assumed that the bomb was detonated via remote control, while secondary literature suggests it was though a phone cipher signal.[18] Furthermore, the bomb was probably not underneath the phone stand, as the police report suggested, but built inside the stand. Secondary literature claims that before the assassination, Mossad had broken into Hamshari's home, taken as many pictures as possible, and sent the photos to the agency's technical department. Mossad mechanics apparently noticed the marble phone base and decided to create a replica with the explosives hidden inside, which was swapped for the original during a subsequent break-in.[19] Finally, the secondary literature reveals the real and cover names of the Mossad officer who posed as the Italian journalist: Nehemia Meiri, who used the cover name Carl.[20]

Given that the low amount of TNT did not kill Hamshari right away, the question arises as to whether Mossad erred in the conception of the assassination plot. Allowing the police to learn about the fake Italian journalist and other details of the operation increased the risk, even if just by a little, that the police would discover one of Mossad's officers. Since Mossad made sure that the wife and daughter were out of the house, could they not have increased the bomb's capacity? But a higher amount would have risked harming a neighbour. Prime Minister Meir gave very clear instructions that Operation Wrath of God should 'not harm a hair' on a European citizen's head.[21]

Another hypothesis is that it may have been deliberate – that Mossad wanted the police to interrogate Hamshari after the explosion. In the covert action logic of '*im*plausible deniability', it would actually be advisable for Mossad to leave some traces behind. In order to have a deterring and terrorising effect upon Palestinians, the agency would not have wanted people to assume that it was an accident. Instead, it needed to be clear that there was intent and agency behind the murder – intimating that Mossad was behind it, without leaving any incriminating evidence. The victim telling the police how the murder happened ensured that the police knew this was a carefully planned killing operation, without leaving any incriminating material on site. Furthermore, because Hamshari employed so few security measures, Mossad could have easily shot him on the street. Killing him with a bomb in his own apartment was a lot more spectacular. It was likely meant to instil fear among the Palestinian leadership that they were no longer safe anywhere, not even in their own homes. Indeed, Palestinians were frightened, and their public reactions were not long in coming. The day after Hamshari's murder, Arab diplomats gathered in Paris and officially demanded that French authorities protect them. At a press conference, Fauzi Gariani, the senior Libyan representative in the city, deplored 'the atmosphere of Zionist terror in France'.[22]

PLO leaders in Europe now feared for their lives and a great deal of agitation went through the ranks of the Palestinian leadership. This was also reported in Club de Berne intelligence, such as by the BVD. Two weeks after the explosion in Hamshari's home, Dutch intelligence informed its partners about the very worried reactions of other Fatah representatives in Europe.[23] It had received a report from a 'reliable and extremely delicate' source that all such Fatah representatives had been summoned to Beirut to an emergency meeting with the Fatah leadership, which was to be held before the end of the year.[24] The BVD knew that the Fatah representative in the Netherlands, Mahmud Salim al-Rabbani, was going to be in Beirut on 27 December 1972 to attend this meeting.[25]

Two days later, the BVD sent an urgent message confirming that the Fatah leadership meeting was going to take place on 6 January 1973.[26] Rabbani and Daoud Barakat (the Fatah representative in Geneva) were said to be in Beirut around 1 January 1973. Dutch intelligence specified that the source of this report was 'different from the source of Watt 9036 [sent on 19 December 1972] but also extremely delicate'.[27] The cable specified, however, that the reliability of the source was 'untested'. Interestingly, the BVD added that it wanted to test the reliability of this source and therefore requested confirmation from other agencies concerning intelligence about the Fatah meeting.[28] This is interesting as it provides insight into how intelligence agencies may use intelligence-sharing as a means to corroborate received intelligence and thus assess an informant's reliability.

The next day, MI5 confirmed the Dutch reports and concurred that there was going to be a high-level PLO/Fatah meeting very soon.[29] The meeting was scheduled for 4 January 1973 and the top Fatah leadership was expected to participate, such as Yasser Arafat, Ali Hassan Salameh, and Saleh Khalaf (alias Abu Iyad).[30] The Fatah representative in London, Said Hammami, was also attending the meeting in Beirut. The meeting details were based on reliable information and MI5 asked that Kilowatt members 'please treat this information discreetly'.[31]

Shortly afterwards, MI5 informed its partners that it had received intelligence that the meeting with the European PLO/Fatah representatives following Hamshari's death was now going to take place on 7 January 1973 in Cairo and not in Beirut.[32] MI5 specified that this source too was delicate and assessed to be reliable. From a later cable, sent by Mossad in February 1973, we know that this meeting indeed took place. The gathering was referred to as the meeting of the Palestinian Council to discuss matters after Hamshari's death. It took place in Cairo in early January 1973.[33]

From Kilowatt correspondence after Hamshari's assassination, one can see that Mossad's second killing operation generated quite a bit of turmoil within Fatah. From the perspective of Mossad, things were going its way: Palestinian activists in Europe now feared for their lives. However, this did not lead to a halt of terrorist activity. The next terrorist operation happened before the end of the year, on 28 December 1972, in Bangkok.

BLACK SEPTEMBER ATTACKS: A HIT IN ASIA AND ATTEMPTED MISSILE ATTACKS IN ROME

ATTACK AGAINST THE ISRAELI EMBASSY IN BANGKOK

With increased awareness among Israeli security, Black September had to search harder to find a vulnerability that it could exploit. In December 1972, the group found a weak link at the Israeli embassy in Thailand. A few weeks before the attack, Tel Aviv ordered a change in the security rules at this embassy, but these measures had not yet been implemented.[34] The embassy in Bangkok was low on the government's list of priorities and had relatively lax security.

On 28 December 1972 – almost three weeks after Hamshari's assassination – Black September managed to infiltrate the embassy with four of its militants. Two operatives dressed up in elegant suits to look like diplomats while the embassy was hosting a party. They sneaked past the security guards and once inside the embassy compound, met up with two Black September armed gunmen, who entered by climbing the surrounding walls.[35] Once the embassy was in the terrorists' hands, they let most of the staff members leave and kept six Israeli diplomats as hostages. Similarly to the Munich Olympics attack, the terrorists rounded up the hostages, handcuffed them together in an upstairs room, and threatened their lives. A leaflet with demands was thrown out of the window: in exchange for the hostages, Black September demanded the release of thirty-six Palestinian detainees from Israeli prisons, including Kozo Okamoto, one of the perpetrators of the Lod Airport massacre of May 1972. This had been a very brutal terrorist operation in which members of the terrorist group known as the Japanese Red Army managed to take guns into the airport's arrivals hall, where they indiscriminately shot at people who were waiting for their luggage. The attack was co-organised with the PFLP and killed twenty-six people, injuring seventy-three others.[36] (See Figure 9.)

Figure 9 Aftermath of the Lod Airport massacre on 31 May 1972. Source: Keystone/ Getty Images.

Coincidentally, the Israeli ambassador to Thailand, Rehavam Amir, was not at the embassy during the attack. He and his wife were attending the coronation of Crown Prince Vajiralongkorn, the heir to the Thai throne. However, the Israeli ambassador to Cambodia, Simon Avimor, was visiting at the time, and he was at the embassy when Black September took control and was immediately taken hostage.

The Thai authorities considered the timing of the embassy siege to be a serious insult and were furious that it took place at the same time as the investiture. They were decidedly on the side of the Israeli government and offered any support they could. Local authorities mobilised the police and hundreds of troops surrounded the building where the hostages were being held.[37]

Negotiations ensued, which were led by the Israeli ambassador to Thailand, the Thai authorities, and, additionally, the Egyptian ambassador to Thailand, Mustapha Falmay el-Essaway. During the protracted negotiations (which lasted for nineteen hours), the Egyptian ambassador and Thai authorities applied very strong pressure on the kidnappers. The Thai authorities shamed them for the timing of the embassy siege and insisted that this was a gross insult to them. Meanwhile, an Israeli special operations team was on its way and the kidnappers feared a Munich-like rescue operation, which could cost the terrorists their lives.

Carefully assessing the risks, the kidnappers eventually accepted the offer to release all the hostages in exchange for impunity and safe passage to Egypt. The terrorists were taken to a nearby airport where they released the hostages and boarded a plane to Egypt. (See Figure 10.) The Egyptian ambassador had continuously offered reassurance and even joined the terrorists on their flight to Egypt to guarantee safe conduct.[38]

Back at Fatah headquarters in Lebanon, Saleh Khalaf, who had recently been made deputy chief and head of intelligence for the PLO, saw the terrorists' abandonment of their mission as an embarrassment.[39] Similarly, Ali Hassan Salameh, one of the Black September masterminds behind this operation, was outraged. Rumours circulated that the Black September leadership ordered the assassination of the failed kidnappers or other retaliatory measures against them.[40]

Indeed, these death threats against the Bangkok perpetrators can be confirmed through Club de Berne correspondence. A few weeks after the attack, in mid January, MI5 shared intelligence about the whereabouts of the perpetrators. A reliable source claimed that they had recently left Damascus for Europe via Beirut.[41] The cable explained that initial reports suggested that Black September was going to severely punish the Bangkok

Figure 10 Released Israeli hostages after the Bangkok embassy attack. Source: UPI/
Bettmann Archive/Getty Images.

perpetrators and take heavy disciplinary actions against them. But, as the
cable continued, the British agency had recently obtained additional intelligence that suggested the perpetrators would instead be given the opportunity to redeem themselves.[42]

Thanks to the numerous journalistic accounts, the course of events at
the Bangkok embassy siege is relatively well known. What has thus far not
been known is that Black September had plans for a parallel attack that was
meant to happen simultaneously. This attack was thwarted by the British
authorities. The story of this other attack begins with an arrest at a London
airport on 24 December 1972.

On that day, MI5 alerted its Kilowatt partners that an Arab man,
Mohammed Abdul Karim Fuheid, had been arrested at the airport in possession of a pistol, ammunition, explosives, and electronic detonators.[43] He
had come from Beirut and was on his way to Stockholm.[44] He had two passports with him – a Bahraini one and a Guatemalan one. The Guatemalan
passport had forged visas for the United Kingdom, Brazil, and France. After
some interrogations, Fuheid claimed that his real name was different and
that he was a first lieutenant in the Jordanian army. He was supposed to go
to Stockholm for a terrorist operation against Israel.[45]

Two days later, on 26 December 1972, Israel thanked MI5 and shared the information Mossad had regarding these names.[46] It asked several very specific follow-up questions. This is a typical example of intelligence cooperation after an arrest. Mossad's questions were as follows:

Were all weapons in false-bottom or only the explosives and the timer?
Was subject in transit only or did he attempt to leave the airport? Did he meet anyone?
Were any further suspects on this particular flight?
We attach utmost importance to clarification whether suspect was part of a group or a 'lone wolf'.
Is Bahrein [sic] passport also a forgery?
Would appreciate earliest possible photo and fingerprints of suspect which would aid in identification. Also description of luggage.
In view of improbability of one terrorist acting alone, we assume further members of gang may have arrived in Stockholm. Would appreciate list of suspects, which we could check for you.[47]

The next day, 27 December 1972, MI5 replied to all the queries.[48] It confirmed that all weapons and explosives were in a false bottom, and that Fuheid was only in transit. He was not seen meeting anyone before his arrest. Police investigations were attempting to establish whether any other travellers on the same flight were associated with the suspect. As of the time the cable was sent, no connection had been established.[49] MI5 believed that the Bahraini passport was also a forgery and promised to provide the fingerprints and photos of Fuheid as well as pictures of his luggage to the Israeli representative at the next liaison meeting. The cable added that Fuheid was being charged with illegal possession of weapons and was going to appear before a magistrate shortly.[50]

Following up further, Shin Bet provided additional intelligence about Fuheid.[51] It knew of a Fatah operative who matched his personal details. The Israeli domestic intelligence agency provided all known details about him, including his birthplace, the date he joined Fatah, his military training, and his last known address in Syria. This person was said to have attended a meeting in early 1971 when Fatah decided to establish Black September.[52]

After some further questioning by UK intelligence, some crucial puzzle pieces came to light about Fuheid's likely operation. He stated that the attack in Norway was planned for 29 December 1972 and would have coincided with a Fatah anniversary.[53] MI5 reckoned that since Fatah was established in the summer of 1962, the date of the planned attack corresponded to the creation of its military wing, Assifa, whose first operation was 30

December 1964. The UK ended the cable with a warning that the security threat remained extremely high for the last days of the year.[54]

After some more extensive interrogations, on 9 January 1973, MI5 sent a very long cable with further information.[55] Importantly, it mentioned that the electrolytic timing devices and the explosives were identical to those found in Halloum's baggage at Schiphol Airport on 23 October 1972.[56] This suggested that Fuheid may have been preparing to sabotage an aircraft.

MI5 also investigated the travel agency that Fuheid had used to purchase his SAS flight tickets to London and Stockholm. The company that had issued the tickets was called Strand Travel Agency and was located in Beirut. MI5 requested further information about this company from its Kilowatt partners and alerted them that it might have previously been involved in terrorist activities in Europe.[57]

Fuheid had changed his story in the meantime and dropped the claim that he had been in the Jordanian army. He confirmed that he was a member of Fatah but claimed that he only worked as a 'weapons instructor' based in Syria. He admitted that he had attended a training course in Algeria in 1969 and that his real name was the one engraved on the back of his watch (which was shared among Kilowatt). Regarding his involvement in the terrorist plot that was thwarted by his arrest, he insisted that he was only a weapons courier. He explained that he was supposed to send a telegram from Stockholm and that somebody would then have come to pick up the suitcase. The telegram was going to be addressed to Mohamed Abu Yussuf, PO Box Beirut 4880. MI5 wanted to know if any Kilowatt member had records of this post office box.

In assessing Fuheid's terrorist involvement, MI5's conclusion was that he must have been far more than a simple weapons courier, being certain that he was an essential operative in a terrorist plot.[58] It based its assessment on his experience with weapons and on the fact that his terrorist kit contained all that was required for aircraft sabotage, either connected with or independent of hijacking a plane. MI5 thus inferred that at least one other terrorist was involved in this operation, probably somebody who was based in Scandinavia.

Regarding Mohamed Abu Yussuf, the addressee of the telegram that Fuheid was supposed to send, it is interesting to note that he was killed by Mossad in April 1973 as the fifth assassination of Operation Wrath of God. This took place in Lebanon and is known as Operation Spring of Youth.[59] Mossad certainly knew of Mohamed Abu Yussuf and receiving intelligence that he was likely connected to a terrorist plot may have strengthened the decision to put him on the kill list. If Mossad had not already known about it, receiving Abu Yussuf's PO box number may have been helpful as well.

Finally, new evidence appeared that linked this thwarted attack to the siege at the Israeli embassy in Bangkok.[60] MI5 read a letter that Fuheid sent to Damascus from prison. It was addressed to Abu Jihad. MI5 determined that this was the alias of Khalil Wazir of Fatah general command, whose name was closely associated with Black September. Fuheid wanted to make sure that Abu Jihad was aware that his mission had failed owing to his arrest and advised that a visit was not desired given the circumstances. In the same cable, MI5 informed its partners that it had obtained intelligence that Black September members in Bangkok had enquired about news of operations in other parts of the world. This was another indication that a parallel attack had been planned.

After prolonged interrogations and investigations, the details of which MI5 shared among the Kilowatt group, it crystallised that Fuheid had been tasked (presumably by Abu Jihad) with carrying out a terrorist attack in or around Stockholm. This attack was meant to coincide with the Bangkok embassy siege on 28 December 1972.

In April 1973, a UK court sentenced Fuheid.[61] While MI5 promised to circulate a detailed report about the case at a later stage, it sent a summary of what it thought to be relevant from an intelligence and counterterrorism perspective right after the verdict was issued. The cable informed its partners that Fuheid was sentenced to prison and MI5 estimated that this would result in 'an appreciably increased risk of an indefinite duration to British interests both at home and abroad'.[62] Namely, Fuheid's release was highly likely to figure in terrorists' demands in future Palestinian operations.

In late January 1973, four Black September members were arrested in Vienna.[63] MI5 was allowed to interrogate these detainees. One of them, as MI5 stressed, expressed no doubt that Black September was going to seek to secure the release of any of its members imprisoned in a foreign country, including the UK. While MI5 anticipated that an attack could take any form, it attributed the highest risk to hostage-taking through the hijacking of a British ship or aircraft. In the UK, likely scenarios were the siege of a foreign embassy, kidnapping, or hijacking.[64]

The British agency further claimed to have found more evidence that confirmed previous intelligence reports that Fuheid had been tasked by Black September to attack Israeli targets in Stockholm. Because his operation had failed, MI5 reported that he was now in disfavour with the Fatah and Black September leadership. The group was therefore less likely to organise attacks that were aimed at obtaining his release. Other Palestinian groups, the cable continued, might nevertheless undertake an operation on his behalf.[65] The UK was thus very worried that having this member of Black September detained could pose a risk to UK interests.

As would become clear a month later, these fears were largely unfounded. In May 1973, MI5 expressed its relief that there had been no public reaction to Fuheid's conviction in Arab countries or the Arab press.[66] Provided his good behavior led to remission of part of his sentence, he was scheduled to be released in December 1973. Pro-Palestinian circles in the UK seemed to have accepted that the trial was fair and the sentence reasonable.[67] As a consequence, MI5 believed that the threat to British interests through an operation specifically designed to secure the detainee's release had diminished appreciably. The British agency could not, however, rule out the possibility of actions by groups acting independently of the Fatah and Black September leadership. Fuheid's release could still appear on any list of terrorist demands in future Palestinian operations, not necessarily directed against a British target. Lastly, MI5 thanked everyone for any actions they may have taken in response to its strong concern regarding terrorist actions against British targets.[68]

A few weeks after the arrest in London, in February 1973, warnings circulated among the Kilowatt group that the Bangkok terrorists were planning another attack. West German intelligence forwarded an alert from Interpol India, which warned about five Arabs who had plans to hijack a plane to obtain the release of Palestinian prisoners in the United Kingdom, Italy, and Austria. In the same cable, West German intelligence commented on each of the suspects and complemented the Interpol list with BND and BfV intelligence.[69] Interpol had given the personal details of five suspects, including their names, passport numbers, passport issue dates, dates of birth, and places of birth. West Germany added further information and specified that the first four names were identical to the aliases used by the hostage-takers in the Bangkok embassy attack. The fifth person was suspected to have been the person who visited the four perpetrators in their hotel room in Bangkok prior to the operation.[70]

German intelligence provided further details about the suspects, such as their level of English mastery, their physical appearances, and their likely rank or role in their next terrorist commando unit. Other details were also included such as their weaknesses (for instance, a 'proclivity for girls'), character traits, or level of education. These additional details were certainly useful to identify them should they travel, but this kind of intelligence would also have been useful if an agency was going to try to acquire them as informants.

In sum, Kilowatt cooperation around the Bangkok embassy siege and its thwarted twin attack reveals how British law enforcement gradually gained more information. Kilowatt cooperation was very detail-oriented and allowed a clear connection to be established between the arrest and the attack in Bangkok. This allowed the UK to determine the sponsor of this twin attack.

Furthermore, the West German comments on the Interpol alert also reveal new aspects of the mechanisms of intelligence cooperation. Namely, while general information about terrorist suspects – as issued by Interpol – was widely accessible, more specific pieces of intelligence were reserved for only a select intelligence circle such as the Club de Berne's Kilowatt group. These additional details included further explanation of the context, the suspects' likely connection to terrorist actions, their physical appearance, their character, and their role within terrorist groups.

THWARTED SURFACE-TO-AIR MISSILE ATTACKS

In late 1972, the Pope invited Israel's prime minister, Golda Meir, for a visit to the Vatican. As part of Israel's foreign policy goal to obtain full international recognition, Meir readily accepted the invitation.[71] Her flight was scheduled to arrive in Rome on 15 January 1973. Black September learned of this upcoming visit and allegedly planned a surface-to-air missile attack to shoot down the plane carrying her.[72] This attempt to shoot down the plane was apparently explicitly meant as retaliation for Operation Wrath of God. Furthermore, after the Bangkok fiasco, Black September was in dire need of a terrorist success, ideally a spectacular attack like the killing of Israel's prime minister, which would make international headlines.[73]

Few accounts exist today about this attempted downing of Meir's plane. British journalist Simon Reeve and former Mossad case officer Victor Ostrovsky tell a riveting story about how Mossad ultimately thwarted this attack, apparently only at the very last minute, according to both accounts.[74] According to Ostrovsky, who provides the most detail about this event, Black September heard about plans for Meir to visit Rome and decided to make a daring attempt on her life. It allegedly possessed Russian-made Strela missiles, which were based on the US Redeye missile system, with a handheld launcher that was slung over the shoulder. The Black September leadership is said to have organised the transfer of these missiles from a training base in Yugoslavia to Rome, where they remained hidden in an apartment.[75]

With Meir's upcoming trip to Rome, Mossad would have been particularly sensitive to any Palestinian activities in Italy. Two days before the visit, it was said to have intercepted a phone call to Rome by a Fatah member in Brussels, saying 'clear the apartment and take all fourteen cakes'.[76] Mossad allegedly traced the call and broke into the apartment, which was empty except for a small strip of torn paper with part of a picture of a Strela surface-to-air missile and Russian instructions on how to use it.[77]

According to Ostrovsky and Reeve, Mossad knew now that Black September had missiles and was likely planning to use them to shoot down Meir's plane. At that point, Israeli security was said to have informed the Italian authorities about the Black September assassination plans against Meir. Following this, local police and Mossad frantically searched the area around the two main runways of Rome Fiumicino Airport. Purportedly, only on the day itself, 15 January 1973, was the Palestinian commando apprehended. The terrorists apparently had missiles pointed towards the sky, ready to be fired at Meir's plane at any moment.[78]

The books by Reeve and Ostrovsky are among the very few accounts that mention this incident and the veracity of the attempted attack has thus far not been proved. In the Club de Berne files, however, there is an important piece of evidence that adds some credence to their story.

On the evening of 15 January 1973, Mossad sent a cable to the Kilowatt group in which it warned that terrorists were now using surface-to-air missiles to attack aircraft.[79] Based on 'recent indications', the cable warned that terrorist tactics now involved hiding near the runway and firing rocket launchers at planes during takeoff or landing. Mossad stated that hijacking planes had become more difficult and therefore it suggested that Palestinian organisations had adopted this new, deadlier tactic.

What makes this cable most remarkable is the date it was sent: the evening of the day that Mossad allegedly thwarted exactly such a surface-to-air missile attack, as described as a tactic in the cable. While this cable does not substantiate all the details of Ostrovsky's story – which at times sounds overly dramatic and possibly embellished – it lends more credibility to Black September's intention to organise such an attack.

Reviewing Club de Berne correspondence over the next few months in relation to this attempted attack in Rome, it is interesting to note that surface-to-air missiles allegedly in the hands of Palestinian terrorists were mentioned and in one case confirmed later. It was mentioned for the first time in February 1973, when Mossad was again expressing its fear that Palestinian groups could prioritise deadly attacks against planes.[80]

This cable, with Kilowatt number 6093, was sent in the context of the downing of a Libyan civilian plane that flew over sensitive Israeli military installations.[81] On 21 February, Libyan Arab Airlines flight 114 entered Israeli airspace over the Sinai Peninsula (then occupied by Israel). The plane flew over sensitive Israeli military installations and an important air-base at Bir Gifgafa. Israel thus believed that the plane was on an aerial spy mission.[82] Israeli fighter planes approached the Libyan plane and demanded its immediate landing. When it refused (allegedly over a period of fifteen minutes), the Israeli fighter jets attacked, which caused the Libyan plane to crash.[83] Egypt had a nearby airbase with fighter jets ready for flight but refused to respond to the distress call of the Libyan plane. All 108 passengers and crew died instantly.[84]

Libya then urged Egypt or Syria to retaliate on its behalf. Since these attempts were of no avail, the Libyan president, Muammar Qaddafi, was allegedly furious and even more determined to support Palestinian terrorist organisations. In retaliation, as Shin Bet feared, Palestinian groups were likely to receive Libyan help to destroy an El Al plane on the ground or during takeoff or landing through one of four possible methods.[85]

As specified in cable 6093 sent in February 1973, Israel was concerned that Palestinian terrorists were going to attack a plane on the ground with remotely controlled toy planes carrying explosives.[86] This is interesting from today's perspective and in view of most recent terrorist practices where everyday appliances, such as toys, have been turned into deadly terrorist weapons. This method as described in the cable also nods at today's small drones that can carry explosives and thus be turned into lethal weapons that can be directed against civilians.

Mossad also expected attacks on planes through use of rocket launchers, and it received reports that Palestinian groups had acquired very large suitcases that could hold and camouflage rockets. With the rocket hidden in a suitcase, a terrorist could approach planes and shoot at them from close up. The Israeli agency assessed that Palestinians could also attack a plane with small arms during landing or takeoff. Lastly, and most relevant to the Rome aircraft attack, Shin Bet received reports that Palestinian terrorists were in possession of 'man-portable' air-defence systems (MANPADS or MPADS), namely surface-to-air missiles that could shoot down a plane using an infrared homing device.[87] This is again the same type of missile that Black September was said to have tried to use against Meir's plane.

A few months later, in August 1973, the German BfV informed its Kilowatt colleagues that it had received confirmed intelligence that Palestinian terrorists were about to obtain a 'Fliegerfaust I Redeye' in order to shoot at aircraft from the ground as they took off or landed.[88] The Redeye, as the West German cable specified, was an American one-person weapon, which could be held on the shoulder. The target would be reached via an infrared seeker-head.[89]

The cable did not specify how the Palestinians were going to obtain these weapons. From the secondary literature it is known that Chadian rebels received Redeye MANPADS, portable surface-to-air missiles, from Libya.[90] Given Palestinian–Libyan relations and Libyan resolve to retaliate for the downing of its plane over the Sinai, it is conceivable that Libya was facilitating Palestinian acquisition of these missiles. Nevertheless, there are today no confirmed accounts that Palestinians had American-built weapons. It is possible, as the cable suggests, that Palestinian groups were trying to obtain them, while it remains unlikely that they succeeded. As mentioned, the cable classified this piece of intelligence as 'confirmed'.[91]

Similar to the hideout where Black September allegedly stored its Soviet-built Strela missiles in January 1973, in early September of that year the Italian authorities indeed found such Strela missiles in an apartment in Ostia, on the outskirts of Rome. The apartment was in the name of a Lebanese national, who was arrested when the police found two Soviet Strela anti-aircraft rocket launchers with infrared pointer heads there.[92] The Italian police apprehended four of his accomplices in a hotel in Rome. The four had Iraqi, Libyan, Algerian, and Syrian passports, and the Italian authorities traced all their movements before arriving in Italy. Two weeks before their arrest, in late August, they had all arrived in Rome from Beirut on different flights, and each was travelling on a passport from a different Arab country. The arrest of these five Arabs is henceforth referred to as the 'Ostia arrests'.

The apartment that the Lebanese national had rented and where the missiles were stored was located very close to Rome Fiumicino Airport. Italian intelligence thus assumed that their plan had been to shoot rockets at aircraft when they landed or took off.[93]

Shortly after, Italy sent a detailed description of the missiles and included pictures of them.[94] The weapons were indeed Soviet-built shoulder-fired SA-7 Strela rockets, like the ones Black September was said to have planned to use for the attack on Meir's plane on 15 January 1973. The cable stressed that, at relatively close range, these highly portable and robust missiles could down an aircraft. Their shooting range was estimated at a rectangle of twelve by five kilometres, and Italian intelligence added that downing a plane with these missiles could very well be possible from the runways at Fiumicino Airport.

Replying to these technical details of the Strela missile, Israel reminded the Kilowatt members that such an anti-aircraft attack could happen at any international airport.[95] As immediate preventive measures, Mossad recommended two courses of action. First, all places at risk, such as frontier posts, ports, airports, and custom areas for incoming cargo, should be alerted about terrorist plans to smuggle rockets near planes or ships. Staff members should carefully search personal luggage, packages, and parcels exceeding 1.4 metres in length. Second, Mossad suggested increased vigilance on the periphery of airports. The Israeli cable reiterated the estimated effective range of the missiles, as stated in SISDE's cable, namely a rectangle of twelve by five kilometres with the runway at its centre. Mossad strongly recommended that the areas within this range around the runways should frequently be checked and patrolled.[96]

Just as when the UK authorities arrested the Black September operative tasked with the parallel operation to the Bangkok embassy attack, in September 1973 Italy was also worried that Italian interests had now become terrorist targets. SISDE assessed that the risk was high that Palestinian terrorist groups would attack Italian citizens or interests to obtain the release of the five Palestinian terrorists who had been arrested in connection with the surface-to-air missiles found in Ostia.[97] Particularly the PFLP, under the leadership of Wadi Haddad, was believed to be planning an attack involving Italy. An attack aimed at freeing these five prisoners was viewed as a strong probability because some intelligence reports suggested that at least three of them were prominent figures within the Palestinian armed struggle. The fact that highly valuable weapons were conferred on them also suggested that they were important terrorist operatives.[98]

Italian intelligence thus assessed the threats against Italian interests as very high. It strongly requested that all Kilowatt countries intensify their surveillance of Italian diplomatic representations, of Italian diplomats, and any Italian political figures who were present in a Kilowatt country. It also asked that security measures for Italian air and sea traffic and important Italian industrial representations be increased.[99]

In October 1973, MI5 followed up on the surface-to-air missiles thread and shared a report on how the terrorists were believed to have been able to obtain the Soviet SA-7 Strela missiles.[100] According to UK intelligence, these weapons had been part of a small consignment passed to an Arab terrorist group by the Libyans. The Libyan government gave it to the group for operations against El Al planes as reprisals for the destruction on 21 February 1973 of the Libyan airline in the Sinai. Interestingly, this cable confirmed intelligence that Shin Bet and Mossad had shared shortly after the downing of the Libyan plane. In the above-mentioned cables with Kilowatt numbers 6093 and 6094, Mossad precisely warned that Palestinian commandos, instigated by and with the help of Libya, were trying to obtain and use surface-to-air missiles against El Al planes in order to retaliate for this incident.[101]

MI5 added the following comment on its intelligence: 'in view of the delicacy of the information, we must insist that it is for internal use of your service only. Rome only: regret information cannot be given to judicial authorities investigating case.'[102] Normally the shared intelligence would just be classified as 'top secret' or 'for your service only', but this time the cable added an entire paragraph to emphatically request no circulation of this information. One cannot but wonder how MI5 obtained this intelligence based on such sensitive sources. The agency ended the cable with the assessment that the threat of SA-7 missiles at airports was going to last. The UK authorities responsible for the protection of airports were advised of this, and MI5 had no objections to relevant authorities in the Kilowatt countries being given similar advice.[103]

Around the same time as MI5's cable, in October 1973, Dutch intelligence also followed up on the Ostia arrest. Because some leads were pointing towards the Netherlands, the BVD carried out an investigation and shared the police report among the Kilowatt members.[104] One of the five terrorists who were arrested in connection with the missiles cache in Ostia had six postcards on him. He had written but not yet mailed the cards. Four of the postcards were addressed to people living in the Netherlands and the Dutch intelligence service went to interrogate these people. The report detailed the content of each postcard that the suspect had written. From these, Dutch intelligence learned that this Black September member had met Dutch nationals in a hotel in Cairo that was popular with Dutch tourists. When shown his picture, they all remembered him. However, the terrorist operative had assumed various identities and told each Dutch tourist a different story about himself. As a commonality, he tried to impress them all with money and paid for their expenses when they were out in Cairo. He also tried to recruit some of them as Fatah activists and assured them that he had other friends who were Dutch and Fatah members. He asked them all for their addresses, as he claimed that he was planning a visit to the Netherlands in August or September and he needed a place to stay.[105]

Besides sharing the preliminary results of this investigation, Dutch intelligence compared their findings with a warning issued by the FBI on 28 August 1973. The FBI report itself is not in the Club de Berne files, but one can glean what it said from the Dutch cable. The FBI warned that, in early August, Saleh Khalaf (Abu Iyad) of Black September had completed the planning and logistical support for the first of a series of operations aimed at destroying planes at airports outside the Arab world.[106] The weapons and explosives to be used were reported to already be cached at the scene of the operation, which would be carried out in the last week of August or the first week of September. Dutch intelligence pointed out the striking similarities between this FBI report and the actual preparations that took place for missile attacks in Rome, which were prevented through the 5 September 1973 Ostia arrests.[107]

Looking at Kilowatt correspondence about Palestinian possession and use of surface-to-air missiles all together, one can say that the risk of Palestinian terrorists obtaining and using these weapons was very high throughout 1973. In particular, the cables between August and October 1973 suggest that they were indeed in possession of such rockets and likely planning an attack at Rome Fiumicino Airport. This too makes the 15 January 1973 attempted downing of Meir's plane more plausible.

From a tactical terrorist perspective, when doing a form of terrorist cost-benefit analysis, shooting down a plane was very lucrative. If an entire plane was downed successfully with all its crew and passengers, it would inflict very heavy material and physical harm. This would no doubt capture global headlines. Furthermore, it was a way of circumventing luggage checks and body searches, which had increasingly become an obstacle for hijacking or air sabotage. On the other hand, even with state sponsorship, as was believed to have come from Libya, such weapons were very expensive, difficult to obtain, required adequate training to operate, and owing to their size, were hard to smuggle to the target location.

As far as is historically known, no such attacks ever succeeded. This may have been because Mossad and European and American intelligence indeed prevented them, either through a spectacular last-minute operation as allegedly happened in Rome on 15 January 1973, or by the discovery and confiscation of the missiles before they could be used, like in Ostia in September 1973.

One can further speculate on the extent to which the Club de Berne and its transnational intelligence-sharing links had helped to prevent the September 1973 Rome missile attack. Italy did not specify how it managed to find and arrest the Ostia suspects and confiscate the missiles. While it is not clear how Italian police found the hideout, cooperation had at least made sure that the warnings from Mossad and the FBI about the preparations for such attacks reached Italian intelligence in time. As a result, the Italian authorities knew what to look out for and could act quickly.

Cooperation around Palestinian missile attacks also demonstrates the effectiveness of the Kilowatt platform to counter Palestinian terrorism. It allowed the partners to share specific and to-the-point information, all grouped under one channel and sent directly to the right office in the respective agency. These direct connections were indeed highly appreciated by the practitioners.[108] In this context it is again understandable that any agency would want to keep this cooperation going, even if it risked being abused for targeted killings or other covert operations.

TERRORIST TACTICS AND INNOVATION

After Hamshari's death, Club de Berne correspondence was, of course, strongly concerned with the Bangkok embassy siege and the parallel attack that was thwarted in Scandinavia. Besides this, in the winter of 1972/1973, agencies were concerned with anticipating the next likely targets and methods of Black September. Warnings were quite precise and, as will be shown, one sounds very familiar when compared with the later terrorist events of 11 September 2001. Besides warnings, agencies tried to collectively understand terrorist groups' operational methods. Cables focused on terrorism financing mechanisms, organisational structures, and individual terrorist operatives who were suspected to have entered Europe to carry out an attack.

In mid December 1972, MI5 issued an alert that Italy had become the centre of recent terrorist attention.[109] More specifically, it warned that the Italian airline Alitalia was going to be the next target of Black September operations, with the objective to release Palestinian prisoners held in Italy. Difficulties in finding accomplices in Alitalia had prevented the hijacking from being carried out in November 1972.[110] Given that in the autumn and winter of 1972 there were indeed substantially more terrorist incidents involving Italy than other countries, this MI5 alert seems plausible.

Another warning was issued by Shin Bet in mid December 1972.[111] It provided a detailed assessment in which it gauged Palestinian terrorists' next targets. Israeli intelligence had received information from several sources that Arab terrorists were planning to carry out 'drastic acts of terror during the holiday season'.[112] The possible targets were believed to be Israeli and Jewish institutions and installations mainly in Western Europe and the United States, and, with a lesser likelihood, in other parts of the world such as Africa. Israel anticipated that the attacks would take the form of kidnapping or killing Israeli officials or VIPs; maybe Shin Bet assumed this because it feared that Black September was trying to retaliate in kind for the Operation Wrath of God killings.

Shin Bet also deemed it likely that the Palestinians were planning acts of sabotage against sea or air transportation, particularly now with increased tourism during the holiday season. Similarly, in terms of taking advantage of the Christmas season, with increased postal traffic, Israeli security expected more letter bombs to be sent to Israeli and Jewish people and institutions mainly in Western Europe. Another wave of letter bombs from the Far East camouflaged as presents was deemed likely. In terms of the threat level, Shin Bet suspected that the perpetrators were already in place in the vicinity of their intended targets.[113] In the same cable, Israel confirmed MI5's warning of 12 December 1972 that Alitalia was at high risk because there were several terrorists who had been arrested in Italy.

This warning, which was sent on 18 December 1972, is interesting in light of the Bangkok attack and the attempt to shoot down Meir's plane. In retrospect, Shin Bet was correct in its assumption that Israeli VIPs were being targeted – including Israel's prime minister and diplomats, such as at the Israeli embassy in Thailand. Anticipating the target location proved more difficult, however. Shin Bet expected an attack in Europe or maybe Africa, but was taken by surprise when Black September hit in Bangkok.

Shin Bet's next warning was shared in early January 1973 in the form of a very carefully drafted and detailed account of a hijacking scenario that it was believed the PFLP was preparing.[114] According to this Shin Bet field report, PFLP terrorists were planning to hijack an El Al plane from Europe to Lod Tel Aviv. While cruising above the Israeli capital, the hijackers would begin negotiations with the Israeli government for the release of detained terrorists. In the air, the hijackers would observe movements on the ground, for instance by tracing the movement of cars, and try to spot in which building the decision-makers might stay. Once this concentration of high-level personnel was identified, the hijackers would crash the plane into it and trigger an explosion. The number of terrorists involved in this suicide mission was expected to be large and composed of various nationalities.

Shin Bet further commented on the quality and veracity of the intelligence and the likelihood of the potential scenario. It determined that the source of the report was reliable, but that Shin Bet had no experience with what it called the 'subsource', namely the informant of the informant. The agency did not know whether the informant's informant had actual access to terrorist circles. It further indicated that this scenario was plausible because it had received earlier reports about terrorist plans to hijack an aircraft in order to crash it on Lod or Tel Aviv. The assumption that the perpetrators would be of different nationalities seemed credible to Shin Bet, as George Habash, then head of the PFPL, had previously employed people of diverse backgrounds in sabotage operations. Lastly, Shin Bet alerted its partners that while El Al was the main target, terrorists could attempt to hijack planes from other airlines as well.[115]

From today's perspective, this cable is remarkable given its striking similarity to the events of 9/11. It reads like a warning nearly thirty years before the planes crashed into the World Trade Center in New York. Interestingly, the very first time a commercial airliner was used as a weapon was only a couple of months before this warning was issued. On 10 November 1972, three men hijacked Southern Airways flight 49 from Birmingham, Alabama to Miami, Florida. Their goal was apolitical, mainly for financial gain. The hijackers demanded that $10 million be paid as ransom, or else they threatened to crash the plane into a nuclear research plant in Oak Ridge, Tennessee. During the 29-hour incident, the hijackers forced the crew to land the plane nine times. On the fifth landing, in Chattanooga, Tennessee, the three abductors received $2 million (of the requested $10 million) and forced the crew to depart again. At a stopover in Orlando, FBI sharpshooters shot out the jet's four tyres, but the plane took off once again. Finally, the aircraft landed in Havana and the perpetrators were arrested by the Cuban authorities.[116] While the cable did not refer to this hijacking, it is conceivable that Israeli intelligence and Palestinian armed groups had heard about it. Learning from other hijacking cases, it is possible that the tactic of using a plane as a weapon may indeed have been part of terrorism strategic thinking in the early 1970s.

A few months later, in May 1973, Israeli intelligence followed up and sent a cable with reference to this 4 January 1973 warning.[117] This follow-up cable confirmed that intelligence had been received from a reliable source with good access that the PFLP was still planning to execute such an attack. A possible variation was that if the Israeli authorities were to reject the terrorist demands, the hijackers would blow up the aircraft over an Israeli town, possibly Jaffa.[118]

The claim that Israeli intelligence received a warning about such a terrorist scenario was briefly mentioned by terrorism scholar Adam Dolnik.[119] It was also referred to by journalist Michael Bar-Zohar. As will be mentioned below, Bar-Zohar also claimed that Mossad believed Basil al-Kubaisi, Operation Wrath of God's fourth assassination victim, to have been part of the planning for this attack.[120]

In addition to anticipating innovations in terrorists' tactics, agencies at that time also tried to understand terrorists' operational methods, including understanding how they financed their operations. In mid December 1972, Belgian intelligence informed its partners that Belgian oil companies had recently been blackmailed by Black September.[121] Either the companies should pay 50 million Belgian francs (a very large sum at the time) or they would suffer a heavy hit. Black September demanded that the ransom be delivered on the night of 20 December 1972 by means of an aircraft. The plane was to fly at a low altitude and drop the money in a bag after receiving an optic signal. Black September insisted on the highest level of secrecy and threatened to severely sanction any police intervention.[122] This was a one-off cable and Belgian intelligence did not follow up on it. It is known that ransom extortion was a common terrorism financing method. However, we do not know whether the oil companies mentioned in this cable resolved the issue or whether they eventually paid the ransom.

A central element of intelligence-sharing at the time concerned information exchanges about terrorist suspects. Agencies either warned about specific people or sent lists of names, where everyone was recommended to be put on a watchlist. Typically, the BfV sent long lists of suspects. This was the case in late December 1972, when it forwarded intelligence it had received from its embassy in Colombia.[123] The West German ambassador in Bogotá received a list of Arab terrorist suspects who were refused entry to Colombia and were deported right away. West German intelligence shared the details of these ten suspects with its Kilowatt partners. The list included the terrorist suspects' names, passport or ID numbers, ages, marital status, professions, and physical descriptions. Owing to a sense of urgency, the BfV had no time to translate the list and sent it in Spanish. According to the agency, some people on the list of deportees were prominent members of the Palestinian armed struggle. Similarly, a week before, the BfV had sent a list of names of Palestinians living in West Germany who were suspected of terrorist activities.[124] Many of the people mentioned were alleged members of the GUPS, which had been forbidden in West Germany in the course of the post-Munich security measures.

In a similar effort to trace terrorist suspects, Mossad shared intelligence about a Fatah operative, Mahmoud Abdalla bin al-Hamid Tuda, who was believed to work in the group's intelligence section, called Rasd.[125] Rasd had been mentioned in Kilowatt correspondence a few times already, for instance in a BfV cable about Black September operational methods.[126] Mossad reminded the Club de Berne that 'RASD is Fatah intelligence which contains a department for "special operations". This department is in charge of terrorist operations outside Israel. Most Black September members are estimated to belong to Fatah intelligence.'[127]

Based on a source that was assessed as 'reliable, with access to terrorist circles', Mossad gave Tuda's birth date and the number of his Jordanian passport that he was expected to use soon for travel to Europe. It added that in mid November 1972, he had entered Lebanon with this passport and visited the Rasd office in Beirut. Israel alerted the Kilowatt services that the purpose of Tuda's upcoming visit to Europe was likely to be to prepare for a terrorist operation. Should he enter any of the Kilowatt countries, Mossad requested to be informed about his movements, the people he contacted, and any other relevant details.[128]

Around the same time, Italy shared a report about a puzzling asylum request.[129] A self-proclaimed former Black September operative had allegedly sworn off terrorism, was therefore wanted by his former Fatah bosses, and consequently needed political asylum. He claimed that he was originally sent by Fatah to carry out a terrorist operation in Europe. He had allegedly received a passport and funding for it and flown to Italy. But he ended up spending the money on other items and was now threatened by Fatah and thus asked for political asylum in Italy. He also claimed that he had spent some time in prison in Haifa under charges of espionage because he had been a Fatah operative. Italy did not consider his story to be credible, but requested that Kilowatt members send any antecedents about this suspect.

CONCLUSIONS

After Hamshari's death, despite fingers pointing at Mossad as the assassin (especially by Arabs living in Europe), it is interesting that the French intelligence agency acted as though these claims did not exist and shared details about the murder case and its investigations. This, as will be shown later, was also the course of action following other assassinations in Europe.

Compared with later Operation Wrath of God killings, Hamshari's survival of the explosion was an exception. In making sure that the 'message' reached Palestinian terrorist activists and frightened them, Hamshari's survival may have worked in favour of Mossad. By permitting him to tell the surprised Parisian police about the circumstances of the offence, Mossad could leave some traces to suggest that Israeli intelligence was behind the murder, without leaving any incriminating evidence. Nevertheless, his initial survival was likely based on a miscalculation, especially given that in all other Operation Wrath of God killings the victims died on the spot. Regardless, the assassination of Hamshari seemed to have achieved its goal of causing turmoil among Fatah's ranks. Club de Berne reporting suggests that the Fatah leadership was indeed agitated and worried for its staff in Europe.

Analysing the subsequent attacks by Black September, besides cables relating to the Bangkok attack itself, the Club de Berne files reveal a parallel attack that was meant to happen in Stockholm around the same time as the Bangkok operation. Intelligence-sharing about this parallel attack was a typical example of Kilowatt cooperation where one piece of information led to the next. Finally, one agency, MI5, was able to 'connect the dots' and link it to events in Bangkok. Cooperation over the Bangkok attack further revealed two different systems of information-sharing: a more widespread Interpol channel and a more exclusive circle with more specific details and intelligence shared among the Kilowatt group.

The Club de Berne files in relation to the Black September surface-to-air missile attack at Rome Fiumicino Airport are remarkable too, as they relate to one of Palestinian terrorism's most brazen terrorist plans. If successful, the attack could easily have counted among the most spectacular terrorist events of the decade. The fact that Kilowatt mentioned several reports that Palestinian terrorists possessed surface-to-air missiles further lends credibility to accounts that the 15 January 1973 and similar attacks were indeed being planned by Black September.

Kilowatt reports about Black September terrorism preparations show that agencies were generally trying to be one step ahead of the group. For this, the Club de Berne was essential as it was an effective attempt at gaining a collective comparative advantage over terrorist conspirators. Lastly, assessing the accuracy of warnings that were issued during this period, one can conclude that some elements were indeed predicted correctly. Namely, that the likely next target would be Israeli VIPs or diplomats. The location of the next attack was, however, wrongfully assessed and an attack in Bangkok was simply not expected. Some warnings that were issued in 1973 sound surprisingly familiar compared with more recent events. Mossad's cable of 4 January 1973 reads at times like a warning of 9/11, almost thirty years before it happened and a decade before the first Palestinian suicide attack took place.

5

ASSASSINATIONS IN NICOSIA AND MADRID, ATTACKS IN JORDAN AND SUDAN

UPDATING THE MURDERERS: THE ASSASSINATION OF HUSSEIN ABU-KHAIR

Shortly before midnight on 22 January 1973, Hussain Abu-Khair[1] the recently appointed 36-year-old PLO representative in Cyprus, went to bed in his hotel room. Minutes after he turned off the light, six small bombs hidden underneath his bed were activated remotely and ripped him to pieces. This time, Israeli intelligence wanted to make sure of killing Khair at once. If he survived the explosion, like Hamshari, he too could have told the police incriminating details that could implicate Mossad. By the same token, Golda Meir's standard remained that no innocent bystanders whatsoever were to be hurt. Hence, the explosives could not be too powerful either. The amount seemed to have been measured just right: it killed Khair while the explosion remained contained to his room only.

Khair was Mossad's third Operation Wrath of God victim. In contrast to Hamshari, he was classified as a 'hard target' by the agency, because he spent a lot of time outside its field of operation, mainly in Syria.[2] However, since Khair had only recently arrived in Cyprus, he had not yet rented a flat. It was his temporary housing that made him most vulnerable: even though he had different daily routines and frequently travelled abroad, in Nicosia he always returned to the same hotel in the centre of town, incidentally called Hotel Olympia. Unaware that he might figure on anyone's hitlist, he did not have weapons or bodyguards. Given he was unprotected and always stayed at the same hotel, which was relatively easy to break into, Mossad figured that his room in the Hotel Olympia was the best location to end his life.[3]

THE CHARGES AGAINST KHAIR

After the second kill operation, Mossad changed the requirements for a Palestinian to be included on the Operation Wrath of God kill list. A direct connection to the Munich massacre was no longer needed. Anybody found to be an outspoken supporter of the Palestinian armed struggle or actively involved in the preparation of terrorist events was a potential target of Mossad's killing team.[4]

This new standard applied to Khair, who had not been directly involved in the Munich massacre. In addition to being the head of Black September Cyprus, there was another principal element that made him a top target: Khair was the Fatah liaison to the Soviet foreign intelligence agency, the KGB.[5] Cyprus, particularly Nicosia, was known at the time to be an intelligence hotspot. For instance, the US, Russia, and several Western and Eastern European countries ran their Middle Eastern intelligence missions through Cyprus.[6]

In the early 1970s, the Soviet Union supported Fatah by providing weapons (including powerful AK-47 assault rifles) and arms training in Eastern European countries.[7] Khair was in charge of selecting the Palestinian guerrillas who were to receive training.[8] Israeli intelligence also believed that he forged close ties with senior Soviet intelligence officers who covered part of the Middle East from the Soviet embassy in Cyprus.[9]

In line with common operational methods and the typical reasoning of intelligence agencies, Mossad likely killed Khair to dissuade other Fatah members from taking on the role of KGB liaison. In other words, it wanted to break the Fatah–KGB link by sending the signal that any Palestinian managing the connection to Soviet intelligence would be killed. Indeed, a few months later, Khair's replacement, Zaid Muchassi, was also killed under Operation Wrath of God.

On top of Khair's links to Soviet intelligence and his role as an arms training facilitator, author Marc E. Vargo suggests that he was also preparing a Black September attack on a ship bound for Haifa. The alleged terrorist plot involved smuggling weapons and terrorists aboard a ship departing Nicosia for the Israeli port. Once there, the terrorists, masquerading as passengers, were to seize the weapons and launch an attack against the ship and the port itself.[10] According to Vargo, Mossad wanted to kill Khair in order to prevent this attack.

The Club de Berne files suggest that just such an attack was indeed being prepared only a week before Khair's assassination. On 12 January, the Cypriot authorities arrested a four-man terrorist squad on an Italian passenger boat called the *Messapia*, which followed the route Bari–Piraeus–Cyprus–Haifa.[11] They were arrested at the Cypriot port of Famagusta because the authorities believed their Afghan passports had been forged.

In their cable, Italian intelligence explained that they had received a report about this arrest in Cyprus, which suggested that the detainees were part of a terrorist operation. Because the terrorists embarked on the boat in Bari, Italy, its agency SISDE was planning to investigate this case. In the cable, SISDE included the names and backgrounds of the four terrorist suspects and asked the Kilowatt group whether any of them was known to other agencies.[12]

On 26 January 1973 (after Khair's assassination), Italy provided an update on the Famagusta arrests based on some further investigations.[13] Neither the Italian consulate in Paris nor the Greek consulate in Venice had issued transit visas for any of the visas found in the four passports. Italy was now certain that these passports were fake. Italian intelligence also investigated the purchase of the tickets for the boat tour. They had first been reserved by a woman in Rome on 28 December 1972. She didn't have her passport with her and so the travel company, Adriatica, refused to sell them to her. A week later, on 4 January 1973, a man came in person and claimed that he was the husband of the woman who had tried to buy the tickets earlier. The name in his passport was given to Italian intelligence, but he had not yet been identified by the Italian authorities.[14]

On 11 April 1973, three months after the Famagusta arrests, an attack was thwarted at Rome Fiumicino Airport.[15] After further investigation, Italian intelligence was able to connect this to the Afghans arrested in Famagusta. It confirmed that the four arrested terrorist suspects had indeed planned an attack on the *Messapia*, but they were stopped by their arrest. But, as SISDE explained, only four of them were arrested, while two more terrorists had remained aboard the ship. They eluded the police in Cyprus and later went back to Italy. There they began the preparations for the attack at the airport in Rome, which was thwarted in April. This cable further substantiates the assumption that there was indeed a shipping attack planned aboard the *Messapia*, similar to Vargo's description.[16]

Based on the messages sent by Italy in January 1973, one can speculate that Kilowatt cables first informed Israeli security about the Famagusta arrests and the suspects' plan to attack this shipping route. However, the hypothesis that Mossad wanted to avert the attack by killing Khair is unlikely to be true, since the arrests had already achieved that. Nevertheless, if it was able to connect the terrorist boat attack plot to Khair, given that the arrests were in Cyprus itself, then Mossad held further evidence that he was involved in the preparation of terrorist attacks. This provided yet another reason for Mossad to kill him.

More generally, besides the Famagusta arrests, the risk of attacks involving the shipping industry or Israeli ports was mentioned numerous times by Kilowatt members before and after Khair's assassination.[17] These warnings also lend more credibility to Vargo's story, as intelligence agencies indeed reported that such attacks were being planned by the Black September leadership.

The Club de Berne files hint at yet another possible attack in which Khair may have been involved. However, the links to him are much fainter in this instance. Correspondence between Mossad and the BfV suggests that the person called Hussain Khair was allegedly involved in the Black September assassination of Wasfi Tal in Cairo on 28 November 1971.[18] As mentioned above, Tal was the Jordanian prime minister who commanded parts of the operations that expelled the Palestinians from Jordan in September 1970.[19] However, Khair was a common Arab name, and of course so was Hussein. It may thus have been sheer coincidence that the name of the assassin of Wasfi Tal and that of the person killed by Mossad were the same.

There is no further mention of Hussain Khair (or Chir or Hir or Bashir) in the Club de Berne files. Because Cyprus was not part of Kilowatt, unlike France and Italy, no cables were sent about the murder investigation.

Assessing Khair's terrorism involvement altogether, most accounts stress his role as the contact point between Fatah and the KGB and as a facilitator of arms training in the Soviet Union. Vargo further mentioned Khair as the organiser of an attack against the shipping industry via the port of Haifa. Through the Club de Berne files it is apparent that such an attack was indeed in preparation. However, an irrefutable direct link between this attack and Khair could not be established through the sources. There is nevertheless a striking temporality between the preparations for this attack and Khair's death. This substantiates the claim that Mossad believed he was not only an important KGB liaison, but also actively preparing terrorist actions. As mentioned earlier, another important similarity between both accounts concerned the boat's final destination: the *Messapia*'s last stop, after Famagusta, was indeed Haifa.

BLACK SEPTEMBER ATTACKS: A KILL IN MADRID, AND ATTACKS IN JORDAN, SUDAN, FRANCE, AND ITALY

This section looks at cooperation within Kilowatt from the murder of Khair in January 1973 until Mossad hit again in April 1973. During this time, Black September heavily increased its terrorist activities and ramped up its capacities to retaliate 'in kind'. This included the assassination of an alleged Mossad officer in Madrid. Black September also aimed to hit in an unexpected location again; this time it was the Saudi embassy in Sudan. Besides Israel, Black September's declared main enemy was the Jordanian state and in February several of its operations targeted Jordanian interests.

Around the time of Khair's death, another Middle Eastern player became more involved with Palestinian terrorism: the Libyan government increased its support for Palestinian terrorism and established ties with Palestinian groups, including Black September. During this period, security agencies were further able to thwart several attacks, as will be demonstrated, through Club de Berne cooperation. One such example was when Kilowatt intercepted arms being smuggled and discovered that the weapons were meant for an attack in France. Lastly, during this time Rome Fiumicino Airport once more became the centre of a Black September operation. The following pages look at cooperation in the Club de Berne around these various incidents. Some of these events, especially the thwarted attacks, are only known about today through the Club de Berne files.

ASSASSINATION OF BARUCH COHEN

With Mossad cold-bloodedly killing Black September members one after another, it is not surprising that the group aimed to find Mossad officers and attempt to kill them too. It found a weakness in Baruch Cohen, who was Mossad's senior officer in Europe at the time. Cohen was a native Arabic speaker, descended from an old Jewish family who had lived in Haifa for five generations, and had started his career with Shin Bet in 1959. After the 1967 war, he served with the security service first in Nablus and then in the Gaza Strip. He rose through the ranks quickly and became known in the Israeli security community as a talented, charismatic, and confidence-inspiring case officer.[20] In 1970, Mossad requested his services and sent him, under diplomatic cover, to the Israeli embassy in Brussels.[21]

Cohen's task was to gather intelligence about Palestinian political activities in Europe. Having worked in the occupied territories and refugee camps, he was familiar with Palestinian life in Israel and Palestine. He therefore knew how to speak to and charm an (often homesick) Palestinian expatriate. Shin Bet sent him intelligence on their families that he could use against them, and he had copious amounts of money available to pay them for information. With a natural talent and flair for the profession, he amassed a large collection of Palestinian informants, many of whom were students. While based in Brussels with his wife and four children, he travelled around Europe and developed his network of informants throughout the continent.[22]

By 1973, Cohen's spy network was compromised, and the Black September leadership knew about his work. The organisation pretended to let him 'recruit' some of its members in Spain, who led him to believe that they were cooperating with him.[23] After a while, he realised that they had failed to complete their allocated tasks; they gave false pretexts and he became suspicious of their loyalty. At this stage, Black September decided to execute him before he left for his next mission and before he could do more damage. They needed to hurry, because in early January 1973, he announced that he was planning to leave Spain to attend to other duties.[24]

On the eve of his death, he called his wife from the Spanish capital to let her know that he would be a day late, but she could count on him to return home before Shabbat, on Friday evening. Samir, a Palestinian medical student, had pushed back their rendezvous by a day and they were scheduled to meet at Café Morrison, on Calle José Antonio in downtown Madrid. Once their meeting was over, they stepped out of the coffee shop. Two men approached, and Samir ran away. As a seasoned officer, at that moment Cohen probably understood that he had been betrayed but had no time to react. The killers shot him in the chest, and he collapsed in a pool of his own blood. His killers escaped. The police arrived minutes later, and an ambulance drove him to the hospital, where he died in surgery.[25] Later the same day, Black September published a note in which they took credit for killing a Mossad agent. In the evening, the Israeli government also published a note acknowledging that Baruch Cohen was an agent of Israel's security services.[26]

How was he compromised? In 1970, the Israeli army had published an official album of photographs to mark one thousand days since the Six Day War, in which Cohen appeared in a photograph standing in military uniform next to his best friend, Zadok Ofir. Ofir was a Shin Bet officer who had also been working undercover in Brussels in the early 1970s. In mid September 1972 – just five days after the Munich massacre – his cover was blown and one of his informants turned on him. As with Cohen, this double agent lured him into a trap in a coffee shop, in Brussels, and Ofir was shot. He survived, but he was the first Israeli intelligence officer on active duty abroad to be shot.

It is safe to conclude that publishing a photo of two Israeli spies working undercover in Europe was more than careless, especially since it was known that Arab intelligence agencies collected such clippings. Even though Cohen concealed his Israeli identity when he handled Palestinian students, it is possible that this picture gave him away. Especially after Ofir had been identified, this picture made it particularly easy for Black September to connect the dots.[27] There was further carelessness by Mossad in relation to Cohen's death. A few months before his murder, Arab newspapers reported that Black September had sentenced an Israeli officer in

Europe to death. As a precaution, Baruch Cohen should have been sent home, and certainly should not have been allowed to meet an informant unprotected and by himself in Madrid.[28]

After Cohen's assassination, Mossad was devastated and outraged. It was the first time that an Israeli intelligence officer had been killed by terrorists, and this sent shockwaves throughout the service.[29] Cohen had also provided crucial intelligence on Black September in Europe and his death impacted Mossad intelligence collection. For many members of the Israeli intelligence community, his death required retribution, and many in the service called for an intensification of Operation Wrath of God.[30]

Mossad immediately set about trying to identify and track down Samir, the Palestinian student and Black September double agent who betrayed Cohen, and the two killers. There are conflicting accounts about whether Cohen's killers were indeed executed. Journalist Aaron Klein claims that they all escaped and survived.[31] Cohen's widow, Nourit, gave an interview in 1988 to the left-wing Israeli magazine *Monitin*.[32] She mentioned that she had received information from Mossad that her husband's killers had been eliminated. Namely, she received calls where the person on the line mentioned a newspaper article about the death of a Palestinian. The caller would add that this death was to 'avenge' her late husband. Furthermore, rumours allegedly circulated within Mossad that the three Palestinians involved in Cohen's execution had been liquidated.[33]

One former Mossad case officer, Victor Ostrovsky, confirmed that Baruch Cohen was killed by Black September, but refutes the claim that he was a Mossad officer. He posits that the public confirmation of his death and his role in the Israeli security services was so-called 'white noise'.[34] In intelligence jargon this means stories that were planted in newspapers by Mossad itself in order to sow confusion in the public record. Given the overwhelming source evidence in all other accounts, including many details about Cohen's career in Shin Bet and later Mossad, this claim seems rather farfetched.

Because Spain had not yet joined the Club de Berne or its Kilowatt exchanges at that time, there are no Kilowatt intelligence records about Cohen's death. Interestingly, two weeks after his assassination, Italy's SISDE warned that a dissident Black September operative had planned to execute an Israeli official in Europe.[35] SISDE's source mentioned Israeli personnel in Geneva as the next likely target, but the cable added that Israeli officials all around Europe were at risk. Given the operational hit and blow to morale that Baruch Cohen's death inflicted on Israeli intelligence, it is very possible that Black September was indeed planning another strike akin to his murder.

ATTACKS AGAINST JORDAN

After the Jordanian civil war, which evicted Palestinian armed groups from Jordan (known as 'Black September' in Palestinian circles and as 'White September' in Jordanian circles), Palestinian terrorists also prepared and executed attacks against Jordanian people and interests. As mentioned in Chapter 1, one of the first Black September operations was the assassination of the Jordanian prime minister, Wasfi Tal, in Cairo on 28 November 1971.

After this killing, terrorist activities centred on Israel, although Jordanian targets were nevertheless still a substantial part of the group's terrorist plots. Black September targeted especially high-level representatives such as Jordan's King Hussein himself. This tendency to attack Jordan was also reflected in the Club de Berne, and around January and February 1973 warnings about Jordanian targets grew in number and intensity.

In a warning issued by SISDE in mid February 1973, the agency mentioned specific Black September plans to kill the Jordanian king. This intelligence was based on information that came from someone the agency assessed as 'a well-informed member of Black September'. The informant further gave information on when the attack was planned; the assassination was going to happen by 17 February 1973 at the latest.[36] Three days later, Italian intelligence sent an addendum and shared the name and personal details of its source for this information. The warning had come from an Algerian national detained by Italian police. He had tried to leave the country while he was forbidden to travel owing to legal proceedings against him (the cable did not mention the context of his trial).[37] During the interrogations, he claimed that he worked for Algerian intelligence, but did not provide further information about the planned attack against Jordan. A search of his luggage proved fruitless and Italian intelligence asked to be advised if the other partners knew anything about him.[38]

Surprisingly, in mid February 1973, Fatah and Black September were indeed planning to overthrow and assassinate King Hussein. (See Figure 11.) According to journalist Aaron Klein, Palestinian terrorists devised a daring plan to mobilise thirty-two terrorists and have them storm the office of the Jordanian prime minister and block the exits with explosives. Once in control of the building and the government staff within, the attackers were to take ministers hostage and demand the release of many Palestinian prisoners in Jordan. The plan was to ambush and kill the king while he was on his way to the exchange site.[39]

However, the attack was thwarted, and according to Yezid Sayigh, a specialist in the Palestinian armed struggle, the Jordanian authorities

Figure 11 Jordan's King Hussein in 1973. Source: Bettmann/Getty Images.

announced the arrest of a seventeen-member Fatah team that had entered the kingdom in mid February. Its assignment had been to take the prime minister and the US ambassador hostage, or, alternatively, to attack the parliament or the royal palace.[40] Consequently, Black September operatives were sentenced to death, and the Jordanian army stepped up its purge of Palestinians, reportedly expelling two hundred and placing another thousand on deportation lists.[41]

Terrorist plans against Jordan were not limited to spectacular attacks such as the one thwarted in February 1973. A month earlier, in January 1973, MI5 informed its partners that on 1 January 1973, four parcel bombs had been intercepted before delivery to Jordan.[42] They were posted in Kuwait and two were addressed to Jordanian ministers in Jordan, one Jordanian official in Muscat (Oman), and one Jordanian official in Qatar.

Another warning involving Jordanian targets was issued by the Jordanian authorities themselves. In early March 1973, MI5 informed its partners that the Jordanian ambassador in London had advised the British Foreign Office about an impending terrorist attack on his embassy.[43] The ambassador claimed that this intelligence came from reliable sources. The British agency asked Kilowatt members for any hints in relation to this and similar attacks.

Attacks against Jordan remained a cause for concern in the Club de Berne in the coming months as well. In April 1973, Mossad believed that Black September was planning an operation against Jordan or attempting to seize an Arab embassy where there were Jordanians present.[44] For this and other operations, a team headed by Abu Daoud was said to be conspiring against Jordan in order to get Palestinians released from the country's prisons. Abu Daoud was also mentioned by Klein as the main Palestinian lead in charge of organising attacks against Jordan.[45]

Regarding the Black September plans to attack Jordan, it is interesting to see a mutually confirming interplay between the secondary literature and the Club de Berne files. Not every attack that the Club de Berne was warned about was based on accurate information, but the alerts often corresponded to general terrorist intentions and plans. Hence, intelligence agencies were right to warn about Jordanian interests being at risk.

In February and March 1973, Jordan remained the target of Black September attacks. The section below about arms smuggling via a Mercedes trade network will show how Kilowatt cooperation intercepted an arms transfer, which prevented an attack against a Jordanian embassy in France.[46] But first, Black September hit again in a surprising location: the next attack was in Sudan.

ATTACK AGAINST THE SAUDI EMBASSY IN KHARTOUM

On the evening of 1 March 1973, the Saudi embassy in Khartoum held a goodbye party for George Curtis Moore, the chargé d'affaires at the US embassy who was returning to the United States for reassignment. Many diplomats attended this event to bid their colleague a fond farewell.[47] When the soirée was getting going at around 7 p.m. – the Saudi ambassador and Moore had just finished their speeches – eight heavily armed Black September terrorists stormed the embassy compound. They fired indiscriminately at the guests who were in the reception area, shot the Belgian chargé d'affaires, Guy Eid, in the leg, and created chaos among the guests.[48]

When the terrorist squad entered the embassy through the front door, the panicked diplomats tried to either hide or escape. Some dispersed throughout the building, while others ran through the rear exit towards the garden. The Black September team combed through the residence, specifically searching for diplomats from Western countries. Witness accounts mention that diplomats hid behind bushes in the garden, on the rooftop, and two Arab diplomats even squeezed together in the bathtub.[49] Some attendees were able to escape. The French ambassador, Henri Costilhes, jumped over a six-foot wall and ran away. The Soviet ambassador, Feliks I. Sevastyanov, hid in the garden until all the attackers were inside the embassy, then fled.[50]

Within minutes, the terrorist group controlled the residence. The commander of the raid, Rizk al-Qas, sorted through the detainees and only kept the ones who were of interest. The others, representatives from Eastern European or Asian countries such as Hungary, Yugoslavia, and Japan, were permitted to leave. In the end, the Black September team kept six hostages: the US ambassador and the US chargé d'affaires, the Jordanian and Belgian chargés d'affaires, and the Saudi ambassador and his wife.[51]

Later that same evening, the hostage-takers issued their demands. In exchange for the hostages, Black September called for the release of Palestinian prisoners in various countries. First, it demanded the release of all current Palestinian prisoners in Jordan. They specifically mentioned Abu Daoud – the alleged head of Black September at the time. Second, they asked that all female Palestinian prisoners in Israel be acquitted. Compared with previous attacks, this was an unrealistically high number of prisoners to be released. Third, Black September demanded the release of prisoners in the US, including Sirhan Bishara Sirhan, the Christian Palestinian who had been tried and convicted for the murder of Robert F. Kennedy.

The next day, 2 March 1973, the concerned governments – Israel, the US, and Jordan – declared their refusal to make any concessions to the terrorists. They made it clear that the terrorists' demands would not be met in any way.[52] Instead, hundreds of Sudanese troops surrounded the embassy and threatened to attempt a rescue operation. Black September had rigged explosives on the ground floor and warned that the embassy would blow up, and kill everyone inside, should the military dare to intervene.[53]

On 3 March 1973, the Egyptian president, Anwar Sadat, offered to intercede to help resolve the crisis peacefully. However, with pressure mounting, and the realisation that the terrorists' demands would not be met, Black September decided to kill the three Western hostages. The commander did this without any prior communication and in an appallingly sadistic and brutal way. He first beat the hostages badly and then shot them 'for sport', aiming at their feet and legs, before shooting to kill.[54] The diplomats' bodies were later found in pools of blood and their bodies were mutilated nearly beyond recognition.[55]

After killing the Western hostages, the Black September commandos released the Jordanian and Saudi hostages unharmed and gave themselves up to the Sudanese authorities. Reports about what happened to them after their capitulation are inconclusive. Allegedly, they were tried and sentenced

Figure 12 Transport of dead US embassy staff after the Khartoum attack.
Source: Bettmann/Getty.

to death by a Sudanese court, but then flown to Egypt and handed over to the PLO for an intra-Palestinian trial.[56]

In the secondary literature, the Khartoum attack is seen as a 'show of force' by Black September. Most authors believe that the terrorists' goal was to prove the group's striking power, rather than to obtain the release of Palestinian prisoners. An argument for this interpretation is the unrealistically high number of prisoners that the terrorists asked to have exchanged for the hostages.[57] The fact that they left no room for negotiation also suggests that it was not really about liberating the prisoners. With this attack, Black September thus intended to show the world that it had not lost its resolve and remained committed to the revolutionary Palestinian cause.[58] (See Figure 12.)

However, their plans backfired, and reactions around the world were overwhelmingly negative. A year before, a similar kind of action at the Munich Olympics attack – the cold-blooded murder of civilian country representatives – was cheered in many Arab countries and Black September gained several recruits.[59] This time, the killing of state representatives was universally condemned, and Arab and Muslim countries threatened to withdraw their support for the Palestinian cause.

The situation became even more complicated for the Palestinian umbrella organisations when the Sudanese police investigations revealed that the official Fatah representative in Sudan, Fawwaz Yassin, was the mastermind behind this operation.[60] This revelation confirmed the long-time claims of Israel and other countries that official Palestinian representation, such as PLO or Fatah, was in fact part and parcel of the same terrorist organisation as Black September.[61]

While relations between Fatah and Black September were indeed ambiguous in 1972, by the spring of 1973 the Palestinian leadership's attitude towards international terrorism had changed. Fatah's core leadership under Yasser Arafat concluded that obtaining diplomatic recognition and government support would be more fruitful to secure subsidies, territorial bases, and diplomatic success. Consequently, Arafat and the Fatah leadership insisted on two main aspects. First, they demanded that official Palestinian representation only organise attacks against Israel in the occupied territories. Second, outside Israel, they intended to seek international recognition through a purely diplomatic route of entirely peaceful means.[62] However, other factions within the very divided Palestinian movement disagreed, and groups such as the PFLP continued to perpetrate terrorist attacks.[63]

One of the consequences of the Khartoum attack was that diplomats around the world were reminded of the dangers of Palestinian terrorism. It meant that not only could Israel be directly affected, but also other European states – like Belgium, which had not been as directly targeted before – or other Arab states. According to historian Bernhard Blumenau, another European country, West Germany, had also been targeted, but was spared by pure chance. Blumenau recounts the story through the records of the German Foreign Office. Based on these sources, the hostage-takers allegedly demanded the release of members of the German terrorist organisation called the Baader–Meinhof gang.[64] The West German ambassador to Sudan was supposed to attend the party in the Saudi embassy, but on that evening he and his colleagues had to welcome a high-ranking delegation of West German politicians. Since none of the hostages in the embassy was West German, the terrorists had to drop their demands about prisoners being held in that country.[65]

West German interests featuring as a terrorist target in Khartoum was never officially confirmed by the German Foreign Office. Blumenau's account stems from internal foreign office correspondence, while officially West Germany did not acknowledge that it had been targeted by international terrorism.[66]

Interestingly, West German intelligence acknowledged it unofficially in their Kilowatt correspondence. The BfV sent a cable on 9 March 1973, and claimed that during the Khartoum embassy siege, Black September had primarily intended to take West German diplomatic staff hostage.[67] Similar to Blumenau's account, the cable also mentioned that the ambassador was not present by sheer luck.

The BfV further warned that Black September was planning more embassy sieges like that in Bangkok. The goal would be to take German and other embassy personnel as hostages and exchange them for Palestinian terrorist prisoners. Allegedly, the West German embassy in Beirut was at high risk. Lastly, the BfV worried more generally that Black September saw West Germany as an opportune operating field in Western Europe.[68]

A month later, Israel briefly mentioned the Khartoum attack in Kilowatt. This was, however, rather in passing, in the context of a warning about the US remaining a high-risk target for Palestinian terrorism.[69] Otherwise the Khartoum attack received relatively little attention in the Kilowatt channel. The likely reason is that Sudan was relatively far away and no agency apart from the BfV and Mossad had intelligence to contribute. The attack also stirred a lot of media attention and most facts about the course of events could already be read in the news at the time.

LIBYAN SUPPORT FOR BLACK SEPTEMBER ATTACKS

A recurring theme in Kilowatt correspondence was reports that the Libyan government provided support for Palestinian terrorism. For instance, Libya was believed to have provided substantial support for the organisation of the Munich massacre. Muammar Qaddafi's administration was suspected of having delivered the weapons for the attack through the Libyan embassy in West Germany.

After the Kiel Lufthansa hijacking of 29 October 1972 (see Chapter 3), Qaddafi enraged the Israelis further not only because he readily accepted the three freed Munich perpetrators, but the Libyan government also gave them an extravagant reception when they arrived. They were granted sanctuary in Libya and were welcomed as heroes. When the bodies of the Munich perpetrators who had died during the attack were also taken to Libya, Qaddafi arranged a state funeral. He called them 'martyr heroes', accorded them the highest military honours, and held Muslim prayers and symbolic ceremonies in memory of their 'righteous struggle'. Later it transpired through the cables that the Kiel Lufthansa hijackers were Libyans and that Libya also helped with the organisation of the hijacking.[70]

Based on the assumption that Qaddafi helped organise the Munich Olympics attack, and following his stated support for it, Israel declared him its public enemy. Then, on 21 February 1973, there was the downing of the Libyan civilian plane, which strained Libyan–Israeli relations even more.[71] As mentioned in Chapter 4, with the subsequent discovery in February 1973 that Palestinians held MANPADS, Israel was worried about Libyan support for the shooting down of an El Al plane.[72] Israel and European intelligence agencies continuously warned about Libyan support for Palestinian terrorism. In February and March 1973, warnings about such cooperation were particularly intense.

In late February 1973, West Germany warned that a 'quite reliable source, with access to local activist Palestinian organisations' had informed the BfV that on 23 February, forty Palestinian terrorists had flown from Beirut to Europe.[73] The goal was again to organise attacks in retaliation for Israel's downing of the Libyan airraft. The attack would be against Israeli and/or Jewish targets in Europe. Belgium was targeted because the Palestinians believed that there were 'many' Jewish and Israeli institutions. Similarly, the US and Poland were at risk because apparently Palestinian activists thought that 'a lot of money came from there to Israel'.[74]

In early March of that year, cables provided more detailed descriptions of Libyan–Palestinian cooperation, outlining meetings that allegedly happened and describing specific plans for Libyan-supported attacks. For instance, the West German BfV informed its partners that the Black September leader Saleh Khalaf (Abu Iyad) personally met with Qaddafi to discuss Libyan sponsorship of the group's next terrorist attack.[75] Qaddafi wanted the Libyan-sponsored attack to happen quickly so that it would clearly be seen as retaliation for Israel's downing of the Libyan plane the month before. Khalaf allegedly outlined two terrorist scenarios that Black September could carry out: either the destruction of an Israeli civilian plane in Tel Aviv or a European city, or simultaneous arson in several Israeli embassies in Europe. Libya promised to invest as much money as needed, to generously reward the successful outcome of an attack, and to provide hands-on resources for such a Palestinian terrorist operation.[76] (See Figure 13.)

Also in early March 1973, Shin Bet informed its partners that senior Libyan officials had met with Palestinian terrorist leaders to plan sabotage attacks with Libyan support.[77] The main motivation for Libya was again believed to be vengeance for its destroyed civilian plane. Its officials were said to have met with Fatah leaders, including Saleh Khalaf, which confirmed West German intelligence that had been sent before. Shin Bet

Figure 13 Tunisian president Habib Bourguiba, Yasser Arafat, and Muammar Qaddafi in 1973 during the fourth anniversary of the Libyan Revolution. At the time, intelligence reports suggested that Qaddafi personally met with various Palestinian leaders to discuss Libyan support for terrorist attacks. Source: Michel Laurent/Gamma-Rapho/Getty Images.

believed that Libyan officials also approached the PFLP and Jibril PFLP-GC leadership. The cable noted that 'naturally the organisations will accede to these requests for obvious reasons'.[78] Namely, given the immense resources a non-state actor received by cooperating with Libya, a terrorist group could massively increase its striking power. Shin Bet further warned that Palestinians had already entered Europe to organise attacks in collaboration with Libya. The Israeli agency ended its cable with the prediction that Libya was going to give 'massive aid' to the perpetrators, who were likely to travel from that country to Europe.[79]

A few days later, on 12 March, Israel followed up on its earlier cable and gave further details about the terrorists who were said to have travelled to Europe for a Libyan–Palestinian terrorist mission.[80] They were going to arrive at their targets in Europe from Libya and Beirut. Israel therefore requested 'greater surveillance' of suspicious movement from Libya and Beirut to Europe as well as of Libyan embassies and PLO offices. While it was, of course, sensible to request further details about Libyan embassies or PLO offices, hearing about activities happening around PLO offices might also have been useful for Operation Wrath of God.

In April 1973, Israel warned that Libya was again meeting with the leaders of Palestinian armed groups.[81] For instance, representatives of the PFLP-GC (Jibril) group were said to have been in Libya since the end of March and to be preparing an attack on an aircraft. Mossad believed that Palestinian terrorists were 'strongly encouraged' by Libya to choose aircraft as targets in retaliation for the downing of the Libyan airliner over the Sinai. More concretely, Mossad knew 'from a reliable source' that Qaddafi had met with Arafat and Ahmed Jibril and urged them to attack an El Al airliner, promising big rewards for carrying out such an operation.[82]

Libyan–Palestinian cooperation continued to be followed closely by Club de Berne intelligence agencies. They were right to fear such state-supported attacks because they indeed happened a few months later. The most brutal attack happened at Rome Fiumicino Airport on 17 December 1973. There, a Libyan-organised terrorist commando threw phosphorus-incendiary hand grenades into a Pan American plane that was waiting on the runway for departure. The terrorists blocked the exits and trapped the passengers in the fire. The death toll was twenty-seven people who died in the flames, with an additional thirty-one heavily wounded. Right after setting the Pan Am plane alight, the terrorists hijacked a Lufthansa plane, with which they escaped to Dubai.

Kilowatt correspondence revealed that the attack was organised by the highest echelons of the Libyan state, in cooperation with radicalised elements of the Palestinian armed struggle.[83] While this attack saw the heavy involvement of a state, in the 1970s Arab state support generally concerned weapons sales, training, and asylum. This type of Arab state support for Palestinian groups remained in place throughout the 1970s and 1980s.

ARMS SMUGGLING VIA MERCEDES SALES

In mid March 1973, Italian border police searched a car with two Jordanians inside. The police officers had no idea that this routine car search would lead to a large international intelligence investigation. The investigation would later reveal important details about Palestinian terrorist operational methods and the car search effectively thwarted an attack in France. This episode is a prime example of successful Kilowatt cooperation, where one piece of information allowed agencies to find further pieces of the puzzle.[84] Episodes like this show how much Club de Berne members valued these intelligence exchanges.

The story begins on 14 March 1973, when the Italian intelligence agency, SISDE, sent a warning to its European partner agencies through the Kilowatt channel, as follows: 'We have received intelligence from a friendly service that an Arab man called Omar Muhammed Talab has left Damascus for Paris on 9 March 1973, in a dark-grey Mercedes 230 with a German licence plate. The Mercedes carries weapons for an attack against an Israeli embassy in France.'[85] The cable further mentioned that the day before, on 13 March, two Jordanians had arrived by ferry from Patras (Greece) at the port of Ancona (Italy). One of them had the same name as the person in the warning from the 'friendly service'. The men drove a dark grey Mercedes 230, and the cable shared the car's West German licence plate. Once the car reached the Italian–French border crossing station in Ancona, the Italian police searched the car but did not find anything suspicious. They thus let the car continue its journey to France.[86]

Then, on the same day, France intercepted the same dark grey Mercedes 230 with the same West German licence plate and the same two Jordanians inside.[87] When, just a few hours later, the French police searched the vehicle, they found weapons and elements to create a bomb: six detonators, two horology engineering devices, and 16 kg of THT explosives.

The explosives were well hidden in the three caches buried in the car's front heating system, in the stringer of the boot, and the engine crankcase. The French authorities confirmed what the Italian alert had said – that the car came from Beirut via Greece and Italy. The DST believed that the two Jordanians were part of a Palestinian terrorist commando unit and interrogated them.[88] It is not clear whether the Italians missed the weapons and explosives when they checked the car, or whether they were added in France. Nevertheless, it was Italy's warning that led France to intercept the weapons smugglers.

Two days after the arrests, and having interrogated the two Jordanian Palestinians, on 16 March 1973, the DST reported to its Kilowatt partners that the explosives were meant for an attack on the Jordanian embassy in Paris.[89] This cable, marked as 'very urgent', further gave the name and personal details of the terrorist who was believed to be the commander of this terrorist operation, using the alias Yaneil. According to French intelligence, Yaneil was the main person in charge of Fatah in Syria, based in the Syrian town of Dimechk.

The operation was allegedly meant to be carried out by Yaneil and two other terrorists. The weapons were to be handed over to a person named David Cross, who had received a letter with instructions in a postal box in the 8th arrondissement in Paris. As will be shown below, France later arrested the person who stole Cross' passport and found further details about the thief's role in this operation. French intelligence was further able to identify the real name of one of the drivers and shared it among the Kilowatt group. He too was working for Fatah and was based in the Syrian town of Dimechk.[90]

Given that the Mercedes had a West German licence plate, the West German police undertook some investigations into the plate's official owner. On the same day as the arrests, the BfV informed Kilowatt that this licence plate had been given to a Syrian national, Mohamed Bachir Taha, in Düsseldorf on 12 January 1973.[91] Taha had entered West Germany legally on 4 December 1972, and his visa was valid until 14 February 1973. The plate was apparently meant to be used on a Daimler-Benz PKW, not a Mercedes. The cable listed all the details of the truck and its supposed owner, including his name, passport, birth date, residence, and travel history in West Germany. The BfV promised to investigate whether Taha was still in West Germany.[92] In another cable, it added that it had no records of the people who were arrested in the Mercedes.[93]

MI5 checked its databases too for previous records of the arrestees and, on the same day, shared that 'a reliable source with good access to fedayeen affairs' had reported in January 1972 about one of the two Mercedes drivers, Omar Muhammed Talab, whose *nom de guerre* was Abu Urubat. This source warned that Rasd (Fatah intelligence special operations) was training new recruits at Shatila camp, near Beirut. The training was for new secret missions. Talab, believed to be from Gaza, was one of the trainees mentioned in this intelligence report.[94]

In the coming days, French intelligence 'diligently pursued', as they said, further investigations about this intercepted Mercedes and its drivers. Their investigations led to the arrest of more members of pro-Palestinian circles and to the discovery of precise details about the preparations for an attack and an arms transfer. The results of these investigations were sent on 20 March 1973, in the form of a long report outlining step by step how the French police and intelligence proceeded.[95]

As a first step, French intelligence investigated the planned weapons transfer. As mentioned before, the weapons in the Mercedes were meant to reach David Cross in Paris' 8th arrondissement. French police went to this address and found Jamil Abdelhakim there and arrested him. He confessed that he was a Fatah officer who had been trained to become a terrorist operative in Syria at Hamuria camp near Damascus. He also admitted that he participated in commando operations on the Golan Heights from 1968 to 1970. French police found the British passport of David Cross in his possession. This passport had been reported as lost in Kabul in December 1972 and French police thus assumed that Black September had stolen it from Cross in Afghanistan. Abdelhakim also had a Jordanian passport and an Austrian passport.[96]

French intelligence was able to reconstruct the plan for the terrorist operation as follows: in autumn 1972, Abdelhakim had stayed at a Fatah-dominated Palestinian refugee camp near Damascus, which was managed by a person called Aziz. Aziz sent Abdelhakim on a terrorist mission to Paris, gave him $1,000, the three passports, and the London address of a British doctor and Palestinian advocate, Dianne Campbell Lefevre.

At the time the cable was sent, Campbell Lefevre too had been arrested by the French police. She was British and had just finished her medical studies. The cable mentioned her parents, brothers, uncles, and cousins who were all living in the UK. It also included her current address in Paris, her last known address in London, and her family's exact addresses in Surrey and London.[97]

The task that Abdelhakim performed in Paris, based on his own claims during the DST interrogation, was solely to buy a car, wait for Black September to organise and deliver weapons to him, and then drive the car and the weapons to Israel with Campbell Lefevre under the cover of going on a tourist trip. However, the French authorities found in Abdelhakim's possession sketches of the area around the Israeli embassy in Paris and the Israeli trade mission. The DST thus suspected that he was in fact preparing an attack against the Israeli embassy in Paris, and that the intercepted Mercedes was carrying the weapons for this attack.[98]

In their second step, French police had arrested Dianne Campbell Lefevre. She denied any knowledge of Abdelhakim's terrorist intentions but confirmed that they were planning a trip to Israel together by car. She gave the names and PO boxes in Lebanon and Syria of some of her Palestinian connections. The DST knew these people as 'active terrorists' and shared their details with the Kilowatt partners.[99]

Third, French police carefully searched the confiscated documents in Abdelhakim and Campbell Lefevre's possession. The DST was thus able to crack the code for the secret messages that Abdelhakim was supposed to use when communicating with his Fatah handler, Aziz, in Syria, and provided its Club de Berne partners with Aziz's PO box number and examples of the codes. For instance, Abdelhakim would send Aziz the message 'George is sick', which meant 'everything ok we start'. Other examples were 'photo mailed', which meant 'I am in prison'. The word 'university' was used for Israel, 'academy' for France, and 'museum' for England.

This French intelligence report was sent as 'very urgent', classified as 'top secret', and prohibited distribution to intelligence agencies outside

Kilowatt channels.[100] It is interesting to see the large amount of detail that French intelligence was willing to share, presumably in the hope that other agencies would be able to follow up.

The next day, on 21 March 1973, France provided additional information about the types of weapons that were found in the Mercedes and how they were hidden in the car.[101] After careful study of the weapons' concealment, it became clear that they were built into the car itself, being completely integrated into its ventilation system and the car boot. This made them very difficult to detect, which possibly explains why the Italians had not found them when they searched the car a few hours before the French searched the same car.

The DST was further able to ascertain the identities of the two drivers of the Mercedes. One of them, Omar Muhammed Talab, was known to have been a Fatah operative for many years and had joined Black September six months before his arrest. His Black September commanders had instructed him to go to the city of Dimechk in Syria, where he picked up the Mercedes with the weapons inside. He told French intelligence that his Fatah handler in Syria, nicknamed Yaneil (his full name was Mohamed Hacene Djaffar, also alias Daniel), was the one who built the weapons into the car, gave it to Talab, and tasked him with driving it to Paris. Yaneil allegedly affixed the relevant visas into Talab's passport.[102]

The two drivers of the Mercedes left Syria on 4 March 1973, and drove through Turkey and Greece. On 12 March, as mentioned in the very first cable on this issue sent by Italy, they got on the ferry at Patras, arriving in Ancona on 13 March. Driving through Italy, they entered France at Montgenèvre on 14 March at 7 p.m., which is when they were arrested.[103]

The second driver also acknowledged his Fatah membership in Syria and confirmed that he too had recently joined Black September. He was the one who had David Cross' address in his papers, which led the police to the arrests of Abdelhakim and Campbell Lefevre. The two drivers had meanwhile been transferred to a prison in Marseille.[104] France also included many relevant and timely details in this cable in order for it to be as useful as possible for the Kilowatt partners.

In a reply to the results of the French investigation, Mossad sent a detailed report that commented on every aspect of the French cables of the days before.[105] Point by point, it assessed whether it was likely or unlikely to be true. For instance, it brought up Abdelhakim's downplaying of his alleged terrorist tasks; namely his claim that Aziz had only instructed him to buy a car and drive it and the weapons to Israel. The Israelis stressed (the slightly obvious point) that Abdelhakim was probably lying to avoid incriminating himself as a participant in an act of terrorism in France.[106] This passage in Mossad's cable reads as though the Israelis were scolding France for taking Abdelhakim's words at face value and they felt the need to point out that he might be lying.

Mossad further pointed out that the PO box numbers provided for Fatah members in Beirut were all wrong. It corrected them one by one and explained that the letters were slightly mixed up for each. For instance, the French cable claimed that Fatah was using PO boxes 2181 and 9364, while Israel knew these same Fatah PO boxes as 1812 and 9463.

Regarding the UK national and suspected participant in a terrorist plot, Dianne Campbell Lefevre, Mossad knew her as a foreigner who served in Fatah's medical service in 1971.[107] Furthermore, Campbell Lefevre gave the names of Fatah people in Egypt. Mossad had no records of them and suggested that these names were probably made up. This passage too intimated that France was naïve for assuming that a terrorist supporter would tell the truth during investigations. Interestingly, however, one of the contacts given by Campbell Lefevre was Hamid Shibli, who was assassinated by Mossad in June 1973 while he was preparing a terrorist attack.[108]

Mossad further curtly dismissed France's success at cracking Fatah's communication code as commonplace. It was entirely unimpressed by it and said: 'The maintenance of contact between the terrorists abroad and their hqs in Beirut by means of code telegrams is standard operating procedure.'[109] In contrast, one might argue that France's main insight was not the fact that the terrorists were using a code, indeed a rather common practice, but that its intelligence agency managed to crack the codes by obtaining and sharing the encryption keys.

To stress its point that most terrorists were using codes to communicate with their handlers abroad, Israel mentioned the case of Rubhi Halloum.[110] Halloum was arrested on 23 October 1972 at Schiphol Airport with a suitcase full of weapons. As outlined in Chapter 3, there were many Kilowatt cables about him, which included the practice of using codes and invisible ink (with lemon and iodide). Mossad specified that Halloum's papers included details of one of the PO boxes that the French had got wrong in their last cable. This was a subtle hint that French intelligence could have known that the PO box numbers provided by Campbell Lefevre were wrong based on information that had been available to them through previous Kilowatt correspondence.

Overall, Mossad was not impressed with French intelligence, and the tone of the cable was very dry and borderline arrogant. In its cables after the Mercedes arrests, the DST had clearly made an effort to diligently and quickly inform its partners about the course of the investigation. French intelligence was mainly transmitting initial insights and sometimes this included near-verbatim phrases from what the interrogated suspects had said. The DST was, of course, not suggesting that it was all true, but it likely hoped that the results of the investigation, even preliminary and still in progress, would be useful for the Kilowatt group.

In its reply, Mossad either downplayed French intelligence as obvious pieces of information or presented the French police as naïve or uncritical. This may have been the stereotypical 'direct way' of Israeli communication. It may also have been related to a competition between the agencies about who was better informed about Palestinian armed groups. Nevertheless, it seems unfair to present France as naïve. The DST simply reported what the Palestinians said, without assessing its validity, which was common practice among the Kilowatt group after an arrest. It did not react specifically to this cable, and it is not clear whether it appreciated Mossad's excessively detailed assessment of every step and point in the investigation.

Meanwhile, the West German authorities pursued investigations at their end and followed up on the alleged owner of the Mercedes' West German licence plate number. At a Berlin border crossing, their police arrested the latest owner of this licence plate, a Jordanian national, Mohamed Bachir Taha, whose personal details were shared among the Kilowatt group.[111] This was the same name that the BfV had already indicated in cable 1079 of 15 March as the alleged owner of the licence plate.[112]

The West German police arrested three other men who were in the car with Taha. The four, whose details were shared with Kilowatt partners, claimed to be motorists who had come to West Germany with the intention of buying spare parts for the Mercedes in Düsseldorf.[113] The BfV shared their names with the Kilowatt group and asked if the partner agencies knew anything about the licence plate owner and the people with him.[114]

The BfV pursued further investigations about the licence plate owner, Mohamed Bachir Taha, and two days later, on 23 March 1973, updated its Kilowatt partners.[115] A 'well-informed source' confirmed that Taha and his brother were Syrian car dealers, as they themselves claimed. Taha had been in West Germany between 29 December 1972 and 15 January 1973, and bought four cars in Düsseldorf from a company called Mazloum. Three of these cars were shipped to Syria and one, the Mercedes 230 with construction year 1966, was driven to Damascus by Taha. There, in a custom-free area, the vehicle was sold to the Jordanian Omar Muhammed Talab, who was the driver of the Mercedes with weapons when the French intercepted it at the Italo-French border.[116] Talab claimed that he was very sick and needed the Mercedes to drive to Yugoslavia to get medical treatment or an operation.[117]

Taha confirmed that he usually kept the German plates because it was too cumbersome to send them back. In the cable, it is clear that West Germany was not happy that he kept them on the cars after selling them. Taha and the three other arrested men denied having connections to Arab terrorist organisations or to the explosives and weapons found in the Mercedes 230. At the time of their arrest, Taha and a companion were in possession of large amounts of Deutschmarks in cash. Taha had 2,100 DM and his associate had 43,150 DM. Both claimed that the money was meant to buy more used Mercedes cars and spare parts in Düsseldorf at the car company that was also mentioned in the previous cable, Mazloum.

Since the West German police could not prove any involvement in terrorist actions, other than legally selling the car to terrorist suspects, the authorities had to release them and deported the men back to East Berlin, from where they tried to enter West Germany. Taha and his colleague were thus not allowed to travel to Düsseldorf. The men indicated that they now planned to go back to Damascus.[118]

Prompted by these German cables, Dutch intelligence shared their prior investigations into a Lebanese car dealer. The Dutch BVD had discovered a few months ago that a Lebanese businessman, Antoine Daou, was using car sales as a cover for terrorist activities.[119] The cable shared all known details about these fake car dealings and about the businessman, including his Interpol file and his exact itinerary in and around Europe. Most recently, in December 1972 he had been in the Netherlands on a ninety-day visa, for his alleged profession as a car merchant. He reapplied for another ninety-day visa, claiming 'to buy cars in Amsterdam and Brussels'.[120] But after his second visa application, Dutch intelligence understood that this was only a cover to facilitate terrorist activities.

Based on the cables sent after the Mercedes arrest and adding this Lebanese case to the equation, Dutch intelligence concluded that the agencies had thus uncovered a terrorism modus operandi of using legal car dealings to smuggle arms.[121] In other words, cooperation allowed them to link various elements together and to identify them as a terrorist operational method and the related smuggling techniques. The BfV replied to this and mentioned that the West German consulate in Kuwait had received an anonymous letter in December 1970 about Daou, the alleged Lebanese car/arms dealer.[122] The letter claimed that he was part of an Arab terrorist commando unit and that he had left Kuwait for West Germany to perpetrate terrorist attacks.

Figure 14 Palestinian advocate and suspect in a terrorist plot, Diane Campbell Lefevre.
Source: William Lovelace/Daily Express/Hulton Archive/Getty Images.

France had meanwhile continued its investigation. Before sending its final report in April 1973, it sent a few updates at the end of March. As some Kilowatt members had requested, the DST provided more technical details about the Mercedes, including the car's chassis number and the serial number of the motor.[123] In another cable, it further informed its partners that it had expelled the above-mentioned two terrorism supporters, Dianne Campbell Lefevre and Jamil Abdelhakim, to whom the weapons were meant to be delivered (to the apartment in the 8th arrondissement of Paris).[124] The French police deported Abdelhakim to Damascus and Campbell Lefevre to London. (See Figure 14.) In the cable, French intelligence included a description of their physical appearances and the clothes they were wearing that day.[125] After her deportation, the French and British press at the time suggested that Campbell Lefevre might have been working with British intelligence, which could explain why she was expelled as opposed to tried.[126]

In mid April 1973, France sent a comprehensive report that summarised the conclusions of its investigations in relation to the arrest of the Mercedes drivers.[127] Having collected and assessed all available intelligence on the matter, it inferred that the arrest had allowed them to 'neutralise' a Palestinian commando force that had been tasked with carrying out an attack against the Jordanian or Israeli embassy in Paris.[128]

The fact that not only Israel but also Jordan and its embassies in Europe were targets fits generally with Black September operational priorities at the time.[129] This is further underpinned by a warning from MI5 in early March 1973 about an imminent attack against the Jordanian embassy in London.[130] With the London embassy as a possible target, it is likely that the Jordanian embassy in Paris was targeted too.

Looking at the exchanges since the arrests on 6 March 1973 all together, it is interesting to see how one warning led to a car search, how this car search led to an arrest, how information about the car dealers led to the discovery of a terrorism modus operandi, and how the whole cooperation effort ended up thwarting a terrorist attack in Paris. While France was the driving force behind these investigations, cooperation involved a high degree of international and national coordination. For instance, one can look at the cooperation about the licence plate. The licence plate number was identified in Italy and France, issued in Düsseldorf, and its owner was arrested in Berlin. This cooperation effort is also remarkable from today's perspective, considering that it happened at a time when there were barely any computers assisting the work of security professionals. This episode has also shown that Club de Berne cooperation could be very useful and that members trusted one another with sensitive intelligence.

MORE SUITCASES CONTAINING ARMS IN ROME

Very similar to the aborted attack at Rome's Fiumicino Airport on the night of 25/26 November 1972, four suitcases filled with arms were again found abandoned at the same airport on 19 March 1973.[131] A day later, on 20 March, Italy reported this to its Kilowatt partners. Each of the suitcases contained a gun (with the series number filed off), magazines with thirty-eight cartridges, a grenade, a smoke bomb, and clippings from a Lebanese newspaper with reports and pictures of Israeli actions against Palestinian camps in Lebanon. On these clippings was written 'Naher al Bared' and 'Badawi', the names of Palestinian camps in Lebanon.[132]

The Italian authorities gave the same reason for why they assumed that the terrorists had aborted their attack. As in November 1972, Italian intelligence believed that the terrorists were planning an attack but decided to abort because of the 'efficacity and visible constant surveillance of the security forces at the airport'.[133] Italy again included an element of self-praise here and presented this case as a success for its security forces and their deterrent effect on terrorists.

Interestingly, this exact reason was given by a Black September operative in a cable sent by the BfV a few months later.[134] In late May 1973, the West German authorities arrested and interrogated a Palestinian terrorist suspect, who confessed to his earlier involvement in Black September terrorist actions. He mentioned to the BfV that during an arms transfer in September 1972, he did not collect a suitcase full of weapons at Rome Fiumicino Airport 'due to the heavy security measures and constant control'.[135]

Italian intelligence sent a follow-up cable with the personal details of the passengers they thought had abandoned the suitcases full of weapons.[136] In another striking parallel to the aborted attack in November 1972, the terrorist suspects caught the Italian authorities' attention again because they hastily tried to change their flights. All three arrived from Tripoli, meant to travel further to Belgrade, and hurriedly tried to change their flight at the last minute. Two of them wanted to reroute to Beirut, while the other wanted Tunis. At the time the cable was sent, the two were still in Rome and were being interrogated. The third man had bought his ticket right before the flight and managed to fly to Tunis. Italy gave a description of the men's physical appearances and asked for any intelligence about them.[137]

According to Kilowatt etiquette, in the following days, Italian intelligence sent more details about the contents of the suitcases. These included pictures of the arms found inside and a careful description of each weapon (Sterling submachine gun, MK2 grenade, MK1 smoke bomb), including the manufacturer's serial numbers of the guns and grenades.[138] The Italian security agencies studied the newspaper clippings and empty envelopes found in the suitcases.[139] The envelopes had handwritten numbers on them and the following text: 'Nahr al-Bared [a Palestinian refugee camp in northern Lebanon] Black Sep' and the sentence 'Palestinian never dead'. Italian intelligence assumed that the letters and the newspaper clippings were prepared so that the perpetrators of the aborted attack could send these to claim responsibility for the attack.[140]

WAITING CROWDS AS A TARGET AND A LINK TO KHAIR

Three weeks after Black September aborted the attack in March 1973 at Rome Fiumicino Airport, this airport became the scene of terrorist activity yet again. On 4 April, two Middle Eastern men with Iranian passports were arrested in the transit hall because they were carrying combat weapons.[141] Each was found to be in possession of three grenades and pistols. The two men had boarding passes for Paris and large sums of cash in French, English, and Italian currencies.

The two men caught the attention of the authorities when they refused to board the plane at the last minute, even though they had gone through all the departure procedures.[142] From today's perspective, it might be puzzling that terrorists were able to carry weapons with them right up to the gate. At the time, however, body checks were mainly conducted shortly before boarding and the terrorists' refusal to board thus raised suspicions.

Shin Bet replied to the Italian intelligence agency about this arrest and assessed the incident within a larger context. It expressed worry that this airport sabotage attempt was a reaction to El Al's increased security, which made it more difficult for terrorists to hijack planes.[143] Terrorist organisations were therefore believed to be carrying out operations that aimed to kill El Al passengers and passers-by before boarding. Shin Bet warned that it had several reports from different sources indicating that preparations for this type of operation were underway in various airports in Western Europe.[144]

Later that same day, in the evening of 4 April 1973, Italian intelligence sent more precise information about the weapons that were in the possession of the terrorists.[145] The cable provided the exact models, serial numbers, and all manufacturing details available. Italian security believed the weapons were produced in Czechoslovakia. Italian police ascertained that the two terrorists had come to Rome by train from Barcelona. Italy asked if any Kilowatt members knew anything about these suspects.[146]

The next day, 6 April, MI5 consulted its database about these names.[147] The British agency found that two passports in these names had been reported to belong to two members of a group of six terrorists who were in Athens in November 1972. This terrorist squad had allegedly been planning an operation against Israeli shipping in Greece. For unknown reasons, the group decided to abort the mission.[148] DST replied immediately to MI5 and acknowledged that it had not known about these links between the Rome and Athens terrorists. It suggested that Club de Berne members share any intelligence that could further link the arrestees to the November 1972 aborted attack in Athens.[149]

A week after the arrests, on 11 April, Italy sent the most important cable that linked the two Iranians to the above-mentioned shipping attack in January 1973 that allegedly had been coordinated by Khair in Cyprus.[150] It shared intelligence that strongly suggested that the detainees were not Iranians but two of a party of six Afghans who, on 6 January 1973, boarded a ship in Bari that was bound for Haifa. As mentioned above, four terrorists had been arrested at the Cypriot port of Famagusta. But the group was now believed to have consisted of six terrorists in total. Two of them were believed to have left the boat undetected and, a few months later, on 4 April, to have tried to perpetrate another attack at Rome Fiumicino Airport, which is when they were arrested.

Over the following weeks, Italy conducted a thorough investigation and was updating its Kilowatt partners bit by bit. A few days after the arrest, having studied the Iranian passports in depth, it reported that the visas and entry stamps were completely identical in both passports, which meant that the two men went everywhere together.[151] Italy listed all the stamps in detail and determined that their route was Shiraz airport in Iran, Paris, Munich, Athens, Madrid, and Barcelona. Interestingly, the cable included whether the stamp was rectangular or hexagonal. This was a control mechanism to verify the validity of entrance stamps, since on some days the customs officers used only rectangular stamps and on others hexagonal ones.

The level of detail with which the police studied the passports is exemplified through Italy's mention of an entry stamp at Paris Orly Airport.[152] The cable specified that the stamp looked extremely similar to the stamp found on page 9 of a forged Israeli passport that was held by a Palestinian who was arrested in January 1973 near Tarvisio in Italy.[153] Italian intelligence noticed that the two entry stamps in Paris and Munich must have been forged because the print of the date was more discoloured compared with the other stamps of the same type.[154] These rather technical cables are interesting for what they reveal about the operational level of cooperation and how important entry stamps were at the time. It was sensible for an agency to study the passports as this revealed where the terrorists had been and what network they might have been part of. A forged entry stamp meant that the terrorists crossed the country illegally and forged the stamp so as not to attract the attention of the police.

SISDE later also sent pictures of the two arrested terrorists, every page in their passports, and the weapons that were in their possession.[155] It further followed leads about their weapons and determined that the pistols had been purchased in Sofia, Bulgaria.[156] The Italian agency provided the name of the company from which the terrorists had bought the pistols, the precise dates of purchase (in 1968 and 1969 respectively), and the manufacturing number.[157]

In July, three months after the arrests, Italy sent an update about the court ruling regarding the detainees.[158] The two were sentenced to four years and eight months in prison for illegal possession of arms, which was a much higher sentence than in other similar cases. However, the two appealed their sentences and Italian intelligence later informed its partners that the investigative judge had given them temporary freedom of movement until their trial was to commence.[159] This meant that the two were allowed to leave the country and were likely able to avoid prison.

After some more investigations, in late July 1973, Italian intelligence was able to identify the organiser of the terrorist attack.[160] It found out that this terrorist coordinator paid the two perpetrators a terrorist commission when they all met in Spain before the attack. The terrorist commander was in Spain to undergo medical treatment in a specialised clinic for the loss of an eye and three fingers on his right hand. He was there with his Algerian accomplice, whose name was also shared among the Kilowatt group.[161]

A month later, Shin Bet's warning of April 1973 turned out to be accurate when on 5 August, a terrorist attack was carried out at Athens Airport. Shin Bet had warned that terrorists were changing their tactics from hijacking planes to harming passengers waiting for their flights to Israel. This is indeed what happened, and the attack was very similar to the one that was thwarted at Rome Fiumicino in April. In the transit lounge of Athens Airport, two Black September operatives threw grenades and fired machine guns at passengers waiting for two Trans World Airlines (TWA) flights – one for Tel Aviv and the other for New York City. The shooting killed three people and injured fifty-five. The Black September commandos took thirty-five people hostage and started negotiations with the police. Shortly after negotiations began, the group surrendered.[162]

In the Club de Berne, this terrorist incident was discussed in terms of its direct connection with the attempted attack on 4 April in Rome.[163] Mossad assumed that because the terrorists feared being discovered at El Al departure checks, as they had been at Fiumicino Airport in April, they were now targeting passengers travelling to and from Israel via other airlines. Israel believed that TWA was specifically selected for its American connection, as Mossad noted that American interests had increasingly become terrorist targets.

Altogether, Club de Berne exchanges regarding the aborted and thwarted attacks at Rome airport show two interesting elements. First, cooperation and cross-referencing of suspects' names led the agencies to identify the wider network of the two terrorists. Of interest here is especially the link to the shipping attack that Khair was suspected to have organised. Second, Israeli intelligence seemed to have read the Palestinian tactics correctly and accurately predicted their shift in target.

TERRORIST TACTICS AND INNOVATION

The period after Khair's death saw comparatively more Black September attacks, as described above, that were either carried out or thwarted; some of these attacks were even prevented through Club de Berne cooperation. In the spring of 1973, Club de Berne members were also horizon scanning more broadly and issued warnings about Black September's tactical advances. A particular concern was the group's ability to obtain passports that could be used for their next operations, particularly stolen or forged Israeli passports.

From late January 1973 onwards, the Club de Berne files suggest that Palestinian groups were trying to obtain passports from various nationalities. The worry was, of course, that with a false but credible identity, Palestinians would be able to infiltrate embassies or other secure places, and that they could travel unnoticed across Europe. Warnings about stolen or forged passports were taken very seriously and every case was meticulously reported.

The first incident involved Palestinian terrorists in Europe using Turkish passports. In late January, the West German intelligence agency sent a warning in which it unusually named its informant: a Jordanian national who lived in Nordenham and who had for years given valuable information to the BfV about planned criminal actions.[164] On 22 January, this informant told the police that he had received a visit from two compatriots, who spoke Arabic with Palestinian accents. The two Jordanians asked to stay with him and told him that they were in West Germany with a group of twenty people to perpetrate terrorist actions against various targets. The targets included a fuel depot of a British petroleum company, an attack on the 'Israeli embassy in Cologne', and an assassination attempt against a member of the West German parliament, Franz-Josef Strauss.[165]

The Jordanian host refused to let them stay, however, and when he gave them back their winter coats as they were leaving, he swiped three Turkish passports from the pockets of one. He gave the passports to the West German police and the BfV shared their details with the Kilowatt partners. Other than these three passports with Turkish-sounding names, the informant believed that he had also seen four Libyan and Moroccan passports and each of the visitors had a pistol in his waistband. The cable ended with a detailed description of the two Jordanians based on the informant's account. West German intelligence requested that Kilowatt members send any hints about the people or passport details mentioned in the cable.[166]

Israel replied to this German cable, stating that Mossad had no information on the suspects mentioned but that there were Turkish nationals within the ranks of terrorist organisations.[167] Mossad knew that the PFLP in particular enlisted foreign nationals for their operations and furthermore, if Palestinians were to perpetrate attacks, they would often use non-Arab passports from Afghanistan or Persian Gulf countries.[168]

A few weeks later, in early February 1973, Italian intelligence followed up on one of the three Turkish names mentioned by the BfV.[169] It had records about this person and could match their passport number with the number indicated in the German cable. This suspect arrived in Italy in May 1971 and worked first as a technical consultant for a firm called Chicago Bridge Italiana Montaggi based in Milan, and then for a firm called Sarpon based in Novara. In May 1972, he left Italy and claimed that he planned to return to Turkey.

Tunisian passports were also believed to be in the hands of Palestinian armed groups. The Belgian intelligence agency, Sureté d'État, informed its partners that there had been a burglary at the Tunisian general consulate in Brussels, in which 159 blank passports had been stolen.[170] It provided all the passport numbers and urged Kilowatt members to inform it immediately should they see a passport with one of these numbers. Since these passports were for Arab nationals, Belgium stressed that Palestinians could use them for their operations.[171]

Similarly, the West German BfV shared intelligence from leftist Palestinian circles in West Germany that terrorists had managed to obtain Polish passports.[172] Using fake Polish identities, Black September operatives were allegedly planning to enter the Israeli embassy in Bonn and attack it once they were inside. The next day, Mossad replied to West Germany's cable and suggested that, given the different physical appearances, it was improbable that an Arab national would operate under a Polish cover.[173] However, Mossad nuanced, 'non-Arabs' could indeed be included in such an operation. As it happened, a couple of months later, in May 1973, Shin Bet informed its partners that a Polish passport had indeed been stolen by Arab nationals.[174]

Agencies also reported on Palestinians possessing stolen or fake Israeli passports, which was a major concern for Israel. In late January 1973, Mossad received reports that some Palestinians had been able to acquire Israeli passports and were learning Hebrew.[175] It warned that this was likely part of a new terrorist tactic to gain entrance to and attack Israeli embassies. Namely, according to its intelligence, Palestinians were going to disguise themselves as either local security guards, police officers, army personnel, or (Hebrew-speaking) Jewish clergy, that is rabbis.[176]

Mossad warned that Black September had already managed to steal uniforms of the following: the British police and army, the Swiss army, various European airlines, and possibly also the US army. Most concerningly, Black September had been teaching Hebrew to its members who were meant to perpetrate attacks abroad. The source for this intelligence was estimated to be 'reliable, with access to terrorist circles'.[177]

Given that Palestinians had similar physical appearances to Israelis, if they also spoke Hebrew and presented Israeli passports they could easily pass as Israelis and would thus be able to approach Israeli targets. An indication that this was already part of Black September's tactics came in the hijacking of a Sabena flight in May 1972, when the perpetrators spoke fluent Hebrew and used Israeli passports.

Given the considerable risks associated with this new tactic of high-level disguise and acquisition of Hebrew language skills, agencies were very concerned when, in January 1973, a Palestinian terrorist in possession of an Israeli passport was detected in the Netherlands. It was only a simple case of a forged passport, but it triggered a lot of interest among the agencies. The following correspondence shows that Palestinians with illegitimate Israeli documentation were very high on the agencies' priority list.

Cooperation over this case began in late January 1973 with a cable sent from Dutch intelligence. The BVD informed the Kilowatt members about a Palestinian terrorist suspect called Sharif Abdel Hafiz a Shanti and noted that he was staying in a hotel using an Israeli passport (in the name of Chanti Charie).[178] According to Dutch intelligence, Shanti did not match the person on the passport and the agency presumed that the passport was not his true identification document. It undertook some investigations about him and knew that he had been living in London until 18 January. Upon his arrival in the Netherlands, he was said to have tried to contact Palestinian circles.[179] Given the dangers emanating from Palestinians using Israeli passports, The Hague urgently requested any information that its Kilowatt partners had on Shanti.[180]

A day later, Israel replied and explained that the passport with the number indicated in the Dutch cable indeed corresponded to a passport that was issued in 1958.[181] The Israeli authorities, however, had records that the passport had been destroyed. They thus assumed that the passport was not stolen but rather a fake document. Mossad reminded all Kilowatt partners again that enhanced vigilance about Israeli passports was needed and it reiterated how grateful it would be to receive any further intelligence about Palestinians using Israeli passports, fake or stolen.

A day later, Swiss intelligence replied and sent a long report with background information about Shanti.[182] In November 1967, he had provisionally requested asylum in Switzerland. Swiss intelligence shared what they knew about him from his interrogation during the asylum application, providing details about his identity, biographical background, and identity document, which at the time was a Jordanian passport. According to his own account, he was born in 1933 in Jaffa to a family with nine children and later moved to Qalqilya (in the West Bank). He trained in electromechanics and later worked as an electro-engineer for the British air force in Baghdad and Kuwait in the 1950s. The cable included a very detailed account of his travels and residences during the 1960s. He left Switzerland in January 1968 for London, and Swiss intelligence asked MI5 to check whether they had any documentation about him.[183]

While West Germany informed its partners that Shanti was not in their records,[184] MI5 indeed knew him. It first thanked Switzerland for its helpful cable and confirmed that Shanti had arrived in the UK in January 1968, then departed from London for Sydney on 23 March 1969.[185] MI5 believed that he had married an Australian national, who accompanied him. It was going to send a picture of him.

With immediate effect, Shanti was put on a Kilowatt watchlist, and his picture was included in the so-called 'terrorist album'. From the cables it becomes apparent that the agencies assumed a direct link between the possession of a forged Israeli passport and terrorist intent.

Other passports that were allegedly in the hands of Palestinian groups were those of Chad. In April 1973, Mossad informed its partners that Fatah had received ten forged Chadian passports.[186] It warned that Black September was going to use them in an operation against Jordan, or in an attempt to seize an Arab embassy when there were Jordanians present.[187] Following up on this Israeli intelligence report, the West German BfV confirmed the information. It too had received reliable intelligence that a group of Fatah members had been able to illegally acquire Chadian passports and that they were on their way to Western Europe.[188] The BfV estimated that the passports were authentic, not forged as was assumed in the Israeli alert. It mentioned that it was unaware of any targets where the group would use these passports. It assessed the source for this intelligence to be a 'B-rated source' (A-rated being the most trustworthy source).

The second part of the cable included a note that reminded the agencies that 'nationals of the African state Chad have a very black skin colour'.[189] The BfV thus pointed out that the 'much lighter-skinned' Palestinians should therefore be easily spotted at the border, should they carry a Chadian passport. While this reminder about Chadians' skin colour might seem like stating the obvious, one should add here that Chad had a large Arab diaspora at the time. If a Palestinian terrorist were going to use a Chadian passport, they could simply claim that they were part of the Arab minority (with a lighter complexion) living in Chad.

Another area where Black September was believed to have made tactical advances was in intelligence gathering for their next attacks. In late January

1973, the Dutch agency received intelligence from a 'friendly service' about a leading PFLP member, who had come to Europe to help select the next terrorist targets.[190] His reconnaissance mission was to gather intelligence about passenger and luggage control at the borders of the different countries.

Dutch intelligence gave this man's name and details of his Lebanese passport, with which he was believed to be travelling around Europe. His exact itinerary was not certain, but informants suggested his route was Beirut–London–Frankfurt–Brussels–Amsterdam, then back to Beirut. As a cover identity, he posed as the general manager of a company called Albert Abela and Co.[191] He was said to possess valid visas for France, Norway, and Belgium.[192]

Similarly, in February 1973, a terrorist 'belonging to the top echelons of Black September' was believed to have arrived in Europe to perpetrate attacks.[193] Mossad shared this person's personal details and asked to be kept informed about any background information on him or if he were to enter a Kilowatt country.[194]

With airports and planes as the main terrorist targets at the time, Palestinian groups were trying to get airport personnel to work with them on terrorist operations. In early March 1973, West German intelligence informed its partners that an airport staff member turned to the police because he was approached by a Sudanese national who offered him large sums of money to throw iron filings into the tank of a El Al Boeing 747 plane. The Sudanese suspect had immediately been arrested (even though he was in this case only the informant) and his details were shared among the intelligence agencies. The Sudanese national had previously been involved in several criminal procedures (in West Germany and some Arab countries) concerning kidnapping, passport forgery, imposture, fraud, deception of authorities, rape, and theft. The West German authorities had not yet heard, however, that he was connected to Palestinian terrorism.[195] It is interesting to see that the use of airport personnel – an operational method that had long been part of Palestinian terrorists' repertoire – was now believed to be resurging again.

Another tactical advance and technological innovation concerned a new type of bomb for air sabotage attacks, which was said to be in the hands of the PFLP.[196] The alert came from the West German BfV, which described this alleged technical innovation in detail and assessed that it was likely that Palestinian terrorists possessed this new technology. The bomb had a 'two-way trigger' activated by a steel bullet that linked the two triggers. The weapon was believed to weigh 25 kg, which was heavy, but it could still be hidden in the bottom of a suitcase.[197]

The danger of this bomb stemmed from the fact that if the bullet was not yet activated, it was difficult to detect during luggage screening. The reason was that the two separate parts of the device did not look like a traditional bomb on the screen and could well be hidden among personal items and clothes in the suitcase. As the cable specified, only a thorough search by hand would allow airport security to detect it. Once the bullet was set loose, however, any movement of the suitcase could trigger the bomb. The BfV thus recommended that in the future they should always first screen any abandoned suitcase via a portable X-ray unit before it was moved or placed upright.[198]

Reports about another new terrorist tactic concerned the use of duty-free items as cover to smuggle weapons on to a plane. In March 1973, Mossad undertook a general horizon scanning to assess potential loopholes that terrorists could exploit to smuggle weapons or sabotage material aboard.[199] Israel thought about the following scenario. Terrorists buy something in the duty-free shop. They would then have an accomplice come to them in the transit hall. This accomplice would bring them a bag with identical items to the ones they had bought at the duty-free shop – but in this replacement bag they would hide weapons.

Airport personnel tended not to check duty-free bags too carefully, especially since the terrorists would have the invoices proving that they had purchased the items at the airport on the same day. Such an operation was possible, Mossad reckoned, at airports where the early checks (including the use of a magnetometer) were not capable of detecting items hidden in hand luggage. It thus recommended that the second examination of hand luggage right before boarding be stricter. Duty-free bags should also be checked thoroughly.[200] To better understand Mossad's reasoning, one has to remember that in the 1970s the transit lounge was reached relatively easily, and only right before boarding were passengers checked more thoroughly.

CONCLUSIONS

From winter 1972 to spring 1973, Palestinian terrorist activities intensified in Europe and Jordan, and intelligence agencies increased their efforts to anticipate and prevent them. After the assassination of a Mossad officer, Black September increased its terrorist activities in Jordan and started to form ties with the Libyan government. In February 1973, Palestinian armed groups began specific discussions and negotiations with President Qaddafi personally about Libyan sponsorship of Palestinian terrorism.

While the agencies were tracking these Palestinian–Libyan connections, Black September hit once more and, as in Bangkok, they struck again in an unexpected extra-European location. The embassy siege in Khartoum took the agencies by surprise. Tactically, for Black September the Khartoum attack was a mistake, as international reactions were very negative and the group's actions roundly condemned. Not just Western actors but also Arab or Muslim spokespeople strongly condemned the brutal and sadistic murder of Western diplomats. Khartoum was one of the last major attacks by Black September.[201] Before Khartoum, this chapter has shown that Rome had again been the centre of Palestinian terrorism.

Today, we only know about several of these terrorist incidents, such as the thwarted attack in France or the aborted attack at Rome Fiumicino Airport, because the agencies shared intelligence about them. The analysis of the Kilowatt files has thus allowed terrorist incidents that were unknown publicly until now to be brought to light. Kilowatt correspondence has also confirmed claims made in secondary literature about suspects' terrorism involvement and thus substantiated claims made by journalists or scholars.

Another interesting aspect of the cooperation described in this chapter is that it could be very effective and useful in preventing attacks and uncovering terrorists' operational methods. This was particularly salient after French authorities arrested at the Italian border the two occupants of a car who were later revealed to be preparing terrorist attacks in France.

Altogether, Operation Wrath of God achieved its intended goal of inflicting fear on the Palestinian leadership in Europe. But it also stirred greater rage and anger among Palestinian armed groups and motivated their terrorist activities further. The escalation of the violence was far from over, and the next deadly hits – by both sides – were not long in coming.

6

A 'BATTLE OF THE SPOOKS' IN PARIS, BEIRUT, NICOSIA, AND ROME

UPDATING THE MURDERERS: THE ASSASSINATION OF DR BASIL AL-KUBAISI

In the early evening of 5 April 1973, Dr Basil al-Kubaisi had just finished a luxurious dinner at the high-end Parisian restaurant Café de la Paix, in the 9th arrondissement. Before returning to his hotel at the Place de la Madeleine, he went to see a prostitute for an hour. When he walked out afterwards, a Mossad hit team of two men snuck up behind him. They crossed the street with him at Rue Chauveau Lagarde. Once they reached the other side, Kubaisi saw their weapons and begged them not to fire. They shot him nine times point-blank with their silenced Beretta .22 pistols. Kubaisi collapsed and died alone on the sidewalk in a pool of blood.[1] According to Bergman, Mossad later commented about the timing of the killing and explained that it was similar to the last request of a death penalty inmate: Kubaisi was granted sex as his last act before he met his maker.[2]

Kubaisi was born and raised in Iraq, went to the US for his studies, and received a PhD in international law in Canada. At thirty-eight years old, in 1971, he returned to the Middle East, moving to Lebanon where he taught law at the American University. (See Figure 15.) He travelled a lot, including to Europe. Mossad had trailed his movements for several months before the killing. Despite his frequent travels, he too was what intelligence officers called a soft target. He had no bodyguard, visited European cities regularly, and during his stays in Europe he stuck to a relatively fixed daily routine.

THE CHARGES AGAINST KUBAISI

The reason for Kubaisi being placed on Mossad's kill list is generally given as his active role within PFLP terrorism. Some authors, such as Reeve and Klein, interviewed Israeli intelligence officers who suggested that Mossad believed Kubaisi was moonlighting as a senior official not only with the PFLP but also with Black September.[3] He was allegedly the quartermaster

Figure 15 Portrait of Dr Basil al-Kubaisi, assassinated by Mossad in Paris, 5 April 1973.
Source: Jean-Pierre Tartrat/Gamma-Rapho/Getty Images.

for many Palestinian terrorist operations in Europe, with his main tasks the supply and transfer of weapons and explosives. His profession as a university professor was believed to serve as the ideal cover. Travelling back and forth between Lebanon and Europe, so as to attend conferences or meet research connections, was not uncommon for an academic and thus had not aroused suspicion among border and customs officials.[4]

Israeli security apparently also thought that he was involved in various terrorist plots. One attack associated with him was an attempt on Golda Meir's life when she visited the United States on 6 March 1973. A large car bomb was parked next to where her convoy was going to pass on the way from JFK Airport to the city. The bomb was defused before her convoy arrived.[5]

Mossad was said to have further intelligence about Kubaisi that implicated him in the planning of the 30 May 1972 Lod Airport massacre.[6] This attack was a particularly brutal and bloody massacre perpetrated jointly with the Japanese Red Army Faction.[7] One author, journalist Michael Bar-Zohar, referred to the 9/11-like warning related to the attack and claimed that Mossad also linked Kubaisi to the preparations for this suicide hijacking.[8]

With many terrorist charges again him, Kubaisi was a 'typical' Operation Wrath of God target: a seemingly low-level PFLP affiliate, who, in fact – as Mossad believed – was a critical element in Palestinian terrorism in Europe. Killing him, Mossad likely reasoned, would thus send a signal to his fellow travellers that Israeli intelligence knew about every Palestinian who was involved in terrorism. The message was clear: even the best cover identity could not protect a violent Palestinian actor from Mossad's vengeful hands.

THE KUBAISI MURDER INVESTIGATION

After his assassination, the French authorities led an investigation and diligently sent the latest police reports to the Kilowatt group. As had been the case after previous assassinations, Mossad received updates from its Club de Berne partners about police investigations into a murder it had itself committed.

The first cable about Kubaisi was sent four days after the assassination, on 9 April 1973. The French intelligence agency DST sent an 'urgent' cable with 'restricted distribution' to the Club de Berne members, asking them to immediately send any intelligence about Raoul Basil al-Kubaisi.[9] It was interested in any piece of information that the agencies held or could collect concerning his recent activities and travels. The DST added that Kubaisi was an Iraqi professor who had been assassinated in Paris on 5 March 1973. However, his actual date of death was 5 *April*, which suggests that the French officials wrote this message in a hurry.

As part of its investigation, French intelligence was trying to determine who Kubaisi had met before his death. The DST sent another 'very urgent' cable informing its partners about his closest contacts.[10] In particular, a friendly service allegedly informed the DST that Kubaisi had been in close contact with his Iraqi compatriot Omar Jamal Wamidh Nadhmi. Nadhmi was said to have been living in the UK for a while and to be a member of Arab and Iraqi student unions in France and the UK.[11]

Nadhmi was mentioned earlier in Club de Berne correspondence by Swiss intelligence, when it had informed its partners in January 1972 that he was on a Swiss entry ban from February 1972 onwards.[12] French intelligence stressed how important any information about Nadhmi or Kubaisi was for the recently opened investigation. DST insisted again on the urgency of the matter.[13]

On the same day, MI5 replied to the DST's cable and informed its partners that, based on a reliable source, it knew that Kubaisi had been working for the PFLP in Paris for three months prior to his assassination.

He had allegedly also been in touch with the South Yemeni embassy in the city.[14] In another cable a few days later, MI5 commented on Kubaisi's alleged connection to Nadhmi.[15] The British agency expressed doubts that the two men were in contact. It nevertheless provided further intelligence it held on Nadhmi. The UK authorities had records of him living in the UK since 1966. He was active in Arab student affairs and, since 1973, was, as the French cable suggested, an executive board member of the general union of Arab students. In this capacity, he was in regular contact with the London representatives of the PLO. He was known by MI5 to be associated with left-wing Arab groups, including the PFLP and the DFLP. Lastly, the agency shared the details of the Iraqi passport that he used when he travelled in 1972.[16]

A month later, in mid May 1973, the DST finalised a report about Kubaisi's travels and contacts since 1971. It consulted his address book and passport, led some further investigations, and completed this data with intelligence from Kilowatt members. French intelligence thus created a long and detailed list of all Kubaisi's travels to countries in the Middle East, Europe, and North America. It listed chronologically every country that he had visited, along with the exact meeting dates and personal details of every person that he had allegedly come into contact with.[17]

The French agency asked for the utmost discretion in this regard and insisted that the people mentioned in the report should not be interrogated by the respective agencies. The investigation was still ongoing and should not be compromised. However, if an agency had any relevant intelligence on any of Kubaisi's contacts, the DST was keen to receive it. It specifically asked about these contacts' political orientation. French intelligence explained that by knowing about their political affiliation, it was hoping to obtain a clearer picture of Kubaisi's 'true personality', the nature of an individual's relationship with him, and his exact role in the PFLP.[18]

Two months later, on 19 July 1973 (incidentally two days before the Lillehammer murder, see below), the DST once more sent the same list of people who had been in contact with Kubaisi in the months leading up to his death.[19] It asked again for any information that the Kilowatt agencies might have on them. This time, the Italian intelligence agency, SISDE, replied right away. It informed the Kilowatt members about Kubaisi's stay in Rome in December 1972, where he met up with his compatriots who worked at the Iraqi embassy. The passport details of Kubaisi and his contacts were given, including their names. SISDE added that the Iraqi ambassador frequently received guests, while the embassy secretary led a more reserved life. It was thus unusual for her to come to see Kubaisi.[20]

FRENCH INTELLIGENCE AND KUBAISI'S
MURDER INVESTIGATION

Analysing in total the Kilowatt reports after Kubaisi's death shows that it was once more very useful for Israel to be kept in the loop about the French investigations. The French authorities ostensibly did everything in their power to obtain more details, to reconstruct Kubaisi's networks and find out who among his contacts might have had a motive to kill him.

The question arises as to whether French intelligence knew or had suspicions that Mossad was behind Kubaisi's death. At the time, rumours about Operation Wrath of God were spreading, especially in Arab circles but also in French mainstream newspapers. A few days after the assassination, for instance, the French newspaper *Le Monde* published an article suggesting that Mossad was likely behind Kubaisi's murder.[21] George Habash, head of the PFPL, published an obituary for him. He accused the Israelis of the deed but also specifically blamed the French authorities for allowing this killing to happen on French soil.[22] If the French authorities knew that Mossad was behind it, why would they include Mossad in their requests for help with the murder investigation?

There are four possible answers to this question. Either French officials, or most of them, had not known that Mossad was behind the assassination and genuinely sent these cables to all Kilowatt partners. In this case, the DST routinely shared updates and hoped to receive further clues that could help with the investigation.

Alternatively, whether it knew about Mossad or not, the DST may have simply aimed to collect as much information about Kubaisi as possible. Kilowatt reached seventeen other intelligence agencies besides Mossad. Thus, it made sense to send an enquiry via Kilowatt, even if the likely murderers were included in the correspondence as well. From the perspective of the DST, it was especially important to cross-reference what they had already found out about him and what partner agencies might tell them. Mossad itself remained suspiciously silent and did not send any cables on the topic of Kubaisi or the French investigations.

A third interpretation is also possible, which relates to the very limited amount of people who knew about Kilowatt and its participating intelligence agencies. For instance, in Switzerland at the time only five government officials in total were in the know about the Club de Berne and the Kilowatt channel.[23] Other countries had a similarly intense veil of secrecy, even among colleagues within the same country. It is therefore conceivable that only a very limited number of French intelligence officials knew that Mossad was part of Kilowatt. Even if some suspected that Mossad was responsible for the assassinations, it is possible that operatives did not know that these cables, sent simply under the code word Kilowatt, would in fact reach the Israeli agency. Furthermore, nowhere on the cable was Mossad or Shin Bet mentioned, since all agencies operated under concealed code names. In the case of Israel, it was 'Orbis' for Mossad and 'Speedis' for Shin Bet. The officers who sent the Kilowatt cables might thus have assumed that they would only reach Western European intelligence agencies, not necessarily Mossad.

If, however, French intelligence strongly suspected that Mossad was behind Kubaisi's death and knew that the agency would see the cables, there is also a fourth possible interpretation. It is conceivable that the DST's cables were meant as a signal to Mossad that it was not going to dig too deep in the investigations. In this case, the cables were a covert message for Israel that France would continue to 'look the other way' – namely, that the French authorities would tacitly accept Mossad eliminating Palestinians on their territory. If this were the case, French intelligence would have implied that it would neither directly confront Mossad about it nor inform on it. Hence, it is conceivable that the cables were sent mainly to give the *impression* that the DST was trying to find the murderer with the help of its liaison partners, while in reality they signalled that France accepted – or maybe even approved of – killing Palestinians as a way of eliminating Palestinian terrorism.

Recent scholarship has revealed French intelligence's practice of targeted killings throughout the 1960s and 1970s.[24] It is therefore possible that the French authorities shared this Israeli counterterrorism or counterinsurgency mentality. In this vein, they would have seen the killing of Palestinians as a logical component of Israel's counterterrorism strategy, one in which France would not interfere.

Since French records about intelligence cooperation, including Club de Berne cooperation, have either been destroyed or remain classified for several more decades, one cannot know at this stage which interpretation is the correct one. From the perspective of Mossad, either way it was highly beneficial that France never addressed any suspicions about Israel's involvement in the murder case. This helped maintain Mossad's official cover and nurtured French–Israeli intelligence relations.

Lastly, one cannot but wonder whether any of the names of the people who were listed as Kubaisi's contacts or meetups may have been the cover identity of the Mossad officer who eventually killed him.

153

OPERATION SPRING OF YOUTH

Only four days after Kubaisi was killed, Mossad undertook the next Operation Wrath of God killing – one of its most daring and spectacular covert operations. It was daring because it took place in Lebanon, which was hostile territory and therefore a lot more dangerous if the operatives were caught.

The operation was given the poetic name 'Spring of Youth' and is also (less poetically) known as the 'Beirut raid'. It was organised jointly by Mossad's elite combat units and the Israeli military, namely the Israel Defense Forces (IDF). This was the first time that Mossad and the IDF cooperated in a ground assault operation.[25] Because the planners of the operation assumed that it would be difficult to strike again in Lebanon after this raid, they decided to hit a maximum number of targets.

The operation consisted of three components. First, Mossad and elite IDF combat units killed three prominent Fatah leaders in their apartments in central Beirut. The three were Abu Yussuf, who was Fatah deputy leader; Dr Kamal Butros Nasser, who was the PLO spokesperson; and Kemal Adwan, who was the Fatah operative in charge of operations in the West Bank. All three men lived in neighbouring buildings in the same compound in central Beirut's Verdun Street. (See Figure 16.)

Second, and almost simultaneously with the targeted assassinations, another combat unit drove to the headquarters of the Democratic Front for the Liberation of Palestine (DFLP), where they planted explosives and destroyed three floors of the building. The DFLP was a radical Palestinian faction mainly active in the West Bank and led by Naif Hawatmeh.

Third, the IDF attacked various targets that it knew had been used by Palestinian terrorists. These included an arms factory near the village of Ouzai, a machine shop in the Dora suburb north-east of Beirut, and a garage in the city of Sidon, twenty-five miles south of Beirut.[26]

The whole operation lasted 2.5 hours and was what one can call a 'show of strength'. It combined precise intelligence with military force to hit at the very heart of the terrorists' camp. The main body of the assault force arrived quietly by boat and docked at various beaches at the western end of Beirut. They were met by members of Caesarea, Mossad's operations division, who had flown in earlier from Europe.[27]

The incursion was meticulously planned with careful attention to detail, including the camouflage of the gunmen. To avoid suspicion, the six-people hit team was paired up and three of them were disguised as

Figure 16 Apartment with a bullet-riddled table after the assassination of Kemal Adwan, PLO chief of operations. Source: Associated Press/Harry Koundakjian/Alamy.

women. Apparently, their disguises were very convincing, and the Mossad officers indeed looked like enamoured couples going for a romantic late evening stroll in the neighbourhood. The disguises also allowed them to hide their weapons more easily.[28]

At first, the plan ran like clockwork. In the late evening of 9 April 1973, the three Palestinians were taken by complete surprise and gunned down instantly as soon as the explosives blasted their apartment doors open. Once their targets were dead, the Mossad operatives took as many documents as they could find from their victims' desks. After the executions were completed, the team faced some precarious moments. Open firefights broke out between the assault force and the building's security guards. However, the Israeli team managed to escape and made it safely back to the boat. The victims, besides the three targets of the operation, included Abu Yussuf's wife, local security guards, and two Lebanese police officers who were killed in gunfights as the assault force made its escape, plus a seventy-year-old Italian woman who was killed by a stray bullet.

Around the same time, other Israeli military commandos placed bombs around the DFLP building and detonated the dynamite. This second team also encountered resistance from the local security guards and DFLP guerrillas. Though most Israelis made it back to safety, one soldier died and three were wounded. Five of the building's security guards were killed in the exchange of fire.

Overall, the operation attacked seven targets (three men and four installations), and thus the number of mobilised troops was enormous compared with the usual amount of military personnel for a targeted killing operation. The raid required the participation of a total of twenty-three IDF soldiers from the elite unit Sayeret Matkal, thirty-four naval commandos, and twenty paratroopers from the military reconnaissance unit.[29] The army mobilised an additional three thousand soldiers as support troops. Assessments at the time highlighted the enormous size of the assault, with *Time Magazine* calling it one of the most spectacular raids ever undertaken by Israel.[30] Ronen Bergman, author of a book about Israel's history of targeted assassinations, claims that it was one of the biggest counterterrorism missions in twentieth-century history, if not the biggest.[31]

There is one aspect of this operation that receives less attention but is of crucial importance from the perspective of countering the Palestinian armed struggle. The Israeli raid managed to obtain files in Adwan's possession that contained details of PLO cells and their clandestine operations in the occupied territories.[32] The documents concerned Fatah and PFLP operations, as they had recently started to coordinate their activities. Both groups regarded the loss of these documents as a 'catastrophe'.[33] In return this was later confirmed by Israeli security, which called the seizure of these documents a 'bonanza' that immediately led to a wave of arrests by Shin Bet in the occupied territories.[34] This effectively wrecked most Fatah and PFLP networks in the West Bank.[35]

Two of the three Fatah leaders who were killed had barely been mentioned in Club de Berne channels. Only Mohamed Abu Yussuf had figured in a cable by MI5 in January 1973 as the sponsor of the Black September attack that was planned to take place in parallel with the Bangkok attack.[36] Given that the Club de Berne was primarily concerned with Palestinian terrorism in Europe, it is not surprising that these Fatah leaders were not mentioned by the agencies.

According to secondary literature, Abu Yussuf and Adwan were the masterminds of several terrorist operations and were actively planning more attacks.[37] The killing of Kamal Nasser, the PLO spokesperson,

Figure 17 Apartment after the assassination of Kamal Nasser, PLO spokesperson. Source: Associated Press/Harry Koundakjian.

however, was controversial among Israeli decision-makers. Weeks prior to the raid, Mossad headquarters debated whether to include him on the target list. Eventually he was condemned to death because he allegedly sanctioned and encouraged terrorism against Israeli citizens, which made him a legitimate counterterrorism target in the eyes of Israeli security.[38] (See Figure 17.)

With the military involved, and considering the number of mobilised troops, Israel had taken official responsibility for the assault. As a consequence, unlike Mossad's covert actions in Europe, Operation Spring of Youth could be mentioned among Kilowatt members. The first time was a week after the raid, on 16 April 1973. Mossad sent a cable in which it mentioned Palestinian claims that US intelligence helped the IDF plan the 'Beirut operation'.[39] While American intelligence had not, in fact, helped with Operation Spring of Youth, as Mossad specified, Israeli intelligence assumed nevertheless that the next Palestinian attacks were likely to involve American interests.[40]

The next time Spring of Youth was mentioned in a cable was in mid April 1973, just a few days after the operation had ended. Mossad warned about the increased risk of terrorist attacks due to Israel's upcoming festivities celebrating the twenty-fifth anniversary of its independence.[41] On

6 and 7 May 1973, Israel, its representations abroad, and Jewish communities around the world were planning festive events, which presented a likely target for Palestinian terrorism. Mossad added some context and specifically mentioned Operation Spring of Youth as a reason for Palestinians to plan a strike: 'In view of the terrorists' recent lack of success in their operations abroad, and in view of the IDF operation in Beirut [Operation Spring of Youth], it seems that their thirst for revenge will be particularly strong on this day.'[42] Here Mossad not only, *en passant*, acknowledged Operation Spring of Youth, but also expected Palestinian retaliation, both against Israeli representations in Europe and/or against facilities in Israel. The cable continued by emphasising a drastic increase in alerts about terrorist plots that aimed to disrupt these festivities. An exceptionally large number of foreign guests and tourists were expected to attend the events in Israel. Mossad reckoned that this represented a convenient target for attacks.

The agency further highlighted that the large number of tourists travelling to Israel made it easier for terrorists to enrol foreigners in their operations. Attempts to smuggle explosives into Israel via foreign travellers had already been reported by others in the Club de Berne.[43] Mossad thus asked for extra vigilance concerning Palestinian attacks in Israel or Europe that could be perpetrated with the help of radicalised European organisations.[44]

A month after the raid, in May 1973, MI5 reported on the current state of Fatah as an organisation, mentioning that it was in 'disarray following events in Beirut on 9/10.4.73'.[45] According to secondary literature, this can largely be confirmed. Operation Spring of Youth indeed left the Fatah leadership in a panic and in acute fear for their lives. Key Fatah representatives became even more cautious, went into hiding, and changed addresses at least once a month.[46] Seeing their comrades killed in a place where they thought they were safe – their homes in central Beirut – was perceived as an escalation. Many other top-level PLO and Fatah officials also lived on Verdun Street or nearby, including Yasser Arafat and Ali Hassan Salameh.[47] High-ranking Fatah members frequently slept at each other's homes and only by coincidence did none of the killed Fatah leaders have a guest on their couch that night.[48] In Palestinian circles, the operation was remembered as the Verdun Mission, named after the street where their peers had lived and died. (See Figure 18.)

Half a million people attended the funerals of the three men, which was yet another sign of how much this mission resonated in Lebanon.

Figure 18 Yasser Arafat alongside portraits of the assassinated PLO members. Source: AFP/ Getty Images.

Lebanese citizens were dismayed that the army had been unable in any way to resist the Israeli operation. The headlines of major Lebanese newspapers read 'A Day of Humiliation'. The administration of the Lebanese prime minister, Saeb Salam, was unable to survive this embarrassment and resigned shortly after.

Around the world, Operation Spring of Youth made a huge impression and received a lot more attention than the previous assassinations in Europe. (See Figure 19.) Reactions in the Arab world were a mixture of horror and awe, but mainly shock and outrage that the IDF was able to orchestrate such a brazen violation of Lebanese sovereignty.[49]

In Israel, the operation was perceived as a resounding success. All targets had been met, and expectations exceeded. Israeli citizens viewed it as legitimate vengeance for the Munich Olympics attack. As Golda Meir put it in the Israeli parliament: 'We killed the murderers who were planning to murder again. Shining pages will be written about this.'[50] Altogether, Mossad demonstrated its might and capacity to strike anywhere, even in its enemies' supposedly safe bedrooms. The myth of the agency's long reach had reached its peak with the Lebanon raid.[51]

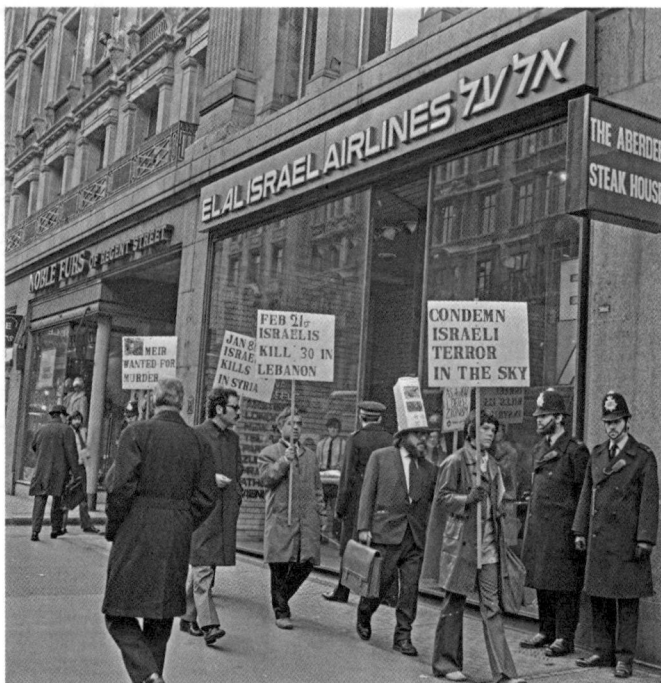

Figure 19 Protest at the El Al office in London. Source: Evening Standard/Hulton Archive/ Getty Images.

UPDATING THE MURDERERS: THE ASSASSINATION
OF ZAID MUCHASSI

Zaid Muchassi, the new PLO representative in Cyprus, travelled to Athens. On 11 April 1973, after a day out, he returned to his hotel room, turned off the lights, and lay on his bed. A switch flipped, remotely detonating a bomb under his mattress, and Muchassi died within seconds.[52]

Muchassi was the PLO envoy who had replaced the murdered Hussein Khair in Cyprus. Khair had been killed two months previously as the third victim of Operation Wrath of God. Mossad used the same method to kill both Khair and Muchassi, a bomb hidden underneath the bed in their hotel room. The message too was the same in both cases: anyone who held the role of KGB liaison was going to be killed by Mossad. In this vein, the aim of Muchassi's assassination was deterrence, intended to disrupt the links between the PLO and Soviet intelligence.

Furthermore, Mossad believed that Muchassi had been involved with Black September and other Palestinian terrorist operations.[53] Two days before his death, two Palestinian terrorist attacks were perpetrated, and it is conceivable that Mossad suspected Muchassi to have been involved in the planning. The first, on 9 April 1973, was an attempted attack against the Israeli ambassador's residency in Nicosia. The second attack was directed against an Israeli plane on the runway at Nicosia Airport. Both attacks failed, and the perpetrators were taken into custody in Cyprus.[54] The Arab National Youth Organisation for the Liberation of Palestine (ANYOLP), a Libya-backed Palestinian terrorist group, claimed responsibility for these attempted attacks.[55]

Given the proximity in time between the ANYOLP attacks and Mossad's assassination, and considering that Muchassi was based in Nicosia where the attacks happened, it is possible that Mossad assumed he was involved in their planning. At the time, Cyprus and Greece were both excluded from the Club de Berne or Kilowatt exchanges. There are unfortunately no Club de Berne records about Muchassi himself or his assassination.

A month later, MI5 referred to the attacks in Nicosia as part of a general threat assessment.[56] The British agency estimated that shipping and aircraft were at high risk, both in the Middle East and in Europe. In particular, transportation hubs that were connected to Israel, Jordan, or the United States were believed to be terrorist targets. MI5 further thought that Cyprus was among the highest risk countries for an attack for as long as the terrorists responsible for the operations in Nicosia on 9 April remained in Cypriot custody.[57]

BLACK SEPTEMBER KILLS VITTORIO OLIVARES

In the afternoon of 27 April 1973, in the centre of Rome on the famous Via XX Settembre, an Italian-Jewish employee of the local El Al office, Vittorio Olivares, aged thirty-four, was shot twice in the stomach and in the chest. The Black September killer ambushed him on a crowded pavement outside a department store and fired at him out of a briefcase. The murderer tried to escape, but a bystander in the street screamed 'This is the assassin – stop him!' The killer turned around, fired shots in the air, and ran. Two blocks away, police officers on duty guarding the Labour Ministry caught and arrested him. As he was put in the car, he smiled and made the V for victory sign with his fingers.[58]

The next day, on 28 April, the Italian intelligence agency SISDE sent a long report about this killing and summarised what the police knew about it.[59] SISDE shared the details of the assassin, his name as indicated in his passport – Zakaria Kamel Abou Saleh – age (twenty-three years), and the issuance details of his Lebanese passport.[60] Saleh told the police that he had arrived in Rome on 19 April, specifically to kill Olivares. He explained that he was personally instructed to commit this murder by Black September and, as he specified, it was in direct retaliation for the killing of Wael Zwaiter.[61] Zwaiter was Operation Wrath of God's very first target, killed on 16 October 1972 in Rome. The Italian cable did not explain who Zwaiter was but added a reference to the Kilowatt cable sent by SISDE on 17 October about Zwaiter's murder investigation.[62]

SISDE gave more details about the murder weapon, a Helwan gun manufactured in Egypt with a 9-calibre silencer. Saleh's passport was assessed as authentic, but the photograph had been replaced. The Italian intelligence agency promised to send more details about the investigation, but in the meantime, it asked everyone to 'urgently' send any information they might have on the assassin.[63]

A week later, Italy further updated the Kilowatt members about the investigation. Saleh had revealed more details about the operational planning of the assassination. He had apparently received direct orders from his Black September superior in Beirut, known by his *nom de guerre* of Abu Mustafa, who had organised the weapons transfer for the murder. On the inner edge of Saleh's shirt, the police found inscribed in Arabic the name Moulham al-Mamoun, which they thought was the real name of the assassin. SISDE asked its counterparts whether they knew any details about him.[64]

In the same cable, the Italian agency speculated about the motives of the assassin. For this, the Italian authorities were looking into whether the victim's past might have triggered the ire of Black September. To their surprise, as the cable mentioned, their investigation revealed no anti-Palestinian rhetoric or activities on Olivares' part and he was not connected to the Middle East conflict in any way.[65]

In line with what SISDE's cable said, a 'World News Brief' in the *New York Times* on 29 April 1973 suggested that Saleh might have killed the wrong El Al staff member.[66] The newspaper interviewed a friend of the victim, who stated that Olivares bore a strong resemblance to Moshe Adad, a forty-year-old Israeli who was head of the El Al office in Rome. Adad, as the *New York Times* speculated, may have been connected to Mossad and might have been the actual man marked for assassination. This would explain why the Italian authorities found no connection between Olivares and the Middle East conflict.

The hypothesis that Black September shot the wrong person is, however, based on rather thin grounds. In the same *New York Times* article, it was also mentioned that Saleh insisted that he thought Olivares was a spy and that his instructions about whom to kill were crystal clear.[67] There is also no evidence that Adad was involved with Mossad or that he would have been a more 'legitimate' target of Black September. On 28 April 1973, the day after the killing, another *New York Times* article also mentioned that Saleh told the police that he believed Olivares was spying for Mossad.[68]

Even though Saleh must have mentioned to the police that he thought Olivares was connected to Mossad, this was entirely omitted in all Kilowatt cables, even the ones that specifically shared police reports about Olivares' death. The cables only mentioned that Saleh claimed to have killed Olivares as revenge for the murder of Zwaiter. About this claim of vengeance, however, SISDE expressed doubts and instead suggested that the two murder cases were not linked at all. It is conceivable, as will be discussed further below, that Italian intelligence feigned ignorance and pretended not to really understand the context of this murder or its relation to Zwaiter.

In a final update on the matter, SISDE sent pictures connected to the case. These included, among others, a picture of the murderer, copies of his Lebanese passport, and pictures of the weapon that he used.[69]

Similar to the French cables after Kubaisi's death, the question arises here as to how much the Italian authorities had known about Mossad's involvement in Zwaiter's murder and whether they could raise this issue in a Kilowatt cable. In October 1972, when Zwaiter's murder happened, Italian intelligence seemed to genuinely not know who was behind the killing. By late April 1973, when the Olivares murder happened and was allegedly undertaken to avenge Zwaiter, Mossad's covert action had become widely known. Especially in intelligence circles, one would assume, rumours must have spread.

However, Italian intelligence reported on the Olivares murder in a dry and matter-of-fact way. When SISDE mentioned Olivares' unsuspicious prior behaviour and 'no apparent anti-Palestinian activities', it expressed doubts about the validity of the murder's objective. The murderer's own claim for why he selected Olivares was not mentioned, namely that Olivares was allegedly a Mossad agent and that his murder was tit-for-tat for Operation Wrath of God victims.

Similar to earlier instances when agencies reported on Mossad murder cases, the Club de Berne kept the information at a strictly technical level. One can argue that precisely in order to keep cooperation up despite political differences, one needed to black out all political questions in the correspondence. It is, however, possible that Italy addressed the issue with Mossad separately on a bilateral level. However, the Club de Berne was not the right medium for it.

Furthermore, naming or accusing Mossad over its covert actions in a multilateral framework might have alienated it. Kilowatt exchanges were simply too important to risk alienating any cooperating party, especially Mossad, which was one of the most important contributors to the liaison.

TERRORIST TACTICS AND INNOVATION

Operation Spring of Youth left Palestinian armed groups in deep shock. The costs of international terrorism had increasingly become clear, and Arafat and the Fatah leadership began to pressure Black September to give up terrorist campaigns abroad.[70] Nevertheless, intelligence agencies at the time detected Black September preparations for further terrorist attacks. Club de Berne correspondence shows that Black September used this time to lay the operational groundwork for future terrorist actions. Namely, cables reported that it was organising a weapons transfer, had stolen European passports, raised money for its operations, and recruited airport personnel to help with attacks.

A few weeks after Operation Spring of Youth, a failed weapons transfer happened at Fiumicino Airport. Rome's main airport remained a prime target for terrorist actions. On 24 April 1973, Italian intelligence reported that the police had found an abandoned cakebox there that contained three grenades (MK1) and a small anti-personnel mine (manufactured in the UK) with a 25 cm fuse.[71] The Italian authorities presumed that the weapons were meant for a terrorist attack, but SISDE had not been able to attribute them to a specific terrorist plan.[72] A few weeks later, it sent additional information and pictures of the bombs and the mine.[73]

While the intelligence agencies believed that Black September already had Turkish, Polish, Tunisian, Israeli, and Chadian passports, West German intelligence now alerted the Kilowatt group to the theft of passports from two more countries. First, the BfV alerted its partners that a blank visa page from a West German passport was missing at the West German consulate in Algiers. It cautioned that it might be in the hands of an armed group.[74] Second, a few days later the BfV received intelligence from Beirut and forwarded it to Kilowatt. The source in Lebanon claimed that Palestinian terrorists had obtained Belgian passports and were on their way to West Germany via East Berlin. These operatives were allegedly planning an attack in Munich in September 1973, which would have marked the one-year anniversary of the Munich Olympics massacre.[75]

To obtain money to finance their terrorist missions, in late May 1973, a Palestinian group attempted to extort money from CEOs in West Germany.

The BfV reported that a so-called 'Palestine People's Fighting Fund' sent threatening letters to people who held influential high-level positions in West German industrial companies. The letters demanded that the addressees give generous financial support to this fund, or else their security was at risk. These 'donations' were to be paid into a Credit Suisse bank account in Geneva, Switzerland. The letters were sent from Frankfurt am Main and the letterhead included the name of this organisation and an emblem of two fists holding a gun.[76]

Because the letters mentioned a Credit Suisse account, Swiss intelligence investigated the matter.[77] BuPo reported that these threats had been sent in English and French all around Western Europe to several high-placed businesspeople.[78] On a 'strictly confidential basis', BuPo obtained details from Credit Suisse indicating the name of the owner of this foundation. His details, shared via Kilowatt, stated that he was a Lebanese national residing in Amsterdam, alongside his exact address in the city. Given the strong suspicion that the foundation had fraudulent intentions, Credit Suisse had blocked all payments into its account.[79]

Swiss intelligence asked Kilowatt agencies to inform their local Interpol branches about the Swiss findings, as some requests in this regard had already been submitted by Interpol London and Copenhagen. This is an interesting example of coordination between Club de Berne and Interpol, but also between Swiss intelligence and the banking industry.

On the same day, Dutch intelligence followed up and informed the Kilowatt agencies about the address in Amsterdam that the owner of the foundation had given to his banker at Credit Suisse. He apparently held a PO box connected to this address, but he was unknown at that location. He was in the Netherlands illegally and the BVD was going to continue the investigation. To facilitate tracking, Dutch intelligence included the passport details that he used when he opened the PO box.[80]

In the agencies' efforts to track the local support networks, in early June 1973, the Luxembourg intelligence agency, SREL, reported on the discovery of a terrorist support system for Palestinian operatives who were passing through Luxembourg.[81] The cable mentioned cases where Maoist groups helped Palestinian terrorists enter the country illegally, hosted them, gave them cash, and accompanied them to their onward train. Maoist or anti-Zionist groups had allegedly organised several such clandestine passages.[82]

The BfV also reported on a Palestinian terrorism support system. This time it was about terrorism facilitators not in Europe, but in Saudi Arabia. The West German consular mission in Jeddah had received intelligence from another embassy in the city. The intelligence report contained two main points. First, the legal adviser to the Saudi Ministry of Trade and Industry, an Egyptian national, was suspected to have been involved in the planning and execution of terrorist actions and hijackings. His real and cover names and details of another alleged terrorist conspirator were shared among Kilowatt.[83]

Second, the West German consulate in Jeddah had received intelligence suggesting that female flight attendants of Western airlines collaborated with Palestinian terrorists. Some Palestinian terrorists, often based in Beirut and Jeddah, were believed to have close relationships with airport and airline staff members. These relations were prone to exploitation for terrorist operations, and some female attendants were said to have already helped smuggle weapons to Europe. Two from the Belgian airline Sabena were believed to have collaborated in this way, and their names and details were shared among Kilowatt. West Germany asked for any hints about the people mentioned in its cable.[84]

The day after, Dutch intelligence confirmed West German suspicions about the Egyptian legal adviser in Jeddah.[85] He had indeed been placed on a watchlist in the Netherlands as he was a suspected member of the PFLP. The two Sabena employees mentioned in the German cable were Belgian and thus the Sureté d'État replied with a detailed and meticulous list of all the records they had on the two women.[86] These included their addresses, family backgrounds, and their professional roles or tasks at Sabena. The Belgian agency confirmed that both were engaged to Arab men, one of them a Palestinian. The cable also included a detailed report on the fiancés, their professions, and previous stays in Belgium.

Alongside these reports, the cable from Belgian intelligence included an assessment from its diplomatic representation in Jeddah. Belgian diplomats considered the relations between the flight attendants and their Arab suitors as 'dubious' and harboured suspicions that the two men were indeed planning to involve the women in terrorist actions. However, Belgian intelligence indicated that its own investigation had not led to any evidence that suggested tangible terrorist intentions.[87]

After reading these reports, Mossad in return shared its assessment of the likelihood that these flight attendants helped terrorist operations. It reckoned that, for some time, terrorists had tried to establish new methods of smuggling arms and explosives into Europe. Using Western airline personnel, Mossad believed, was an effective way for them to circumvent controls in order to smuggle arms across the Mediterranean. Another element that supported this assumption, among others that had been reported in Kilowatt in October 1972 and January 1973, was that terrorists had already tried to obtain airline uniforms with which they could disguise themselves as flight crew.[88]

Finally, after a six-week investigation, Belgian intelligence shared the results of its inquiry and declared that the two flight attendants were probably innocent. One had married her fiancé, moved to Jeddah, and stopped working for Sabena. In dry security language, the cable concluded: 'Investigations about a potential collaboration between her and Palestinian terrorism had been unsuccessful.'[89] While it made sense at the time to be extra careful and report any suspicious behaviour, these two Belgian women and their fiancés clearly caught the security agencies' watchful eyes only because of their intercultural relationships.

Intelligence reports between April and June 1973 suggest that Palestinian armed groups were operating rather disjointedly. While there were some tactical advances, such as obtaining passports or enhancing financing methods, during that time there were no terrorist attacks. This may have been because, after the Khartoum attack in March 1973, the Fatah leadership changed its priorities and ordered Black September to halt its terrorist operations. Another reason could be that intelligence agencies had improved their spy networks among Palestinian circles and were able to disrupt terrorist plans. Such was the case with Mossad's next targeted killing operation: bombing the bombers before they could strike; a story that could have been taken from a spy movie, as will be discussed next.

UPDATING THE MURDERERS: THE ASSASSINATION OF HADI NAKAA AND HAMID SHIBLI

On a summer's day in Rome, two Palestinians, Abdel Hadi Nakaa and Abdel Hamid Shibli, sat in a green Mercedes and drove through the city centre's slow-moving morning traffic. In their car was a bomb meant for an imminent attack at an El Al office. But before the two could strike, their car exploded. The bomb was detonated remotely by a Mossad officer in a car behind them. This was Operation Wrath of God's seventh killing operation, a rather spectacular one that prevented an attack shortly before it was carried out.

Secondary literature has conflicting accounts about the exact target of their attack. Author Marc E. Vargo claims that the two Palestinian terrorists were driving out of the city with a bomb meant for an El Al office at the airport. He further suggests that Mossad had been able to rewire the remote control of the bomb, which then blew up the car on the Israelis' remote command.[90] Israeli journalist Ronen Bergman suggests that Mossad simply planted an additional bomb underneath the car and was able to activate this bomb remotely, which seems more likely.[91] Author Aaron Klein describes the execution of the killing in a similar way to Bergman. Both Klein and Bergman claim that the two terrorists were about to blow up the El Al office in the centre of Rome at Via Barberini 67, the same office where Vittorio Olivares had worked.[92] Klein also suggests that the car exploded very close to this El Al office in the centre of the city.[93]

Bergman provides further details about how Mossad found out about this imminent terror attack. It had allegedly managed to recruit a Palestinian highly placed in the PFLP, who agreed to spy in exchange for money.[94] He gave the agency crucial intelligence based on what it called 'excellent and exclusive access'.[95] The code name for this informant was 'Sadness'. Mossad received intelligence from Sadness on 10 June 1973, suggesting that two PFLP hit men had been sent to Rome to carry out an attack on the El Al office.[96] Mossad's Operation Wrath of God team immediately reacted to this intelligence and travelled to Rome. All three authors agree that Israel successfully thwarted an imminent attack by killing the two men.

Killing terrorists who were on their way to execute a terrorist attack sounds like it was taken from the plot of a James Bond film. But, as unrealistic as it might sound, this story can indeed be confirmed by official Italian police records that were shared through the Kilowatt channels. On 18 June 1973, a day after the explosion, Italian intelligence sent a detailed police report about the explosion of a Mercedes with two passengers in it.[97] The report explained that at 9.30 a.m., a green Mercedes exploded at Piazza Barberini in Rome. The location of the explosion solves the puzzle about the likely target: Piazza Barberini was a two-minute walk from the El Al office in the centre of town. By car, one could reach the office within seconds. This meant that Nakaa and Shibli were about to reach their target when Mossad pre-empted the attack.

Further indications that the terrorists' target was the El Al office in the city centre (as opposed to the one at the airport) come from the above-mentioned *New York Times* article after Olivares' murder. Journalists speculated at the time that Black September might in fact have planned to shoot the head of the El Al office, Moshe Adad, and not Olivares.[98] Incidentally, both looked very similar. The newspaper therefore suggested that Olivares might have been killed by mistake and that Adad might still be a target. If these assumptions were correct, it is conceivable that Black September wanted to attack the same office again, this time to make sure to kill Adad.

THE NAKAA AND SHIBLI MURDER INVESTIGATION

When the Italian agency, SISDE, sent the first cable with the initial police report, the two terrorists were severely wounded and burnt, but had not yet passed away. Their names were given as Abdel Hadi Nakaa and Abdel Hamid Shibli, both born in Damascus. Shibli had a driver's licence in the name of Rjad Shibli al-Ramleh. His clothes had a name tag that said Abu Khaled.[99]

Inside the car, the Italian police found items for constructing a bomb, like watchmaking devices for the timer, chemicals, and more than 800 g of plastic explosives hidden in eight cartons of Dunhill cigarette boxes. This account confirms Bergman's version of events, namely, that an additional bomb was planted on the car, since the terrorists' bomb, or elements to make it, was still in the car. This differs from Vargo's claim that the terrorists' bomb had been rewired.

The Italian authorities traced the movements of Shibli and Nakaa prior to their deaths and found that they had reached Rome from Lyon only a few days earlier. On 15 June, the two made a call from a public phone booth in Rome to a landline in Lyon, and the cable provided this number and another that was written on a note found in their car. The timing of Shibli and Nakaa's arrival in Rome also aligns with Bergman's account that Sadness informed Mossad on 10 June about two hit men travelling to Rome. The fact that the two had only reached Rome recently reinforces the hypothesis that they may have specifically come for the attack, as warned by Sadness.

Italy urged its Kilowatt partners to send any intelligence they had on Shibli and Nakaa or the Mercedes. France was asked for help with identifying the owners of the landlines in Lyon.[100] During the following weeks, the Italian authorities pursued their murder investigation. On 26 June, SISDE shared its latest findings about the personal details of the killed men and their itineraries before entering Italy.[101] Italian intelligence gave as many details as possible about Nakaa and Shibli's personal information, their visa requests, the passports they used when they requested the visas, and their alleged profession, namely engineers. Shibli had tried to enter Italy with the exact same Mercedes on 10 June 1973, but his entry was refused because he did not have a visa. This further confirms Bergman's account, since Sadness allegedly informed Mossad about the two hit men on 10 June, the same day Shibli had tried to enter Italy.

While French intelligence never replied to Italy's request (at least in the group; it is possible that it replied bilaterally), German intelligence updated its partners with what it knew about Nakaa and Shilbi.[102] The BfV had no records of Nakaa but provided details of a visa application by Shibli and two others to enter West Germany in July 1971. At the time, Shibli and the two others, whose names were also given in the cable, went to the West German embassy in Paris and submitted their visa application. When they were told that the West German authorities needed to call Beirut to check their identities and that they had to pay for these phone calls, the three stormed out of the embassy and never came back.[103]

Because the Mercedes that blew up had been manufactured and sold in West Germany, the BfV gave all known details about the previous owners of the car. It was a green Mercedes Benz 220d, and the BfV included the motor manufacturer number, chassis number, and signature physical features. This car was first known to have belonged to a West German citizen, under a licence plate registered in Essen. On 17 April 1973, a Syrian citizen registered the car and kept the same licence plate number that was on the car when it exploded. The BfV shared the names of the two previous car owners but stated that it had no intelligence on them.[104]

A month later, on 30 July, Italian intelligence sent a long list of attachments that it thought were useful for the Kilowatt group to help make sense of these killings.[105] SISDE sent copies of documents that were found on Nakaa and Shibli. These included every page of their passports, their drivers' licences, and pictures of them both. The cable also included pictures of what was found in the car's boot, such as an ignition system and the still intact explosives that were packed in the Dunhill cigarette cartons. These were, of course, the explosives that were meant to blow up the El Al office, not the explosives that were placed by Mossad that killed them.

Interestingly, this cable was sent after the Lillehammer affair, which publicly exposed Mossad's Operation Wrath of God, as will be described further below.[106] As a result of that incident, Italy and other countries had become aware that Mossad was behind some of the killings, and Italian intelligence was likely to have harboured suspicions about this bombing too. Given that, as the cable states, the explosives in their car were intact, the Italian police must have deduced that the two men had been killed by a separate bomb. This would have left the police with two possible assumptions: either the terrorists had two bombs, namely one that had yet to be built and a second one that was already built and exploded accidentally, or somebody, like Mossad, added a second bomb. After the Lillehammer revelations, this latter was not an unreasonable assumption. Bergman claims that the Italian police believed the former possibility and concluded that the explosion was caused by incorrect handling of the terrorists' own bomb.[107]

Lastly, in a slightly absurd administrative act, on 13 August 1973, the Roman investigative judge granted Shibli and Nakaa posthumous freedom of movement until their trial for the illegal possession of explosives. Very scrupulously, SISDE shared this piece of intelligence with its Kilowatt partners.[108]

THE CHARGES AGAINST SHIBLI AND NAKAA

Shibli and Nakaa's preparations for their terrorist attack against El Al in Rome are mentioned numerous times in the secondary literature. However, most books about Operation Wrath of God go over this assassination rather quickly and do not mention further details about the two victims. With the Club de Berne files, it becomes apparent that the two were involved in other terrorist plans. These revelations started with an MI5 investigation from May 1973 about terrorist plans to attack synagogues in the UK and the Netherlands. Later, MI5 was able to connect Shibli and Nakaa to these plans. Namely, their investigation revealed that the planned attacks against the UK and Dutch synagogues and the El Al office in Rome were two legs of the same terrorist operation.

In early May 1973, MI5 noticed the suspicious behaviour of an Arab man named Mahmoud Hassan Fowel. He entered the UK on 2 May and MI5 had intelligence that he had come to prepare a terrorist operation. His alleged immediate task was to obtain accommodation and weapons on behalf of another Black September operative, called Ghafour. Ghafour was said to have been the Fatah liaison and supply officer in Libya since 1970. Shortly after Fowel, on 11 May, Ghafour also entered the UK.[109] Both men reconnoitred the Israeli embassy and three Jewish synagogues in the country. MI5 received intelligence that suggested the two were planning to attack the synagogues with automatic weapons, pistols, and grenades. The shooting was planned for a Saturday evening, at a time when prayers had finished and worshippers would be leaving after the Shabbat ceremony.[110]

MI5 gave further details about the preparation of this attack. The two men first travelled from Lebanon to the Netherlands, where they met a third unidentified person and discussed an attack against a synagogue in The Hague. Dutch intelligence was later briefed bilaterally by MI5 and confirmed that its security agency had records on Fowel and Ghafour. MI5 further identified another operative, code-named Abu Osame, whom the terrorist team met in Libya, Lebanon, and then in Rome in March 1973. According to MI5, the plans to attack synagogues in the UK and the Netherlands had been at an advanced stage. Two groups of five to six men each were in the final stages of preparations to move to the two countries from Libya and other Middle Eastern states.

When Fowel and Ghafour appeared at a London airport on 20 May, they were arrested. Despite these precise details outlining a planned attack and potential charges against them, UK officials felt the evidence obtained during the investigation and detention was insufficient to ensure successful prosecution. Both men were thus allowed to leave on a non-stop flight to Beirut on 22 May.[111]

In early June, German intelligence added more pieces to the puzzle and revealed that Fowel was a drug and car dealer.[112] He was believed to have been the provider of heroin in various drug abuse cases in Hamburg since July 1972. In August 1972, the German public prosecution office issued an arrest warrant for him on suspicion of drug dealing and other drug crimes.[113]

The BfV investigated further and interrogated one of Fowel's clients in Hamburg to whom he had supplied 1kg of heroin.[114] This led West German intelligence to a car manufacturing firm in Hamburg, which confirmed that it had sold Fowel several cars and that he had contacts with second-hand car dealers around the city.[115] Following the findings of the UK investigation into Fowel's activities, the BfV now connected the dots: it believed that Fowel's drug and car dealing financed Black September terrorist operations. As previous investigations and Kilowatt cooperation revealed, car dealing could serve two terrorist purposes: the gains from the sales could help finance terrorist operations and the cars themselves were useful to smuggle weapons across borders.[116]

The investigation of Fowel and Ghafour went quiet for a while, until Nakaa and Shibli were killed in the bomb explosion on 17 June 1973. After the killing, various agencies checked their records for Nakaa and Shibli and shared their knowledge with the Kilowatt group. The first to do so was MI5, which sent its reply on 19 June, two days after the killing. In this cable, MI5 mentioned that it had evidence (without further details) that linked Shibli and Nakaa to Fowel's thwarted terrorist operation.[117] It thought that Fowel and Ghafour, and Shibli and Nakaa were two teams that were part of the same overall operation. This aligned with what MI5 had mentioned in an earlier cable, where it assumed that in late May 1973 several terrorist teams had travelled to Europe from the Middle East.[118]

In the same cable, the British agency confirmed intelligence provided by the BfV that Fowel had been to West Germany on several occasions to purchase second-hand cars, mainly Mercedes, ostensibly for resale in Lebanon.[119] Given that Shibli and Nakaa were driving a Mercedes, it is possible that the car that blew up in Rome had been purchased by Fowel and given to Shibli for the Rome El Al office attack.

This cable had a second part, which connected Shibli to another planned terrorist attack. MI5 noticed that in a cable sent by the DST on 23 March 1973, the alleged terrorist supporter Dianne Campbell Lefevre had included Shibli as one of her contacts in a fedayeen camp in Lebanon when she was there in 1971/1972.[120] MI5 thus considered it likely that Shibli had supported terrorist activities with her in France in March 1973.[121]

Lastly, MI5 compared the physical appearance of Ghafour, who had been arrested with Fowel in London in May, with the description of a 48-year-old man whose documents had been found in the wrecked car. The two matched, and UK intelligence thus suggested that Ghafour might have been the third team member of the Shibli and Nakaa terrorist squad.[122] Given that Ghafour had been released from detention in the UK on 22 May, this would have given him plenty of time to travel to Lyon and Rome to help prepare the El Al bomb attack.

Dutch intelligence also checked its records about Shibli and Nakaa and shared what information it had on them.[123] The BVD noticed that Shibli and his Beirut telephone number had been found on Rubhi Halloum's contact list, which was shared among Kilowatt partners on 23 October 1972.[124]

This means that Shibli had already been mentioned in Kilowatt cooperation at least twice, in October in connection to Halloum and in March in connection to Dianne Campbell Lefevre. These Kilowatt signals may have been the first indications that alerted Israeli intelligence about Shibli as a terrorist suspect.

A month after Shibli and Nakaa were killed, Mossad warned that three terrorists were allegedly on their way to Europe on a sabotage mission.[125] Their names and physical appearances were given; two of them were said to hold Lebanese passports, another a Syrian passport. A European man with tattoos, named Hans, was allegedly going to help the group with their mission. Mossad suspected that the Jibril organisation was behind this terrorist squad. It pointed out that the PFLP-GC (Jibril) had not carried out any terrorist activity since the air sabotage attempt through a booby-trapped record-player in August 1972.[126] Mossad believed that this could be a new attempt by the group to show its pugnacity.

In a follow-up to this cable, Mossad specified that the group's target was El Al offices in Europe.[127] The cable repeated the names of the three terrorists who were said to be on their way from the Middle East, gave descriptions of their physical appearances, and mentioned the names of their European helpers. It reiterated that the risk of attacks against El Al offices was very

173

high. Based on this cable, it is conceivable that Mossad worried that Black September wanted to 'finish the job' that Shibli and Nakaa were meant to do, and maybe even that Olivares' killer was meant to do: execute the head of the El Al Rome office, Moshe Adad.

CONCLUSIONS

What we have seen in this chapter can be described as a true 'battle of the spooks'. Over a few days, Mossad assassinated members of the Palestinian armed struggle in Paris, Beirut, and Athens. In retaliation, Black September assassinated Olivares and accused him of being a Mossad officer. In retrospect, it was highly unlikely that Olivares was linked to Mossad, but his murderer clearly believed so and saw his death as revenge for Operation Wrath of God.

After each of the murder cases in Europe, Club de Berne members diligently sent updates about the police investigations. Agencies asked Kilowatt partners (including Mossad) for help in tracking down the killers (namely Mossad). In no instance was Israel mentioned in connection with the killing missions in Paris or Athens, even though at the time it became increasingly clear that Mossad was behind them.

Similarly, Italian intelligence questioned Saleh's claim to have shot Olivares as vengeance for the death of Zwaiter. SISDE was feigning ignorance and seemingly unsuspiciously wondered whether Olivares might have had any anti-Palestinian past that could explain his killing. Kilowatt members, of course, handled assassinations in Europe differently compared with Mossad's assassinations in Lebanon. Since Israel claimed official responsibility for the raid, Kilowatt members could address the Israeli assassinations in Beirut.

Looking at estimative and warning cables, Mossad and other agencies were expecting a strong Black September reaction after Operation Spring of Youth. All agencies were on very high terrorist alert in Europe and in Israel. However, the Fatah leadership was terrified after the Beirut raid. Palestinian leaders at the highest level feared for their lives and were busy organising hideouts that they hoped Mossad could not find. MI5's assessment that Fatah was in 'disarray' after the Lebanon raid was, by all accounts, accurate.

By the same token, the Fatah leadership had already started to exert pressure on Black September. By April 1973, Fatah had largely managed to reintegrate Black September into its structures and forced it to give up international terrorism. Noticeable from the Kilowatt warnings and estimative intelligence at the time, it seems that Palestinian terrorists in Europe indeed worked without clear operational plans. Furthermore, comparatively more Kilowatt investigations concluded that people were innocent or that suspects were not involved in terrorist activities.

However, Palestinian terrorism was not yet over. While Black September was less active, splinter groups like the Libyan-backed ANYOLP or PFLP continued to pursue terrorism as a tactic. Indeed, Mossad's next assassination disrupted a Palestinian terrorist attack right before the bomb was planted.

The Club de Berne exchanges about Shibli and Nakaa reveal an interesting aspect of Mossad's selection of its targets. Namely, this case further substantiates the claim that Operation Wrath of God mainly targeted key operatives in Palestinian terrorism. The targets were Palestinians who were actively involved in the preparation of at least one if not several terrorist attacks.

The secondary literature has accused Mossad of selecting targets more for their convenience than for their role or importance in Palestinian terrorist activities. Club de Berne files do not confirm this. Kilowatt correspondence instead suggests that Mossad killed a person only after the agency had clear suspicions that they were deeply involved in terrorist planning, either in a strong support function (like the first operation against Zwaiter) or as a planner (like the eighth operation against Boudia; see below) or as a hit man (like this seventh operation against Shibli).

From the intelligence exchanges we also gather that Shibli had been on Mossad's radar for quite some time. It may even have been European intelligence that alerted Mossad to his terrorist network. Knowledge of his previous terrorist involvement possibly allowed Mossad to act so quickly when the news came via Sadness that Shibli had been on his way to Rome for an attack. Given that the agency already had European intelligence that classified Shibli as a potentially dangerous terrorist operative, it is conceivable that this led Mossad to decide to take this warning so seriously.

After the assassination, SISDE was useful in keeping Mossad up to date with the investigation (of Mossad's own killing operation). The Italian intelligence agency provided many details about what was found in the car and on its occupants, including the intact second bomb that was likely meant for the imminent attack against the El Al office. Its cable remained quiet about the likely cause of the explosion and did not comment on the fact that the bomb found in the car was intact, which suggested that there was a second bomb that detonated. The secondary literature assumes that the Italian police believed this to be a 'work accident'.[128] In this case, the police likely believed that the terrorists had two bombs, one that had not yet been assembled and a second one that exploded prematurely because they had not handled it correctly.

Overall, it is quite an incredible and spectacular story that an agency eliminated terrorist operatives on their way to carry out a terrorist act. The Club de Berne files do confirm this, and with the files we can now ascertain the exact address where the car exploded: at Piazza Barberini, which was a stone's throw away from the El Al office on Via Barberini. This confirms that the terrorists were most likely planning to attack the nearby El Al office in the centre of town, not the one at the airport.

7

A CAR BOMB IN PARIS, A FIRING SQUAD IN DC, A THWARTED ATTACK NEAR VIENNA

UPDATING THE MURDERERS: THE ASSASSINATION OF MOHAMED BOUDIA

Algerian native Mohamed Boudia, a core nodal point and manager of Palestinian terrorism in Europe, was a man of several passions. He loved women (and women loved him); he was a *bon vivant* and a partygoer.[1] He was passionate about the arts and his official role as the manager of a small theatre in Paris provided him with the perfect cover for his other passion, the Palestinian armed struggle. (See Figure 20.)

Boudia was acutely aware of Operation Wrath of God and knew that he might be next on its target list. It is likely that he knew he was also watched by French, Italian, and Swiss police and that there was an Interpol search warrant out for him. Italy had issued an Interpol arrest warrant against him for an attack on an oil pipeline near Trieste, which will be discussed further below. The Swiss authorities led an investigation into him for another attack, which too will be discussed below. In France he was known for his involvement in the Front de Libération Nationale (FLN) during Algeria's war of independence and served three years in prison for the organisation of FLN terrorist attacks on French soil.[2] When Algeria gained its independence, he was released and first lived in Algiers for a few years, then moved to Paris.

In France, while leading a very active social life, he was also very careful, frequently using disguises and makeup from his theatre to avoid detection. For instance, he would spend the night at a woman's home and then leave in the morning disguised as an old woman to trick any surveillance teams that may have been following him.[3] As another precaution, he frequently changed his daily routines, travelled a lot, and in Paris spent his nights at different locations. However, there was one constant element in his life, which was his weak point: he always drove a grey Renault R16 with a Parisian licence plate. This habit was what Mossad called his 'capture point', the weakness that would allow it to organise his execution.[4]

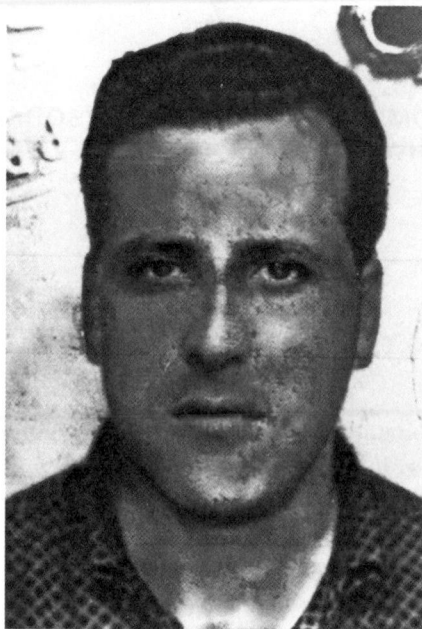

Figure 20 Portrait of Mohamed Boudia, killed by Mossad in Paris on 28 June 1973. Source: Associated Press/Alamy.

On the evening of 27 June 1973, Boudia went to see one of his many girlfriends. Late at night, Mossad broke into his car and planted a pressure-sensitive bomb underneath the driver's seat. The plan was smart: even if Boudia left the apartment in disguise, the person entering his beloved Renault R16 was likely going to be him. The bomb still had to be activated remotely and this was only going to be done once a Mossad operative nearby was certain that it was indeed Boudia.

The bomb was purposefully designed to look like a home-made bomb. Mossad used a pressure-activated 'land mine', which was packed with heavy nuts and sharp scrap iron. This was meant to make it look like Boudia was the victim of an accidental explosion of a bomb that Black September had itself built for an attack, but which had exploded prematurely while Boudia was carrying it.[5] As will be shown later, the French police indeed came to this conclusion (at least in the Kilowatt reports that were shared after the explosion).

Mossad further knew that Boudia always checked for explosive devices around the outside of his car before he would get in. Hence, by planting the bomb inside the car, hidden underneath the driver's seat, they knew he

Figure 21 Car after the assassination of Mohamed Boudia. Source: STF/AFP/Getty Images.

was unlikely to spot it.[6] He did not find it, and the bomb detonated at 10.57 a.m. on 28 June 1973, while he still had one foot on the pavement. The blast ripped him to pieces and when the French police arrived ten minutes later, they found his flesh and body parts scattered around the surrounding cars. (See Figure 21.)

CHARGES AGAINST BOUDIA

Boudia's involvement in terrorism was clear to everyone. Secondary literature and Club de Berne files describe him as a central figure in most of the operational planning and execution of Palestinian terrorist activities in Europe. He was said to have replaced Hamshari as the new head of Black September operations in France, after Hamshari was killed in Paris in December 1972, as Operation Wrath of God's second victim.[7]

Boudia was not only in charge of coordinating the planning and execution of specific attacks, he also linked Fatah/Black September with PFLP terrorism units and liaised with other terrorist groups around the world, notably the German Baader–Meinhof Group, Carlos' network, the Japanese Red Army Faction, and the Irish Republican Army (IRA).[8] According to a contemporary journalistic account, he was allegedly a 'terrorism ambassador', who planned to create an interconnected global terrorist network that would work together, share intelligence, organise weapons transfers, and undertake joint attacks around the world.[9] He organised military training in Lebanon for members of these partner terrorist groups as part of his goal to help them connect.[10]

Most accounts place Boudia at the heart of all operational terrorism links in Europe and assign him a central role in many spectacular terrorist events. For instance, he is alleged to have masterminded a major attack that was thwarted, but which would have taken the lives of many Israeli citizens and tourists if it had been successful, namely, the simultaneous bombing of nine big hotels in Tel Aviv during the first night of Passover in spring 1971.[11]

According to Jewish tradition, on the first night of Passover families and friends come together for the Seder, the collective reading of the Bible passage about how the Jewish people escaped oppression and slavery in ancient Egypt. It usually involves large gatherings, and Jews from around the world travel to Israel to spend the occasion with friends and family in hotel catered events. Through the previously mentioned source code-named 'Sadness', Shin Bet had been able to thwart the plans to place bombs at the hotels during the Seder and arrested all operatives involved before they could strike.[12]

In the summer of 1971, the subsequent military trial took place in Lod, Israel, where all the operatives confessed. They revealed how Boudia 'charmed' them and persuaded them to perpetrate this terrorist attack. The operatives entered Israel as 'walking bombs', carrying explosive chemicals embedded in their coats. If the substances were mixed, they would have made a potent type of Napalm. The female terrorist recruits hid the powdered and liquid explosives in their underwear, shoes, makeup, and hygiene products such as a tampon box. They all named Boudia as the brains behind the operation.[13]

This same informant, Sadness, who helped thwart the Passover attack and had access to the inner circles of the top Palestinian leadership, in the months before Boudia's killing warned of other major attacks that were being organised by him.[14] With the help of Club de Berne files, it is possible to reconstruct his detailed plans for some of them. One was an attack against a transit camp in Austria for Jewish refugees, called Schönau. As will be explained below, this attack was the cause of extreme worry for Mossad. The thwarting of this attack led to a Kilowatt-wide investigation. The resulting intelligence, which was sent to Mossad via its European partners, was extremely helpful in tracking Boudia and eventually organising his assassination.

Many other attacks, however, were indeed carried out, such as in Rotterdam and Trieste, which were directed against oil tanks. Intelligence agencies ascertained that Boudia was the core strategist behind these sabotage attacks. In Rotterdam, in the Netherlands, he initiated an attack against a Gulf Oil refinery on 15 March 1971. In Trieste, Italy, the attack was carried out against oil storage tanks on 4 August 1972.[15] This explosion was huge and caused serious damage. Forty-four pounds of explosives were used, which burned more than 250,000 tons of crude oil at a cost of $2.5 billion.[16] However, the worst was prevented as the firefighters extinguished the fire right before it could ignite an outsized fuel tank.[17]

Through Club de Berne files about the Schönau and Trieste investigations, more details about the attacks come to light for the first time. In particular, Boudia's operational methods become apparent: he used his charm again and again to recruit unsuspecting women, who fell in love with him and agreed to become terrorist operatives.

These investigations relating to the attacks in Schönau and Trieste also highlight how Mossad was using ongoing investigations as cover to collect operational intelligence about Boudia. As will be shown, this intelligence was very useful to organise his assassination. Hence, the next sections bring more details to light about important terrorist attacks and demonstrate once again how the European intelligence agencies contributed to the execution of Mossad's killing operation on their own soil – Europe.

A PARKING TICKET THAT KILLS: USING THE SCHÖNAU INVESTIGATION TO TRACK BOUDIA

The Schönau investigation started with an arrest in Tarvisio, Italy, from which point onwards collective investigations and intelligence exchanges provided clue after clue. Eventually, the Kilowatt network uncovered the terrorists' elaborate plan to attack the Jewish transit camp in Schönau.

It began with a warning by Mossad on 29 January 1973. The Israeli agency alerted its partners that some Israeli passports had been stolen and were in the hands of Fatah operatives who had been sent abroad for terrorist actions.[18] As mentioned in Chapter 5, in late January 1973, several warnings about Palestinians possessing Israeli passports had been issued and were all taken very seriously. Mossad gave the first three digits of the stolen passports' serial numbers: 595. It also specified that it was possible that other serial numbers were also in the hands of Palestinian terrorists.

Israel asked that Kilowatt partners alert their border controls and inform Mossad or Shin Bet immediately if a suspect Israeli passport was noticed.[19]

In an extraordinary case where a warning directly led to an arrest (and eventually the exposure of terrorist plans), the next day Palestinians with exactly these stolen passports were taken into custody. Namely, on 30 January 1973, Italy informed the Kilowatt group about the detention of three Palestinians who held Israeli passports with serial numbers beginning with 595, the same series that was indicated as stolen by Mossad the previous day. The three Palestinians had tried to illegally cross from Austria into Italy at the border town of Tarvisio.[20]

The Italian agency, SISDE, gave a detailed account of all the travel stamps in the passports, which included entry and admission stamps from the airports at Lod Tel Aviv, Munich, London, New York, and Paris, and all stamps were from December 1972. The three Palestinians confessed to the Italian authorities that they were not Israelis but Palestinians, and that they were in Europe as part of their 'engagement in the Palestinian resistance'. They acknowledged that the names in their passports were false and gave the police their supposed real names, which were shared in the cable. Because the passports had no visas to enter Italy, the Palestinians needed to be deported back to Austria. The Italian authorities were waiting to hear from Austrian border control whether they would be allowed to return to the country.[21]

After a week, SISDE shared that the three detainees had not been sent back to Austria.[22] Instead, they had been taken to Udine where they were waiting for a judgment in their trial for forgery of documents and false identity. Importantly, the Italian agency reported on documents found in the terrorists' possession that provided hints about the possible target locations of their attacks. The three detainees carried maps of Europe, with spots marked in Austria, Switzerland, and West Germany. One of the detainees had with him a topographical map of Vienna, on which a trail was indicated. SISDE promised to send copies of the maps as soon as possible.[23]

The three detainees had meanwhile been interrogated by the Italian and Austrian police. The Austrians were further able to link this arrest in Tarvisio to another arrest the week before in Vienna. On 20 January 1973, another group of three Palestinians had been arrested in Vienna possessing stolen Israeli passports with the same serial number that Mossad had reported missing. Intense interrogations ensued in Italy and Austria, and Mossad was allowed to send Arab-speaking translators to the hearings that took place in both countries.[24] In this way, Mossad was providing a service while, of course, obtaining vital intelligence right from the Palestinian terrorists themselves.

By synthesising all the available information, it was established that both groups were part of an attack on a target located on the outskirts of Vienna. This operation was planned and coordinated through a handler in Geneva. Furthermore, both terrorist squads, the ones arrested in Vienna and in Tarvisio, started their missions in Geneva. This led the Swiss authorities to open a new investigation specifically about the case and to share intelligence about the current state of knowledge in Switzerland relating to these terrorist operations.

TRACING BOUDIA WITH HELP FROM THE SWISS

Swiss intelligence enquired among any individuals or institutions in Geneva that might have been in contact with the terrorists. Through Kilowatt, BuPo shared a very long report about its findings.[25] The Swiss investigation brought to light a panoply of further leads and, most interestingly, through this cable one can understand in detail how Swiss intelligence was operating. Among others, the cable reveals that Swiss intelligence had very close ties to the tourism industry, with informants in restaurants or bars throughout Geneva. The classic spy cliché of rummaging in garbage bags was apparently a practice that was indeed used at the time, for instance to find out the intentions of suspicious pro-Palestinian students.

Through talks with representatives of the Genevan hotel industry, Swiss intelligence found that the three Arabs arrested in Vienna had stayed in the Hotel Continental in Geneva from 17 to 19 January 1973; the cable even indicated their room number. At the hotel in Geneva, the three registered with Syrian passports, which contained valid Swiss tourism visas that were issued in Damascus in December 1972. Their Syrian passports had different names from the ones in the Israeli passports and these were also different from the names the three claimed to Italian intelligence were their real names.

One of the three had 'for inexplicable reasons' not filled out the hotel register, and Swiss authorities scolded the hotel manager for this mishap. Swiss police were nevertheless able to find personal details about him and shared them with the Kilowatt partners. Swiss intelligence enquired among its sources in Palestinian circles, but it could not establish whether the three Arabs had any contact with the Palestinian underground in Geneva.[26]

Furthermore, in their interrogation by Austrian police, the three Palestinians claimed that a Genevan bar named Escale was used as a meeting point with their handler. In this bar, they received the stolen Israeli passports that were meant to be used for the operation in Austria and they gave their handler their Syrian passports. The Swiss interrogated the owners of the bar and tried to find out more about this meeting. They expected that soon more information would come through from this investigation and promised to send further updates to any interested intelligence agency.[27]

The Austrian authorities led further interrogations, which concluded that a fourth person was meant to join the terrorist squad in Vienna. The Austrians had not found out who it was but reported that this person was supposed to give the three operatives their next instructions for the planned attack. Swiss intelligence found a plane ticket and other evidence suggesting that this fourth person, who was meant to meet both groups in Vienna, was in fact the same person who gave one of the groups their Israeli passports in the Escale bar in Geneva. This person, the Swiss informed their partners, held the strings of the attack and was none other than Mohamed Boudia.[28]

Swiss intelligence came to this conclusion, among others, through the interrogation of two women who were active in 'pro-Palestinian circles' and who had apparently helped Boudia with practical tasks related to the operation. Among others, they hosted him during his stays in Switzerland. The first woman was Anne-Marie Bollier, a student in pharmacy at the University of Geneva, who was originally from Zurich. Bollier was known to be associated with pro-Palestinian groups and to support, as the cable said, 'all kinds of revolutionary causes', like the Black Panthers in the USA or Latin American armed groups.[29]

On 18 January 1973, she made a flight reservation for Boudia under his cover name R. Bertin from Geneva to Vienna, departing on 19 January (the next day) with an open return ticket (which meant that he could choose the date of his return). She acknowledged that Boudia had personally instructed her to make this reservation, though she insisted that she knew him only under his (cover) name of Bertin.

Swiss intelligence searched her garbage bin and found, torn apart but clearly readable, Boudia's return ticket (still using the name Bertin) of 21 January from Vienna to Geneva. She acknowledged that she hosted Boudia before and after his trip to Vienna, and that he ripped up his ticket and threw it in her bin on 21 January. On that same day, according to her account, which Swiss intelligence believed to be true, she drove him to the airport for a flight to Paris.

In the search of her apartment, Swiss intelligence officers found another lead. There was a note with handwritten instructions on how to build an explosive bomb and how to use it. The note was in an envelope that was addressed to Zohair Shibl, at an address in Vienna.[30] Bollier confirmed that

Boudia had left this envelope with her, and that she was instructed to send the letter and get in contact with Shibl once Boudia gave her the signal to do so. The Swiss service enquired about Shibl with Austrian intelligence, which confirmed that it knew him as a Fatah operative in Vienna in charge of gathering operational intelligence for Black September operations.

The second person who the Swiss interrogated was Catherine Erschoff, a French citizen, who worked as a translator at conferences, residing in Geneva.[31] Like Bollier, Erschoff was also known to be associated with the Palestinian movement in Geneva. She was known, for instance, to have regularly met the former head of the PLO, Fouad al-Shamali (before his death in the summer of 1972). She was also known to be closely linked to Daoud Barakat, who was officially accredited to the Arab League in Geneva and held a diplomatic passport, but who *de facto* was known semi-officially as the Fatah representative in Switzerland.[32]

Both women were further 'close friends' with Zeinat Abdel Majid, who worked for Barakat but was officially in Geneva in his capacity as secretary of the Kuwaiti embassy. The cable stressed further that, before his death, all the people mentioned in the cable had also been in close contact with Palestinian leader Mahmoud al-Hamshari (who was Operation Wrath of God's second assassination victim in Paris in December 1972). In terms of the two women's role as terrorism supporters, the cable concluded that Bollier and Erschoff hosted Boudia whenever he was in Geneva and the two also regularly went to Paris. It was further mentioned that Erschoff was co-owner of a restaurant and an apartment in Paris, and the cable included the exact addresses of both places.

Lastly, a parking fine led to another important clue about Boudia's network and routine. In December 1972, Boudia was fined in Geneva for a wrongly parked car of which he was the driver. But the car was in somebody else's name. The cable from Swiss intelligence provided details of the car's French licence plate number (7699 WG 75), its colour and brand (a dark grey Renault R16-TS), and its owner: Adria Guerrar, Boudia's former wife. She was Algerian and lived in Paris. Her date of birth and exact home address in the 12th arrondissement were also included in the Swiss cable. Cross-checking this cable with the cable French intelligence sent after Boudia's death shows that this was indeed exactly the car – with the same licence plate number – in which Boudia met his death.[33] At the time the Swiss cable was sent, Mossad was still searching for a way to kill Boudia. With this context in mind, it seems that Swiss intelligence had inadvertently drawn attention to Boudia's car and facilitated the Israelis' efforts to track it down.

The Swiss cable noted that Boudia was, of course, well known to Kilowatt intelligence services for his involvement in the Palestinian armed struggle. It specifically mentioned the 'Barge Evelyne et Consorts' affair in April 1971, which was the above-mentioned thwarted Passover terror attack. Evelyne Barge was one of the operatives who entered Israel with the chemicals to mix the bomb.

The cable further mentioned that the Swiss knew that French intelligence had interrogated Boudia in April 1971, and had issued a travel ban on him. In a subtle justification for why Switzerland let him stay in Geneva, the Swiss message mentioned that Boudia had been released without sentence by the French authorities and that in October 1972 this travel restriction was lifted. When Boudia claimed he needed to travel to Geneva for professional engagements linked to the management of the theatre in Paris, Swiss authorities thus let him come.

Swiss intelligence insisted that there was no doubt about Boudia's identity and involvement in this operation in Vienna. Though the end of the cable hinted that it was likely that Boudia himself handed out the stolen Israeli passports in the Escale bar, BuPo stated that it could also have been someone acting under his leadership.

Because of the revelation of Boudia as the string-puller behind this operation, BuPo further provided as many personal details about him as possible. The cable included his nationality (Algerian), family details and information about his wife, his profession (director of a small theatre in Paris), current place of residence (Paris), and his exact address (23 Rue Claude Bernard) in the 5th arrondissement.[34] All this, plus the details about his car, was, of course, very useful for preparing a killing mission against him!

The Swiss authorities knew that Boudia had been in Switzerland between 24 and 25 January 1973, only a few days before the arrests in Tarvisio. 'Unfortunately he could not be apprehended,' they said, and reckoned that he had left Switzerland by the time the cable was sent on 30 January.

The cable ended with a recommendation to check any travels since 1 December 1972 to a Kilowatt country under the name Bertin, either Roland, Robert, Rodrigue, Roger, or Pierre Bertin as the first name of Boudia's cover could vary. Given the operational involvement of Bollier and Erschoff, Switzerland suggested that their records should be checked too in the Kilowatt services, and in particular France should follow up, given their numerous visits to Paris. The investigation was still ongoing, and BuPo promised to continuously update its partners about new information.[35]

Over the course of a week, Switzerland liaised directly with Austrian intelligence to find out if anyone under the cover name R. Bertin had been in Austria. Austrian intelligence searched all hotel records for all of January 1973. Indeed, as the Swiss then reported to the Kilowatt group, a Roland Bertin had stayed in Vienna in the Hotel Bellevue between 6 and 8 January. Bertin had a French passport. According to Austrian intelligence, these dates corresponded to when one of the terrorist squads was believed to have also been in Vienna.[36]

In early February, Mossad replied to the Swiss cable and provided further intelligence it had on Boudia. It listed the attacks it thought Boudia was responsible for, mentioning, among others, the Passover attack of spring 1971, the sabotage attack against oil refineries in Rotterdam in March 1971, and the murder of a Syrian journalist in Paris on 13 November 1972.[37]

Mossad confirmed that the operational methods as described in the Swiss cable corresponded to what it knew about Boudia's habits of 'paying particular attention to the rules of clandestine activity'.[38] Namely, Boudia was known to travel in Europe using various passports under assumed names, to stay in private flats (as opposed to hotels), and to frequently change his place of residence. Mossad knew that he maintained contact with other terrorists through 'female couriers', who had legitimate reasons to travel. He was known to refrain from establishing direct contact with known members of terrorist organisations. Similarly, for his journeys he often sent women to buy tickets for him so that he did not have to go to the travel office himself. Lastly, through his work in the theatre he had easy access to makeup and disguises, which he was known to use to alter his appearance and avoid identification. As indicated above, this practice is also mentioned in the secondary literature.

Mossad highlighted the role that Geneva played and suggested that it was because of the presence of a large terrorism support network. The Israeli agency believed, however, that Geneva was only a point of transit, while the core of the operation was controlled from Paris, which was, of course, where Boudia was based. The cable confirmed again that the current state of all investigations led to Boudia as the main controller of the operation.[39]

Lastly, the cable summarised key details about the suspects involved in the operation who were mentioned in the Swiss cable. Bollier, Erschoff, and Majid were classified as Boudia's middle (wo)men and terrorism supporters in Geneva. Zohair Shibl was believed to be a Black September operative permanently based in Vienna and responsible for helping with logistical and operational support for attacks.[40]

Soon afterwards, Italian intelligence updated its partners about an administrative matter. The three Palestinian detainees held in Udine had been transferred to Austria and handed over to the Austrian federal police.[41]

BOUDIA AS THE MASTERMIND BEHIND THE SCHÖNAU ATTACK

Three weeks after the Tarvisio arrests, on 23 February 1973, Mossad sent a detailed description of the attack that was believed to have been prepared by Boudia and the two terrorist squads arrested in Tarvisio and Vienna.[42] The attack was directed against the Schönau transit camp near Vienna, which at the time was used as an overnight stopover by Jews who were emigrating from the Soviet Union to Israel. In line with Swiss, Italian, and Austrian intelligence reports, Mossad identified Boudia as the overseer and leader of the whole operation.

Mossad's investigation led to the following assessment: on 20 January 1973 in Vienna, three men bearing Israeli passports were detained because of the suspicion that their passports had been forged. During the interrogations it became clear that the three were Arab nationals, members of Black September, who arrived in Vienna to carry out an attack against the immigration transit camp at Schönau.[43] Then, on 30 January, a second group of three Palestinians with passports of the same series were detained at the Austro-Italian border as they were trying to cross from Austria into Italy without visas. Investigations revealed that these three were connected to the first group.

What followed in the cable was a detailed description of the planned attack on the Schönau transit camp. What is remarkable is the level of detail that Mossad was able to ascertain. Even more remarkable is that an attack against Schönau eventually did happen several months later, on 28 September 1973. A comparison between the originally planned and actually executed attack will follow below.

In the cable, Mossad explained that the purpose of the attack was to gain control of the Schönau immigration transit camp, hold its occupants as hostages, and demand the release of terrorists held in Israel. It also identified the intended method: twelve people armed with Kalashnikovs were supposed to arrive at the camp in rented cars in the early hours of the morning (between 1 and 3 a.m.). The cars would have been rented using the Israeli passports. The plan was to infiltrate the camp via the back fence and gain control. At this point the operatives would start negotiations with the Austrian authorities and demand the release of terrorists held in Israel.

Depending on how the negotiations unfolded, the terrorists had planned for two scenarios. If their demands were met, they were to:

- depart with the hostages for the Vienna airport;
- board a plane, which would take them to an Arab country;
- release the Jewish emigrants before boarding the plane;
- take the crew of the plane as hostages to ensure the terrorists' safe arrival at their destination;
- receive notification of the release of the terrorists held in Israel by a code word, which Black September would pass on to the Austrian police.

In the event that their demands were not met, they were to take the emigrants of military age with them to an Arab country and continue the negotiations from there. The instructions for the perpetrators were not to use their weapons against local residents, but to be ready to kill the hostages as a means of increasing pressure.[44]

In the cable, Mossad further shared what it knew about the preparations for the attack. Israeli intelligence believed that the operation had been planned and organised from Lebanon, and that Black September was controlling its operatives from there. The organisation's base in Lebanon was thought to have recruited the perpetrators, trained them, dispatched them to Europe, coordinated their movements there, and organised the meetings. In Beirut, the heads of the squads who went to Europe were briefed about the outline of the operation using maps and sketches, which were later found in their possession when the Italian police arrested them.

Boudia was assumed to be responsible for the preparations in Europe related to the attack. He kept travelling from place to place and maintained contact with Black September logistical support members in Europe, and with the terrorist squads that arrived from Lebanon. The centre of activity was believed to be Paris. Preparations for the attack had begun very early, and the European leg began setting the scene at least two months before the squads left Lebanon.

The way the operation was organised, according to Mossad, was so that the different collaborators did not know the entire plan of the operation. In other words, the agency believed that the Schönau attack reflected a 'need-to-know' organisational basis: individuals or specific squads only knew as much as was needed for them to fulfil their specific task, but without knowing the overall plan. Only towards the end, a day or two before the attack, would they have come together and learned about the arrangements for how to execute it. This tactic was useful to minimise damage in case one unit got caught. Since they did not know much about the other squads, they could not compromise each other. Essentially this was a way to ensure that, in case of capture, the operation as a whole would not be blown.

The centre of the web was Mohamed Boudia, who received orders from Beirut and passed them on personally to the people in the field in Europe. He coordinated the work of the contact people and couriers and was himself in Geneva and Vienna when the respective Schönau squads arrived.[45]

In terms of gathering intelligence for the perpetration of the attack, Mossad informed the Kilowatt members that the leader of the Vienna Schönau squad, Ali Zibag, and the Black September man in Vienna, Zohair Shibl, went to Schönau at least twice to find out how and where the terrorists could sneak into the camp.

Mossad compared the operational methods for this planned attack with previous attacks or attempted attacks and believed that they corresponded with Black September tactics more generally.[46] The operational leader, in this case Boudia, knew all the details of the plan, while informing the operatives step by step on a strictly need-to-know basis.

In terms of Black September techniques for attack preparations, according to Mossad there were three main types of operatives. The Schönau attack was allegedly organised along these lines. First were the non-disguised, openly recognisable operatives. These were officially accredited personnel who worked at offices such as the Arab League and held diplomatic passports. Second were the operatives in disguise who lived in Europe as regular citizens and pursued no official political activities while working undercover for Black September. An example, the cable specified, was Zohair Shibl, who had lived in Vienna for several years and had been very actively involved in the planning and initial execution of the Schönau attack. He met the Schönau squad that came to Vienna and was seen previously at the Black September headquarters in Lebanon.

The third type of operative were local European helpers who travelled around and worked as couriers, rented cars and apartments on behalf of Black September, or transmitted written or oral messages. Examples were the Swiss women Anne-Marie Bollier and Catherine Erschoff. Other examples were two Austrians who were members of a right-wing association and organised a private apartment for the second Schönau squad after the first one had been arrested and helped them to illegally cross the Italian–Austrian border.

Two important points where both squads had met were Geneva and Vienna. The cable indicated who exactly met whom, where, and when. It also included a list of the names and all known details of the participants of the attack, and members of its support network. The cable specified whether the people had been located, and what connections they had to other terrorist suspects.[47] Interestingly, it mentioned that Boudia had not yet been located. It was a very detailed account about the different connection points, and it was intended that Kilowatt agencies could follow up. Mossad specified that any tiny piece of information, however minor, could result in a new and possibly important lead.

Despite the high degree of detail that could be ascertained about the operation, Mossad emphasised that some elements to complete the picture were still missing. Israeli intelligence had, for instance, no information on the origins and whereabouts of the weapons, and how they were supposed to reach the terrorists. It added, though, that it knew Zohair Shibl had connections with the Iraqi embassy in Vienna and thought it possible that the weapons were hidden there.[48]

Furthermore, based on the interrogations, Mossad suspected that there was a third six-person terrorist squad that was also supposed to participate in the attack. It speculated that they had been in Western Europe but managed to leave via Eastern Europe, after having been warned about the arrest of their colleagues. Alternatively, it was also possible that the squad had not reached Europe yet.

As concluding remarks, the cable again compared the operational methods of this attack with what was generally known about Black September tactics: 'The planned operation is reminiscent in several significant details of the Munich and Bangkok operations, such as the early preparation, the fact that only the leader of the group knew the details of the plan, the size of the group, the quantity and type of the weapons etc.'[49] In this vein, there was no doubt that Black September was behind the attempted Schönau attack.

Given previous experiences, Mossad stressed that despite having thwarted this attack, Schönau remained a popular target for Black September terrorist operations. Indeed, the transit camp was attacked on the eve of the Yom Kippur War, on 28 September 1973.

TRACING BOUDIA AGAIN WITH THE SWISS

On 23 February 1973, the same day as Mossad sent the long cable in which it pieced all the details together, the agency wrote a Kilowatt cable addressed to Swiss intelligence.[50] It asked if BuPo could interrogate Anne-Marie Bollier again to find out about her and Boudia's connections to Zohair Shibl. Mossad was hoping that Swiss intelligence would ask her about the instructions on how to build a bomb that were found in a letter addressed to Shibl. It reiterated that it was still not yet known how the arms were supposed to be delivered to the Schönau perpetrators. It expected that further interrogation of Bollier could lead to information on this.

Because Boudia changed addresses so frequently, Mossad explained that it did not know where he resided at the moment.[51] In the same cable it asked Swiss intelligence to kindly interrogate Catherine Erschoff to find out about his current whereabouts, his place of residence, and what additional identification papers he was using.[52] This Mossad request is somewhat surprising, since BuPo had already sent the exact address of Boudia's apartment in Paris in a previous cable. It is possible that Mossad assumed that Boudia had already changed his address and wanted Swiss help to find his most recent location.

Given that Mossad was preparing an assassination mission to kill Boudia, this cable can be seen as one of the most direct uses of the Kilowatt channel for Operation Wrath of God, albeit hidden under the mantle of the Schönau operation. In this vein, the agency used a current investigation as a pretext to ask a partner to help find a terrorist who was on its kill list.

Swiss intelligence followed up on Mossad's request and sent a reply on 6 March. Unfortunately, and unlike most other cables, this Swiss cable was not archived. It is, however, possible to infer what it said based on Mossad's reply on the next day and based on an internal report that summarised all known facts about the Schönau operation. In this internal report, Boudia was mentioned again as the leader of the attack and therefore the report focused strongly on him. Swiss intelligence was able to ascertain not only that Bertin was the cover name that Boudia was using, but also the following additional names: he was posing as a French citizen with passports in the names of Roland Bertin, Pierre Bertin, and Maurice Boyer. He sometimes pretended to be a Moroccan citizen under the names Said Ben Ahmed, Abu Khalil, and Abu Khaled, and was also using the family name Betanschan.[53]

The cable sent by Swiss intelligence mentioned these other cover names being used by Boudia. BuPo also sent a draft report that summarised the known elements at the time and the progress of the Schönau investigation. The Swiss agency further informed its partners about its intention to publish some parts of the report in an official press communiqué. The cable was sent before it published the communiqué, possibly as a courtesy to give Mossad a heads up.

The next day, on 7 March 1973, Mossad sent a most unusual direct reply to BuPo.[54] The cable was addressed personally to Dr André Amstein, the head of Swiss intelligence, which is rare. Mossad sent this message from its station in Paris and exceptionally had a Mossad official, 'S. Cohen', personally sign the cable, which too is rare.

Mossad urged the Swiss authorities not to divulge any information relating to the investigations that they had undertaken in Geneva about Boudia and Schönau. It insisted that the Swiss authorities should seriously reconsider the publication of the communiqué. Mossad gave two arguments as to why it was important to keep absolute secrecy about this Schönau investigation and why it was best not to publish the communiqué.

First, in Austria the investigation was still ongoing. Mossad thought that the detained terrorists had provided more information than they should have been allowed to tell according to their orders. They were able to cooperate with Austrian police precisely because the affair was kept top secret. If the Swiss government were to publish anything in relation to their statements, it risked silencing them. This could undermine the Schönau investigation altogether. Mossad also strongly advised the Swiss to consult with 'our common Austrian friends' and to wait for their comments and guidance before publishing the communiqué.[55]

Second, at the time the cable was sent, Boudia was not aware that the intelligence services knew about his involvement in the Schönau operation. If the Swiss authorities were to publish information about his involvement, or even mention the cover names/aliases that he used during his stays in Geneva (Mr Bertin), they would provide him with valuable information. Boudia could henceforth be much more careful, change aliases, and avoid meetings in Switzerland. 'As a consequence, the hope to one day be able to apprehend him would diminish,' the cable stressed.[56] Mossad thus emphatically requested that the Swiss authorities leave out any reference to Boudia and his cover names in their statements.

This cable is of interest for several reasons. First, it is interesting that the Kilowatt channel was used in this case as a means to communicate a state-to-state message in the fastest possible way. Mossad had this direct line to the heart of the Swiss state and used it to prevent the publication of this communiqué.

Second, it reveals that Israel wanted to keep the Schönau investigations completely secret. While it makes sense to want not to jeopardise an ongoing investigation, it is also plausible that the Israeli government was afraid that even the publication of the intention to attack a Jewish transit camp would attract negative publicity. It could also alert other terrorists to the idea of attacking the Schönau camp.

Additionally, Mossad did not want Switzerland to ruin its efforts to get close to Boudia. Officially, it claimed that Israeli security wanted to 'apprehend' Boudia. Unofficially, as we know, Mossad wanted to eliminate him. Therefore, it needed Switzerland to keep complete silence on this, and even used the Kilowatt channel to make sure it stayed quiet. Switzerland never issued a press communiqué about the Schönau investigation, though it wrote a lengthy internal report that summarised the investigation and especially detailed the Palestinian network and links between Boudia and his Genevan and Viennese terrorism support system.[57]

Interestingly, the report was finalised on 6 June 1973, nearly three weeks before Boudia's murder. Since the draft report was shared with Mossad, it is possible that this final report was also shared with Israeli intelligence. Independent of this June 1973 report, over the course of the Schönau investigation Swiss intelligence shared with Mossad a vast amount of crucial operational details about Boudia, his network, routine, cover identities, and most importantly, where and how to find him.

A week later, another cable in relation to the thwarted Schönau attack was sent through the Kilowatt channel.[58] This time it was not Mossad, but its fellow service Shin Bet that sent it. The cable contained revelations obtained after further interrogations of the team leader of the Vienna squad, the above-mentioned Ali Zibag. He was arrested together with his peers in Vienna on 20 January 1973 carrying the forged Israeli passports.

Zibag admitted that he was involved in other terrorist attacks, including an attempt to assassinate King Hussein of Jordan. This operation was organised by Abu Nidal with the goal of killing the king during a visit to London. Zibag described the plan as follows: in 1971, Abu Nidal heard that King Hussein was flying to the US and that he would return via London. Zibag and two others were selected to kill the king at his hotel during his stopover in the UK.[59]

In Beirut, the three each received false identities and documents, a 9 mm pistol, and two magazines with fourteen bullets. Abu Nidal forbade them to take silencers and ordered them to surrender to the British police after the murder. The three flew from Beirut to London and managed to smuggle the weapons through customs. They first stayed together at a hotel and then moved separately to furnished apartments in the city. Every morning the three met at the hotel where King Hussein was to stay.[60] After a week, their handler was supposed to meet them at a rendezvous in a café with detailed instructions about the murder, or with an alternative plan to attack a Jewish library in London. However, their contact man never appeared and after a month of waiting, the three returned to Beirut together.

Shin Bet assessed that the plan as described by Ali Zibag corresponded to the modus operandi of Black September. In particular, it believed it was common for a terrorist squad to meet their handler in situ and only shortly before the operation. This also corresponded to the way the Schönau attack was organised. Similarly, the preference for private apartments over hotels seemed to be a common terrorist practice, as private dwellings were better for avoiding police surveillance.

Shin Bet, however, thought that Zibag confused the time of the operation. King Hussein was in the US with a return via London in April 1972, not 1971. Commenting about the people involved in the attack, it added: 'Abu Nidal and those mentioned in para 1 above [the terrorists who accompanied Zibag to London] are not known to us.'[61] Later, in 1974, Abu Nidal created his own group and this was likely one of the first times that intelligence agencies noticed him as a potential terrorist leader. As mentioned above, ever since the Jordanian civil war in September 1970 that expelled Palestinians from Jordan, several terrorist groups indeed continuously planned and executed attacks against Jordanian targets.[62]

At the end of March 1973, Mossad had fact-checked some of the statements made by Ali Zibag during the interrogation.[63] He apparently lied about working at a hotel in Gaza. The hotel owner, when asked about it by Mossad, insisted that only his own family members were allowed to work at the hotel and that it was impossible that Zibag ever worked for him. Similarly, Mossad compared a photograph of one of the Vienna detainees and found out that he had lied about his name. It was able to identify his real name and shared all available personal details, including a physical description and information about his family and network.[64]

These fact-checking investigations were important elements to determine the trustworthiness of the detainees' testimonies. This was especially important since secondary literature suggests that some of this intelligence was used by Mossad for operational planning of further killing missions. Namely, historian Thomas Riegler, who researched the thwarted Schönau attack, among others, based on Austrian intelligence sources, believes that some of the information that Mossad obtained through these interrogations in Austria served as the basis to plan Operation Spring of Youth.[65] This claim was first mentioned in a newspaper, arguing, among other things, that Mossad knew the area extremely well and possessed strong operational intelligence for the mission.[66]

Riegler reinforces the claim by highlighting an internal Austrian security document that said that in detention, one of the Palestinians drew a sketch of Black September offices in the south Beirut neighbourhood of Sabra.[67] During Operation Spring of Youth, Mossad was allegedly able to operate with 'surprising familiarity with the area'[68] and destroyed a seven-storey building that belonged to Black September. If it was indeed able to obtain the information from the interrogations, it was yet another example of Mossad using intelligence obtained through cooperation with its European partners for Operation Wrath of God.

COMPARING THE PLANNED AND THE EXECUTED SCHÖNAU ATTACK

The Schönau attack was thwarted in February 1973, and a few months later, in June, Boudia was killed. Several months later, in September 1973, under new operational leadership, Palestinian terrorists again planned an attack on the Schönau transit camp. This time, the attack was indeed carried out. In the literature, it is commonly referred to as the 'Schönau ultimatum'.

The target was, of course, the same, but the way the terrorists gained access to the site was different. In the first plan, the idea was for the Palestinians to arrive by car, climb over the fence, and gain control of the camp. Then negotiations with Austrian authorities were to start, with demands for the release of fellow Palestinian activists in Israeli prisons.

In the successful attempt, the Palestinians were not actually trying to infiltrate the camp itself; instead they managed to establish control over a train that was bringing Jewish Soviet refugees to Schönau.[69] Two terrorists boarded the train in Czechoslovakia and once they crossed the border to Austria, they raided the train controller. The two terrorists were heavily armed with guns, grenades, and a ring of dynamite on their hips. Of approximately one hundred Jewish migrants, they selected five as their hostages and forced them to leave the train when it stopped at Marchegg station in Austria. Two of the hostages, a young woman and her baby son, were able to escape. The terrorists added a custom official to their hostages and were thus in control of four in total.

As a result of an unbelievable blunder by the Austrian police forces that reached the site very quickly, the terrorists managed to hijack a car and carefully drive it with their hostages towards the nearby Schwechat Airport. The car stopped in the middle of the runway and negotiations started at this point. The terrorist demands were for a plane to take them to an Arab country and from there they would negotiate with Israel over the release of hostages in exchange for prisoners in Israel. (The same demand was made at the Munich Olympics attack).[70]

After seven hours and after Arab diplomats were able to talk to the terrorists, a new and much more political demand was made of the Austrian government: in exchange for the release of the hostages, Austria should in future prohibit all transit of Soviet Jews to Israel via Austria. Meanwhile, the Austrian chancellor, Bruno Kreisky, called for an emergency cabinet meeting and began consultations with his ministers and, in parallel, with Arab diplomats.

Finally, despite the concerns of some ministers about undermining Israeli interests, Kreisky offered to 'postpone and probably stop'[71] Austria's role as a transit place for Jewish emigration from the Soviet Union, if the terrorists were to release the hostages. The terrorists agreed to this in principle, but demanded an official statement from the Austrian government. At 1.15 a.m. on 29 September, Austrian national TV and radio broadcast the official communiqué that the Schönau transit camp would be closed because Austria could no longer guarantee the safety of the migrants. After this, the two terrorists agreed to release the hostages. They subsequently boarded the plane that had been organised for them to travel to Algeria, where they were free to go.[72] The political repercussions of Kreisky's decision resonated around the world and it was particularly negatively received in Israel.

IMPORTANCE OF THE SCHÖNAU ULTIMATUM FOR ISRAEL

After the severance of diplomatic relations between Israel and the Soviet Union in 1967, no flights were offered between Eastern Bloc countries and Israel. Austria's neutral position made the country an important transit stop for Jewish immigration to Israel. This is why Schönau held such strategic importance for Israel.[73] Instead of flying directly to Israel, Jewish migrants from the Soviet Union, Romania, or Czechoslovakia now went by train to Vienna and from there took a plane to Tel Aviv. Before their flight, the Austrian government allowed the migrants to stay at Castle Schönau. It also allowed the Jewish Agency for Israel to administer the camp. After the thwarted Schönau attack, Israeli forces were allowed to guard the premises in partnership with local police.[74]

The Kreisky administration had wanted to close Schönau for a while because these arrangements infringed on Austrian sovereignty and risked undermining its official neutral status.[75] For as long as Austria's role as a facilitator of Jewish migration to Israel stayed low-profile and was not well known to the wider public, the Kreisky administration could tolerate it. When the attack was carried out, it forced the Austrian government to take an official stance on the issue. As described above, without much consultation of his ministers, Kreisky chose to close the camp in exchange for a bloodless resolution of the crisis.

However, in terms of the effects of the attack, as much as Schönau was a symbol of Soviet Jewish migration, its closure too was mainly a symbolic gesture. It did not affect the actual numbers of Soviet Jews migrating through Austria. The main change was that on their way out of the Soviet Union, the migrants stayed overnight at a facility administered by the International Committee of the Red Cross and not one that was overseen by a Jewish agency or guarded by Israeli security.[76]

Nevertheless, strategically the target was important because it put the spotlight on something Israel preferred to keep under the radar. The reason for this lies in the question of refugees' rights to enter Israel. Palestinians at the time were using human rights discourse to argue that Palestinian refugees from the 1948 war should be allowed to return to Israel.[77] Because of Israel's raison d'être as a homeland for Jewish people, it strongly encouraged Jewish migration into the country, especially Ashkenazi Soviet Jewry (among others, to counterbalance the increasing Sephardic Jewish migration). Accepting Jewish refugees but refusing Palestinian refugees bore a certain degree of hypocrisy. Schönau was a symbol of Soviet Jewish migration to Israel and attacking it put the spotlight on a debate which the Israeli government preferred to avoid.

But not only was it a strong symbolic choice; the timing of the attack, 28 September 1973, was also strategically well planned. The crisis and Israeli outrage about its resolution distracted the Israeli government for about a week right before Egypt and Syria hit the country with the Yom Kippur surprise attack. In November 1973, a month after the attack, the German news magazine *Stern* published an interview allegedly with one of the two Palestinian perpetrators of the Schönau ultimatum. He claimed that the attack was specifically organised as a distraction, or a 'trap' meant to divert the attention of the Israeli leadership.[78] This later sparked a controversy over whether the timing of the attack indeed meant that Schönau was a deliberate deception and diversion orchestrated by the attackers to increase the likelihood of surprise.

Secondary literature that supports this idea points at Syria and its alleged sponsorship of the Palestinian Schönau terrorist squad. The hit team was allegedly recruited by a pro-Syrian Palestinian terror organisation called As Sa'iqa, which closely collaborated with the Syrian army and its secret services.[79] Club de Berne files confirm that Mossad already suspected this Syrian connection right after the Schönau attack and before the Yom Kippur War started.[80] In a report on 1 October 1973, it shared intelligence that the attack was perpetrated by Fatah/Black September 'with the assistance of members of Sa'Iqa, [which means] Syrians have known about the attack'. If Syrians were involved, it is conceivable that they helped set the date of the Schönau incident so that it would fall within a week before the date of the surprise attack on Israel.

It should be noted, however, that literature about the Yom Kippur War suggests many other reasons for Israel having been taken by surprise. Among others, intelligence analysts knew about Egyptian and Syrian intentions to attack but believed their militaries did not yet have the capacity to do so.[81] This misreading of Egyptian and Syrian forces led to fixed ideas that they would not attack.[82]

Furthermore, one can question whether Syria would share its top-secret surprise attack plans with the Palestinian hit team. The risk of them being caught and interrogated by Austrian police was very high, especially since the previous team had been caught a few months before. Even if Schönau was a deception or distraction, it is unlikely that the perpetrators would have known this in advance. This calls into question the validity of the claims made by the hit man in the interview given to *Stern*. The fact that Black September had tried to attack Schönau months before suggests that it was primarily a Palestinian operation. Constant Jewish immigration into Israel was a thorn in the Palestinians' side, especially since a lot of the newcomers settled in the post-1967 occupied territories.

Overall, while Palestinians planned and executed the attack, it is very possible that Syria tried to influence the timing of it so that it would occur shortly before the surprise attack on Israel. In this view, Schönau can, at best, be an additional element that contributed to Israel's surprise.

BOUDIA AND THE OIL PIPELINE ATTACK

After the investigation that uncovered the plans to attack Schönau, in March 1973 more material came to light in Italy that incriminated Boudia in further terrorist operations. Secondary literature attributes the Trieste oil reserve explosion to Boudia, but rarely discusses the attack and its perpetrators. With the Club de Berne files, one can now know more about it and the investigation that finally revealed the perpetrators and how they operated.

On 4 August 1972, a Black September terrorist squad composed of Arab, Italian, and French operatives detonated forty-four pounds of explosives in a large oil terminal at Trieste.[83] The resulting fire consumed four oil tanks, lasted for two days, and burned more than 250,000 tons of crude oil at a cost of $2.5 billion.[84] Black September claimed responsibility for the attack via a communiqué from Wafa (the Palestine news agency) in Beirut.[85] Other than this official claim, Italian intelligence stressed that it had no indication whatsoever about the possible perpetrators of this sabotage attack.[86]

While Italian investigations reached a dead end, West German police identified a possible suspect. This terrorist suspect had only had poor-paying jobs and, as an informant would mention, suddenly received a large payment from an unknown source right around the time of the Trieste attack. The BfV found out that he was in Italy between 30 July and 6 August (the attack happened on 4 August), and in the interrogations of his wife, she confirmed that he was in Trieste on the date of the attack.[87] The West Germans put him under very tight surveillance and undertook 'intensive investigations', but no charges could be made against him.[88] After several months, the people responsible for the attack were still at large.

Six months later, in mid March 1973, based on investigations conducted together with France, Italy identified four main suspects.[89] The investigation had been rekindled when the Italian authorities found out that a known French terrorism sympathiser, Thérèse Lefevre, was near Trieste at the time of the attack on the oil refinery. Lefevre had already been under investigation for suspicion of being an accomplice to the murder of Syrian journalist Khodr Kannou.[90] Kannou was gunned down in his home in Paris on 13 November 1972. The car that the killers used to escape was registered under Lefevre's name. At the time, suspicions circulated that Kannou was not a Syrian journalist but in fact an Israeli officer.[91] The murder case has never conclusively been solved, with speculations ranging from the Syrian government to Black September as the murderers.

When Lefevre was arrested again in February 1973, the Italian cable explained that she confessed to French intelligence that she carried out the Trieste attack under the direct order of Mohamed Boudia.[92] He was her lover and, under his spell, she agreed to carry out terrorist activities in the name of Black September.[93] She named three others as accomplices, giving their names and descriptions of their physical appearances. One of the alleged accomplices, an Italian citizen, was arrested on 25 February 1973, and was put on trial in Trieste. Lefevre's name was further written in the notebook of an Algerian terrorist, who was also suspected to be involved in the killing of the Syrian journalist Kannou and of having committed a number of other terrorist crimes.

The cable named Boudia as the mastermind behind the Trieste attack and explained that he was very highly placed within Black September (which most agencies by then probably already knew). Italian intelligence concluded that in its assessment, he was the most active director of terrorist operations in Europe. It thus requested to receive more intelligence on him, because his name appeared in several ongoing terrorist investigations (these exchanges occurred simultaneously with the Schönau investigations).[94]

Mossad must have agreed with the Italian assessment that Boudia was among the most active and dangerous terrorist masterminds. While he was on the Israeli agency's target list, Club de Berne cooperation provided more rock-solid intelligence about his past, present, and future terrorist involvement, and also about his whereabouts, routine, and networks. Mossad thus received useful operational intelligence on how to capture him. By late June 1973, it had enough intelligence to strike: the Israeli agency killed the 41-year-old Algerian in Paris in his beloved Renault.

BOUDIA'S MURDER INVESTIGATION

On 29 June 1973, a day after Boudia died in the fancy St Germain district of Paris, the French DST sent a long report through the Kilowatt channel.[95] Boudia was referred to as an Algerian national and an active pro-Palestinian militant. The report described first how, where, and when the car exploded. Like the Italian agency in the Nakaa and Shibli Rome killing, the DST gave details about the car, a Renault R16, its matriculation number, and where precisely it was parked.[96] The murder happened at 32 Rue des Fosses-Saint Bernard in the 5th arrondissement, which was a vibrant quarter in the heart of Paris. At 10.57 a.m., the bomb exploded and killed him on the spot.[97]

Boudia was known to French intelligence as a central player in several clandestine and terrorist groups. First, as the cable highlighted, according to the most recent intelligence, he was believed to be the key person in the PFLP in Paris. Second, he was known to have been an important coordinator of the RUR, a secret Algerian movement against the Boumediene government.

The explosives were placed right under the driver's seat and, based on first examination, the French police assumed that it was an accidental explosion; as the cable said in French: 'une detonation fortuite'.[98] The French word 'fortuite' can be translated as 'by chance' or 'unexpected'. The DST thus suggested that Boudia's death was caused by a bomb that was not meant to explode at that time, but exploded prematurely, unexpectedly, and accidentally. Given Boudia's terrorist activities, French intelligence might have assumed that the bomb was planned for a terrorist attack but exploded in his car instead.

As mentioned above, Mossad had designed the bomb in a simple way on purpose so as to make it look like terrorists had built it themselves with nuts and bolts inside. Based on this cable, at least in the initial police report, this deception seemed to have worked.

France, as the DST pointed out in the cable, had been trying to capture Boudia for a while already and the cable mentioned that he was wanted by all French security forces. There was an international search warrant to capture him, issued by Interpol. This search warrant was placed by Italy, for charges against him relating to the Trieste oil pipelines attack of 4 August 1972.

French intelligence added a short justification as to why they had not arrested him even though he was on French territory. The cable stressed that despite 'intensive investigations to find Boudia', he had until then escaped all French attempts to capture him.[99] French intelligence emphasised that he moved around very frequently and travelled a lot within and outside France. On a near daily basis, the French claimed, he changed his hideout. As mentioned above, Boudia was indeed extremely careful, using several cover names and makeup and disguises from his theatre, and frequently moved apartments. Nevertheless, he also led a very active social life and was obviously not hidden enough to prevent Mossad finding him.

France shared another 'very new piece of intelligence' with its partners, one that had just come in shortly before Boudia's death and was based on a 'vulnerable source'. An RUR disciplinary commission had allegedly just removed Boudia from his position and stripped him of all responsibilities in the organisation. This disciplinary measure was taken because he had slept with the daughter of a militant of this group.[100]

As a consequence, the cable continued, Boudia was preparing to leave France to move to Syria and was about to get rid of all his possessions in France. Ironically, as the cable had not failed to point out, he was also trying to get rid of the car in which he met his death, which was still registered to his former wife, Adria Guerrar. The cable speculated that this disciplinary measure and the dispute with the RUR could have had something to do with his death. France promised to keep all partners updated about the police and judicial proceedings of the Boudia case.

Similar to all Kilowatt cables after an Operation Wrath of God killing, the DST did not mention any suspicions about Mossad's involvement in the murder. At the time, however, Israeli covert assassinations in Europe had become more widely known. For instance, the day after Boudia's assassination, the French newspaper *Le Monde* clearly blamed Mossad for Boudia's murder.[101] The French cable, on the contrary, even drew suspicions away from Mossad: it suggested that either the bomb exploded by accident or, if it was murder, that the RUR may have been behind it, given the group's irritation with Boudia's behaviour.

BLACK SEPTEMBER KILLS YOSEF ALON

On a late summer night, 1 July 1973, in a quiet suburb of Washington, DC, Colonel Yosef (Joe) Alon and his wife, Devora, drove back home after a dinner party with friends. At 1 a.m., the two reached their house and parked in the driveway. Devora left the car and headed towards the house. Joe was getting his jacket from the car, when a man suddenly appeared and shot five bullets into his chest. Devora returned and found her husband lying in a pool of blood. She and her oldest daughter (seventeen years old) tried to help him. When the ambulance arrived, the younger daughters (aged fourteen and six) had also woken up. Joe died at the hospital a few hours later.[102]

Later that night, a Voice of Palestine radio broadcast, which was aired from Cairo, claimed responsibility for the assassination of Alon as retaliation for the killing of Boudia in Paris a few days earlier. US officials at the time were not sure whether Palestinian armed groups indeed were responsible for the attack, or whether they used this murder as an opportunity for propaganda.[103]

Alon was a former Israeli air force officer and military attaché at the Israeli embassy in Washington, DC. He was one of the founders of the Israeli air force and had served in it for twenty years. He became one of its icons and was relatively well known in Israel. Three years before his assassination, he was appointed military attaché at the Israeli embassy to the US. He was heavily involved in integrating the F-4 fighter planes from the US to Israel, which later became the backbone of the Israeli air force.[104]

Until this day, numerous theories about Alon's murderers prevail. A book by Fred Burton, published in 2011, rekindled new interest in the case. Burton was a former deputy chief of the counterterrorism division of the US State Department's Diplomatic Security Service and vice-president of the private intelligence and consulting firm Stratfor. He became personally interested in this murder case and over thirty years followed different leads about Alon's assassins. He concluded that Black September was responsible for the assassination. The order was given by Saleh Khalaf, alias Abu Iyad, and Ali Hassan Salameh was in charge of organising the operation.[105] Both were prominent Black September leaders and were believed to have been the main organisers of the Munich Olympics massacre.

Burton claims he discovered exactly who shot Alon on that summer night in 1973.[106] He says that he then gave Israeli intelligence the name and likely whereabouts of this Palestinian who allegedly killed Alon. Allegedly, he later received a message back from one of his Mossad contacts that read:

'The [Ali] matter has been resolved.'[107] According to Burton, this means that Mossad killed Alon's murderer based on the personal details that he gave them. His claims are persuasive but have, to date, never been confirmed by any other official or non-official source.

With the murder investigation in the hands of the FBI, in the 1970s the Club de Berne networks were barely used to find more details about Alon or his murderers. Nevertheless, Alon was mentioned a few times in the Kilowatt channel. Such was the case a week after his murder. Shin Bet sent a warning that Black September and the PFLP were planning attacks on military attachés along the lines of the murder of Alon in the US.[108] The agency had received this warning from a 'sub-source' which was connected to the PFLP in Amman and Damascus. This agent or 'sub-source' also explained the terrorists' tactical reasoning for targeting military attachés: the source explained that the attachés were usually not closely guarded.[109]

CONCLUSIONS

Overall, the Schönau and Trieste investigations and the cables sent after Boudia's assassination reveal several insights into how cooperation in the Club de Berne was used for Operation Wrath of God. Most importantly, the Schönau investigation was used by Mossad as a pretext to gather information on Boudia. Mossad was able to directly apply this information as operational intelligence for its hit teams. Swiss intelligence in particular was extremely helpful, since BuPo provided Boudia's most recent address in Paris and gave specific details about his car, its official owner, and the owner's address in Paris. It further shared with Mossad Boudia's cover names, the details of his fake French passport, and the personal data of his middle (wo)men in Geneva. The Israeli agency also received more details about his marital situation, the name and background of his wife, and his family's history in Algeria.

In particular, the information about Boudia's car is noteworthy. In secondary literature, it is assumed that the dark grey Renault was in Boudia's own name, and that this made it particularly easy for Mossad to track him down.[110] However, through the Club de Berne it becomes clear that the car was in someone else's name, and it was Swiss intelligence that gave the name and address in Paris of the owner of the car. The car was Boudia's weak point, and it was Swiss intelligence that enabled Mossad to exploit this weakness.

Furthermore, the Schönau investigation provided further incriminating material about Boudia's terrorism involvement. He attracted attention as the mastermind behind this attack and as an important figure in Black September operations in Europe. Mike Harari needed to present the past terrorist record and risks for future terrorist acts for each person who was going to be put on the Operation Wrath of God kill list. Boudia's role in the Schönau attack made it clear why Mossad needed to eliminate him, especially if killing him might prevent another attempt to attack the transit camp. However, in effect, Boudia's death only delayed things, and the actual attack in September 1973 happened right before the Yom Kippur War. As some have argued, the attack in part distracted Israel from Egypt and Syria's war preparations.

However, the fact that Boudia was killed but then replaced a few months later by someone who carried out a similar attack raises questions about the effectiveness of targeted killings. Essentially, you can kill a terrorist leader, but then someone else just becomes the leader. Typically, the idea behind killing a leader is that it disrupts the group, which then takes a while to reassemble and reorganise. However, once the group does reorganise, its members might be even more motivated to strike back as revenge for their peers. Many of the Operation Wrath of God assassinations seem to have intensified Black September's resolve to retaliate. And in many instances, they did. This includes the case of Joe Alon, who was shot only a few days after Boudia's death.

PART III

BLUNDER AND COOPERATE

8

LILLEHAMMER FIASCO: OFFICIAL CONDEMNATION, COVERT APPROVAL

Late in the evening of 21 July 1973, in a small, quiet Norwegian vacation town called Lillehammer, a couple walked home from the movies. The woman was seven months pregnant and was thus walking slowly when a grey Volvo suddenly stopped nearby. Two Mossad hit men leapt out of the car, shot the man in the torso and head, and then drove off as quickly as they had come. A level-headed bystander wrote down the licence plate number and later gave this to the police.[1]

The person killed that night was Ahmed Bouchiki, a Moroccan waiter and cleaner, who – apart from looking very similar to Ali Hassan Salameh – had absolutely nothing to do with Middle Eastern terrorism. Mossad thought it had achieved the crowning success of its mission, finally killing the 'Red Prince', but instead had stumbled into one of the agency's worst blunders, which left embarrassing scars on it for years to come.

'The most damaging exposure ever of Israel's clandestine activities abroad'[2] or 'one of the greatest disasters in the history of Mossad'.[3] Authors who describe the Lillehammer fiasco are not hesitant to use superlatives and to present it as a major blunder with fatal and drastic consequences for the agency. It was so disastrous because it was the combination of two unforgivable mistakes: first, Mossad killed the wrong man and, second, it got caught doing it. (See Figure 22.)

How did this happen? There were several contributing factors at play. First, the assassination in Lillehammer was organised and executed by a new team. After Boudia's elimination, Mossad gave this very active special operations team a break. The team had organised eight killing operations in eight months, a non-stop operation that required a high degree of precision, planning, and hard work. While it was sensible to give them a break, the choice of their successors was less astute. The team for the Lillehammer killing operation was assembled at the last minute, and some members had no prior experience in covert operations abroad.[4]

Second, unlike Rome or Paris, Scandinavia was unfamiliar terrain for Mossad, which had never mounted an operation in Norway before.

Figure 22 Lillehammer crime scene where Ahmed Bouchiki was killed by Mossad, 21 July 1973. Source: NTB/Alamy

Furthermore, Middle Eastern-looking officers could blend in less easily than in Italy or France. Finding anonymity after a kill was much harder in a town of fourteen thousand inhabitants, where strangers were highly conspicuous and where there had not been a murder case in forty years. This mission took place on difficult operational ground, and a much more seasoned team was needed.[5]

Third, Operation Wrath of God was a victim of its own success. Some authors mention that the previously successful operations, especially Operation Spring of Youth, instilled a sense of invincibility, authority, and mastery. It was believed that Mossad could do anything, anywhere, to any adversary. Its hubris led it to devise more audacious plans and to take greater risks.

Fourth, Mossad and the directors of Operation Wrath of God needed to have a major success. Even though Operation Spring of Youth and other killings in Europe were considered great achievements, the agency had at that time only eliminated relatively 'small fish' among Palestinian terrorists. Its main Palestinian targets were still at large, and Mossad needed to kill one of them to make this operation a real success.

The leader of Operation Wrath of God, Mike Harari, personally needed this too. He was ascending very high on the career ladder – even eyeballing the position of head of Mossad. Catching a Palestinian leader like Salameh would catapult him into prime position for the top role.[6] Hence, when the opportunity to get Salameh presented itself, to save time he was willing to overrule security procedures. For instance, as will be shown below, he should have ordered an extra background check on Salameh and not used only a picture to confirm his identity. Some authors also observed a certain obsession with Salameh among Mossad's special operations units. The potential prestige of finally catching the infamous 'Red Prince' was so great that it clouded their judgement when they weighed the risks before approving the operation.[7]

With the Club de Berne files, it is possible to add another important factor: since late 1972, reports had grown in number and intensity about terrorist cells operating in Scandinavia. Gradually, more warnings reached Mossad about attacks involving targets in a northern European country. It thus appeared entirely credible to the agency when intelligence reports claimed that its most wanted terrorist, Ali Hassan Salameh, was in Norway planning an attack.

SCANDINAVIA AS A TERRORIST HUB

When cooperation started in the Club de Berne Kilowatt channel, no Scandinavian country was part of the exchanges. Over the course of 1972, especially towards the end, more warnings and reports were issued that concerned terrorist activities in northern European countries. The Scandinavian countries began to be regularly included in some Kilowatt correspondence on an ad hoc basis, and by late 1972 they were receiving copies of intelligence reports more frequently.

In May 1973, Denmark joined Kilowatt as a full member, which was a sign of its increased strategic importance for European counterterrorism cooperation.[8] As a full Kilowatt member, the country received all cables and was tasked with relaying any intelligence that concerned other northern countries. Sometimes other Scandinavian countries could be copied in if a warning concerned them directly.

Since the end of 1971, agencies had shared intelligence that claimed Scandinavia was a target of Palestinian terrorism. For instance, Mossad sent several cables in December of that year outlining step by step how

Palestinian terrorists had allegedly built a terrorist network in Scandinavia, with Stockholm as their base.[9] Around the same time, as mentioned in Chapter 4, the UK authorities thwarted a parallel attack to the Bangkok attack on 28 December 1972. This terrorist operation was planned for a target in Stockholm (or if Stockholm was not possible, the terrorists were tasked to find another target in Scandinavia).[10]

Earlier cables also included warnings about terrorist events in Scandinavia, like a warning issued by the West German BfV on 30 September 1972 about two Black September members arriving in Copenhagen to perpetrate sabotage attacks.[11] In January 1973, Mossad believed it had uncovered an operative of the PFLP-GC (Jibril organisation) in Denmark, Ahmad Misbah Omrin, who wanted to organise an attack there. Omrin had allegedly failed in his task and returned to another country in Europe (which one was unknown).[12] He was known among the Club de Berne agencies as the main person in charge of Jibril terrorist activities outside Israel, and his picture figured in the so-called 'terrorist album', the shared database of portraits of known terrorists.[13]

Mossad assessed that it was likely that Jibril was trying to organise another attack in Europe, since its last operation had been a failed attempt at sabotage of a plane from Rome to Tel Aviv on 16 August 1972.[14] Since then, Jibril had continuously tried to perpetrate attacks in Europe and had now attempted to include Denmark.[15] The BfV replied and informed its partners that the country where Omrin had gone after Denmark was West Germany. He entered Berlin illegally and asked for political asylum. This was denied and he was deported to Beirut.[16]

Several months later, in September 1973 (a few months after the Lillehammer fiasco), more cables about Omrin appeared. He was allegedly on his way from Beirut by Mercedes to collect operative intelligence for PFLP-GC (Jibril) to carry out attacks in Europe.[17] Mossad shared the Lebanese licence plate number but assumed that Omrin was going to exchange it for a less conspicuous plate. In October 1973, Dutch intelligence offered to help track Omrin and said it could share a picture of him again.[18]

In February 1973, Mossad shared another warning about an imminent attack in Scandinavia.[19] A PFLP operative residing in London, Abdalla al-Biyafi, had allegedly travelled to a Scandinavian country to plan another attack. In April, Mossad sent an update about al-Biyafi and wished to be informed if he passed through a Kilowatt country and if so, what his connections and activities were.[20]

In June 1973, a month before the Lillehammer fiasco, Mossad received more warnings about terrorist plots involving Scandinavia. One of them came from MI5 about Ahmed Makhlouf, a terrorist suspect resid-ing in Sweden.[21] Makhlouf flew from Stockholm to London, applied for political asylum, which was refused, and was deported back to Sweden. MI5 examined his documents and found that he had connections to Palestinian armed groups.

An interesting case concerned the warning about an attack against the Israeli embassy in Stockholm. Author Marc E. Vargo mentions that Mossad intercepted messages that showed plans for an attack against the embassy and that a terrorist meeting was being planned there.[22] This can be con-firmed with Club de Berne records. In early July 1973, Mossad informed its Kilowatt partners that it knew of a very concrete plan to attack the Stockholm embassy, but that this operation had temporarily come to a halt because the terrorists were not able to smuggle weapons to Sweden.[23] It described the plot and how it obtained the intelligence as follows: Israel received this intelligence report from a reliable source that 'had access to subject', which meant that the spy who gave the intelligence had been in direct contact with the terrorists mentioned in the cable. The cable outlined a detailed plan by Black September members to attack the Israeli ambassador in Sweden. Preparations for the attack had allegedly already started.[24]

The cable stated further that, on 14 June 1973, two weeks before it was sent, two Black September members, whose names were mentioned, were believed to have left Damascus for East Berlin, from where they continued to Warsaw. They allegedly travelled on Syrian passports and carried two pistols and five hand grenades in a cache in a suitcase.[25]

Their plan, as Mossad specified, was to smuggle these weapons into Stockholm with the help of an Arab man who lived there. This local helper and the two terrorists were then going to overpower the Israeli ambassador and his family during the changing of the guards at his residence. After tak-ing them hostage, the three were to demand that the Swedish government give them a plane to fly them and their hostages to Libya. The date of the operation was fixed to be 17 June 1973. However, the two terrorists were believed to have returned to Syria in the meantime because they had not been able to smuggle the weapons into Sweden.[26]

At the end of the cable, Mossad assessed the intelligence report and added that the two terrorists who came from Syria might only have been the couriers for the transfer of weapons. It believed that the actual attack would have been more likely to be executed by other Arabs who were already in Sweden.

The presence of Arab terrorists in Scandinavia, the cable pointed out, had continuously increased. Palestinian terrorists had begun their activities already in late 1972 when a Fatah member was arrested in London as he was trying to smuggle weapons to Sweden.[27] Overall, Mossad's cable shows that Israeli intelligence presumed that there was an increasing group of Arabs in Sweden who were preparing terrorist attacks.

All these warnings, especially the last one about the attack against the Israeli ambassador in Stockholm, suggested to Mossad that Palestinians had a considerable presence in Scandinavia. When it heard that Salameh was going to meet a fellow traveller in Sweden, the agency had no problem believing it and acted upon the intelligence very quickly to catch him.

THE ASSASSINATION OF AHMED BOUCHIKI, BELIEVED TO BE ALI HASSAN SALAMEH

Ali Hassan Salameh was born into a wealthy family from Ramle in 1942 and was the first-born child of Sheikh Salameh, a famous commander who died in combat during the 1947–1949 Palestine War (called the War of Independence in Israel and part of the Nakba in Arabic). His father was celebrated as a martyr in Palestinian memory, which weighed heavily on Ali Hassan.

In one of the few interviews he gave, he commented on the burden of living with his father's legacy: 'I wanted to be myself [but] the fact that I was required to live up to the image of my father created a problem for me.'[28] His important stature in the Palestinian movement and the high expectations of him stemmed not only from his father's legacy, but also from his marriage into one of the Arab world's most prestigious families, the Husseini clan, who were notorious for their hatred of Jews.[29] The pressure from family and the Palestinian leadership eventually compelled him to enrol with Fatah and join the struggle against Israel.

Salameh was a good-looking young man who studied at the American University in Beirut and in West Germany. Even though he was married, he was known to be a 'playboy'. His Middle Eastern charm, obsession with fashion and tailor-made suits, his athletically trained body, and handsome face worked like a magnet for beautiful women, whose presence he thoroughly enjoyed. (See Figure 23.)

Salameh's charisma, family status, and intellect helped him to rapidly rise through the Fatah ranks, where he specialised in intelligence and in Yasser Arafat's personal security. He was among the founding members of Black September and oversaw the organisation's key terrorist

Figure 23 Ali Hassan Salameh in 1975; he was later assassinated by Mossad on 22 January 1979. Source: Associated Press/Alamy.

operations in Europe. According to American intelligence files, from the early 1970s he acted as the informal and secret liaison between the Fatah leadership and the Central Intelligence Agency (CIA).[30] He was not an informant or agent, but he helped foster relations between the PLO and the US agency.[31]

In 1972, the Israeli government did not yet know about this secret link between the PLO and the US, nor did they know about Salameh's role in it.[32] Mossad still wanted him gone mainly for his crucial role in Black September terrorism. Correspondence via the Club de Berne channel confirms that Mossad and European agencies had been chasing after Salameh for several months before Lillehammer. They held him responsible for a great number of terrorist operations and believed he was actively planning future attacks.

CHARGES AGAINST SALAMEH

On 21 July 1972, exactly a year before Mossad killed the person it thought was Salameh in Lillehammer, the Israeli agency sent a cable about Black

215

September's organisational structure. Notably, this message was sent before the Munich Olympics massacre and before Black September had become a better-known terrorist group.[33] Mossad mentioned that Salameh was working in Fatah intelligence's special operation branch (called Rasd) and was 'Fatah's man in charge of attacks abroad'.[34] According to the agency, Salameh had two main assistants for his next terrorism plan and their names were shared among the group.

His team was allegedly in regular contact with Daoud Barakat to plan the next terrorist attack, which was believed to be a hijacking.[35] Barakat was at the time working for the Yemeni mission to the United Nations and he later became the official PLO representative in Geneva. He was regularly accused of terrorism involvement but had always vehemently rejected these claims.[36]

In late September 1972, after the Munich massacre, West German intelligence sent a very long and detailed cable explaining the operational methods of Black September.[37] This cable, with Kilowatt number 1032, also mentioned Rasd, the secret intelligence arm of Fatah, and the belief that Salameh was its officer in Europe. He was allegedly heading a division in charge of collecting operational intelligence for Black September attacks. This division would also investigate who and what institutions in Europe worked together with Israel.

Most authors indeed believe that Salameh had key responsibilities within Rasd.[38] He joined Rasd in 1968 and received training in intelligence and counterintelligence from the Egyptian government. In his early assignments, Salameh worked in counterespionage. He was in charge of identifying and killing Arabs who collaborated with Israelis, vetting Fatah volunteers, and spotting members who might have been recruited by Mossad to penetrate the group.[39] Here it is interesting that both German Kilowatt cable 1032 and journalist Ronen Bergman describe one of Salameh's main tasks as the identification (and liquidation) of collaborators with Israelis.

Secondary literature also confirms that Salameh was a major figure in Palestinian terrorism more generally. He is believed to be among the founders of Black September, together with Abu Iyad, in September 1971,[40] and he allegedly masterminded the first major Black September operation, the killing of Jordanian prime minister Wasfi Tal on 28 November that year.[41] Later he rose through the ranks and became close to several members of the Fatah leadership, including Arafat, who asked him to head his group of bodyguards.[42]

Throughout 1972 and 1973, Salameh is said to have been heavily involved in planning and organising major Black September attacks in Europe. Among others, he is held responsible for the hijacking of a Sabena airliner on 8 May 1972.[43] There is, however, controversy over his involvement in the planning of the Munich Olympics operation. The alleged mastermind behind the Munich massacre, Mohamed d'Aud Awadh (with the *nom de guerre* Abu Daoud), later insisted that Salameh had no role in the operation whatsoever and that he was not present in Europe at the time.[44] Others insist not only that Salameh was present in Munich, but that he helped with many details of the operational planning for the attack.[45]

Interestingly, MI5 sent a cable on 6 September 1972, the day that the Munich Olympics attack ended. It first mentioned Salameh more generally as 'Fatah chief of intelligence and planner of Black September operations'.[46] Second, and crucially, in the same cable MI5 reported that a delicate and reliable source had informed it that Salameh had been in Europe since early August to prepare the Munich Olympics attack and might still be in the area.[47]

The MI5 cable also mentioned that with Salameh was Saleh Khalaf (*nom de guerre* Abu Iyad) and that they arrived in Europe around the same time. This confirms that Mossad received foreign intelligence in which Salameh was connected to the Munich attack and which mentioned he had been in proximity before and after the massacre.

In early December 1972, Mossad mentioned Salameh again in its cables. The Israeli agency enquired about a terrorist suspect, who, according to Mossad, worked closely with Salameh on Black September psychological warfare and sabotage operations in Europe.[48] It asked whether the Europeans had any leads on either of the two, but nobody responded via the Kilowatt channel.

TRACKING SALAMEH

After months of unsuccessfully tracking Salameh, Mossad finally thought it had achieved a breakthrough. On 14 July 1973, intelligence came in that suggested a meeting had been set up in Scandinavia between Ali Hassan Salameh and Kamal Benaman, a 28-year-old Algerian living in Geneva. Benaman was believed to have served as a European liaison for Black September. A Mossad team trailed him on his plane from Geneva to Copenhagen and saw him board a plane to Oslo. After an intense search, they located him in the Norwegian town of Lillehammer and believed this was where the meeting with Salameh was going to take place.

On the afternoon of Friday 20 July, Benaman was seen relaxing on the balcony of a coffee house in the centre of town. Mossad watched him closely and saw two Middle Eastern-looking men join him at his table. They spoke French together, a language Salameh was presumed to have mastered. The surveillance team was pleased to report that one of the men strongly resembled Ali Hassan Salameh.[49] (See Figure 24.)

The Operation Wrath of God team leaders were euphoric, but before authorising the hit, Mike Harari needed additional confirmation. Mossad, despite months of chasing Salameh, had very scarce intelligence on him. The Israeli agency only had one recent picture of him, which it used to check his identity.[50] Harari asked that an officer approach the men and compare the suspect with the picture of Salameh they had. It was confirmed again: the suspect apparently looked exactly like the man in the photograph, 'like two brothers resemble each other'.[51] The officers in charge of confirming Salameh's identity indeed believed that, based on this picture, they had found him.[52]

Figure 24 Ahmed Bouchiki, assassinated by Mossad on 21 July 1973. Source: NTB/Alamy.

Interestingly, this picture had in fact been sent by MI5 right after the Munich Olympics massacre. At the time, agencies tried to help Mossad with as much intelligence as possible about Black September. In September 1972, MI5 thus sent a picture of Salameh to facilitate the search for him.[53] The British agency, of course, had not known at the time that Mossad would later use the picture for an attempt to kill Salameh.

In retrospect, it is very clear that one matching picture was not enough evidence to authorise an assassination mission. To approve a kill based on such circumstantial evidence was highly unusual for Mossad. However, as mentioned above, the mission was organised and greenlighted in haste. What was also quite unusual was that concerns that it might not be the right target were overruled. According to Bergman, some members of the surveillance team questioned Salameh's identity, despite the resemblance to the picture.

Additionally, it is baffling that nobody asked some common-sense questions such as why would a top terrorist, technically known to be a wealthy playboy residing in Lebanon, lead a double life in a small town in Norway together with a heavily pregnant Norwegian girlfriend? Why would Salameh, Mossad's most wanted man, not show any sign of caution, try to hide, or change his habits to prevent being tracked by the Israeli agency? If one believed Salameh to be a master of deception, a quiet life in Lillehammer would have been the perfect cover and hiding place. Nevertheless, basic logic would have suggested that this man was not Salameh. Mossad took a huge risk in killing him and paid a huge price for it.

THE LILLEHAMMER AFFAIR

When the hit team reported back to Harari after the kill, they mentioned that it was a success, but that a witness had been able to write down the licence plate number of the Volvo as it drove away. Harari advised that they abandon the car in a side street and dump the keys in a gully. The whole team was to fly out of Norway within hours of the killing.[54]

One team member, Dan Aerbel, thought differently. Aerbel was a Danish-Israeli businessman who was selected for this operation at the last minute, mainly for his language skills and to help with logistics. He had used this travel opportunity to shop for kitchen appliances for his new house in Herzliya (a town near Tel Aviv) that needed to be furnished.

Figure 25 The car used by Mossad during the assassination of Ahmed Bouchiki.
Source: SCANPIX Arkiv/NTB/Alamy.

With these heavy and bulky purchases in the boot, he did not feel like abandoning the car. Instead of following Harari's instructions, he and his colleague simply drove the car back to the rental place at Oslo Airport. That is where the Norwegian police were waiting for them.[55] (See Figure 25.)

Aerbel had only occasionally participated in Mossad operations, and it was his first big mission. He was not used to upholding a cover identity and used his real passport on this occasion.[56] Most importantly and problematically, he was claustrophobic. Later, Mossad headquarters checked his file, where he had indeed mentioned it.[57] Normally, he would have been suspended from all operational duties, but somehow this was overlooked. This was yet another grave professional mistake by Mossad, a very costly one.

As soon as Aerbel was taken into a closed room for interrogation, he gave the whole game away. He told the Norwegians literally everything. He even gave them the emergency number of Mossad headquarters, the Hadar Dafna building in Tel Aviv, so that they could call to verify his statements. He also revealed the cover identities, locations, and escape routes of his Lillehammer team members. Within days, six Mossad agents ended up in

Norwegian custody. By pure chance, Mike Harari and the two assassins managed to leave Norway just in time.[58]

By that point, the Norwegian authorities understood that this was a targeted killing by Mossad. They found documents on the captives, which the operatives should have destroyed after reading. These documents contained incriminating material on them, but worse, it led to the discovery of Mossad collaborators, communication channels, operational methods, and safe houses across Europe.[59]

On one of the suspects, the police found the keys to a safe house in Paris. When French police searched the apartment, they found more keys that led to the discovery of more safe houses in France.[60] The police search of these safe houses brought to light more incriminating material and evidence that linked Mossad to previous Operation Wrath of God assassinations.[61] In this way, European intelligence was able to understand the murders that had happened in their countries and to piece together how Mossad had organised the hit teams.[62]

Overall, in terms of operational consequences, Mossad's infrastructure in Europe was exposed and its ongoing operations entirely compromised. As a result of Lillehammer, the Israelis needed to withdraw agents, leave safe houses, pull back informants, and change phone numbers all over the continent.[63]

Internally, Lillehammer had long-term consequences too. Mossad headquarters became more cautious before authorising missions abroad. Critics within the agency further saw their beliefs confirmed that killing Palestinians in Europe was a waste of time and resources.[64] More importantly, Lillehammer was a blow to its officers' morale and belief in the agency.[65] This very publicly exposed failure marked itself deep into the conscience of Israeli intelligence. It is commonly remembered with remorse, and the Israeli intelligence community refers to Lillehammer in an unfortunate pun, as *Leyl-ha-Mar*, the Night of Bitterness.[66]

On an official diplomatic level, the Lillehammer affair and the public trial of the six Mossad officers caused a mass outpouring of international outrage and hostile press towards Israel.[67] Diplomatic relations between Israel and Western Europe were embittered. Norway in particular was incensed; it had no prior knowledge of Operation Wrath of God.[68] The incident further damaged Israel's reputation because it became clear that it had carried out its own terror operations.[69]

While the Norwegians publicly showed outrage and indeed refused to cover up the story in any way, it also showed relative leniency towards Israel. In February 1974, a Norwegian court ruled that Mossad was responsible for

Figure 26 A Norwegian police van driving Mossad officers to their trial in Oslo.
Source: NTB/Alamy.

the murder. Five of the six captured agents were convicted and sentenced to prison, with terms ranging from one to five and a half years. (See Figure 26.) However, after twenty-two months they were all pardoned, probably through a secret Israeli–Norwegian deal.[70] Furthermore, Norwegian police had not pressed too hard in their investigation and apparently did not follow up on all leads.[71] Other Western European states also showed solidarity with Israel. The PLO demanded that investigations into the unresolved murder cases of Palestinians in France and Italy be reopened, but both governments ignored these calls.[72]

Finally, it seems that diplomatically Israel got away with a black eye, but it had to live through a major public embarrassment and operationally it had its infrastructure in Europe largely destroyed. As a logical step, Operation Wrath of God was temporarily suspended by Meir. Only after several years did Mossad organise the next targeted assassination against a Palestinian involved in the planning and execution of the Munich massacre. On 22 January 1979, Ali Hassan Salameh was killed in a car bomb in Beirut. (See Figure 27.)

Figure 27 The scene in Beirut after the assassination of Ali Hassan Salameh, killed in a car explosion on 22 January 1979. Source: AP/As Safir/Alamy.

COOPERATION AFTER LILLEHAMMER: BUSINESS AS USUAL

If one were to solely look at the correspondence of the secret Club de Berne channels, it would appear as if the Lillehammer scandal never happened. There was no qualitative or quantitative difference in terms of intensity and engagement in the Kilowatt exchanges. The same topics were covered, in the same way.

In what follows, four examples are discussed in detail, starting with a hijacking that happened a day before the assassination in Lillehammer. On 20 July 1973, in a joint operation, the PFLP and the Japanese Red Army Faction hijacked Japan Airlines flight number 404 (referred to as JAL404). The Club de Berne channel was very active with hectic back-and-forths during and after the hijacking. This terrorist event is barely covered by the secondary literature and, through an analysis of the Club de Berne files, a range of hitherto unknown details about the attack come to light.

JAL404 HIJACKING OVER AMSTERDAM

Japan Airlines flight 404, with 123 passengers and 22 crew members on board, was scheduled to fly from Amsterdam to Tokyo. Shortly after takeoff, still over Dutch airspace, the plane was hijacked. A joint commando unit of five Japanese

Red Army (JRA) and four PFLP terrorists gained control of the plane. One of them carried a hand grenade, which detonated and killed one of the hijackers and injured a flight attendant. When the Israeli authorities heard about this hijacking, they were very worried because they thought this was the '9/11-type attack' about which they had been warned in January 1973.[73]

The hijackers wanted to land in a Middle Eastern country, but were not given landing permission. Finally, the plane landed in Dubai, where the abductors made their demands. In exchange for the hostages, the terrorists demanded that Israel release Kozo Okamoto from prison. Okamoto had perpetrated the Lod Airport massacre in May 1972, a particularly brutal attack where the terrorists created a bloodbath by indiscriminately shooting at people in the waiting hall. He was sentenced to life in prison and the Israeli government made it clear that it was certainly not going to release him. (See Figure 28.)

The terrorist squad then kept the plane in Dubai for two days before flying it to Damascus (Syria) and finally to Benghazi (Libya). On 23 July, all passengers and crew were finally released, and the empty plane was blown up.[74] (See Figure 29.) The leader of this terrorist unit was JRA terrorist Osamu Maruoka, who managed to escape. Years later, when he tried to

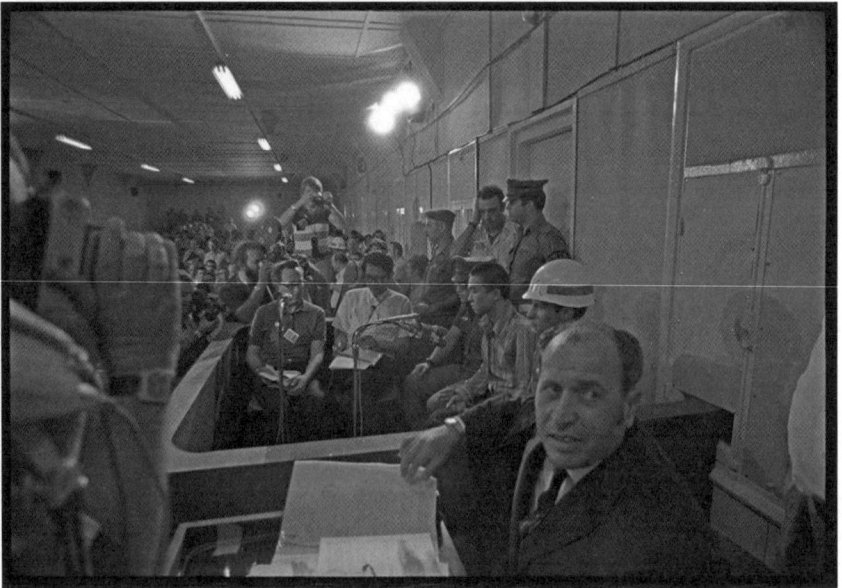

Figure 28 The trial in Israel of Japanese Red Army militant Kozo Okamoto for the Lod Airport massacre in May 1972. Source: David Rubinger/Corbis/Getty Images.

Figure 29 JAL404 plane that was blown up after the hostages were released.
Source: Genevieve Chauvel/Getty Images.

enter Japan on a false passport he was arrested and sentenced to life in prison. He died in prison in May 2011.[75]

The Kilowatt exchanges show a very intense back-and-forth among the agencies while the hijacking was ongoing. At first, the main goal was to find out who the hijackers were, based on the passenger list. On 20 July, just a few hours after the plane had been hijacked, Dutch intelligence sent the passenger list to an American intelligence agency (the cable did not specify which) and asked for help in identifying the hijackers from it.[76] American intelligence carefully checked the list and sent back the names of twenty-eight people who 'could possibly be of potential terrorist interest'.[77] From these twenty-eight, American intelligence further narrowed down the list to four people who were the likely perpetrators. The Dutch agency then forwarded these lists of twenty-eight and four names to the Kilowatt members.[78]

Each of the twenty-eight passengers' personal details were included, such as their addresses, professions, passports, birth dates, and birthplaces. If known, their political affiliation or connection to any student union was mentioned, since this could indicate that they might have been part of the hijacking commando unit. The Americans were cautious, though, and only stated that one person on the list that they mentioned was almost certainly among the hijackers. Three more people also mentioned as likely members of the terrorist unit had a 'rebellious', communist, or leftist history, but were otherwise not previously known to American intelligence.[79] It is interesting that Dutch intelligence asked colleagues in the United States for help in identifying the hijackers.

In the same cable, Dutch intelligence shared information that it had intercepted in a conversation between the hijackers in the plane and Schiphol air traffic control. The leader of the hijackers was called Iso Kassay and reached Schiphol via an earlier plane from Paris, together with someone called Akbar. Kassay said he wanted the flight to be called 'Mount Carmel'. The Dutch cable outlined the flight route of the plane and added that it had meanwhile landed in Dubai because of a lack of fuel.[80]

A few hours later, Italian intelligence checked whether they had any records of the twenty-eight people included on the list and provided additional details on them.[81] Israel informed its partners that it had no traces of the suspicious people mentioned in the JAL404 passenger list and that it was continuing the investigation.[82]

On 23 July, while the crisis was still ongoing, Mossad gave an update and a warning.[83] Other than demanding the release of Kozo Okamoto, Israel specified that the hijackers had at that point not disclosed their intentions or their specific target. Israeli intelligence thought that they were thus still waiting for instructions. It also pointed out that in the past, terrorists had aimed for multiple simultaneous hijackings. The cable listed a few incidents, including the simultaneous hijackings that took place on 6 September 1970, which is known today as 'Skyjack Sunday'.[84] Israel informed its partners that alongside the JAL404 hijacking, there had already been some attempted attacks against the El Al office in Athens on 19 July.

Since the simultaneity of attacks was a common feature of terrorists' modus operandi, Mossad deemed it very probable that the planning of other attacks, which would coincide with the JAL404 hijacking, was ongoing. It had already received indications that groups of Arab terrorists were on their way from the Middle East to Europe and the United States. Their goal was to perpetrate terrorist acts, but at that stage no further details were known to the Israeli agency.[85]

Israel reminded everyone that weapons and sabotage material could be smuggled aboard with hand luggage and duty-free shopping bags (referring to its Kilowatt cable 6098 of 19 March 1973).[86] Accordingly, and in view of the enhanced risk of simultaneous attacks, Mossad strongly recommended upholding strict security measures at airports and including a very thorough search of all passengers as they boarded their planes. It emphasised that the danger was not limited to flights to the Middle East, as terrorists were believed to include non-Arab nationals in their operations.

The next day, 24 July, Israel obtained the first hints about the Palestinian organisation behind the attack. Mossad shared intelligence suggesting that the PFLP had organised the JAL404 hijacking. It assessed this information as plausible given the modus operandi of the PFLP in the past.[87] As became known later, it was indeed the PFLP in cooperation with the JRA.

Still on the same day (24 July), France replied to the Dutch-American list of suspicious passengers and likely hijackers.[88] The DST was able to identify two of the four presumed hijackers and found out that they had stayed in Paris right before the hijacking. The two were Pakistani and bought their tickets for JAL404 together on 17 July. The French agency further found the hotel where the two stayed before their departure to Amsterdam. According to the hotel management, the two had no visitors and made no phone calls during their stay. The DST was in possession of a specimen of their handwriting and offered to send it to anyone interested. It also shared all personal and passport details available to them.[89]

On the evening of 24 July, French intelligence also checked the records of other hotels in Paris and found that another alleged perpetrator of the JAL404 hijacking had stayed in Paris too before heading to Amsterdam.[90] His name was Miyazawa Hayoto and the cable shared the name of the hotel where he stayed and his personal details. On 19 July, a day before the hijacking, he went to a travel agency in Paris to book his ticket. The travel agent remembered him and mentioned that he insisted on flying on the JAL404 flight on 20 July. According to the travel agent, there were many visas in his passport, and he spoke in broken English.[91] The DST had also enquired about Hayoto with Japanese intelligence. The Japanese police said they knew his name well because it apparently served as the cover name of (the above-mentioned) Osamu Maruoka.[92]

In the coming days and weeks, after the crisis had been resolved, Club de Berne members France, Italy, and the Netherlands tried to reconstruct which countries the alleged perpetrators had visited, whom they had met, and when. This was standard operational procedure after an attack and yet another indication that everything had stayed the same after Lillehammer.[93] After the three agencies determined which route each of the twenty-eight people on the list had taken, another back-and-forth started in August 1973 when the agencies tried to track who among them might have returned to Europe.[94]

On 25 July 1973, Mossad shared further hints about the group that was behind the hijacking.[95] During the flight, the hijackers had declared that the mission's name had changed. Instead of 'Mount Carmel', the terrorist mission was now 'Martyr Sa'ada', named after the hijacker who had been killed by the grenade on board the plane. Mossad held traces of a PFLP terrorist whose code name was Sa'ada; his real name was known to be Kiti George Thomas. Sa'ada was the chief assistant of Wadi Haddad, who at the time was in charge of the PFLP. Sa'ada was known to have been involved in previous terrorist operations abroad and to have travelled extensively in Europe. Mossad summarised that if Sa'ada was indeed the terrorist killed on JAL404, then it was very likely that the PFLP was the perpetrator of the attack.[96]

After the conclusion of the hijacking crisis, French intelligence wrote an update about the ongoing investigation. The interesting aspect of this cable is that it included a justification or exculpation of French security regarding the terrorists' stay in France before the attack. First, the cable stressed that the DST had no prior records of the hijackers and therefore they appeared as completely unsuspicious to French security.[97] Second, the DST specified that Japan Airlines estimated that the airline was not in danger of air piracy and had thus not asked the French authorities to apply any airport security measures. Therefore, as the cable explained, seventy people boarded the JAL404 plane at Paris Orly without any security checks.

The DST had meanwhile enquired with the travel agency, Flandrac, which had issued a ticket to one of the terrorists. According to the travel agent, that individual too had forcefully insisted on getting a ticket for the JAL404 flight, pretending that he needed absolutely to travel via Anchorage, which was on the JAL404 route, and that he had friends on this flight. The same travel agent mentioned to the DST that the man looked younger than the picture in his passport.[98]

A few days later, the DST had obtained the passenger list from Japan Airlines and closely looked at those passengers who boarded the plane in Paris and Amsterdam. French intelligence was thus able to confirm the identity of the hijackers who boarded the plane in Paris and shared their personal details via Kilowatt.[99]

At the end of July 1973, French intelligence informed its partners that three Japanese suspects, who were on the very first list of twenty-eight names sent by American intelligence to Dutch intelligence, were spotted on a train from Paris to Vienna on the 29th. The three were accompanied by a fourth compatriot, whose name and date of birth were also given.[100] Similarly, on 1 August, French intelligence informed its partners that another group of people on this list had left France. They took a plane to Casablanca and the body search and hand-luggage check before boarding was negative.[101]

Altogether, Club de Berne correspondence revealed several additional elements about this hijacking. Among others, correspondence established the identities of the terrorists who perpetrated the attack and provided further details about the course of events. The cables further confirmed that the PFLP was behind the attack. Agencies went to great lengths in order to track the prior movements of the alleged hijackers. It is likely that they had not previously been involved in Palestinian terrorism and thus French justification is understandable for why they had let them board without security checks. A further interesting element concerns the fact that American intelligence helped identify the hijackers and that Japanese intelligence helped add more personal details about them.

RECRUITING TERRORISTS

In addition to intelligence-sharing about JAL404, another thread started among the Kilowatt partners in mid July. Dutch police arrested a suspect, led an extensive investigation, and sent the other agencies regular and detailed updates. This case too shows how cooperation remained unchanged after the Lillehammer affair, as these intelligence exchanges started before the scandal and continued over several months afterwards.

Correspondence about this case started on 16 July 1973, when the Dutch intelligence service, the BVD, alerted its Kilowatt partners about a suspect, Mohamed Bellabiod.[102] Dutch police detained him on suspicion of theft, but in the interrogations he confessed to membership of Black September. He was said to have been trained in 1968–1971 in the handling of arms, grenades, mines, and bazookas in a training camp called El-Bir in Jordan.

After Bellabiod was deemed ready to be deployed in an attack, his commander sent him to Europe as part of a terrorist team. It was a middleman who organised his commando unit's travel. Once in the Netherlands, their task was to hijack a plane, no matter what airline, in July 1973 from Schiphol Airport and take it to Libya. According to the arrested man, the squad was in possession of two pistols and three hand grenades. The names of his commander at the camp, the middleman, and the other members of the terrorist squad were all included in the cable.[103]

The cable detailed the terrorist team's travel route from the Middle East and their stays in France, Switzerland, and Belgium, before they reached Amsterdam. At the time of sending the cable, the Dutch service had not known where the weapons or the other members of the group were located. The cable asked for urgent help and requested that the Kilowatt agencies send any hints about the people mentioned or information that could help verify Bellabiod's story.

A week later, the BVD sent an update with new details from the investigations.[104] His name and origins could be clarified: he was Algerian and had a different name from that on his (forged) passport. He had been staying in Paris for two years with his cousin, whose name was given and about whom the DST was asked to enquire. He further had a handwritten address (not in his handwriting) of the Libyan embassy in Brussels, which was suspicious given that he claimed to be Algerian. He said that he had been arrested in West Germany in January 1973, and the BfV was addressed directly and asked to 'check these facts'.[105]

The BfV replied with some additional details about Bellabiod. He illegally stayed in West Germany for a while and, as a cover, he pretended to be a construction worker. He was married to a Belgian woman and the cable shared her name and address in Belgium. Bellabiod's mother was said to be living in Lille, France. In April 1973, the West German authorities issued a deportation decree against him, but the BfV had not known when or whether the expulsion had actually happened.[106]

Meanwhile, the Dutch authorities continued investigations and understood that Bellabiod worked in close cooperation with the Libyan embassies in Algiers, Paris, and Brussels. Dutch intelligence traced people Bellabiod had continuously met there since 1969. The BVD suspected that they were preparing attacks in Europe. All their names, personal details, family histories, and physical appearances were given in the cable.[107]

The Dutch agency assessed the various pieces of evidence concerning Bellabiod and came to the conclusion that he was part of a three-man team in charge of recruiting 'terrorists-to-be' on behalf of the Libyan embassy in Brussels. The cable stated that the investigation was still proceeding and urgently requested any intelligence on the matter as soon as possible.[108]

Libya, as a sponsor and supporter of Palestinian terrorism, had already been mentioned as a risk in previous Club de Berne correspondence.[109] However, from mid July 1973 onwards, the agencies noticed increased direct connections between the Libyan government and Palestinian groups.[110] For several months they ran a cat-and-mouse game with the Libyan administration, and Kilowatt members tried to understand Libyan involvement in the Palestinian armed struggle. Agencies needed each other's help to counter this threat.[111] This is another instance that shows how important intelligence cooperation was at the time; too important to let Lillehammer disrupt it in any way.

TRACKING SUSPECTS: MORE TRAILS LEADING TO BANDAK

Another pertinent example of uninterrupted cooperation concerns Yousef Issa el-Bandak. As mentioned above in Chapter 2, in September 1972, Kilowatt members found out that he had helped with the logistics of organising the Munich attack, particularly arranging housing for the terrorists before the operation.[112] In mid July 1973 intelligence reports about him reappeared, which means that correspondence about him started before the Lillehammer affair and continued over several months afterwards.

In that month, MI5 alerted the Kilowatt members that Bandak had flown from Munich to London on 7 July 1973, travelling on a United Arab Republic diplomatic passport. The British agency believed that he was going to Spain on 13 July to meet a German woman, whose telephone number was given in the cable.[113] In addition to this cable, a week later MI5 sent two more messages with updates about Bandak. It had been able to cross-check Bandak's travel route with visa information it received directly from the BfV. It could thus confirm the accuracy of the cable that it had sent a week before and MI5 also knew by then that Bandak had indeed left for Spain.[114] It was further able to identify the German woman, Anna Schulze (name changed), who Bandak was going to meet in Spain. In the second cable, MI5 shared her name, a home address in Munich, a work address in Rome, and three phone numbers linked to her that were found in Bandak's address book.[115]

The West German police drove the investigation further at their end based on the address and the phone number mentioned by MI5. They found out that the address in Munich belonged to the mother of Anna Schulze. BfV further explained that Schulze had worked in Rome for a few years and inferred that she met Bandak there.[116] It had intelligence on him which suggested that he was in charge of organising a forthcoming terrorist operation. He planned to go to Spain to buy an apartment and from there coordinate the attack. The BfV further shared the name of a fake Italian company that served as a front.[117]

On 8 August 1973, which incidentally was almost a year after the first cable about him was sent, Italy replied with intelligence it had about Bandak and Schulze's stay in Italy. It confirmed that he had lived there from 1969 to 1971. The cable gave his address in Rome at the time – a flat that was owned by a company called Societa Immobiliare Nationale. The phone number of this flat that was given in MI5's cable was apparently nearly correct; one number was wrong, according to the Italian cable.[118]

The Italian agency, SISDE, also informed its partners about Schulze. A German national, she stayed in Italy legally from May 1966 to July 1969 and worked for the company Associazione Nationale Industria Saponi. Her passport details, and date and place of birth were given, as well as the addresses and the landlines of where she had been living in Rome during this time.[119] Italian intelligence investigated her phone number that MI5 had mentioned in its previous message. This corresponded to a Rome telephone number but was apparently not attributed to any landline in the city, or anywhere in the Italian phone system.

The German BfV meanwhile collected intelligence about Bandak's family members, some of whom were identified as highly placed Arab diplomats. In late August 1973, it sent a cable informing its partners that Bandak's brother was working as a UN observer in New York and his father served as Jordanian ambassador in Madrid and previously in Chile. Until recently, Bandak had himself been working for the Egyptian diplomatic service and for the Arab League. He was believed to soon be entering the Iraqi foreign service and would work at the Iraqi embassy in Madrid.[120] As a follow-up, a month later the BfV found further traces of Bandak's movement in Europe. He had been seen in Geneva and Munich and was travelling using an Iraqi diplomatic passport. He had visas for Switzerland, Italy, and Spain. On 29 September 1973, he left Munich again for Geneva and was allegedly on his way to Madrid.[121]

Altogether, according to the Kilowatt agencies, Bandak had moved to Spain to work for the Iraqi embassy and continued to covertly support the Palestinian armed struggle with the help of his German friend, Schulze. In the coming months, intelligence about Bandak reappeared frequently in Kilowatt correspondence.

THE SECOND WAVE OF LETTER BOMBS

After the first wave of letter bombs starting in October 1972, letters or parcels containing small bombs remained a continual threat from Black September. Sporadically, it sent further batches of letter bombs to select targets around the world. On 21 March 1973, one such injured a member of the Wallem shipping company in Singapore.[122] The addressee, the managing director, was not Jewish and the company was Norwegian. However, Wallem was the local agency for ZIM, an Israeli shipping company. MI5 sent a report with some context surrounding this letter bomb and speculated that the connection to ZIM was Black September's reason for selecting Wallem as the target.[123]

The next wave of letter bomb attacks was in August 1973. The first warning came in early July when MI5 shared reports that suggested Fatah was planning to re-activate the Black September letter bomb campaign. The British agency believed that some of the booby-trapped parcels and letters were going to be sent from the Persian Gulf. It considered this intelligence to be reliable and assessed that Arab terrorists retained the capacity to mount such a campaign.[124]

This was confirmed in early August by Mossad, which informed its partners that various explosive letters had been intercepted by Israeli post offices. For instance, the Jerusalem post office did an X-ray examination of a letter on 30 July and found that it was booby-trapped. The letter was addressed to an Arab teacher who was employed as a school inspector in the West Bank. The sender's address, written in Arabic, was given as the Ministry of Education and Culture in Nablus.[125]

Israeli intelligence compared the technique of this letter bomb (detonation mechanism, size, and thickness of the letter) with the ones used a year before and found that they were the same. Mossad pointed out that no improvement had been made in the letter bomb mechanism. This suggested that it was likely the same group, Black September, who organised these letter bombs and the ones in September/October 1972. The addressee of the letter bomb, as Mossad highlighted, revealed a new type of target. Namely, this teacher was selected because the terrorists suspected him of collaborating with the Israeli authorities. This was the first case of a letter bomb used as a punitive measure to condemn collaboration with Israel.[126]

Israel had received reports that Black September was planning to dispatch additional letter bombs; one report even spoke of a new wave of such bombs. The bomb intercepted in Jerusalem was believed to be the beginning of this wave. Mossad believed that terrorists were going to involve countries where no letter bombs had yet been received or sent. This was because in those countries the postal services might not have made arrangements for examining suspicious envelopes. Kuwait especially was thought to have served as the letter bombs' distribution centre, in part because the managing director of the Kuwaiti shipping company, whose name was given, had a 'hand in the distribution' and was helping Black September with this operation. Lastly, Mossad highlighted that letter bombs had remained a low-risk terrorist weapon and were thus likely to continue to be used as a tactic.[127]

A CABLE MENTIONS OPERATION WRATH OF GOD

A few months after the Lillehammer affair, Operation Wrath of God was mentioned by the French DST in Kilowatt correspondence, albeit in a very ambivalent way. In late September 1973, French intelligence brought the partner agencies' attention to a complaint by an Iraqi oil industry worker who was temporarily living in Paris.[128] He asked the French municipal police for help because on 11 September he was followed by 'a man of North African type'. He was worried that he could be the next victim like in 'recent events'. This Iraqi citizen was concerned because he felt that he had been under surveillance in another European capital a month before, again, as he presumed, by a Middle Eastern service.

The French cable was neutral in its tone and simply forwarded this Iraqi's concern to the Club de Berne members. It asked whether the Kilowatt members had any intelligence on him that could confirm his identity and verify his claims. Anything or any type of intelligence, as the cable stressed, was welcome.

The cable was rather ambiguous, but it seems that this Iraqi national was worried that he could be the next victim of Operation Wrath of God. While France was relaying this message, was the DST covertly asking whether this person was on Mossad's kill list? The question remains unanswered, but this cable was the closest thing to addressing Operation Wrath of God among the Kilowatt partners.

CONCLUSIONS

When, in late July 1973, one Mossad operative after another was arrested by Norwegian police, the Israeli agency's worst nightmare began. Humiliating weeks and months ensued; operational bases were destroyed that had taken months to build. Mossad's image plummeted just three months after it had acquired an aura of apparent invincibility when its Operation Spring of Youth roared through the streets of Beirut.

How could Mossad get it so drastically and dramatically wrong? A number of factors contributed to the error, including gross operational mistakes in the recruitment of the hit team and the planning of their escape. Another factor was Mossad's reliance on so little intelligence. It only used one photograph of Salameh to verify his identity – incidentally a picture that was sent by MI5 via the Club de Berne. The Club de Berne further contributed, involuntarily, to Mossad's mistake: the many Kilowatt reports about Palestinian terrorist activities in Scandinavia contributed to the plausibility that a top Palestinian terrorist was hiding in Norway.

Nevertheless, cooperation continued unchanged, as was shown through correspondence about the JAL404 hijacking, intelligence-sharing about the suspects Bellabiod and Bandak, and exchanges about the second wave of letter bombs. Other examples where cooperation remained unaffected by the Lillehammer affair included the following:

- Besides Bandak, cooperation about the tracking of terrorists who were believed to have prepared the Munich Olympics attack continued throughout 1972 and 1973 (see Chapter 2).

- Warnings about Ahmad Misbah Omrin were first issued in January 1972. He was believed to be the main terrorist organiser of the PFLP-GC (Jibril organisation), based in Denmark. Intelligence-sharing about Omrin extended until September 1973, when the agencies were alerted that he was on his way from Beirut to Europe (see above in Chapter 8).
- Another example concerns the discovery of arms smuggling through the sales of Mercedes cars (see Chapter 5). While the arrest happened in March 1973, agencies sent continuous updates about the investigation, including months later and well into late 1973.
- Cooperation about surface-to-air missiles allegedly in the hands of Palestinian terrorists started in January 1973, continued after the downing of a Libyan plane in February, and resumed again in September of that year with the Ostia arrests (see Chapter 4). This too shows that cooperation remained unaffected by the Lillehammer affair.
- A further example, and perhaps the most surprising one given the fact that the Lillehammer affair exposed previous Mossad assassinations, Italian intelligence sent updates about the police investigation into the murders of Shibli and Nakaa, which was Operation Wrath of God's seventh killing operation (see Chapter 6). Hence, Kilowatt members continued to update Mossad about its own killings, even though by that point they clearly knew that it was behind the assassinations.
- The same applies regarding the French murder investigation into Kubaisi's assassination (see Chapter 6). Intelligence agencies continued to update the DST's list with Kubaisi's contacts well after the Lillehammer affair.

All these examples show that the Kilowatt members cooperated secretly even though their governments faced an official diplomatic crisis and even though they realised that their intelligence had facilitated Mossad's killing mission. Having been building trust for more than a year, since October 1971 when the cooperation started, the ties among the Kilowatt members were very strong. Cooperation happened as a routine exercise. The exposure of Operation Wrath of God had no effect whatsoever within the Kilowatt group.

As another indication that cooperation among the Club de Berne continued unchanged – or even intensified – a year later, in 1974, the Club installed a second cooperation mechanism. This was done to extend cooperation because, as the heads of various Club de Berne agencies specified, throughout the 1970s the group's cooperation was 'very effective and efficient'.[129] In short, cooperation continued for decades, and there was no change in tone, speed, extent, or content after Lillehammer; on the contrary, cooperation expanded.[130]

CONCLUSION: A SECRET SECURITY ORDER

This volume has advanced three interlinked arguments. First, it has shown that Mossad abused the intelligence it received from European agencies for its own covert operation. During the first months of Operation Wrath of God, European agencies were unaware that the information they were providing was being used for Mossad's killing operation. Thus, through intelligence-sharing the *Europeans had become a key component of Operation Wrath of God*. Initially, this happened without their knowledge or approval.

Second, this book's revelations raise the question of *European complicity* and co-responsibility for the killing of Palestinians in Europe. Namely, counterterrorism intelligence-sharing was so useful and important for the Europeans that once Mossad's assassination campaign became known (before and after the Lillehammer affair), they were willing to turn a blind eye. Cooperation remained unchanged, as intense and trusted as if Mossad's killing operations had never happened. This book argues that the reason for this lies in the *usefulness* for all parties of this Euro-Israeli cooperation.

Third, once it became publicly known that Israel was using Europe as a 'battleground' in its struggle against the Palestinians, European governments heavily condemned the country's actions. This led to an official crisis between the European countries and Israel. However, as mentioned above, the secret Euro-Israeli exchanges remained entirely unaffected by these official condemnations. This shows that *the international relations of intelligence agencies operate according to a separate logic*, independent of the official level. This volume thus furthers our understanding of intelligence agencies as separate international actors in their own right.

MOSSAD'S RELIANCE ON EUROPEAN AGENCIES TO ORGANISE ITS COVERT ACTION

An important new insight that this volume has revealed is that Mossad relied heavily on foreign intelligence agencies to organise its covert actions. This invites us to rethink the often-presented image of Mossad as a near omnipotent and omniscient agency. Instead, it is clear that it did not act alone, and that European intelligence was vital for the successful completion of Operation Wrath of God. This dismantles some of the mystique around Mossad, because this book offers a much more nuanced and realistic view of its strengths and weaknesses.

This volume has further advanced our understanding of an agency's operational methods in organising a covert operation. The secondary literature about Operation Wrath of God has often accused Mossad of having compiled the kill list based on convenience or easy access to a target, as opposed to a person's role in or importance for Palestinian terrorism. For every targeted killing operation, this book has carefully assessed what the Kilowatt agencies had known about each victim beforehand. Given that Mossad was always included in Kilowatt correspondence, it received the same intelligence.

For each of Mossad's killing missions, Club de Berne records suggested that the assassinated person was heavily involved in terrorist activities, except, of course, the mission that mistakenly killed Ahmed Bouchiki in Lillehammer. Each target's role and degree of involvement varied, but all of them had a terrorist past, present, and likely future. Mossad's first kill, Zwaiter, was believed to have a strong support role in terrorist activities, including logistical help with planning the Munich Olympics massacre. The secondary literature often criticises Mossad for this killing, simply because it was not known until now that Zwaiter played such an important role in Palestinian terrorism.

The second Operation Wrath of God victim was Mahmoud al-Hamshari. The secondary literature and intelligence records align on the assumption that Hamshari was the official Fatah representative in France. However, Dutch and Israeli intelligence assumed that part of a Fatah representative's portfolio was to help with preparations for terrorist attacks in Europe, including, for instance, recruiting new operatives from among Palestinian diasporas. Mossad's charges against Hamshari went further than that and Israeli intelligence held him responsible for specific attacks. One attack allegedly planned by Hamshari was a very brutal air sabotage attack, in which a bomb exploded on a plane flying right over the Swiss city of Würenlingen. The crash killed forty-seven passengers and crew. Hamshari is said to also have been in the process of negotiating a non-aggression deal between the PLO and France. If Mossad knew about it, his assassination may have been a signal to France that Israel disapproved of this approach to terrorism and that it was going to undermine it if possible.

The third assassination victim of this covert action was Hussein Abu-Khair in Nicosia. One of the core reasons for eliminating Khair was his role as the link between the PLO and the KGB. Mossad killed him and later his replacement, which indicates a clear motive was deterrence. Mossad wanted to break the ties between the Palestinian armed struggle and Russian intelligence. As such, the message was that Fatah members who worked as a liaison to the KGB needed to fear for their lives. The secondary literature further points to Khair's active role in the organisation of an attack on a boat en route from Cyprus to Haifa. Interestingly, intelligence agencies did indeed report on such an attack, which was thwarted by the arrest of the perpetrators at the port of Famagusta in Cyprus. These arrests took place only a week before Khair was killed. However, looking at the evidence more closely, neither the secondary literature nor the Club de Berne records provide proof that Khair was indeed preparing this attack. Yet, it is striking that the attack was thwarted only a few days before he was killed. Taking all aspects into consideration, it is likely that Mossad had put Khair on the kill list for his role as the Fatah–KGB liaison, but that these additional reports of his involvement in terrorist preparations made his execution a stronger priority and accelerated the preparations for the mission to kill him.

The fourth victim of Operation Wrath of God was Dr Basil Paoud al-Kubaisi. The secondary literature and primary sources agree that he was an important PFLP terrorist organiser. Several attacks, including the particularly horrific Lod Airport massacre in May 1972, were believed to have happened under his command. Some journalistic accounts have suggested that he was also in Black September, which could not be confirmed by intelligence reports. Nevertheless, here, too, Mossad was killing under the clear assumption that Kubaisi had blood on his hands from terrorist activities.

Operation Spring of Youth was the fifth killing mission. The three assassinated men were PLO and Fatah leaders and were close friends of Arafat and Salameh (who both lived a stone's throw away from the raided apartments). The logic for selecting these targets is clear from the secondary literature: all three were very prominent figures in the Palestinian armed struggle. By killing them, Mossad further proved that it could strike anywhere – not just in friendly countries, but also on hostile territory. A Palestinian leader could no longer feel safe, not even in their own bedroom. The Club de Berne files further link one of the three targets, Mohamed Abu Yussuf, to the planning of the Black September attack in Scandinavia that was thwarted in December 1972 (and which was supposed to take place parallel to the Bangkok attack).

The sixth killing mission was to eliminate Zaid Muchassi. Muchassi's death is mentioned relatively little in the secondary literature and was not mentioned in the Club de Berne files. Most likely, he was selected by Mossad because he was the new Fatah–KGB liaison. He needed to be eliminated like his predecessor as a deterrent.

The seventh mission was the car bomb that exploded when Shibli and Nakaa were driving around Rome. The two hit men were on their way to carry out a terrorist attack on an office of the Israeli airline, El Al. This James Bond-esque operation of assassinating terrorists on their way to plant a bomb could be confirmed with Kilowatt cables, especially with reports from Italian intelligence after the car explosion.

The eighth killing mission was the execution of Mohamed Boudia. He was undoubtedly a top terrorist by all accounts. The secondary literature associated him with numerous attacks. Club de Berne reports confirmed most of these charges and attributed even more terrorist actions to him. The Kilowatt records about Boudia further reveal the usefulness of these exchanges in tracking Mossad's targets. Swiss intelligence provided important details about his habits that Mossad could use when it was planning his assassination.

The ninth kill was the murder of Ahmed Bouchiki, which led to the Lillehammer affair. While the Club de Berne files did not mention him, intelligence-sharing influenced Mossad in two central ways. First, it gave Mossad the impression that Scandinavia was a major terrorist hub, and this gave credibility to claims that a top terrorist was in Norway. Second, journalistic accounts claim that Mossad only had one photo of Salameh and that they used this to compare the target's resemblance to Bouchiki before they decided to kill him. The Club de Berne records imply that MI5 had sent this picture to Mossad. The secondary literature stressed that in this picture Salameh indeed had a very strong resemblance to Bouchiki. The tenth killing operation was several years later when Mossad assassinated Ali Hassan Salameh in 1979.

Altogether, when looking at the selection of the victims of Operation Wrath of God as a whole, a clear rationale behind each targeted killing becomes apparent. The Club de Berne files either helped to discern the reasons for the selection of the target or confirmed the accounts in the secondary literature. This has revealed some of Israeli intelligence's methods of planning and executing killing missions, including how they collected information before approving the operations.

INTELLIGENCE COOPERATION AND EUROPEAN COMPLICITY

This volume raises some provocative questions, such as were Europeans accomplices to Israel's covert operations? It has argued that they were, because European intelligence was essential for Operation Wrath of God.

Furthermore, after the second killing mission, rumours were already circulating that Mossad was responsible for the assassination. With every assassination, its responsibility became increasingly clear, and mainstream newspapers openly accused Israeli intelligence of the murders.[1] If European intelligence agencies had vehemently disapproved of Mossad's covert actions, then they could have taken action, such as ending Kilowatt cooperation. The opposite happened: cooperation intensified, as this book shows, and no agency ever directly addressed Mossad's potential involvement in any of the killings. Even more so, after each and every Mossad assassination, European intelligence diligently shared their police investigations with the Israelis.

This leads to two interrelated inferences. First, the informal channels among the Club de Berne members were not the right forum on which to call out Mossad. Cooperation within Kilowatt – a multilateral framework – had a certain performative element. The rules of the game simply did not allow the alienation of a partner agency in that way. Furthermore, with an increased need for information about Palestinian terrorism in Europe, Mossad's intelligence was simply too important for any European agency to risk losing access to it.

Second, maintaining complete silence about Operation Wrath of God or sharing police records about the murder investigations was also a covert signal to Mossad itself. By continuing to update Mossad about these investigations, European intelligence agencies signalled that they would not investigate the murder cases further and hinted that they would let Israel continue its covert operations on European soil. Even if not necessarily approving, European governments secretly agreed to tolerate Mossad's bloodbath on the streets of Europe. An element that supports this further is that once the Lillehammer trial made Mossad's killing operations publicly known, France and Italy refused to reopen the murder cases, despite Palestinian pressure to do so. Both of these elements together suggest that intelligence cooperation was too important for agencies to risk losing Mossad as a partner, and that Mossad therefore was free to use Europe as the theatre for its extrajudicial killings.

Another reason why European governments may have tolerated Mossad operations, despite the numerous risks involved, is that they may have agreed with Israel's counterterrorism policy. For European governments, Palestinian terrorism had increasingly become a problem. Not only did it force the concerned governments to take a political stance on the Middle East conflict (when most countries preferred to stay aloof), but it directly threatened the security of their own citizens.

It is thus conceivable that some European countries were aligned with Israel's approach and believed that targeted killing was an admissible or condonable way to fight Palestinian terrorism. It is known that French intelligence had its own targeted killing programme throughout the 1960s and early 1970s.[2] The UK too had not hesitated to include assassinations in its covert actions, and was also known to have been happy to climb on the bandwagon and hide behind other intervening nations, most frequently the US.[3] Italian intelligence as well is known to have carried out some bloodstained covert operations, including false flag operations, like *Gladio*, that involved its own citizens in Italy.[4]

Using this line of reasoning, one can say that Mossad was doing the 'dirty work' of counterterrorism in Europe, while European intelligence agencies were avoiding being publicly associated with it in any way. They could continue to support Mossad via the informal Club de Berne channels, because it was done entirely in secret. Until now, it was simply not known that European agencies not only tolerated Mossad's covert actions, but also provided vital intelligence to help carry them out.

Another reason to cooperate in the Kilowatt framework was that it was perceived by all parties as an extremely effective framework to counter terrorism. This was most apparent when agencies were able to prevent attacks through intelligence-sharing. Such was, for instance, the case in March 1973, when Italian intelligence alerted their French counterparts about a suspicious Mercedes that was about to cross the border. When French border control checked the car, it indeed found weapons and arrested the car's occupants. This led to a cross-Kilowatt investigation and revealed that the Palestinians planned to attack the Israeli and Jordanian embassies in Paris. While this attack was thwarted, the race between intelligence agencies and Black September was far from being won. For this, Club de Berne cooperation was immensely useful, first to gain a much better assessment of Palestinian groups and their operational structures and, second, to piece together their plans after a suspect had been arrested.

This meant that through intelligence-sharing, the agencies were able to collectively gain enormous amounts of intelligence on Palestinian armed groups and their terrorist plans. In particular, the direct connection from agency to agency and the possibility of sending messages instantly proved very helpful to counter the threat of terrorism.

Altogether, this volume argues that it was precisely this perceived effectiveness and a certain inter-agency dependency that made European agencies 'look the other way' when it became clear that Mossad was killing Palestinians on European soil (behind their backs, but in plain view, and with their intelligence). Some agencies might also have sympathised with Israel, others disapproved, but all continued to work together informally, in full plausibly deniable secrecy.

A COVERT SECURITY POLICY

Operation Wrath of God came to an abrupt halt when its targeted assassinations were exposed and nearly all Mossad's operational structure in Europe was disrupted. This happened during the Lillehammer affair in July 1973. Cooperation in the Club de Berne remained entirely unaffected by this. This means that agencies continued to share intelligence even though by that point they all very clearly knew that their intelligence had served the purpose of a killing operation and might do so again in the future.

Even at the height of the crisis, and thereafter, it was 'business as usual' in the intelligence world, with agencies sharing warnings, reports based on past terrorist attacks, and intelligence about the inner workings of terrorist groups. Among the intelligence files are countless examples where cooperation about a case started before Lillehammer and continued after Operation Wrath of God was exposed. These cases are obviously in stark contrast to all the official statements that condemned Israeli actions. For Israel, this meant that it could use European intelligence without facing any negative consequences.

This discrepancy between official condemnations of Israeli covert action and secret intensification of ties in the Club de Berne furthers our understanding of Western states' collaboration outside the channels of formal diplomacy. It shows that intelligence liaison operated independently of official policies. The agencies found their unique international modus operandi and administered their own intergovernmental relations.

This book thus argues that in the world of intelligence agencies, where everything can be kept secret, plausibly denied, and kept away from the public eye, a different logic applies to that in foreign policy decision-making. When deciding with whom to cooperate, an intelligence agency only needed to consider its perceived national security interests. If cooperation could be kept secret, neither moral considerations about a cooperating agency's human rights record nor public perceptions of a government's image played a role. In this vein, this discrepancy between official condemnation and covert acceptance of Israel's assassinations showed a form of covert security logic. In short, intelligence agencies can work independently of and differently from official state policy.

GENERAL THEMES

THE INTERNATIONAL RELATIONS OF THE SECRET STATE

The insights of this volume have advanced our understanding of how the international relations of intelligence agencies work and reveal a new and secret dimension of international relations. In particular, a core novelty of the book is that these secret relations have been documented. Intelligence-sharing about terrorist attacks, which were discussed in various chapters, showed the following different aspects.

One central theme in this respect is that of *covert diplomacy*. Covert or clandestine diplomacy is defined as the use of intelligence agencies to engage in secret discussions with adversaries.[5] In the case of the Club de Berne and the public outrage relating to the Lillehammer affair, it was not necessarily a means of keeping up secret communication channels with an adversary, but rather a means of keeping European–Israeli ties secret and separated from official Euro-Israeli relations.

Moreover, because the exchange of secret information remained uninterrupted before, during, and after the Lillehammer affair, it likely helped with the normalisation process after European agencies realised the extent to which Mossad operated unlawfully on their territory, in part with their own intelligence. The previously established strong security ties at the technical level arguably facilitated the preservation of friendly and trustful relations in matters of security cooperation.

Furthermore, Chapters 2 and 3 showed that the West German BfV was exceptionally keen to supply Kilowatt members with intelligence about Black September. For West German intelligence, Club de Berne cooper-ation thus served as a platform where they could prove their relevance, competence, and importance as a security partner. This allowed them to reverse their negative image after the debacle at the Munich massacre. The BfV's extensive flow of cables, including the ones that exculpated the West German authorities, can thus be read as an additional layer of communi-cation that went beyond sheer tactical updates about Black September and its likely next targets. This was a form of covert diplomacy in a moment of crisis that was possible only because Mossad and the BfV had direct links to one another and a shared communication channel.

Another theme is the *interdependency* that existed among the agen-cies. Chapters 3 and 4 discussed various cases where each agency con-tributed pieces of information and only by considering all the sources together were the agencies able to infer terrorist intentions. This shows a certain degree of interdependency, mainly because one agency could not have eyes and ears in all of Europe. There is, however, the risk of losing capacity when an agency becomes too reliant on others. Under certain circumstances, it can be very sensible to rely on partners in areas where one's own intelligence service lacks competencies. Reliance, however, may create vulnerabilities. In this vein, the Club de Berne records show that the agencies had collectively gained power over terrorist groups while in relative terms lost power through their inter-agency dependency. Regarding Operation Wrath of God, European agencies had become too dependent on Mossad/Shin Bet and were thus limited in their options. Namely, when they realised that Israel was killing Palestinians on their territory, their dependency meant that they could not 'punish' Israel by stopping intelligence cooperation.

The agencies also used their intelligence-sharing for their own *image cultivation*. This volume has shown that, quite frequently, cables were sent with the purpose of cultivating a certain image of the agency. For instance, MI5 and the BfV often mentioned that their intelligence came from a 'friendly service in the region', thus boasting about their extensive relations with other intelligence agencies around the world. Other agencies, such as smaller ones like the Swiss BuPo, usually replied within hours, thus showcasing the appearance of being swift, conscientious, and reliable.

Italy had to struggle with a reputation for being lax with terrorists, which will be discussed further below. SISDE mentioned very frequently that its security services were strong and strict, implying that it was not lax at all about terrorism. Finally, most cables sent by Mossad included the following addition: 'source reliable, with access to terrorist circles'. The Israeli agency was thus making sure its partners knew that it had been able to infiltrate Palestinian networks and that it received first-hand information. This was a way of boasting about its capabilities and ensuring its partners would see the value in maintaining relations with Israeli intelligence.

The sharing of intelligence demonstrates that these agencies engaged in an *alternative foreign policy* from that practised at the political level. In the early 1970s, the European Commission had a very critical foreign policy towards Israel. The official European policy line heavily criticised Israeli post-1967 settlement policies. However, the countries' intelligence relations were excellent. Not one critical word was ever mentioned in Kilowatt exchanges. Similarly, Switzerland had an official foreign policy of neutrality. A neutral country had to always treat all belligerents in the same way. Switzerland's secret state, however, put itself on the side of Israel and heavily supported it in its struggle against violent Palestinian groups. Hence, Switzerland's intelligence service did not observe the same constraints as its official foreign policy service and deviated from its official adherence to neutrality. This suggests that intelligence agencies were much freer in the maintenance of international relations with other intelligence agencies than their countries' foreign services. Under certain circumstances they operated on a different logic and applied different criteria for cooperation.

Finally, another theme that emerges is that the international relations of the secret state were *practitioner driven*. The exchanges were fostered by low- to mid-level intelligence officials. The intense information exchanges – often daily – enhanced intergovernmental relationships between agencies and established personal connections between intelligence officers themselves. In particular, success stories of attacks that were prevented through cooperation, as discussed in Chapter 5, showed the group that cooperation was useful and effective. After a while, cooperation led to more cooperation and a common sense of Kilowatt as a force multiplier.

EFFECTIVENESS OF COVERT ACTION

Assessing Operation Wrath of God as a whole, one can ask to what extent it achieved its operational, tactical, and strategic goals. On an entirely operational and organisational level, at least until the Lillehammer blunder, the operation was a resounding success. Mossad managed to organise 'clean kills' without harming any bystander. It was also able to leave each crime scene without incriminating evidence, all the while sending a loud and clear message to Palestinian terrorism supporters that anyone could be hit next, anywhere in the world.

In this vein, did Operation Wrath of God achieve its medium-term goal of deterrence? It certainly instilled fear among Palestinian terrorist leaders and forced them to go undercover. Mossad's actions also made it more difficult for them to organise or support terrorist actions in Europe. For some, this motivated them to fight Israel even harder, but for many it was indeed a deterrence. Furthermore, on an operational level, some of Mossad's assassinations directly prevented imminent attacks or disrupted planned terrorist operations. Examples of this are the killing of Khair in Cyprus and Operation Wrath of God's seventh killing in Rome, where terrorists were literally on their way to plant a bomb at an El Al office.

On a tactical level, a major Operation Wrath of God goal was to wipe out Black September terrorism in Europe. Indeed, once the covert action ended, Black September was almost entirely dissolved. However, historians of the Palestinian armed struggle invite us to be careful with attributing this development entirely to Mossad. Around the time that Operation Wrath of God slowed down, in late 1973, shifts occurred within Palestinain circles and rifts opened up between various factions.[6] Two opposing views emerged about the use of international terrorism: by late 1973 and early 1974, Fatah's core leadership under Yasser Arafat opposed terrorism as a tactic. Its assumption was that efforts to obtain diplomatic recognition and government support would be more fruitful to secure subsidies, territorial bases, and diplomatic success.[7] This was countered by radical elements and splinter groups that wanted to uphold terrorist actions at all costs.[8]

For Black September this meant that the core Palestinian leadership, including its umbrella organisation Fatah, gradually began to withdraw support for its terrorist actions. Internationally the same happened: compared with the period of the Munich massacre, in mid 1973 there was much less support for actions where civilians were kidnapped or killed. The embassy siege in Khartoum in March of that year especially showed how few people still stood behind Black September.

By the same token, Operation Wrath of God played its part too, as it made it much more difficult for Palestinian terrorists to operate in Europe. Every Palestinian leader had to live in fear of their life. One can thus conclude that Black September ended because of a number of factors, including tactical changes within Palestinian groups, diminishing public support for its actions, and Mossad eliminating its leadership and operatives in Europe and the Middle East.[9]

Lastly, on the longer-term strategic level, where does Operation Wrath of God sit in the history of the Arab–Israeli conflict? Some Mossad analysts argue that it consumed far too many resources for little more than vengeance. Money and resources were redirected from other priorities, including collecting intelligence about Israel's neighbours. Equally, some authors see the operation as a distraction, which deflected attention from Israel's military enemies like Egypt and Syria. Around the same time as Operation Wrath of God was running, these countries were planning the Yom Kippur War that indeed caught the Israeli security establishment by surprise.[10] One can thus argue that with Operation Wrath of God, Israeli security was pouring too many resources into killing terrorists when attention should have been on Israel's neighbouring countries.[11] Egypt and Syria were planning and executing actual military attacks in 1973, which were cosiderably more threatening than Black September ever could be.

Another unintended negative effect of Operation Wrath of God was that it gave Mossad a dangerous sense of invincibility and overconfidence. This led to reckless operational planning and backfired dramatically with the Lillehammer affair. This international embarrassment had damaging effects on the agency's morale, public image, and global reputation.

Looking at the Palestinian armed struggle over the long term, Operation Wrath of God had relatively minor effects. Mossad's secret assassinations did not eradicate Palestinian terrorism in Europe or elsewhere. While Black September terrorism ended, Palestinian terrorism in Europe reappeared in the next decades in a different form; for instance, in the 1980s the Abu Nidal group was a particularly violent branch that again operated in Europe.

Overall, Operation Wrath of God achieved its short-term operational and tactical goals, but strategically did not solve any deeper issues nor did it in any way bring Israel closer to peace.

NEW INSIGHTS INTO BLACK SEPTEMBER

Even though this volume has analysed terrorist events through the lens of intelligence agencies, the reports, assessments, and warnings nevertheless reveal a great deal about Black September itself. Intelligence records give insights into its organisation, its operational practices, and its planned, aborted, or executed attacks. For some of the terrorist plans, especially the ones that never materialised, these intelligence reports are the only records of the events and they are presented in this book for the first time.

An example of such a failed terrorist attack that was unknown until now is the planned attack in Norway that was supposed to happen simultaneously with the 1972 Bangkok attack. The UK authorities arrested the terrorist operative who was tasked with the attack. Through its own investigation and the Club de Berne exchanges, MI5 concluded that this attack was meant as a parallel operation to the attack in Bangkok that took place on 28 December 1972.

Similarly, the history of Black September includes countless cursory references to terrorist attacks the authenticity of which has remained unverified. Through the Club de Berne records, several attacks could either be confirmed or corroborated with primary source evidence. Such was the case with a planned Palestinian missile attack that attempted to target a plane carrying Israel's Prime Minister Golda Meir. Allegedly in a spectacular last-minute action, Mossad was said to have neutralised the missiles only minutes before Meir's plane landed. On the evening of 15 January 1973, the same day that this attack was allegedly attempted, Mossad alerted its partners about Palestinians using surface-to-air missiles to attack aircraft. Other agencies later confirmed that this weapon was likely in the hands of terrorist groups.

Another such example was the claim that Hussain Abu-Khair had been planning a terrorist attack against a ship travelling from Cyprus to Haifa. The Club de Berne records show that such an attack was thwarted exactly around the time that Khair was assassinated. While the intelligence reports did not confirm any links between Khair and this attack, they lent credence to the claim of Khair's involvement.

The Club de Berne files also substantially advance our current understanding of Black September's operational methods, about which we still know very little today. One method that we can infer from the intelligence assessments is that Black September ran its missions strictly on a need-to-know basis. This meant that before an attack, individual operatives neither knew each other nor knew the nature of the attack itself. Typically, a terrorism coordinator would gather the entire team a few hours before an attack and only at that point explain to them their tasks in the operation. This was an effective way to avoid a terrorist operation being exposed if one of the members of the operation was arrested. If they did not know about the operation in advance, they could not tell the police and the plan could remain intact. According to the BfV, MI5, and Mossad, this was an important feature of any Black September operation. Allegedly this approach was also employed before the Munich Olympics attack.

Kilowatt exchanges in March 1973, after two Arab men were arrested in a Mercedes near the French–Italian border, also revealed new insights about Black September practices. International police and intelligence investigations exposed a transnational terrorist smuggling ring between Europe and the Middle East. It uncovered that Black September ran a second-hand Mercedes sales business as a front to smuggle weapons and to finance terrorist operations. Intelligence agencies also discovered that the Mercedes' occupants were part of a terrorist scheme to attack the Israeli and Jordanian embassies in Paris.

Based on Kilowatt intelligence-sharing, another Black September tactic came to light: the consistent use of young European women for terrorist missions. Young women were sometimes knowingly and sometimes unknowingly drawn into a terrorist action. For instance, in the case of the so-called 'Passover attack' in spring 1972, European women smuggled chemicals into Tel Aviv to create bombs that were meant to explode during festive Passover dinners. An example of women unknowingly becoming involved was the case of an airline sabotage attempt on 16 August 1972. In this, two English tourists were coaxed into carrying a gramophone on to a plane as extra luggage, without knowing that the record-player contained a bomb.

Another contribution of this book is the addition of new details to known terrorist attacks. This was the case with the October 1972 Lufthansa Kiel hijacking, in which Black September managed to obtain the freedom of the three surviving perpetrators of the Munich massacre. The Club de Berne files show that the West German BfV sent a very detailed and prescient warning cable that described the course of events of this hijacking almost exactly the way it indeed happened. This is remarkable because the West German government had been accused of connivance or of letting the attack happen on purpose. The threat of explosive letters is another instance where it was known that such attacks had happened but where Kilowatt exchanges brought forward additional elements. We now know the mechanism of the bombs, the ways in which terrorists aimed to increase their lethality (for instance, by adding poison), and that the threat remained constant, with the most intensive period being September 1972 to January 1973.

Altogether, based on the intelligence reports, one can conclude that Black September was among the most dangerous Palestinian terrorist groups in the early 1970s. According to reports shared in Kilowatt, it was not reluctant to risk civilian victims and was extremely well organised in terms of operational planning, division of labour, arranging logistics, and maintaining a network of sympathisers or supporters. The time period when it posed the biggest threat was September 1972 to March 1973, while March was also the month when most of its plans were exposed or thwarted by the Kilowatt countries.

BLURRED LINES BETWEEN FOREIGN AND DOMESTIC INTELLIGENCE

Kilowatt cooperation further revealed an eradication of the boundaries between foreign and domestic intelligence. The Club de Berne is widely understood to be an association of the domestic intelligence agencies of its member states. However, Mossad (Israel's foreign intelligence service) received all the Club de Berne cables, alongside Shin Bet (Israel's domestic intelligence service). Similarly, France too had its foreign and domestic intelligence agencies present in the Club de Berne. In numerous cases mentioned in this book, one can see that the domestic agencies effectively did the job that a country's foreign intelligence service otherwise had to carry out abroad.

The threat of terrorism is typically considered a domestic security issue. However, terrorist groups operated transnationally and this resulted in the traditional division of competencies into foreign and domestic intelligence agencies being less applicable in matters of counterterrorism cooperation.

This raises the question of the extent to which these analytical distinctions between foreign and domestic intelligence are valid considering the day-to-day work of intelligence practitioners. The division of domestic versus foreign intelligence is assumed to be a central feature of Western intelligence. However, the Kilowatt records invite intelligence scholars to re-evaluate this distinction and to potentially determine different analytical criteria for intelligence organisation.

CENTRALITY OF ITALY

An interesting theme that cuts across this book is the centrality of Italy in both Black September and Wrath of God operations. The terrorist incidents involving the country are strikingly numerous, including several suitcases filled with weapons that were abandoned (November 1972, March and April 1973), two prevented surface-to-air missile attacks in January and September 1973, and the fact that the organisers of the Munich attack used Italy as a base and were connected to terrorist sympathisers there. The 16 August 1972 El Al aircraft sabotage attempt started from Rome, and many more terrorist events were also linked to Italy. Two of the ten Mossad killing missions happened in Rome, and Black September also retaliated in that city with the killing of Olivares.

There was a strong concentration of terrorist activities in and around Rome, involving the city, its airport, and the surrounding outskirts. In December 1972, MI5 warned therefore that Italy had become a terrorist hub.[12] The secondary literature too mentioned Rome as the European centre of Palestinian terrorism.[13] The concentration of Palestinian terrorist activities in Rome therefore explains why Mossad chose several targets in Italy.

The question arises as to why Black September chose Italy as an important base. Unlike in France, there was no Arab diaspora on which they could build. Neither was Italy a particularly central location from which to move in and around Europe. There were some terrorist cells in neighbouring Yugoslavia, but the airports in Paris or London would have been better choices in terms of international connectivity.

One explanation is that Italian security services were known to be 'weak on terrorism'. This is suggested by Ronen Bergman, journalist and author of *Rise and Kill First*, who described Italy as a 'particularly weak country when it comes to counterterror enforcement'.[14] Thus, given the country had a reputation for being lax on security, Palestinian terrorists logically organised attacks there as a place where they estimated they had the highest chances of success.

Interestingly, within Kilowatt cooperation Italy tried numerous times to counter this view. For instance, in all three cases when suitcases were found filled with weapons, Italian intelligence suggested that it was because of 'effective' security measures, hinting that Rome Fiumicino Airport's strong security footprint deterred terrorists and led them to abandon their immediate terrorist plans. It is conceivable that the Italians' claims are correct and that it was precisely their heavy security that captured more terrorist suspects. This would mean that the country's reputation of being weak on terrorism attracted terrorists to Rome, while its actual security apparatus was strong and thus more successful in capturing Black September operatives.

Relatedly, there is the possibility that, compared with other counties, Italian officers simply reported more terrorist incidents. Precisely because it wanted to correct its image, it is possible that Italy reported on each and every incident in order to present its security agencies as active, 'effective', and strong.

Altogether, Italy as a Palestinian terrorist hub was likely the result of an interplay of various factors. Its role as the host of several Palestinian attacks and Israeli covert operations fostered an intense counterterrorist response and brought about a very active Italian contribution within the Kilowatt intelligence-sharing framework.

LENIENCY TOWARDS TERRORISTS

There is another aspect that stands out when looking at the arrests of Black September operatives. European intelligence, law enforcement, and justice systems showed remarkable leniency towards terrorist suspects and perpetrators. Palestinian terrorists were often released immediately without trial, like Halloum (see Chapter 3). Often arrestees were released after a short detention period or a few months of travel restrictions, such as in the case of the perpetrators of an attempted aircraft sabotage. Alternatively, suspects were indeed pronounced guilty of conspiring in terrorism, but were nevertheless released without serving any time in prison.

The case of Halloum and his release right after his arrest is explicable because of his official status as a diplomat. He and other terrorists mentioned here had, however, clearly been preparing attacks and were nevertheless set free (with or without trials) shortly after their arrest. The Lufthansa Kiel hijacking is an extreme case where the surviving Munich perpetrators were even allowed to go to a country, Libya, that welcomed them with open arms and celebrated them as heroes.

One explanation for this is that European laws at the time were not yet adapted to terrorist offences the way they are today.[15] European governments thus had limited resources at their disposal and could not detain perpetrators for the sheer act of planning terrorist offences. This is different from today, when a person can receive a prison sentence for intention to perpetrate an attack or for involvement in a terrorist group such as Al Qaida or Islamic State.

Another possible explanation could be that some European governments concluded secret 'non-aggression' agreements with violent Palestinian groups.[16] A deal of this sort was, for instance, thought to have been sealed by France. In 2018, a former head of French intelligence claimed that there was indeed a secret deal between France and Palestinian terrorists in the 1980s.[17] In this deal it was allegedly implied that no terrorist suspect would be prosecuted or arrested, and in exchange terrorists would spare French targets in their attacks. Similarly, in the mid 1970s, Italy allegedly entered a deal with Libya to help keep Palestinian terrorism away.[18] If such deals had indeed been made, they ought to be seen in conjunction with Club de Berne cooperation. The two policies, a secret deal with Palestinian groups and secret cooperation with Mossad, were not mutually exclusive because each was done in secret. Arguably, they were two sides of the same overall European counterterrorism strategy.

To Israeli stakeholders at the time, however, European policies showed a very high level of tolerance for Palestinian terrorism in Europe. Israeli security officers at the time expressed frustration with European counterterrorism efforts, or the lack thereof.[19] This was, so they claimed, what fostered their decision to resort to a self-administered 'justice' and to prevent terrorist attacks with more drastic means such as Operation Wrath of God.[20]

Furthermore, through its targeted killing campaign, Mossad effectively voided any government–terrorist deals of their substance. Namely, deterring terrorists by killing anyone affiliated with the Palestinian armed struggle sent a clear signal that even if there were secret agreements, Palestinian terrorism in Europe would not be tolerated. No terrorist was safe, even in supposed 'safe havens' provided covertly by European governments.

SUMMARY AND OUTLOOK

Altogether, this volume has revealed entirely new aspects of Operation Wrath of God, the Palestinian armed struggle, and intelligence cooperation in relation to both. One of its core insights is the extent to which Mossad relied on European intelligence to organise its covert action. From an Israeli perspective, this is not very surprising, given that Mossad simply used the pre-established intelligence-sharing channels. It was a sensible decision to use all available means for intelligence collection. Moreover, since European agencies provided intelligence on exactly those suspects who could be included on Mossad's kill list, it would have been foolish not to use it. Furthermore, for Israeli decision-makers, counterterrorism was not limited to collecting intelligence to support law enforcement. Counterterrorism meant eliminating the threat, which included killing terrorists before they could hit.

Nevertheless, from a European perspective the revelations in this book are surprising because one would simply not expect Europeans to help kill Palestinians, even less so Palestinians living in Europe. European governments essentially failed in their duty to keep safe all citizens (irrespective of their nationality) who lived under their sovereignty.

Even though – as this book reveals – Mossad held clear evidence that the assassinated Palestinians were involved in terrorist activities, these Israeli killing missions were still extrajudicial executions. Any government upholding the rule of law should technically refrain from tolerating or supporting such behaviour, especially if it happened on their sovereign territory. Arguably, Palestinians were lulled into a false sense of security.

European behaviour also shows a very high degree of hypocrisy towards Arab states, to which they would never reveal their countries' covert and tacit support for Israel. This volume thus reveals a hidden side to European intelligence, one that would not have been easy to justify on a diplomatic level and that it would certainly have preferred to keep under the table. Simply put, it would have been very uncomfortable for European governments if this book had been published a few decades earlier.

These revelations are also surprising in relation to the image of Mossad. Usually, it is perceived as a very powerful intelligence agency and Operation Wrath of God is considered to have been an impressive show of strength. The fact that Mossad had to rely on European or other foreign intelligence shows a certain degree of weakness and dependency. This, of course, runs counter to the official Mossad narrative. This book contributes to drawing a more nuanced picture of the agency and its capabilities.

New insights have also been offered about counterterrorism intelligence cooperation itself. While in a few instances alerts did indeed lead to the prevention of terrorist attacks, the actual strength of Club de Berne cooperation was to help obtain a much better overall picture of Palestinian terrorism in Europe as a whole. Hence, it was less about sharing operational intelligence to address immediate threats, but rather, through Kilowatt, terrorist suspects in one country could be matched up with records in a different country. As such, crossing borders did not mean crossing into safe havens. Suspects could also be linked to earlier events, which, if they were arrested, could support law enforcement efforts, or it could help create an understanding of terrorist networks and anticipate likely next targets.

In essence, Club de Berne cooperation represented a collective and extensive database of crucial information about terrorist suspects, organisations, methods, and events, which the agencies could retrieve at any moment. In the period before mass digitisation, a network of information such as this was invaluable.

Circling back to the above points, this explains precisely why European intelligence never addressed Operation Wrath of God in the Kilowatt framework and continued cooperation with Mossad as if they had never known about it or the Lillehammer affair. The threat of transnational terrorism was too high for any country to afford to be excluded from Kilowatt. But this also meant that Israel could assume, as it did, that it could get away with Operation Wrath of God without having to face any consequences from the Europeans.

Indeed, cooperation continued for years and decades. It was beyond the scope of this volume to analyse intelligence cooperation for the entire decade. However, the Kilowatt sources from 1973 to 1979, which the author has consulted, show that cooperation continued in the same way as in 1972 and with the same level of detail and commitment by European and Israeli intelligence alike.

These frequent intelligence exchanges developed into a close-knit community of practitioners. While European Union officials repeatedly tried to integrate the Club de Berne into more formal (and more accountable) EU-wide intelligence structures, members of the Club consistently resisted. Even today, Club de Berne has continued to provide an informal intelligence-sharing platform, similar to the way it started back in the early 1970s.[21]

Altogether, this book has told the story of a 'war of the spooks' between Israeli intelligence and its arch-enemy at the time, Black September.

Unlike previous accounts, it is for the first time based on documentary evidence and takes into consideration the role played by the 'hosts' of this secret war, the Europeans. The 'hosts' of a covert action are very rarely considered, and this applies also to Europe in the study of covert action. Instead, the field is largely dominated by studies that analyse American or UK secret interventions.

This needs to change, and indeed is changing. This volume has contributed to this growing field that analyses covert action from various perspectives (actors, reactors, hosts) and understands it as a global phenomenon. It provides a better understanding of Mossad's logic and rationale for selecting the Palestinians who were killed, and especially also the dilemmas of European intelligence agencies: should they criticise Mossad and risk losing it as a vital partner in the fight against terrorism, or keep quiet about it and continue cooperation with Israeli security? Clearly, they chose the latter because they could keep it entirely secret. With this book, the secret has been revealed for the first time.

Acknowledgements

'Kilowatt'. This word opened unforeseen research avenues at the start of my academic career. At the time, I was reading a French encyclopaedia of intelligence concepts. (Who actually *reads* encyclopaedias? I have no idea why I did that!) In it I came across the mysterious Club de Berne. As any historian would do, I went to the archives in Berne to find out more about this secret intelligence group. In a memorandum written in 1978 to a Swiss minister of interior I read about the code word 'Kilowatt', which was used for the secret telecommunication channel between the Club de Berne intelligence agencies. When I put 'Kilowatt' in the search engine of the Swiss National Archives, several entries appeared containing thousands of archival documents. After consulting these documents, it dawned on me: I have uncovered the most extensive intelligence-sharing database currently available to researchers!

Absolutely fascinating research questions emerged from these records. How do the international relations of intelligence agencies work? Do secret links across national agencies operate differently from official diplomatic relations? When everything can be kept secret, and hence does not need to be justified publicly, is there a different foreign political logic at play? These questions gripped me and eventually led me to the topic of this book.

When the European Research Council (ERC) granted me a Marie Curie Senior Researcher fellowship, I had the time and resources to try and find the answers to these questions. I am extremely grateful to the ERC. Besides giving me time and resources, it also provided international distinction and demonstrated belief in the quality of my work.

During the fellowship, I was able to delve into the Club de Berne/ Kilowatt archive, which was a real pleasure. Every day I discovered a new element of how European intelligence agencies contributed to Operation Wrath of God and enthusiastically included it in the book. Eventually, I was able to piece together the overall picture. To my readers I would like to say: I hope the book will be as much fun to read as it has been to write.

ACKNOWLEDGEMENTS

There are numerous people and institutions to whom I owe gratitude for their help and support while writing this book. At Cambridge University Press, I would like to express thanks to Michael Watson. He steered the book through peer review and, together with Rosa Martin, ensured a very smooth publication process. I would also like to extend my gratitude to the three anonymous reviewers of the book, who provided constructive feedback and helped me improve it. I further had the opportunity to discuss this research project with numerous friends and colleagues, who kindly gave me their thoughts, feedback, and encouragement. I would like to thank Natasha Telepneva, Marco Wyss, Damien van Puyvelde, Sten Rynning, Christoph Meyer, Geoff Roberts, and Mike Goodman. Furthermore, Lisa Komar has done a fantastic job proofreading the book.

Finally, to my family, I owe everything. My husband, Nat, is absolutely amazing and his unshakeable belief in me inspires me and drives me forward. My favourite reply from him, when I thank him for believing in me, is: 'I don't believe in you. I *know* in you!' My parents are always there for me and have carefully read all my work. If they liked it, I thought, chances are that others would like it too. My kids are my world, and it is to them, Zenobia and Emrys, that this book is dedicated.

Notes

INTRODUCTION

1. Ronen Bergman, *Rise and Kill First: the Secret History of Israel's Targeted Assassinations* (New York: Random House, 2019), 150.

2. For an account in German about the Munich Olympics massacre and the German authorities' reaction, see Matthias Dahlke, *Demokratischer Staat und transnationaler Terrorismus Drei Wege zur Unnachgiebigkeit in Westeuropa 1972–1975* (Munich: Oldenbourg, 2011), 57–128. For the long-term political consequences of the attack, see Eva Oberloskamp, 'Das Olympia-Attentat 1972. Politische Lernprozesse im Umgang mit dem transnationalen Terrorismus', *Vierteljahrshefte für Zeitgeschichte*, 60/3 (2012), 321–352; Kay Schiller and Christopher Young, *The 1972 Munich Olympics and the Making of Modern Germany* (Berkeley: University of California Press, 2010), 194–207. See also David Clay Large, *Munich 1972: Tragedy, Terror and Triumph at the Olympic Games* (New York: Rowman and Littlefield, 2012), 201–248; Sven Felix Kellerhoff, *Anschlag auf Olympia: Was 1972 in München wirklich geschah* (Darmstadt: Wissenschaftliche Buchgesellschaft, 2022). For an account of the attack from the Palestinian perspective, see Paul Thomas Chamberlin, *The Global Offensive: the United States, the Palestine Liberation Organization, and the Making of the Post-Cold War Order* (Oxford University Press, 2012), 142.

3. 'Operation Wrath of God' was not a term used by Mossad at the time. Later publications about the kill mission coined the operation's name; see Bergman, *Rise and Kill First*, 663.

4. 'Liaison' is the term used in intelligence studies to mean intelligence cooperation arrangements.

5. For an account of the creation of the Club de Berne and its cooperation mechanisms in the 1970s, see Aviva Guttmann, *The Origins of International Counterterrorism: Switzerland at the Forefront of Crisis Negotiations, Multilateral Diplomacy, and Intelligence Cooperation (1969–1977)* (Leiden: Brill, 2018); part III is about the Club de Berne.

6. If interested in the early workings of Club de Berne intelligence cooperation, see Aviva Guttmann, 'Combatting Terror in Europe: Euro-Israeli Counterterrorism Intelligence Cooperation in the Club de Berne (1971–1972)', *Intelligence and National Security*, 33/2 (2018), 158–175; Guttmann, 'Secret Wires across the Mediterranean:

the Club de Berne, Euro-Israeli Counterterrorism, and Swiss "Neutrality"', *International History Review*, 40/4 (2018), 814–833; Guttmann, 'Turning Oil into Blood: Western Intelligence, Libyan Covert Actions, and Palestinian Terrorism (1973–74)', *Journal for Strategic Studies*, 45/6–7 (2022), 993–1020.

7. For an account of the Club de Berne's function in recent years, see Oldrich Bures, 'Informal Counterterrorism Arrangements in Europe: Beauty by Variety or Duplicity by Abundance?' *Cooperation and Conflict*, 47/4 (2012), 495–518, 502; John D. Occhipinti, 'Still Moving toward a European FBI? Re-Examining the Politics of EU Police Cooperation', *Intelligence and National Security*, 30/2, (2015) 234–258, 241.

8. For a journalistic investigation of the Club de Berne and its importance in today's intelligence-sharing landscape, see Jan Jirát and Lorenz Naegeli, 'Der geheime Club der geheimen Dienste', *Wochenzeitung*, 05.03.2020 and the translation into English, 'The Club de Berne: a Black Box of Growing Intelligence Cooperation', by the independent thinktank about:intel, 01.04.2020, https://aboutintel.eu/the-club-de-berne/.

9. Club de Berne messages were sent in English, French, Italian, and German. All translations into English were done by the author.

10. For archival records about the Club de Berne, see Swiss Federal Archives (SFA) ['Schweizerisches Bundesarchiv'], E4320C#1994/77#479*, *Terrorismus / BERNER KLUB / (5)39/5*, 1978–1989.

11. For archival records, filed by year, about the Kilowatt cables, see SFA, E4320-07C#1994/349#806*, *Eingang* KILOWATT, 1971–1972 [this archive record will be referred to as SFA, E4320-07C, Kilowatt, 1971–1972]. These Kilowatt records from 1971 to 1974 have been digitised and can be accessed online via the search engine of the SFA. Occasionally cables will be referenced that were sent by Swiss intelligence to the Kilowatt members. For these records, see SFA, E4320-07C#1994/349#812*, *Ausgang* KILOWATT, 1971–1977 [this archive record will be referred to as SFA, E4320-07C, Kilowatt *Sent by Switzerland*].

12. The Kilowatt members agreed to send all messages to the entire group; today's equivalent would be to 'copy' everyone into an email. Therefore, it is possible to understand cooperation as a whole by consulting the cables that the Swiss received and sent through the Kilowatt communication channel.

13. One of the few studies that looks at intelligence cooperation and targeted assassinations is J. Patrice McSherry, *Predatory States: Operation Condor and Covert War in Latin America* (New York: Rowman and Littlefield, 2005).

14. The first publication about Operation Wrath of God was by David B. Tinnin and Dag Christensen: *The Hit Team* (New York: Dell, 1977). The next was by George Jonas: *Vengeance: the True Story of an Israeli Counter-terrorist Team* (Toronto: HarperCollins, 1984). However, the veracity of *Vengeance* has strongly been questioned and the events as they were described in the book seem highly unrealistic; see Philip Taubman, 'Book on Israeli Avenger-Spy Questioned', *New York Times*, 02.05.1984: https://www.nytimes.com/1984/05/02/books/

book-on-israeli-avenger-spy-questioned.html. *Vengeance* was nevertheless the basis for Steven Spielberg's movie *Munich.*

15. David Hoffman reported on the BBC's interview for the *Washington Post*: 'Israeli Confirms Assassination of Munich Massacre Plotters', *Washington Post,* 24.11.1993.

16. Aaron J. Klein, *Striking Back: the 1972 Munich Olympics Massacre and Israel's Deadly Response* (New York: Random House, 2005); Simon Reeve, *One Day in September: the Full Story of the 1972 Munich Olympics Massacre and the Israeli Revenge Operation 'Wrath of God'* (New York: Skyhorse, 2011). These two books are the most comprehensive accounts of Operation Wrath of God.

17. Bergman, *Rise and Kill First*; Marc E. Vargo, *Mossad: Six Landmark Missions of the Israeli Intelligence Agency, 1960–1990* (Jefferson, N.C.: McFarland, 2015); Dan Raviv and Yossi Melman, *Every Spy a Prince: the Complete History of Israel's Intelligence Community* (Boston: Houghton Mifflin, 1990); Ian Black and Benny Morris, *Israel's Secret Wars: a History of Israel's Intelligence Services* (New York: Grove, 1991).

18. Some of this book's preliminary findings have been presented in Aviva Guttmann, 'Mossad's Accomplices: How Israel Relied on Foreign Intelligence Agencies to Organise its Killing Campaigns', *English Historical Review* (in press).

19. Bergman, *Rise and Kill First*, 156.

20. For works that research the relations between Eastern and Western bloc countries and armed groups, see Adrian Hänni, Thomas Riegler, and Przemysław Gasztold, eds., *Terrorism in the Cold War*, 2 vols. (London: I.B. Tauris, 2020–2021). See also Natalia Telepneva, *Cold War Liberation: the Soviet Union and the Collapse of the Portuguese Empire in Africa, 1961–1975* (Chapel Hill: University of North Carolina Press, 2022). For the East German context, see also Lutz Maeke, *DDR und PLO: Die Palästinapolitik des SED-Staates* (Berlin: De Gruyter, 2017); Jeffrey Herf, *Undeclared Wars with Israel: East Germany and the West German Far Left, 1967–1989* (Cambridge University Press, 2016).

21. The majority of works on covert action focus on CIA or MI6 secret interventions; see, for instance, Rory Cormac, *Disrupt and Deny: Spies, Special Forces, and the Secret Pursuit of British Foreign Policy* (Oxford University Press, 2021); Lindsey A. O'Rourke, *Covert Regime Change: America's Secret Cold War* (Ithaca: Cornell University Press, 2018); Michael Poznansky, *In the Shadow of International Law: Secrecy and Regime Change in the Postwar World* (Oxford University Press, 2020); see also William J. Daugherty, 'Covert Action: Strengths and Weakness', in *The Oxford Handbook of National Security Intelligence,* edited by Loch K. Johnson (Oxford University Press, 2010), 608–628; Rory Cormac, Calder Walton, and Damien van Puyvelde, 'What Constitutes Successful Covert Action? Evaluating Unacknowledged Interventionism in Foreign Affairs', *Review of International Studies*, 48/1 (2022), DOI: doi.org/10.1017/S0260210521000231.

22. A few case studies exist dealing with specific bilateral intelligence cooperation during moments of crisis, such as the case of Franco-German cooperation during the Algerian war; see Mathilde von Bülow, 'Franco-German Intelligence Cooperation and the Internationalization of Algeria's War of Independence (1954–62)', *Intelligence and National Security*, 28/3 (2013), 397–419. See also Hugues Canuel, 'French Aspirations and Anglo-Saxon Suspicions: France, Signals Intelligence and the UK–USA Agreement at the Dawn of the Cold War', *Journal of Intelligence History*, 12/1 (2013), 76–92. Another interesting case using recently declassified sources is cooperation among several Western countries – the United Kingdom, New Zealand, and Canada – during the 1979 Iranian hostage crisis: Don Munton and Miriam Matejova, 'Spies without Borders? Western Intelligence Liaison, the Tehran Hostage Affair and Iran's Islamic Revolution', *Intelligence and National Security*, 27/5 (2012), 739–760. Another case study was published about a multilateral signals intelligence liaison called Maximator (named after the beer that its founders were drinking); see Bart Jacobs, 'Maximator: European Signals Intelligence Cooperation, from a Dutch Perspective', *Intelligence and National Security*, 35/5 (2020), 659–668.

23. For works that see intelligence cooperation as state-centred praxis, only happening on a case-by-case basis, and according to a strict cost–benefit logic, see Melinda Hass and Keren Yarhi-Milo, 'To Disclose or Deceive? Sharing Secret Information between Aligned States', *International Security*, 45/3 (Winter 2020/2021), 122–161; James Igoe Walsh, *The International Politics of Intelligence Sharing* (New York: Columbia University Press, 2012); Jennifer E. Sims, 'Foreign Intelligence Liaison: Devils, Deals, and Details', *International Journal of Intelligence and CounterIntelligence*, 19/2 (2006), 195–217; H. Bradford Westerfield, 'America and the World of Intelligence Liaison', *Intelligence and National Security*, 11/3 (1996), 523–560; Chris Clough, '*Quid Pro Quo*: the Challenges of International Strategic Intelligence Cooperation', *International Journal of Intelligence and CounterIntelligence*, 17/4 (2004), 601–613; Don Munton and Karima Fredj, 'Sharing Secrets: a Game Theoretic Analysis of International Intelligence Cooperation', *International Journal of Intelligence and CounterIntelligence*, 26/4 (2013), 666–692; Stéphane Lefebvre, 'The Difficulties and Dilemmas of International Intelligence Cooperation', *International Journal of Intelligence and CounterIntelligence*, 16/4 (2003), 527–542; Sir Stephen Lander, 'International Intelligence Cooperation: an Inside Perspective', *Cambridge Review of International Affairs*, 17/3 (2004), 481–493.

24. For works that approach the study of intelligence cooperation on different levels, particularly the organisational level of intelligence agencies or individuals as drivers for cooperation, see Björn Fägersten, 'Sharing Secrets: Explaining International Intelligence Cooperation' (dissertation, Department of Political Science, Lund University, 2010); Didier Bigo, 'Shared Secrecy in a Digital Age and a Transnational World', *Intelligence and National Security*, 34/3 (2019), 379–394; Bures, 'Informal Counterterrorism

Arrangements in Europe'. See also Michael Herman's analysis of intelligence cooperation from a practitioner's view in *Intelligence Power in Peace and War* (Cambridge University Press, 1996), 200–218; Sophia Hoffmann, 'Circulation, Not Cooperation: Towards a New Understanding of Intelligence Agencies as Transnationally Constituted Knowledge Providers', *Intelligence and National Security*, 36/6 (2021), 807–826.

25. Covert diplomacy is an understudied state practice and has mainly been researched in the context of covert operations. See Len Scott, 'Secret Intelligence, Covert Action and Clandestine Diplomacy', *Intelligence and National Security*, 19/2 (2004), 322–341, 330. A case of covert diplomacy that is relatively well-researched is British intelligence in the Northern Ireland peace process; see Thomas Leahy, *The Intelligence War against the IRA* (Cambridge University Press, 2020); Peter Taylor, *Brits: the War against the IRA* (London: Bloomsbury, 2001); Michael Smith, *New Cloak, Old Dagger: How Britain's Spies Came in from the Cold* (London: Indigo, 1996), 211–230. For a case study of clandestine diplomacy during a crisis, see Timothy Fursenko and Aleksandr Naftali's account of the Cuban Missile Crisis: *'One Hell of a Gamble': Khrushchev, Castro, Kennedy and the Cuban Missile Crisis, 1958–1964* (London: Norton, 1997). The authors show, based on documentary evidence from both sides of the Iron Curtain, how secret backchannels were used to defuse this crisis.

26. For works about the Palestinian armed struggle, see Yazid Sayigh, *Armed Struggle and the Search for State: the Palestinian National Movement, 1949–1993* (Oxford University Press, 2011); Chamberlin, *The Global Offensive*; Wendy Pearlman, *Violence, Nonviolence, and the Palestinian National Movement* (Cambridge University Press, 2014); John W. Amos, *Palestinian Resistance: Organization of a Nationalist Movement* (New York: Pergamon, 1980); Ariel Merari and Shlomi Elad, *International Dimension of Palestinian Terrorism* (New York: Routledge, 2021; first edition 1988); and for Black September specifically, see Christopher Dobson, *Black September: Its Short, Violent History* (London: Hale, 1975).

27. For analysis of some of the events mentioned in this book and a look at what factors contributed to the successful prevention of the terrorist plots, see Aviva Guttmann, '"We Have Successfully Neutralised an Attack": Historical Case Studies in Terrorism Prevention through Cooperation', *Terrorism and Political Violence* (2024), 1–17, https://doi.org/10.1080/09546553.2024.2400157.

28. For works in the study of terrorism innovation, see Adam Dolnik, *Understanding Terrorist Innovation: Technology, Tactics and Global Trends* (New York: Routledge, 2007); Yannick Veilleux-Lepage, *How Terror Evolves: the Emergence and Spread of Terrorist Techniques* (Lanham, Md: Rowman and Littlefield, 2020); Paul Gill, John Horgan, Samuel T. Hunter, and Lily D. Cushenbery, 'Malevolent Creativity in Terrorist Organizations', *Journal of Creative Behavior*, 47/2 (2013), 125–151; João Ricardo Faria, 'Terrorist Innovations and Anti-Terrorist Policies', *Terrorism and Political Violence*, 18/1 (2006), 47–56.

1 SETTING THE SCENE

1. Vargo, *Mossad: Six Landmark Missions*, 84; Sayigh, *Armed Struggle*, 309; Randall David Law, *Terrorism: a History* (Cambridge: Polity, 2018), 223.
2. In Arabic, the group was called Munaẓẓamat Aylūl al-Aswad.
3. Tinnin and Christensen, *The Hit Team*, 41.
4. Klein, *Striking Back*, 31.
5. Dobson, *Black September*, 12–13.
6. Merari and Elad, *International Dimension of Palestinian Terrorism*, 97.
7. For a discussion of the Club de Berne files about this attack, see Guttmann, *Origins of International Counterterrorism*, 213–214.
8. Klein, *Striking Back*, 32.
9. For Israel's lack of intelligence on Black September prior to Munich, see *ibid.*, 120.
10. Bruce Hoffman, *Inside Terrorism* (New York: Columbia University Press, 2006), 3.
11. Schiller and Young, *The 1972 Munich Olympics*, 194–207.
12. Hoffman, *Inside Terrorism*, 69.
13. Alex P. Schmid and Janny de Graaf, *Violence as Communication: Insurgent Terrorism and the Western News Media* (London: Sage, 1983), 31.
14. Klein, *Striking Back*, 82.
15. Baruch Kimmerling and Joel S. Migdal, *The Palestinian People: a History* (Cambridge, Mass.: Harvard University Press, 2003), 258, note 29.
16. This view of Black September as a covert branch of Fatah is shared by the majority of scholars, both among experts on the Arab–Israeli conflict and among terrorism scholars. See Eliezer Ben-Rafael, *Israel–Palestine: a Guerrilla Conflict in International Politics* (Westport: Greenwood, 1987), 38; Benni Morris, *Righteous Victims: a History of the Zionist–Arab Conflict, 1881–2001* (New York: Vintage, 2001), 379; Hoffman, *Inside Terrorism*, 67.
17. Authors of this view include Abu Iyad and Eric Rouleau, *My Home, My Land: a Narrative of the Palestinian Struggle* (New York: Times Books, 1981), 131–132; Helena Cobban. *The Palestinian Liberation Organisation: People, Power, and Politics* (Cambridge University Press, 1984), 55. Sayigh puts Salameh as the driving force behind the creation of Black September, but adds that recruits came from various organisations not just Fatah. Sayigh also assesses that it is not clear whether Khalaf (the second-in-command after Arafat) had helped in the creation of Black September; Sayigh, *Armed Struggle*, 307, 309.
18. Herf, *Undeclared Wars with Israel*, 167.
19. For Arafat condoning Black September terrorism including the Munich massacre, see Sayigh, *Armed Struggle*, 309; Herf, *Undeclared Wars with Israel*, 167.
20. When, in March 1973, Black September attacked the Saudi embassy in Khartoum (see Chapter 5), evidence was found that local PLO structures and operatives helped carry out the attack. The Lufthansa Kiel hijacking (see Chapter 3) was allegedly also organised with the help of Fatah; Morris, *Righteous Victims*, 379.
21. Sayigh, *Armed Struggle*, 310.

22. For a British intelligence assessment suggesting that Black September was the covert branch of Fatah, see Kilowatt cable no. 5005, sent from MI5, 'Arab Terrorist Activities', comment: 'reference our watt 5004 of 1.9.72', 06.09.1972, in SFA, E4320-07C, Kilowatt, 1971–1972. For the same assessment by the West Germans, see Kilowatt cable no. 1032, sent from the BfV, 'Leiter der Organisation Schwarzer September', 25.09.1972, in SFA, E4320-07C, Kilowatt, 1971–1972 (translated from German by the author). These intelligence assessments will be discussed further below in Chapter 2. For US assessments concerning Black September being part of Fatah, see cable sent by US embassy in Tehran to Washington, 'Arab Government Support for Black September Organisation', 19 March 1973, in US National Archives, Access to Archival Databases (AAD), Series: Central Foreign Policy Files, created 7/1/1973–12/31/1979, document-ing the period ca. 1973–12/31/1979 – Record Group 5; https://aad.archives.gov/aad/createpdf?rid=79977&dt=2472&dl=1345.
23. This poem was allegedly part of an 864 BC agreement between the Greek cities of Elis, Sparta, and Pisa to allow a Sacred Truce so that the Olympiad could take place every four years. Three months in advance, it was forbidden to attack the territory where the Olympic games were to take place to allow athletes and pilgrims to safely travel there and organise the games.
24. Black and Morris, *Israel's Secret Wars*, 271.
25. *Jerusalem Post*, 25 September 1972, and *Yediot Aharonot*, 17 November 1989, cited in Black and Morris, *Israel's Secret Wars*, 271.
26. Victor Ostrovsky and Claire Hoy, *By Way of Deception: the Making and Unmaking of a Mossad Officer* (New York: St. Martin's, 1991), 178; Klein, *Striking Back*, 84.
27. Raviv and Melman, *Every Spy a Prince*, 185–186.
28. Yoel Marcus was the first journalist to expose the existence and activities of 'Committee X' in *Haaretz*, 10.06.1986.
29. Tinnin and Christensen, *The Hit Team*, 51.
30. Peter Taylor, *States of Terror: Democracy and Political Violence* (London: Penguin, 1994), 14.
31. For an analysis of the concept of implausible deniability of covert actions, see Rory Cormac and Richard J. Aldrich, 'Grey Is the New Black: Covert Action and Implausible Deniability', *International Affairs*, 94/3 (2018), 477–494.
32. Mike Harari quoted in Bergman, *Rise and Kill First*, 141.
33. Reeve, *One Day in September*, 172–173.
34. *Ibid.*
35. Samuel Tobias Lachs, *Humanism in Talmud and Midrash* (Rutherford: Fairleigh Dickinson University Press, 1993), 55.
36. Black and Morris, *Israel's Secret Wars*, 272.
37. Reeve, *One Day in September*, 168.
38. 'Caesarea' was Mossad's operations division and 'Kidon' (Hebrew for 'bayo-net') was the killing unit within it. See Bergman, *Rise and Kill First*, 153–155, for the creation and development of Kidon.

39. Tinnin and Christensen, *The Hit Team*, 53–54.
40. Vargo, *Mossad: Six Landmark Missions*, 67
41. Raviv and Melman, *Every Spy a Prince*, 186; Reeve, *One Day in September*, 169.
42. Bergman, *Rise and Kill First*, 154.
43. Note from the Federal Police [author not mentioned], 'Der Berner Klub', and added next to the title in handwriting 'gegründet 1969', [place not mentioned], 24.05.1989, in SFA, E4320C#1994/77#479*, *Terrorismus / BERNER KLUB / (5)39/5*, 1978–1989.
44. Note [author not mentioned], 'Vertraulich. Notiz über den Berner Klub', Bern, 06.04.1978, in SFA, E4001E#1985/152#348*, *Terrorismus: Zusammenarbeit mit dem Ausland*, 1972–1982.
45. Policy briefing note from Rudolf Gerber, at the time attorney general, for Federal Councillor Kurt Furgler in view of an upcoming ministerial meeting, Bern, 04.02.1980, in SFA, E4001E#1985/152#345*, *Terrorismus: Verschiedenes*, 1972–1982.
46. Note from the Federal Police [author not mentioned], 'Geheim. Berner Klub. Partnerdienste', [date and place not mentioned, likely to have been written in 1989], in SFA, E4320C#1994/77#479*, *Terrorismus / BERNER KLUB / (5)39/5*, 1978–1989.
47. Circular note for the commanders and inspectors in the Swiss Federal Police, 'Berner-Club: Subversion/Terrorismus/Spionage', 10.06.1980, SFA, E4320C#1994/77#479*, *Terrorismus / BERNER KLUB / (5)39/5*, 1978–1989.
48. See 'Arms Smuggling via Mercedes Sales' in Chapter 5.
49. Letter by Dr Amstein to Federal Councillor Furgler, 'Notiz an Herrn Bundesrat Dr. Furgler', Bern, 03.04.1973, in SFA, E4001E#1985/152#348*, *Terrorismus: Zusammenarbeit mit dem Ausland*, 1972–1982.
50. In the US, the FBI gave a new priority to counterterrorism, including targeting Arab Americans; see Daniel S. Chard, *Nixon's War at Home: the FBI, Leftist Guerrillas, and the Origins of Counterterrorism* (Chapel Hill: University of North Carolina Press, 2021), 211–228.
51. The term 'terrorist album' was used often, such as in Kilowatt cable no. 6081, sent from Mossad, 'Ahmad Misbah Omrin', comment: 'date of information: 3 January 1973', 19.01.1973, in SFA, E4320-07C, Kilowatt, 1973.
52. The term 'register' was used in Kilowatt cable no. 6119, sent from Mossad, 'Terrorists / Fatah squad armed with revolvers fitted with silencers leaves for Europe', comment: 'source: reliability untested, with access', 02.07.1973, in SFA, E4320 07C, Kilowatt, 1973.
53. Kilowatt cable no. 6143, sent from Mossad, 'Intended attacks by the PFLP-GC (Jibril) in Europe', comment: 'source: reliable with access to subject', 20.09.1973, in SFA, E4320-07C, Kilowatt, 1973.
54. Kilowatt cable no. 45, sent from BuPo, 'Kilowatt – Meldungen', comment: 'an Orbis Paris von BuPo CH', 09.05.1973, in SFA, E4320-07C, Kilowatt *Sent by Switzerland*, 1971–1977.

55. For some cables, Club de Berne archives also include the previous drafts of the text before the cable was sent. Such was the case with a cable sent by Swiss intelligence about a cover name used by Mohamed Boudia (see Chapter 7), Kilowatt cable no. 44, sent from BuPo, 'Identification du soi-disant R. Bertin', 07.02.1973, in SFA, E4320-07C, Kilowatt *Sent by Switzerland*, 1971–1977.

56. An Italian cable was sent to Swiss intelligence near its close of business time. Swiss intelligence immediately replied and asked for cables to be sent during its business hours; Kilowatt cable no. 7040, sent from the Italian SISDE, 'Aéroport de Fiumicino-Rome. Découverte de 4 sacs contenant des armes et des explosifs', 27.11.1972, in SFA, E4320-07C, Kilowatt, 1971–1972 (translated from French by the author).

57. Kilowatt cable no. 5026, sent from MI5, 'Ismail plus five others', comment: 'routine, confidential', 08.12.1972, in SFA, E4320-07C, Kilowatt, 1971–1972.

2 PREPARING THE KILL LIST

1. Black and Morris, *Israel's Secret Wars*, 271.
2. Klein, *Striking Back*, 120.
3. Kilowatt cable no. 5004, sent from MI5, 'Yousef Issa el-Bandak, born 20.7.1924 in Bethlehem, Arab League representative Buenos Aires, Argentina', comment: 'flash, secret', 01.09.1972, in SFA, E4320-07C, Kilowatt, 1971–1972.
4. Klein, *Striking Back*, 79.
5. Kilowatt cable no. 9022, sent from the Dutch BVD, 'Attack in München, 5-9-72', comment: 'confidential', 06.09.1972, in SFA, E4320-07C, Kilowatt, 1971–1972.
6. *Ibid.*
7. Kilowatt cable no. 1016, sent from the German BfV, 'Anschlag auf olympisches Dorf in München', 06.09.1972, in SFA, E4320-07C, Kilowatt, 1971–1972 (translated from German by the author).
8. *Ibid.*
9. Kilowatt cable no. 5006, sent from MI5, 'Reference your telegram no. watt 1016/72 of 6.9.72', comment: 'priority, secret', 07.09.1972, in SFA, E4320-07C, Kilowatt, 1971–1972.
10. Kilowatt cable no. 1024, sent from the German BfV, 'Ermittlungsverfahren zur Aufklärung des Attentats vor München', 13.09.1972, in SFA, E4320-07C, Kilowatt, 1971–1972 (translated from German by the author).
11. *Ibid.*
12. Sayigh, *Armed Struggle*, 309; Bergman, *Rise and Kill First*, 144. See 'Black September Organisation' in Chapter 1 for further background information on the relationship between Fatah and Black September.
13. Kilowatt cable no. 7024, sent from the Italian SISDE, 'Massacre pendant les jeux olympiques', 21.09.1972, in SFA, E4320-07C, Kilowatt, 1971–1972 (translated from French by the author).

14. Kilowatt cable no. 1051, sent from the German BfV, 'Anschlag im olympischen Dorf', comment: 'streng vertraulich – amtlich geheimhalten', 08.11.1972, in SFA, E4320-07C, Kilowatt, 1971–1972 (translated from German by the author).

15. Kilowatt cable no. 1022, sent from the German BfV, 'Anschlag im olympischen Dorf', 13.09.1972, in SFA, E4320-07C, Kilowatt, 1971–1972 (translated from German by the author).

16. See 'Updating the Murderers: The Assassination of Wael Zwaiter' in Chapter 3.

17. Kilowatt cable no. 1021, sent from the German BfV, 'Mordanschlag auf das olympische Dorf in München am 5.9.1972', 11.09.1972, in SFA, E4320-07C, Kilowatt, 1971–1972 (translated from German by the author).

18. For Libyan support for Black September and cooperation with Palestinian terrorist groups, see 'Libyan Support for Black September Attacks' in Chapter 5.

19. It was the Lufthansa Kiel hijacking that freed the Munich terrorists; see 'Lufthansa Kiel Hijacking and German–Israeli Covert Diplomacy' in Chapter 3. For the cable where Libyan support for the hijacking was mentioned, see Kilowatt cable no. 1056, sent from the German BfV, 'Entführung einer Lufthansamaschine am 29.10.1972', 20.11.1972, in SFA, E4320-07C, Kilowatt, 1971–1972.

20. Kilowatt cable no. 6096, sent from Mossad, 'Fatah group leaves for Europe. Source: reliable. Sub-Source: with access to terrorist circles', 12.03.1973, in E4320-07C, Kilowatt, 1973.

21. Ibid.

22. Kilowatt cable no. 1116, sent from the German BfV, 'Angebliche Einreise von arabischen Terroristen in die Bundesrepublik Deutschland', comment: 'nur für den Dienstgebrauch', 04.09.1973, in SFA, E4320-07C, Kilowatt, 1973 (translated from German by the author).

23. Kilowatt cable no. 1024, sent from the German BfV, 'Ermittlungsverfahren zur Aufklärung des Attentats vor München', 13.09.1972, in SFA, E4320-07C, Kilowatt, 1971–1972 (translated from German by the author).

24. Kilowatt cable no. 6048, sent from Mossad, [cable had no title], 11.09.1972, in E4320-07C, Kilowatt, 1971–1972.

25. Bergman mentions Abu Daoud's real name as Mohammed Oudeh; Bergman, Rise and Kill First, 171.

26. Kilowatt cable no. 1031, sent from the German BfV, 'Anschlag auf olympisches Dorf in München', 25.09.1972, in SFA, E4320-07C, Kilowatt, 1971–1972 (translated from German by the author).

27. Ibid.

28. Kilowatt cable no. 1020, sent from the German BfV, 'Terroranschlag auf olympisches Forf [sic] in München', comment: 'geheim – amtlich geheimhalten', 11.09.1972, in SFA, E4320-07C, Kilowatt, 1971–1972 (translated from German by the author).

29. Kilowatt cable no. 1028, sent from the German BfV, 'Terroranschlag im olympischen Dorf am 5.9.1972', 18.09.1972, in SFA, E4320-07C, Kilowatt, 1971–1972 (translated from German by the author).

30. Kilowatt cable no. 6049, sent from Mossad, 'Indication of terrorist activity', comment: 'top priority', 12.09.1972, in E4320-07C, Kilowatt, 1971–1972.
31. Kilowatt cable no. 5004, sent from MI5, 'Yousef Issa el-Bandak, born 20-7.1924 in Bethlehem, Arab League representative Buenos Aires, Argentina', comment: 'flash/secret', 01.09.1972, in SFA, E4320-07C, Kilowatt, 1971–1972.
32. *Ibid.*
33. Kilowatt cable no. 5005, sent from MI5, 'Arab terrorist activities', comment: 'reference our watt 5004 of 1.9.72', 06.09.1972, in SFA, E4320-07C, Kilowatt, 1971–1972 (this cable was also mentioned in Chapter 1, note 22).
34. Kilowatt cable no. 7021, sent from the Italian SISDE, 'Yousef Issa el-Bandak né à Betlem 20.7.1924', 08.09.1972, in SFA, E4320-07C, Kilowatt, 1971–1972 (translated from French by the author). At the top right of this cable, Swiss archives put a stamp in blue ink that said: 'Für jede Akten-Edition gesperrt'. This meant that it was forbidden to include this document in any published volume of archival documents. This stresses the secret nature of these exchanges about el-Bandak.
35. *Ibid.*
36. Kilowatt cable no. 0031, sent from BuPo, 'Mouvement d'éléments arabes suspects – el Bandak, prénom Youssif, né en 1924', 03.10.1972, in SFA, E4320-07C, Kilowatt *Sent by Switzerland*, 1971–1977.
37. Kilowatt cable no. 5012, sent from MI5, 'reference your telegram no watt 0031 of 3.10.72', comment: 'routine, secret', 05.10.1972, in SFA, E4320-07C, Kilowatt, 1971–1972.
38. Kilowatt cable no. 5024, sent from MI5, 'Youssif al-Bandak', comment: 'reference your kilowatt 0031 of 3.10.72', comment: 'routine, secret', 01.06.1973, in SFA, E4320-07C, Kilowatt, 1973.
39. *Ibid.*
40. Kilowatt cable no. 7059, sent from the Italian SISDE, 'Mouvement d'Arabes suspects', comment: 'reference watt 0031 du 3.10.72', 19.02.1973, in SFA, E4320-07C, Kilowatt, 1973 (translated from French by the author; the original French term for terrorism host was 'métier de logeuse').
41. *Ibid.*
42. Kilowatt cable no. 5037, sent from MI5, 'Yousef Issa al-Bandak', comment: 'immediate, secret', 11.07.1973, in SFA, E4320-07C, Kilowatt, 1973.
43. See 'Cooperation after Lillehammer: Business as Usual' in Chapter 8.
44. Kilowatt cable no. 7026, sent from the Italian SISDE, 'Arabes suspects en rapport au massacre de Munich (Bavière)', 02.10.1972, in SFA, E4320-07C, Kilowatt, 1971–1972 (translated from French by the author).
45. For the terrorist cell in Yugoslavia, see 'Two Attempts at Aircraft Sabotage in Rome' in Chapter 3.
46. Kilowatt cable no. 6053, sent from Mossad, 'Terrorists. Dispatch of terrorists to Europe. Source: not always reliable. In contact with terrorist circles', 02.10.1972, in SFA, E4320-07C, Kilowatt, 1971–1972.

47. *Ibid.*
48. Kilowatt cable no. 8000, sent from SREL, 'Passage d'un ressortissant Arabe suspect à Luxembourg', 27.09.1972, in SFA, E4320-07C, Kilowatt, 1971–1972 (translated from French by the author).
49. Kilowatt cable no. 1037, sent from the German BfV, [cable had no title], comment: 'vs-vertraulich, amtlich geheimhalten', 30.09.1972, in SFA, E4320-07C, Kilowatt, 1971–1972 (translated from German by the author).
50. Kilowatt cable no. 7022, sent from the Italian SISDE, 'Rome. 19–29 September 1972 – conference of interparliamentary union', comment: 'trs msgg trés urg[ent]',16.09.1972, in SFA, E4320-07C, Kilowatt, 1971–1972.
51. Kilowatt cable no. 5005, sent from MI5, 'Arab terrorist activities', comment: 'reference our watt 5004 of 1.9.72', 06.09.1972, in SFA, E4320-07C, Kilowatt, 1971–1972 (this cable was also mentioned in Chapter 1, note 22, and above, note 33).
52. Kilowatt cable no. 1032, sent from the German BfV, 'Leiter der Organisation Schwarzer September', 25.09.1972, in SFA, E4320-07C, Kilowatt, 1971–1972 (translated from German by the author) [hereafter cited as 'BfV cable no. 1032'].
53. *Ibid.*
54. *Ibid.*
55. Salameh's role as a Fatah intelligence officer is confirmed by secondary literature; see Bergman, *Rise and Kill First*, 170. For Club de Berne intelligence on Salameh, see 'Charges against Salameh' in Chapter 8.
56. BfV cable no. 1032.
57. Klein, *Striking Back*, 31–32. This need-to-know operational basis was also mentioned in contemporary journalistic publications such as John Kent Cooley, *Green March, Black September: the Story of the Palestinian Arabs* (London: Frank Cass, 1973).
58. Bergman, *Rise and Kill First*, 144–145.
59. Interview given by al-Gashey in the documentary film by Kevin Macdonald, 'One Day in September', 1999.
60. Kilowatt cable no. 1017, sent from the German BfV, 'Terroranschlag der PFLP in Europa', 07.09.1972, in SFA, E4320-07C, Kilowatt, 1971–1972 (translated from German by the author).
61. Kilowatt cable no. 1033, sent from the German BfV, 'Organisation "Schwarzer September". Neue Mitglieder von Operationsgruppen', 26.09.1972, in SFA, E4320-07C, Kilowatt, 1971–1972 (translated from German by the author).
62. Kilowatt [no cable number], sent from the German BfV, 'Fahndung nach Terroristen', comment: 'nur für den Dienstgebrauch', 15.09.1972; Kilowatt [no number], sent from the German BfV, 'Eine befreundete Stelle teilte soeben mit', 30.09.1972; Kilowatt cable no. 1036, sent from the German BfV, 'Arabische Terroristen', 29.09.1972; all three in SFA, E4320-07C, Kilowatt, 1971–1972 (translated from German by the author).

63. Kilowatt cable no. 7021, sent from the Italian SISDE, 'Presumable attack against Jumbo Jet Muenchen-USA', 09.09.1972, in SFA, E4320-07C, Kilowatt, 1971–1972.

64. *Ibid.*

65. Kilowatt cable no. 1019, sent from the German BfV, 'Sicherheit des Luftverkehrs', 11.09.1972; Kilowatt cable no. 1025, sent from the German BfV, 'Gefährdung des zivilen Luftverkehrs', 14.09.1972; Kilowatt cable no. 1026, sent from the German BfV, 'Gefährdung des zivilen Luftverkehrs', 15.09.1972; all three in SFA, E4320-07C, Kilowatt, 1971–1972 (translated from German by the author).

66. For the Lufthansa Kiel hijacking, see 'Lufthansa Kiel Hijacking and German–Israeli Covert Diplomacy' in Chapter 3.

67. Kilowatt cable no. 6050, sent from Shin Bet, 'Black September plans to carry out attacks', comment: 'most immediate', 15.09.1972, in E4320-07C, Kilowatt, 1971–1972.

68. Kilowatt cable no. 1034, sent from the German BfV, 'Beabsichtigte Flugzeugentführung durch die Organisation "Schwarzer September"', 29.09.1972, in SFA, E4320-07C, Kilowatt, 1971–1972.

69. Kilowatt cable no. 1039, sent from the German BfV, 'Geheim / amtlich geheimhalten / Information über Planung terroristischer Aktionen durch Palästinenser', 09.10.1972, in SFA, E4320-07C, Kilowatt, 1971–1972.

70. Kilowatt cable no. 6058, sent from Mossad, 'Terrorists – plans to kidnap children of Israeli diplomats', comment: 'reliable, with access to terrorist circles', 12.10.1972, in SFA, E4320-07C, Kilowatt, 1971–1972.

71. *Ibid.*

72. Kilowatt cable no. 6057, sent from Mossad, 'Terrorists attacks in Europe', 11.10.1972, in SFA, E4320-07C, Kilowatt, 1971–1972.

73. Kilowatt cable no. 5011, sent from MI5, 'Black September', comment: 'immediate, secret', 29.09.1972, in SFA, E4320-07C, Kilowatt, 1971–1972.

74. Kilowatt cable no. 1015, sent from the German BfV, 'Gefährdung des zivilen Luftverkehrs', 07.09.1972, in SFA, E4320-07C, Kilowatt, 1971–1972 (translated from German by the author).

75. Kilowatt cable no. 1018, sent from the German BfV, 'Geheim / amtlich geheimhalten. Planung arab. Terroristen', 08.09.1972, in SFA, E4320-07C, Kilowatt, 1971–1972 (translated from German by the author).

76. For an account of German–Israeli exchanges in the Club de Berne during and after the Munich Olympics attack, see Aviva Guttmann, 'Covert Diplomacy to Overcome a Crisis: West German and Israeli Intelligence after the Munich Olympics Attack', *Journal of Cold War Studies*, 25/4 (2023), 101–126.

77. For intelligence agencies countering the threat of letter bombs at the time, see also Gutttmann, *The Origins of International Counterterrorism*, 207–208, 210–213, 223–224.

78. Cables that warned about a batch of letter bombs and effectively prevented their delivery included Kilowatt cable no. 6509, sent from Mossad, 'letter bombs', 25.09.1972; Kilowatt cable no. 7029, sent from the Italian SISDE, 'Rome – lettre piégée', 07.10.1972; Kilowatt cable no. 1038, sent from the German BfV, 'Sprengstoffbrief-eingegangen beim jüdischen Altersheim in Düsseldorf', 09.10.1972; Kilowatt cable no. 1050, sent from the German BfV, 'Versendung von Sprengstoffbriefen und Briefen von sprengstoffverdächtigem Inhalt', 08.11.1972; Kilowatt cable no. 5020, sent from MI5, 'letter bombs', 10.11.1972; all in SFA, E4320-07C, Kilowatt, 1971–1972.

79. Kilowatt cable no. 5007, sent from MI5, 'flash, secret', 19.09.1972, in SFA, E4320-07C, Kilowatt, 1971–1972.

80. Kilowatt cable no. 5007 [same number as above, but a different cable], sent from MI5, 'flash, confidential', 19.09.1972, in SFA, E4320-07C, Kilowatt, 1971–1972.

81. Kilowatt cable no. 0023, sent from BuPo, 'Envoi de lettres piégées a la mission d'Israel a Genève', 20.09.1972, in SFA, E4320-07C, Kilowatt *Sent by Switzerland*, 1971–1977.

82. Kilowatt cable no. 0026, sent from BuPo, 'Zustellung von Sprengstoffbriefen an die israelische Mission in Genf', 21.09.1972, in SFA, E4320-07C, Kilowatt *Sent by Switzerland*, 1971–1977.

83. Kilowatt cable no. 6509, sent from Mossad, 'letter bombs', 25.09.1972, in SFA, E4320-07C, Kilowatt, 1971–1972. Club de Berne records suggest that this series of letters from Amsterdam was sent to London, Geneva, New York, Montreal, Brussels, and Paris. Journalist Aaron Klein claims that explosive letters from Amsterdam were also sent to Israeli diplomats in Ottawa, Vienna, Buenos Aires, Kinshasa, Jerusalem, and Tel Aviv; Klein, *Striking Back*, 95.

84. Kilowatt cable no. 6054, sent from Mossad, 'Departure for Europe of terrorists to carry out acts of sabotage', comment: 'source reliable, with access, some of his past reports proved to be accurate', 04.10.1972, in SFA, E4320-07C, Kilowatt, 1971–1972.

85. Kilowatt cable no. 9025, sent from the Dutch BVD, 'Letter-bombs', 13.10.1972, in SFA, E4320-07C, Kilowatt, 1971–1972.

86. Kilowatt cable no. 6056, sent from Mossad (reporting about the event in Düsseldorf), 'letter bombs', 09.10.1972, in SFA, E4320-07C, Kilowatt, 1971–1972.

87. Kilowatt cable no. 5017, sent from MI5, 'priority, secret', 03.11.1972, in SFA, E4320-07C, Kilowatt, 1971–1972.

88. Kilowatt cable no. 7030, sent from the Italian SISDE, 'Rome – Lettres explo sives', 12.10.1972, in SFA, E4320-07C, Kilowatt, 1971–1972. A few days later, Italian intelligence sent pictures of the letter bomb that reached Rome from Malaysia: Kilowatt cable no. 7031, sent from the Italian SISDE, 'Rome – Lettres explosives', 16.10.1972, in SFA, E4320-07C, Kilowatt, 1971–1972.

89. Kilowatt cable no. 9024, sent from the Dutch BVD, 'letter bombs', 11.10.1972, in SFA, E4320-07C, Kilowatt, 1971–1972.

NOTES TO PAGES 47–48

90. Kilowatt cable no. 0034, sent from BuPo, 'Bomben-Briefe', 16.10.1972, in SFA, E4320-07C, Kilowatt *Sent by Switzerland*, 1971–1977.

91. Kilowatt cable no. 1041, sent from the German BfV, 'Giftbrief an die israelische Botschaft in Bonn-Bad Godesberg', 19.10.1972, in SFA, E4320-07C, Kilowatt, 1971–1972.

92. German intelligence later confirmed that the letter contained poison and specified that it was sodium cyanide; Kilowatt cable no. 1057, sent from the German BfV, 'Verdächtige Briefsendungen an die israelische Botschaft in Bonn-Bad Godesberg am 2.10.1972', 29.11.1972, in SFA, E4320-07C, Kilowatt, 1971–1972.

93. Kilowatt cable no. 6055, sent from Mossad, 'Letter bombs', 05.10.1972, in SFA, E4320-07C, Kilowatt, 1971–1972.

94. Kilowatt cable 1048, first sent by the Dutch BVD to the German BfV, which forwarded it directly to the Swiss BuPo, 'Ribhi Halloum, Liste mit israelischen und jüdischen Namen und Anschrifen', 03.11.1972, in SFA, E4320-07C, Kilowatt, 1971–1972 (translated from German by the author). For more context about the arrest and the subsequent Club de Berne exchanges, see 'A Terrorist Cell in Latin America and Explosive Letters' in Chapter 3.

95. Kilowatt cable no. 6061, sent from Mossad, 'Letter bombs', 23.10.1972, in SFA, E4320-07C, Kilowatt, 1971–1972.

96. An example where Black September got the addresses via the *Jewish Year Book* was a batch of letter bombs sent from Singapore to Jewish organisations in Munich and Frankfurt in mid December 1972: Kilowatt cable no. 5028, sent from MI5, 'priority, confidential', 13.12.1972; Kilowatt cable no. 5029, sent from MI5, 'priority, confidential, Letter Bombs' 14.12.1972; Kilowatt cable no. 6070, sent from Mossad, 'Letter bombs', 15.12.1972; all three in SFA, E4320-07C, Kilowatt, 1971–1972.

97. Sayigh, *Armed Struggle*, 310.

98. Reeve, *One Day in September*, 152; Klein, *Striking Back*, 96. Klein claims further that Palestinian students in Stockholm and Bonn were hurt by Mossad's letter bombs, but this could not be confirmed by other sources.

99. Kilowatt cable no. 6011, sent from Mossad, 'explosive letters', 05.01.1972, in SFA, E4320-07C, Kilowatt, 1971–1972.

100. Kilowatt cable no. 5000, sent from MI5, 'immediate, secret, Parcel Bombs', 08.01.1973, SFA, E4320-07C, Kilowatt, 1973.

101. The last letter bomb of this wave was intercepted by Italian police on 23 January 1973. The letter was addressed to the Israeli consulate in Milan; Kilowatt cable no. 7047, sent from the Italian SISDE, 'Lettre suspecte piégée parvenue au consulat d'Israël à Milan', 23.01.1973, in SFA, E4320-07C, Kilowatt, 1973 (translated from French by the author).

102. Kilowatt cable no. 5013, sent from MI5, 'routine, secret, letter bombs' 03.04.1973, SFA, E4320-07C, Kilowatt, 1973.

103. For this, see 'Second Wave of Letter Bombs' in Chapter 8.

3 A FIRING SQUAD IN ROME AND FOUR BLACK
SEPTEMBER ATTACKS

1. Bergman, *Rise and Kill First*, 154.
2. Klein, *Striking Back*, 119; Vargo, *Mossad: Six Landmark Missions*, 107.
3. Reeve, *One Day in September*, 170.
4. Black and Morris, *Israel's Secret Wars*, 271. Black and Morris mention that Mossad also held Zwaiter responsible for the organisation of the very first terrorist hijacking, of an El Al plane that was taken to Algeria in August 1968. But the authors also suggest that he was 'more of an intellectual than a terrorist'. See also Vargo, *Mossad: Six Landmark Missions*, 108.
5. Bergman, *Rise and Kill First*, 156.
6. Kilowatt cable no. 6033, sent from Mossad, 'Planned attack on El Al plane at Copenhagen', 07.07.1972, in E4320-07C, Kilowatt, 1971–1972 [hereafter cited as 'Mossad cable no. 6033'].
7. It is possible, based on Sven Felix Kellerhoff's account, that Wolf was Willy Pohl, a German neo-Nazi, who assisted Abu Daoud in the logistics of the Munich attack. See Kellerhoff, *Anschlag auf Olympia*, 32.
8. Mossad cable no. 6033.
9. *Ibid.*
10. Kilowatt cable no. 1022, sent from the German BfV, 'Anschlag im olympischen Dorf', 13.09.1972, in SFA, E4320-07C, Kilowatt, 1971–1972 (translated from German by the author).
11. *Ibid.*
12. *Ibid.*
13. Kilowatt cable no. 7032, sent from the Italian SISDE, 'Meurtre du ressortissant Jordanien Zwaiter Wael – Rome – 16 octobre 1972', 17.10.1972, in SFA, E4320-07C, Kilowatt, 1971–1972 (translated from French by the author).
14. *Ibid.*
15. This cable, no. 7032, was thus also sent to Canadian intelligence.
16. *Ibid.*
17. Kilowatt cable no. 7034, sent from the Italian SISDE, 'Meurtre du ressortissant Jordanien ZWAITER WAEL – Rome 16 octobre 1972', 24.10.1972, in SFA, E4320-07C, Kilowatt, 1971–1972 (translated from French by the author).
18. *Ibid.*
19. Kilowatt cable no. 1054, sent from the German BfV, 'Ermordung des jordanischen Staatsangehörigen Zwaiter Wael – Rom am 16.10.1972', 15.11.1972, in SFA, E4320-07C, Kilowatt, 1971–1972 (translated from German by the author).
20. Kilowatt cable no. 7061, sent from the Italian SISDE, 'Arabes arretés à Come le 12.3.1973', 15.03.1973, in SFA, E4320-07C, Kilowatt, 1971–1972 (translated from French by the author).
21. *Ibid.*

22. Kilowatt cable no. 4016, sent from the French DST, 'Arabes arretés à Come le 12 mars 1973', 'diffusion restreinte, trés urgent', 19.03.1973, in SFA, E4320-07C, Kilowatt, 1971–1972 (translated from French by the author).

23. *Ibid.*

24. Vargo, *Mossad: Six Landmark Missions*, 108; Bergman, *Rise and Kill First*, 151.

25. Vargo, *Mossad: Six Landmark Missions*, 108.

26. The online database of declassified Swiss diplomatic documents 'Dodis' published a collection pertaining to the Würenlingen attack; see 'Würenlingen attack 1970', dodis.ch/T1389.

27. Tinnin and Christensen, *The Hit Team*, 77.

28. Kilowatt cable no. 7010, sent from the Italian SISDE, 'Fiumicino airport – attempt on aircraft El Al company – 16.8.1972', 17.08.1972, in SFA, E4320-07C, Kilowatt, 1971–1972 [hereafter cited as 'SISDE cable no. 7010'].

29. 'Women Duped into Taking Bomb to Their El Al Flight', *New York Times*, 18.08.1972.

30. SISDE cable no. 7010.

31. Michael Bar-Zohar and Eitan Haber, *Massacre in Munich: the Manhunt for the Killers behind the 1972 Olympics Massacre* (Guilford, Conn.: Lyons, 2005), 147; this book was previously published under the title *The Quest for the Red Prince: Israel's Relentless Manhunt for One of the World's Deadliest Terrorists*.

32. SISDE cable no. 7010.

33. *Ibid.*

34. *Ibid.*

35. *Ibid.*

36. Kilowatt cable no. 7011, sent from the Italian SISDE, 'Fiumicino airport – attempt to aircraft El Al company – 16.8.1972', 18.08.1972, in SFA, E4320-07C, Kilowatt, 1971–1972.

37. Kilowatt cable no. 7012, sent from the Italian SISDE, 'Fiumicino airport – attempt to El Al aircraft – 16-8-1972', 21.08.1972; Kilowatt cable no. 7018, sent from the Italian SISDE, 'Attentat contre aéréo El Al. Fiumicino, 16.8.1972', 28.08.1972 (translated from French by the author); Kilowatt cable no. 7020, sent from the Italian SISDE, 'Attentat contre aéréo El Al. Fiumicino, 16.8.1972', 08.09.1972 (translated from Italian by the author); all in SFA, E4320-07C, Kilowatt, 1971–1972.

38. Kilowatt cable no. 7014, sent from the Italian SISDE, 'Attack against El Al aircraft – Fiumicino, 16/8/1972', 23.08.1972, in SFA, E4320-07C, Kilowatt, 1971–1972 [hereafter cited as 'SISDE cable no. 7014'].

39. Kilowatt cable no. 7015, sent from the Italian SISDE, 'Attack against El Al aircraft – Fiumicino, 16/8/1972', 23.08.1972, in SFA, E4320-07C, Kilowatt, 1971–1972.

40. SISDE cable no. 7014.

41. Kilowatt cable no. 7019, sent from the Italian SISDE, 'Attack against El Al aircraft – Fiumicino, 16.8.1972, enclosures', 31.08.1972, in SFA, E4320-07C, Kilowatt, 1971–1972.

42. Kilowatt cable no. 7016, sent from the Italian SISDE, 'Attack against El Al aircraft – Fiumicino, 16/8/1972', 25.08.1972, in SFA, E4320-07C, Kilowatt, 1971–1972.

43. *Ibid.*

44. Kilowatt cable no. 7017, sent from the Italian SISDE, 'Attack against El Al aircraft – Fiumicino, 16.8.1972', 28.08.1972, in SFA, E4320-07C, Kilowatt, 1971–1972.

45. Kilowatt cable no. 6051, sent from Mossad, 'Movement of PFLP-GC leaders', comment: 'source: reliable in contact with PFLP-GC leaders', 18.09.1972, in SFA, E4320-07C, Kilowatt, 1971–1972.

46. Kilowatt cable no. 6063, sent from Mossad, 'Dia Aly Khan', comment: 'source: from a field report dated 16.10.72', 30.10.1972, in SFA, E4320-07C, Kilowatt, 1971–1972.

47. Kilowatt cable no. 6036, sent from Mossad, 'PFLP-GC senior personality sent abroad on mission', comment: 'source: reliable; subsource: with access to terrorist circles', 12.07.1972, in SFA, E4320-07C, Kilowatt, 1971–1972.

48. Kilowatt cable no. 7033, sent from the Italian SISDE, 'Ressortissant arabe Sami Abrahim Adham', 20.10.1972, in SFA, E4320-07C, Kilowatt, 1971–1972 (translated from French by the author).

49. *Ibid.*

50. Kilowatt cable no. 4011, sent from the French DST, 'Activité suspecte de Sami Abrahim Adham', comment: 'diffusion restreinte / urgent', 27.10.1972, in SFA, E4320-07C, Kilowatt, 1971–1972 (translated from French by the author).

51. *Ibid.*

52. *Ibid.*

53. Kilowatt cable no. 9033, sent from the Dutch BVD, 'Palestine terrorists in Yugoslavia', 20.11.1972, in SFA, E4320-07C, Kilowatt, 1971–1972.

54. The Dutch report did not mention the women's names, but referred to them as 'Dutch girl A' and 'B'.

55. *Ibid.*

56. *Ibid.*

57. Kilowatt cable no. 7057, sent from the Italian SISDE, 'Aéroport de Fiumicino – attentat contre avion El Al (16/8/1972)', 16.02.1973, in SFA, E4320-07C, Kilowatt, 1973 (translated from French by the author).

58. John Sibley, 'Few Arab Terrorists Are Punished for Hijackings and Killings', *New York Times*, 20.12.1973.

59. Kilowatt cable no. 9026, sent from the Dutch BVD, 'Ribhi Halloum, born 2.7.39 in Mazara (West Bank, Ramallah district)', 24.10.1972, in SFA, E4320-07C, Kilowatt, 1971–1972 [hereafter cited as 'BVD cable no. 9026'].

60. Klein, *Striking Back*, 151.

61. Kilowatt cable no. 6062, sent from Mossad, 'Rubhi Halloum', 30.10.1972, in SFA, E4320-07C, Kilowatt, 1971–1972.

62. Kilowatt cable no. 9030, sent from the Dutch BVD, 'Ribhi Halloum', 03.11.1972, in SFA, E4320-07C, Kilowatt, 1971–1972 [hereafter cited as 'BVD cable no. 9030'].

63. BVD cable no. 9026.
64. Klein, *Striking Back*, 151.
65. *Ibid.*
66. *Ibid.*
67. Kilowatt cable [no number], sent from the Dutch BVD directly to the Swiss BuPo, 'Ribhi Halloum', 25.10.1972, in SFA, E4320-07C, Kilowatt, 1971–1972.
68. Kilowatt cable no. 9028, sent from the Dutch BVD, 'Ribhi Halloum', 26.11.1972, in SFA, E4320-07C, Kilowatt, 1971–1972.
69. *Ibid.*
70. *Ibid.*
71. *Ibid.*
72. Other agencies replied to mention that they held no records on Halloum in their files, such as Kilowatt cable no. 1049, sent from the German BfV, 'Ribhi Halloum', 07.11.1972, in SFA, E4320-07C, Kilowatt, 1971–1972 (translated from German by the author).
73. Kilowatt cable no. 6062, sent from Mossad, 'Rubhi Halloum', 30.10.1972, in SFA, E4320-07C, Kilowatt, 1971–1972.
74. Kilowatt cable no. 5016, sent from MI5, 'Arab terrorist threat to Brazilian air lines (Varig)', 01.11.1972, in SFA, E4320-07C, Kilowatt, 1971–1972.
75. *Ibid.*
76. BVD cable no. 9030.
77. *Ibid.*
78. These letters were shared alongside Halloum's CV; *ibid.*
79. *Ibid.*
80. *Ibid.*
81. *Ibid.*
82. Kilowatt cable 1048, first sent by the Dutch BVD to the German BfV, which forwarded it directly to Swiss BuPo, 'Ribhi Halloum, Liste mit israelischen und jüdischen Namen und Anschrifen', 03.11.1972, in SFA, E4320-07C, Kilowatt, 1971–1972 (translated from German by the author).
83. For more context on this first wave of letter bombs, between September 1972 and January 1973, see 'First Wave of Letter Bomb Attacks' in Chapter 2.
84. Kilowatt cable no. 5018, sent from MI5, 'Letter bombs', comment: 'Secret, Flash', 09.11.1972, in SFA, E4320-07C, Kilowatt, 1971–1972.
85. *Ibid.*
86. Kilowatt cable no. 5019, sent from MI5, 'Letter bombs', comment: 'Immediate. Confidential', 10.11.1972, in SFA, E4320-07C, Kilowatt, 1971–1972.
87. *Ibid.*
88. Kilowatt cable no. 5020, sent from MI5, 'Letter bombs', comment: 'flash, confidential', 10.11.1972; Kilowatt cable no. 5021, sent from MI5, 'Letter bombs', comment: 'immediate, confidential', 13.11.1972; both in SFA, E4320-07C, Kilowatt, 1971–1972.

89. Kilowatt cable no. 7040, sent from the Italian SISDE, 'Aéroport de Fiumicino-Rome. Découverte de 4 sacs contenant des armes et des explosifs', 27.11.1972, in SFA, E4320-07C, Kilowatt, 1971–1972 (translated from French by the author).
90. *Ibid.*
91. Interestingly, four months later, on 19 March 1973, four suitcases filled with arms were found again at Rome Fiumicino Airport. On this occasion too, SISDE suggested that the terrorists had planned an attack but decided to abort because of the 'efficacy and constant supervision of the security forces in the airport'. See 'More Suitcases Containing Arms in Rome' and note 131 in Chapter 5 about this second aborted attack.
92. Kilowatt cable no. 7042, sent from the Italian SISDE, 'Aeroporto di Fiumicino-Roma. Rinvenimento di quatro borse contenenti armi ed explosivi', 28.11.1972, in SFA, E4320-07C, Kilowatt, 1971–1972 (translated from Italian by the author).
93. *Ibid.*
94. *Ibid.*
95. Kilowatt cable no. 5024, sent from MI5, 'Incident at Rome airport 25.11.72', comment: 'routine, secret', 01.12.1972, in SFA, E4320-07C, Kilowatt, 1971–1972.
96. *Ibid.*
97. Kilowatt cable no. 7044, sent from the Italian SISDE, 'Aéroport de Fiumicino-Rome. Découverte d'armes et d'explosifs', 22.12.1972, in SFA, E4320-07C, Kilowatt, 1971–1972 (translated from French by the author).
98. *Ibid.*
99. Kilowatt cable no. 5025, sent from MI5, 'Incident at Rome airport 25.11.72', comment: 'priority, confidential', 05.12.1972, in SFA, E4320-07C, Kilowatt, 1971–1972.
100. *Ibid.*
101. Kilowatt cable no. 5026, sent from MI5, 'Ismail plus five others', comment: 'routine, confidential', 08.12.1972, in SFA, E4320-07C, Kilowatt, 1971–1972.
102. The following summary of the events of the hijacking are based on Dahlke, *Demokratischer Staat und transnationaler Terrorismus*, 70–75; Schiller and Young, *1972 Munich Olympics*, 215–216; Oberloskamp, 'Olympia-Attentat 1972', 332; Majid Sattar, 'Folgen eines Anschlags. Mit einer Flugzeugentführung preßten palästinensische Terroristen im Oktober 1972 die drei überlebenden Olympia-Attentäter frei', *Frankfurter Allgemeine Zeitung*, 09.11.2006, 10; Klein, *Striking Back*, chapter 20; 'Arabs Hijack German Airliner and Gain Release of 3 Seized in Munich Killings', *New York Times*, 30.10.1972.
103. A telegram was sent to the Israeli ambassador in Bonn and Ambassador Ben-Horin presented the Israeli government's message not to release the terrorists; see Israel State Archives, *The Fortieth Anniversary of the Massacre of the Israeli Athletes in Munich*, 'Aftermath: Hijacking of a Lufthansa Plane and the Release of the Munich Terrorists Cause Outrage in Israel'; https://catalog

.archives.gov.il/en/chapter/aftermath-hijacking-lufthansa-plane-release-munich-terrorists-lead-outrage-israel/.

104. Dahlke, *Demokratischer Staat und transnationaler Terrorismus*, 72. Originally, the Bavarian chief prosecutor, Ammon, was meant to join as well, but he missed the flight and the plane left without him.

105. The German term was 'übergesetzlicher Notstand', cf. 'Erklärung des Landgerichts Münchens zur Einstellung des Strafverfahrens gegen Culmann vom 26. 6. 1973', in Bundesarchiv Koblenz, B 108 Bundesministerium für Verkehr, no. 52058, cited in Dahlke, *Demokratischer Staat und transnationaler Terrorismus*, 73.

106. Sattar, 'Folgen eines Anschlags'.

107. Oberloskamp, 'Olympia-Attentat 1972', 329.

108. *Ibid.*, 332; Dahlke, *Demokratischer Staat und transnationaler Terrorismus*, citing Hans-Dietrich Genscher, 112; see also Bernhard Blumenau, *The United Nations and Terrorism: Germany, Multilateralism, and Antiterrorism Efforts in the 1970s* (Basingstoke: Palgrave Macmillan, 2014), 49.

109. Amnon Rubinstein, 'Bonn's Disgrace', *Haaretz*, 30.10.1972, cited in Yael Greenfeter, 'Israel in Shock as Munich Killers Freed', *Haaretz*, 04.11.2010.

110. Kilowatt cable no. 1018, sent from the German BfV, 'Geheim / amtlich geheimhalten. Planung arab. Terroristen', 08.09.1972, in SFA, E4320-07C, Kilowatt, 1971–1972 (translated from German by the author).

111. *Ibid.*

112. Kilowatt cable no. 1033, sent from the German BfV, 'Organisation "Schwarzer September". Neue Mitglieder von Operationsgruppen', 26.09.1972, in SFA, E4320-07C, Kilowatt, 1971–1972.

113. *Ibid.*

114. Such as in Kilowatt [no number], sent from the German BfV, 'Fahndung nach Terroristen', 15.09.1972; Kilowatt [also no number], sent from the German BfV, 'Eine befreundete Stelle teilte soeben mit', 30.09.1972; Kilowatt cable no. 1018, sent from the German BfV, 'Geheim / amtlich geheimhalten. Planung arab. Terroristen', 08.09.1972; all in SFA, E4320-07C, Kilowatt, 1971–1972.

115. Kilowatt cable no. 1026, sent from the German BfV, 'Gefährdung des zivilen Luftverkehrs', 15.09.1972, in SFA, E4320-07C, Kilowatt, 1971–1972.

116. Kilowatt cable no. 1019, sent from the German BfV, 'Sicherheit des Luftverkehrs', 11.09.1972; Kilowatt cable no. 1034, sent from the German BfV, 'Beabsichtigte Flugzeugentführung durch die Organisation "Schwarzer September"', 29.09.1972; both in SFA, E4320-07C, Kilowatt, 1971–1972.

117. Kilowatt cable no. 1039, sent from the German BfV, 'Geheim / amtlich geheimhalten / Information über Planung terroristischer Aktionen durch Palästinenser', 09.10.1972, in SFA, E4320-07C, Kilowatt, 1971–1972.

118. *Ibid.*

119. *Ibid.*

120. Dahlke, *Demokratischer Staat und transnationaler Terrorismus*, 70–74; Jason Burke, 'Bonn "Faked" Hijack to Free Killers,' *Observer*, 26.03.2000.

121. Published German foreign service record, document no. 367, 'Botschafter von Puttkamer, Tel Aviv, an das Auswärtige Amt', 08.11.1972, in *Akten zur Auswärtigen Politik der Bundesrepublik Deutschland 1972* (Munich: Oldenbourg, 2003), https://doi.org/10.1524/9783486718157, volume III, 1686, note 3.

122. During the Kiel Lufthansa hijacking, the BfV sent a cable to the Club de Berne partners with the passenger list, their names, and nationalities. Among the passengers were one German, six Arabs, one American, one British, one Turkish, and one Spanish. In the cable it was specified that the plane was a Boeing 727. Kilowatt cable no. 1044, sent from the German BfV, 'Entführung eines DHL-Flugzeuges am 29.10.1972', 29.10.1972, in SFA, E4320-07C, Kilowatt, 1971–1972.

123. Reeve, *One Day in September*, 165.

124. Oberloskamp, 'Olympia-Attentat 1972', 329.

125. Klein, *Striking Back*, 128.

126. Golda Meir, *My Life* (New York: G. P. Putnam's Sons, 1975), 385.

127. Political Archive of the Federal Foreign Office [Politisches Archiv des Auswärtigen Amts], B 1, Bd. 509, Letter of the German ambassador, Tel Aviv, 21.11.1972, 'Lufthansa-Zwischenfall', cited in Oberloskamp, 'Olympia-Attentat 1972', 334.

128. Schiller and Young, *The 1972 Munich Olympics*, 188.

129. For an account of relatuons between East and West Germany and Israel in the context of the global Cold War, see Lorena De Vita. *Israelpolitik: German–Israeli Relations, 1949–69* (Manchester University Press, 2020). See also Carole Fink, *West Germany and Israel: Foreign Relations, Domestic Politics, and the Cold War, 1965–1974* (Cambridge University Press, 2019), particularly pages 199–218 for the Munich and Kiel crises.

130. The terrorists needed a visa to go to Turkey because the flight was scheduled to go to Ankara.

131. Kilowatt cable no. 1055, sent from the German BfV, 'Entführung einer DLH Maschine am 29.10.1972', 16.11.1972, in SFA, E4320-07C, Kilowatt, 1971–1972.

132. *Ibid.*

133. Kilowatt cable no. 1056, sent from the German BfV, 'Entführung einer Lufthansamaschine am 29.10.1972', 20.11.1972, in SFA, E4320-07C, Kilowatt, 1971–1972.

134. *Ibid.*

135. *Ibid.*

136. Cable no. 1058, sent from the German BfV, 'Entführung einer Maschine der Lufthansa nach Tripolis', 08.12.1972, in SFA, E4320-07C, Kilowatt, 1971–1972.

137. Willy Brandt, *People and Politics* (Boston: Little, Brown & Company, 1978), 439–441.

138. Kilowatt cable no. 1044, sent from the German BfV, 'Entführung eines DHL-Flugzeuges am 29.10.1972', 29.10.1972, in SFA, E4320-07C, Kilowatt, 1971–1972.

139. Kilowatt cable no. 5015, sent from MI5, 'Antoine Hawa and Elias Loutfallah', comment: 'immediate, secret', 31.10.1972, in SFA, E4320-07C, Kilowatt, 1971–1972.

140. Kilowatt cable no. 5026, sent from MI5, 'George Antoine Hawa', comment: 'Confidential', 16.08.1973; Kilowatt cable no. 9052, sent from the Dutch BVD, 'George Antoine Hawa', 29.06.1973; both in SFA, E4320-07C, Kilowatt, 1973.

141. Kilowatt cable no. 9052, sent from the Dutch BVD.

142. Kilowatt cable no. 6059, sent from Mossad, 'Terrorists / army, police and airline uniforms for terrorist operations', comments: 'source: reliable. Subsource: Lebanese who visited Europe, reliability not known', 16.10.1972, in SFA, E4320-07C, Kilowatt, 1971–1972.

143. Kilowatt cable no. 5013, sent from MI5, 'Bogus use of uniforms by Arab terrorists', comment: 'routine, secret', 17.10.1972, in SFA, E4320-07C, Kilowatt, 1971–1972.

144. Kilowatt cable no. 4010, sent from the French DST, 'Utilisation d'uniformes de compagnies aériennes de la police et de l'armée en vue d'opérations terroristes', comment: 'diffusion restreinte, normal', 24.10.1972, in SFA, E4320-07C, Kilowatt, 1971–1972 (translated from French by the author).

145. *Ibid.*

146. Kilowatt cable no. 1046, sent from the German BfV, 'Zusammenarbeit türkischer Extremisten mit palästinensischen Terrororganisationen', comment: 'vertraulich. Amtlich geheimhalten', 02.11.1972, in SFA, E4320-07C, Kilowatt, 1971–1972 (translation from German by the author).

147. *Ibid.*

148. *Ibid.*

149. Kilowatt cable no. 1066, sent from the German BfV, 'Ausländerrechtliche Massnahmen gegen Funktionäre und Aktivisten radikaler palästinensischer Gruppen', comment: 'nur für den Dienstgebrauch', 30.01.1973, in SFA, E4320-07C, Kilowatt, 1973 (translation from German by the author) [hereafter cited as 'BfV cable no. 1066'].

150. Oberloskamp, 'Olympia-Attentat 1972', 330; Dahlke, *Demokratischer Staat und transnationaler Terrorismus*, 93.

151. Dahlke, *Demokratischer Staat und transnationaler Terrorismus*, 94.

152. *Ibid.*

153. *Ibid.*, 91.

154. Kilowatt cable no. 1042, sent from the German BfV, 'Ausländerrechtliche Massnahmen gegen Funktionäre und Aktivisten radikaler palästinensischer Gruppen', comment: 'vertraulich. Amtlich geheimhalten', 24.10.1972, in SFA, E4320-07C, Kilowatt, 1971–1972 (translation from German by the author).

155. A week later, the BfV sent additional details about the people on the list, explaining, among other things, why they had been deported; Kilowatt cable no. 1045, sent from the German BfV, 'Ausländerrechtliche Massnahmen gegen Funktionäre und Aktivisten radikaler palästinensischer Gruppen', comment: 'vertraulich. Amtlich geheimhalten', 31.10.1972, in SFA, E4320-07C, Kilowatt, 1971–1972 (translation from German by the author).

156. BfV cable no. 1066.

157. *Ibid.*

158. Kilowatt cable no. 1068, sent from the German BfV, 'Ausländerrechtliche Massnahmen gegen Funktionäre und Aktivisten radikaler palästinensischer Gruppen', comment: 'nur für den Dienstgebrauch', 05.02.1973, in SFA, E4320-07C, Kilowatt, 1973 (translation from German by the author).

159. Kilowatt cable no. 1089, sent from the German BfV, 'Ausländerrechtliche Massnahmen gegen Funktionäre und Aktivisten radikaler palästinensischer Gruppen', comment: 'nur für den Dienstgebrauch', 26.04.1973; Kilowatt cable no. 1091, sent from the German BfV, 'Ausländerrechtliche Massnahmen gegen Funktionäre und Aktivisten radikaler palästinensischer Gruppen', comment: 'nur für den Dienstgebrauch', 23.05.1973; both in SFA, E4320-07C, Kilowatt, 1973 (translation from German by the author).

160. Political Archive of the Federal Foreign Office, B 1, Bd. 509, Complaint of the Egyptian ambassador to the Foreign Office, 23.09.1972, 'Ägyptische Demarchen wegen der Sicherheitsvorkehrungen', cited in Oberloskamp, 'Olympia-Attentat 1972', 331.

161. BfV cable no. 1066.

162. Kilowatt cable no. 1043, sent from the German BfV, 'Mahrouf el-din Ghanem, student, geb. 21.10.1940 in Lattakia/Syrien', 27.10.1972, in SFA, E4320-07C, Kilowatt, 1971–1972 (translation from German by the author).

163. Kilowatt cable no. 4508, sent from the French RG (known among Kilowatt as *surenat*), 'Mahrouf el-din Ghanem', comment: 'confidentiel', 03.11.1972, in SFA, E4320-07C, Kilowatt, 1971–1972 (translated from French by the author).

164. Kilowatt cable no. 7035, sent from the Italian SISDE, [cable had no title], 10.11.1972, in SFA, E4320-07C, Kilowatt, 1971–1972 (translated from French by the author).

165. *Ibid.*

166. Kilowatt cable no. 1040, sent from the German BfV, 'Zeid, Muhamad Abdel Ghani', 19.10.1972, in SFA, E4320-07C, Kilowatt, 1971–1972 (translation from German by the author).

167. Kilowatt cable no. 9032, sent from the Dutch BVD, 'Maan Mohamed Ziade, born 1.1.38 in Tripoli (Lebanon)', 10.11.1972, in SFA, E4320-07C, Kilowatt, 1971–1972.

168. *Ibid.*

169. *Ibid.*

170. Kilowatt cable no. 9034, sent from the Dutch BVD, 'Maan Mohamed Ziade', reference: 'Our Watt 9032 of 10-11-1972', 14.11.1972, in SFA, E4320-07C, Kilowatt, 1971–1972.
171. Kilowatt cable no. 6067, sent from Mossad, 'Maan Ziadeh', reference: 'your Watt 9034 of 14.11.72', 23.11.1972, in SFA, E4320-07C, Kilowatt, 1971–1972.
172. *Ibid.*
173. Kilowatt cable no. 6064, sent from Mossad, 'Black September plans operation in Europe', comments: 'source: reliable. Sub-source: has access to terrorist circles', 30.10.1972, in SFA, E4320-07C, Kilowatt, 1971–1972.
174. Kilowatt cable no. 5022, sent from MI5, 'Suspected PFLP operation', comment: 'Immediate. Secret', 14.11.1972, in SFA, E4320-07C, Kilowatt, 1971–1972.
175. *Ibid.*
176. Bergman, *Rise and Kill First*, 154; Klein, *Striking Back*, 119; Vargo, *Mossad: Six Landmark Missions*, 107–108; Reeve, *One Day in September*, 170; Black and Morris, *Israel's Secret Wars*, 271.

4 A BOMB IN PARIS AND TWO ATTACKS IN BANGKOK AND ROME

1. That he stepped back before the explosion was mentioned in Reeve, *One Day in September*, 172. Reeve also explains that the detonator was very sophisticated and that it used the same principle as cipher telephones.
2. Vargo mentions Hamshari as the organiser of Zwaiter's funeral; Vargo, *Mossad: Six Landmark Missions*, 113.
3. Klein, *Striking Back*, 107.
4. Kilowatt cable no. 9020, sent from the Dutch BVD, 'EL FATAH representative in the Netherlands: Rabbani, Mahmoud Salim, born Haifa 2.5.1934', comment: 'confidential', 28.06.1972, in SFA, E4320-07C, Kilowatt, 1971–1972.
5. *Ibid.* ('subversive' was synonym for 'terrorist' in cables from the BVD).
6. Klein, *Striking Back*, 108.
7. For the Würenlingen attack, see Chapter 3, note 26.
8. The ways in which Mossad allegedly assessed Hamshari's terrorism involvement were mentioned in exactly the same way by both authors: Klein, *Striking Back*, 108; Bergman, *Rise and Kill First*, 154.
9. Reeve, *One Day in September*, 171.
10. Bergman, *Rise and Kill First*, 154.
11. Kilowatt cable no. 4021, sent from the French DST, 'Attentat commis contre l'oléoduc Trieste-Ingolstadt le 4 aout 1972', comment: 'diffusion strictement confidentiel, urgent', 30.03.1973 (Hamshari was mentioned in this cable and said to have met the organisers of this attack); Kilowatt cable no. 6086, sent from Mossad, 'Preliminary investigation in Switzerland in connection with arrest of three Arabs', 05.02.1973; both in SFA, E4320-07C, Kilowatt, 1973.

12. 'Mahmoud Hamchari', 10.01.1973, French Diplomatic Archives [Archives diplomatiques], section: Afrique du Nord – Levant, Généralités – Proche-Orient, 1973–1979, b. 375 QO/129, Sécurité des ressortissants arabe en France (février–avril 1973), cited in Valentine Lomellini, *Il Lodo Moro. Terrorismo e ragion di Stato, 1969–1986 [The Moro Agreement. Terrorism and Raison d'État]* (Bari: Laterza, 2022), 95, note 26.
13. Klein, *Striking Back*, 108.
14. Kilowatt cable no. 4013, sent from the French DST, 'Attentat en France contre Hamshari Mahmoud représentant du Fatah en France', comment: 'confidentiel, urgent', 13.12.1972, in SFA, E4320-07C, Kilowatt, 1971–1972 (translated from French by the author).
15. *Ibid.*
16. *Ibid.*
17. Klein, *Striking Back*, 107; Reeve, *One Day in September*, 172; Bergman, *Rise and Kill First*, 155.
18. Klein, *Striking Back*, 107.
19. Bergman, *Rise and Kill First*, 155.
20. *Ibid.*
21. *Ibid.*, 140.
22. Klein, *Striking Back*, 109.
23. Kilowatt cable no. 9036, sent from the Dutch BVD, 'Fatah representatives in Europe', reference: 'watt 4013 of 13-12-1972' [which was the French cable informing about Hamshari's assassination], comment: 'source: reliable and extremely delicate', 19.12.1972, in SFA, E4320-07C, Kilowatt, 1971–1972.
24. *Ibid.*
25. *Ibid.*
26. Kilowatt cable no. 9037, sent from the Dutch BVD, 'Fatah representatives in Europe', reference: 'watt 9036 of 19-12-1972', comment: 'urgent', 21.12.1972, in SFA, E4320-07C, Kilowatt, 1971–1972.
27. *Ibid.*
28. *Ibid.*
29. Kilowatt cable no. 5031, sent from MI5, 'Fatah representatives in Europe', comment: 'priority, secret', 22.12.1972, in SFA, E4320-07C, Kilowatt, 1971–1972.
30. *Ibid.*
31. *Ibid.*
32. Kilowatt cable no. 5035, sent from MI5, 'PLO/Fatah meeting', comment: 'priority, secret', 29.12.1972, in SFA, E4320-07C, Kilowatt, 1971–1972.
33. Kilowatt cable no. 6086, sent from Mossad, 'Preliminary investigation in Switzerland in connection with arrest of three Arabs', 05.02.1973, in SFA, E4320-07C, Kilowatt, 1973.
34. Klein, *Striking Back*, 112.
35. Reeve, *One Day in September*, 175.

36. For a discussion of this attack and its impact on Japanese foreign policy, see Erika Tominaga, 'Japan's Middle East Policy, 1972–1974: Resources Diplomacy, Pro-American Policy, and New Left', *Diplomacy and Statecraft*, 28/4 (2017), 674–701, 683ff.

37. Peter O'Loughlin, 'Arab Terrorists Flown to Cairo after Releasing Six Hostages', *Daily Telegraph*, 30.12.1972.

38. Craig R. Whitney, 'Israeli Embassy in Bangkok Held by Arabs 19 Hours', *New York Times*, 29.12.1972.

39. Sayigh, *Armed Struggle*, 355.

40. Reeve, *One Day in September*, 175.

41. Kilowatt cable no. 5002, sent from MI5, 'Black September', comment: 'immediate, secret', 13.01.1973, in SFA, E4320-07C, Kilowatt, 1973.

42. *Ibid.*

43. Kilowatt cable no. 5032, sent from the British domestic intelligence agency MI5, 'Arab terrorism operation', 24.12.1972, in SFA, E4320-07C, Kilowatt, 1971–1972.

44. *Ibid.*

45. *Ibid.*

46. Kilowatt cable no. 6074, sent from Mossad, 'Arab terrorism', comments: 'immediate. Merry Christmas', 26.10.1972, in SFA, E4320-07C, Kilowatt, 1971–1972.

47. *Ibid.* It is interesting to see that the term 'lone wolf' was used by Mossad at that time.

48. Kilowatt cable no. 5034, sent from MI5, 'Arab terrorism', comment: 'immediate, secret', 27.12.1972, in SFA, E4320-07C, Kilowatt, 1971–1972.

49. *Ibid.*

50. *Ibid.*

51. Kilowatt cable no. 6075, sent from Shin Bet, 'Arab terrorism', comment: 'immediate', 27.12.1972, in SFA, E4320-07C, Kilowatt, 1971–1972.

52. *Ibid.*

53. Kilowatt cable no. 5036, sent from MI5, 'Ref watt 5033 of 25.12.72', comment: 'immediate, secret', 28.12.1972, in SFA, E4320-07C, Kilowatt, 1971–1972.

54. *Ibid.*

55. Kilowatt cable no. 5001, sent from MI5, 'Reference to our telegram no watt 5036 of 28.12.72', comment: 'routine, secret', 09.01.1973, in SFA, E4320-07C, Kilowatt, 1973.

56. For the arrest of Rubhi Halloum, see 'A Terrorist Cell in Latin America and Explosive Letters' in Chapter 3.

57. Kilowatt cable no. 5001, sent from MI5, 'Reference to our telegram no watt 5036 of 28.12.72', comment: 'routine, secret', 09.01.1973, in SFA, E4320-07C, Kilowatt, 1973.

58. *Ibid.*

59. For the assassination of Mohamed Abu Yussuf, see 'Fifth Assassinations: Operation Spring of Youth' in Chapter 6.

60. Kilowatt cable no. 5003, sent from MI5, [no title], comment: 'immediate, secret', 13.01.1973, in SFA, E4320-07C, Kilowatt, 1973.
61. Kilowatt cable no. 5015, sent from MI5, [no title], comment: 'priority, secret', 06.04.1973, in SFA, E4320-07C, Kilowatt, 1973.
62. *Ibid.*
63. For more details about this arrest, see 'A Parking Ticket that Kills: Using the Schönau Investigation to Track Boudia' in Chapter 7.
64. Kilowatt cable no. 5015, sent from MI5, [no title], comment: 'priority, secret', 06.04.1973, in SFA, E4320-07C, Kilowatt, 1973.
65. *Ibid.*
66. Kilowatt cable no. 5019, sent from MI5, 'Mohammed Abdul Karim Fuheid', comment: 'priority, confidential', 07.05.1973, in SFA, E4320-07C, Kilowatt, 1973.
67. *Ibid.*
68. *Ibid.*
69. Kilowatt cable [no number], sent from the German BfV, 'Geplante Flugzeugentführung durch arabische Terroristen', 16.02.1973, in SFA, E4320-07C, Kilowatt, 1973 (translation from German by the author).
70. *Ibid.*
71. Paul Hofmann, 'Mrs Meir to Visit Pope in First Such Call by an Israeli Premier' *New York Times*, 15.01.1973.
72. Reeve, *One Day in September*, 176.
73. *Ibid.*
74. Reeve, *One Day in September*, 176–177; Ostrovsky and Hoy, *By Way of Deception*, 185–196. Other studies that have researched Operation Wrath of God, by such as Bergman, Klein, and Vargo, do not mention this episode. Kai Bird mentions it very briefly, in a list of alleged Black September attacks: Bird, *The Good Spy: the Life and Death of Robert Ames* (New York: Crown, 2014), 140.
75. Ostrovsky and Hoy, *By Way of Deception*, 185. If true, the story of the transfer is quite atrocious. Ostrovsky claims that Black September used unwitting German citizens as cover for the shipment. Once the missiles had safely reached the shores of Italy, Black September did not want to take any security risks, and so slit the throats of the Germans and dumped their bodies in the Adriatic Sea.
76. Ostrovsky and Hoy, *By Way of Deception*, 191; Reeve, *One Day in September*, 176.
77. Ostrovsky and Hoy, *By Way of Deception*, 191–192; Reeve, *One Day in September*, 176. The Strela missiles were called SA-7 in the Soviet Union and code-named 'Grail' by NATO.
78. Ostrovsky and Hoy, *By Way of Deception*, 195.
79. Kilowatt cable no. 6080, sent from Mossad, 'Terrorist plans to attack aircraft', 15.01.1973, in SFA, E4320-07C, Kilowatt, 1973.
80. Kilowatt cable no. 6093, sent from Mossad, 'Possible attack on El Al planes', 23.02.1973, in SFA, E4320-07C, Kilowatt, 1973.

81. For more context on the downing of this civilian aircraft, see 'Libyan Support for Black September Attacks' in Chapter 5.
82. John T. Phelps, 'Aerial Intrusions by Civil and Military Aircraft in Time of Peace', *Military Law Review*, 107 (1985), 255–303, 288.
83. Terence Smith, 'Israelis Down a Libyan Airliner in the Sinai, Killing at least 74', *New York Times*, 22.02.1973.
84. For more context on the Israeli shooting down of the Libyan passenger plane, see Brenda Lange, *Muammar Qaddafi* (Philadelphia: Chelsea House, 2005), 74.
85. Kilowatt cable no. 6094, sent from Shin Bet, 'Libya/plans for attacks on Israeli targets to be carried out by the terrorist organisations', 09.03.1973, in SFA, E4320-07C, Kilowatt, 1973.
86. Kilowatt cable no. 6093, sent from Mossad, 'Possible attack on El Al planes', 23.02.1973, in SFA, E4320-07C, Kilowatt, 1973.
87. *Ibid.*
88. Kilowatt cable no. 1109, sent from the German BfV, 'Sicherheit im Luftverkehr', comment: 'VS-vertraulich. amtlich geheimhalten', 09.08.1973, in SFA, E4320-07C, Kilowatt, 1973 (translation from German by the author).
89. *Ibid.*
90. Nathaniel K. Powell, *France's Wars in Chad: Military Intervention and Decolonization in Africa* (Cambridge University Press, 2021), 142.
91. Kilowatt cable no. 1109, sent from the German BfV, 'Sicherheit im Luftverkehr', comment: 'VS-vertraulich. amtlich geheimhalten', 09.08.1973, in SFA, E4320-07C, Kilowatt, 1973 (translation from German by the author).
92. Kilowatt cable no. 7104, sent from the Italian SISDE, 'Rome – le 5/9/1973 – arrestation d'arabes détenteur de lance-fusées', 06.09.1973, in SFA, E4320-07C, Kilowatt, 1973 (translated from French by the author).
93. *Ibid.*
94. Kilowatt cable no. 7105, sent from the Italian SISDE, 'Tuyau lance-fusées de fabrication soviétique saisi lors de l'arrestation de cinq arabes à Ostia (Rome) le 5.9.1973', 11.09.1973, in SFA, E4320-07C, Kilowatt, 1973 (translated from French by the author).
95. Kilowatt cable no. 6141, sent from Mossad, 'Terrorist attempt to attack airliners by means of shoulder fired AA rockets', 10.09.1973, in SFA, E4320-07C, Kilowatt, 1973.
96. *Ibid.*
97. Kilowatt cable no. 7108, sent from the Italian SISDE, 'Rome, 5.9.1973 – arrestation de cinq arabes détenteurs de fusées lance-missiles', 21.09.1973, in SFA, E4320-07C, Kilowatt, 1973 (translated from French by the author).
98. *Ibid.*
99. *Ibid.*
100. Kilowatt cable no. 5043, sent from MI5, 'Arrest of Arabs with SA-7 missiles – Rome 5.9.73', comment: 'immediate, secret', 15.10.1973, in SFA, E4320-07C, Kilowatt, 1973.

101. For Kilowatt cable 6093, see notes 80 and 86 above; for Kilowatt cable 6094, see note 85.
102. Kilowatt cable no. 5043, sent from MI5, 'Arrest of Arabs with SA-7 missiles – Rome 5.9.73', comment: 'immediate, secret', 15.10.1973, in SFA, E4320-07C, Kilowatt, 1973.
103. *Ibid.*
104. Kilowatt cable no. 9075, sent from the Dutch BVD, 'Arabs with missile rockets arrested in Rome on 5-9-1973', reference: 'watt 7104 of 6-9-1973 and following correspondence', comment: 'urgent', 12.10.1973, in SFA, E4320-07C, Kilowatt, 1973.
105. *Ibid.*
106. *Ibid.*
107. *Ibid.*
108. Guttmann, *Origins of International Counterterrorism*, 183.
109. Kilowatt cable no. 5027, sent from MI5, [no title], comment: 'priority, secret', 12.12.1972, in SFA, E4320-07C, Kilowatt, 1971–1972.
110. *Ibid.*
111. Kilowatt cable no. 6510, sent from Shin Bet, 'Forecast of possible Arab terrorist activities', 18.12.1972, in SFA, E4320-07C, Kilowatt, 1971–1972.
112. *Ibid.*
113. *Ibid.*
114. Kilowatt cable no. 6078, sent from Shin Bet, 'PFLP plans to hijack El Al aircraft', 04.01.1973, in SFA, E4320-07C, Kilowatt, 1973.
115. *Ibid.*
116. For more details about this incident, see 'Hijacked Plane Lands in Havana a Second Time, 31 Hostages Free; 3 Gunmen Seized after 29 Hours', *New York Times*, 12.11.1972.
117. Kilowatt cable no. 6113, sent from Shin Bet, 'PFLP plans to hijack aircraft', comment: 'further to watt 6078 of 4.1.1973', 24.05.1973, in SFA, E4320-07C, Kilowatt, 1973.
118. *Ibid.*
119. Dolnik, *Understanding Terrorist Innovation*, 39.
120. Michael Bar-Zohar and Nissim Mishal, *Mossad: the Greatest Missions of the Israeli Secret Service* (Hopewell, NJ: Ecco, 2014), 175. For Mossad's assassination of Basil al-Kubaisi, see 'Updating the Murderers: The Assassination of Dr Basil al-Kubaisi' in Chapter 6.
121. Kilowatt cable no. 2036, sent from the Belgian Sûreté d'État, [no title], comment: 'secret, routine', 15.12.1972, in SFA, E4320-07C, Kilowatt, 1971–1972.
122. *Ibid.*
123. Kilowatt cable [no number], sent from the German BfV, 'Arabische Terroristen', 28.12.1972, in SFA, E4320-07C, Kilowatt, 1971–1972 (translation from German by the author).

124. Kilowatt cable no. 1059, sent from the German BfV, 'Funktionäre der "Generalunion Palästinensischer Studenten" (GUPS) im Ausland', 21.12.1972, in SFA, E4320-07C, Kilowatt, 1971–1972 (translation from German by the author).
125. Kilowatt cable no. 6076, sent from Mossad, 'Mahmoud Abdalla bin al-Hamid Tuda', comment: 'source reliable, with access to terrorist circles', 28.12.1972, in SFA, E4320-07C, Kilowatt, 1971–1972.
126. Rasd was mentioned by the German BfV, for instance, in Kilowatt cable no. 1032, sent from the German BfV, 'Leiter der Organisation Schwarzer September', 25.09.1972, in SFA, E4320-07C, Kilowatt, 1971–1972 (translated from German by the author). See also 'Understanding Black September' in Chapter 2.
127. Kilowatt cable no. 6076, sent from Mossad, 'Mahmoud Abdalla bin al-Hamid Tuda', comment: 'source reliable, with access to terrorist circles', 28.12.1972, in SFA, E4320-07C, Kilowatt, 1971–1972.
128. *Ibid.*
129. Kilowatt cable no. 7045, sent from the Italian SISDE, 'Soi-disant palestinien [G. L.] né à Haïfa le 16.1.1947, inscrit maritime', 29.12.1972, in SFA, E4320-07C, Kilowatt, 1971–1972 (translated from French by the author).

5 ASSASSINATIONS IN NICOSIA AND MADRID, ATTACKS IN JORDAN AND SUDAN

1. Other Arabic transliterations of his name included Hussain Abd el Hir, Hussein Abad al-Chir, and Hussein Al Bashir.
2. Vargo, *Mossad: Six Landmark Missions*, 115.
3. Klein, *Striking Back*, 113; Bergman, *Rise and Kill First*, 168.
4. Vargo, *Mossad: Six Landmark Missions*, 114–116.
5. Klein, *Striking Back*, 114; Reeve, *One Day in September*, 173; Vargo, *Mossad: Six Landmark Missions*, 114.
6. Klein, *Striking Back*.
7. For Soviet–PLO/Fatah relations, see Galia Golan, *The Soviet Union and the Palestine Liberation Organization: an Uneasy Alliance* (New York: Praeger, 1980); Ray S. Cline and Yonah Alexander, *Terrorism: the Soviet Connection* (New York: Crane Russak, 1986), 34; Roberta Goren, *The Soviet Union and Terrorism* (London: George Allen and Unwin, 1984).
8. Reeve, *One Day in September*, 173.
9. *Ibid.*
10. Vargo, *Mossad: Six Landmark Missions*, 114. Khair as coordinator of this attack was also mentioned in Jonas, *Vengeance*, 221.
11. Kilowatt cable no. 7046, sent from the Italian SISDE, 'Soi-disant ressortissant afghans – soupçonnés de programmes terroristes', 12.01.1973, in SFA, E4320-07C, Kilowatt, 1973 (translated from French by the author).

12. *Ibid.*
13. Kilowatt cable no. 7048, sent from the Italian SISDE, 'Soi-disant ressortissant afghans – soupçonnés de programmes terroristes', 26.01.1973, in SFA, E4320-07C, Kilowatt, 1973 (translated from French by the author).
14. *Ibid.*
15. For this thwarted attack at Fiumicino, see 'Waiting Crowds as a Target and a Link to Khair' in Chapter 5.
16. Kilowatt cable no. 7072, sent from the Italian SISDE, 'Aeroporto di Fiumicino, 4.4.1973 – Arresto di due stranieri', 11.04.1973, in SFA, E4320-07C, Kilowatt, 1973 (translated from Italian by the author). George Jonas also mentions that the Haifa shipping attack was going to be carried out by Afghan nationals; Jonas, *Vengeance*, 220.
17. Club de Berne members frequently warned about possible Black September attacks against seafaring vessels or ports. Before Khair's assassination, there was, for instance, a Dutch warning sent in the context of the above-mentioned Halloum arrest: Kilowatt cable no. 9028, sent from the Dutch BVD, 'Ribhi Halloum', 26.11.1972, in SFA, E4320-07C, Kilowatt, 1971–1972. In April 1973, there was a similar MI5 warning: Kilowatt cable no. 5015, sent from MI5, [no title], comment: 'priority, secret', 06.04.1973, in SFA, E4320-07C, Kilowatt, 1973. After Khair's assassination, Club de Berne members continued to warn that ships or ports were at high risk; see Kilowatt cable no. 9043, sent from the Dutch BVD, 'Possible terrorist plans to hijack shipping', 30.03.1973, in SFA, E4320-07C, Kilowatt, 1973. There were many more, including a warning by Mossad that missiles could be smuggled aboard ships in order to attack ports: Kilowatt cable no. 6141, sent from Mossad, 'Terrorist attempt to attack airliners by means of shoulder fired AA rockets', 10.09.1973, in SFA, E4320-07C, Kilowatt, 1973.
18. Kilowatt cable no. 6066, sent from Mossad, 'Black September plans for an attack in Europe', comment: 'source: usually reliable', 03.11.1972, in SFA, E4320-07C, Kilowatt, 1971–1972; Kilowatt cable no. 1071, sent from the German BfV, 'Schwarzer September', 14.02.1973, in SFA, E4320-07C, Kilowatt, 1973 (translated from German by the author).
19. For more context about the murder of Wasfi Tal, see 'Black September Organisation' in Chapter 1.
20. Klein, *Striking Back*, 118; Black and Morris, *Israel's Secret Wars*, 266–267.
21. The Israeli embassy in Brussels was at the time the centre of Israeli espionage activities in Europe; Raviv and Melman, *Every Spy a Prince*, 185.
22. Klein, *Striking Back*, 119.
23. Iyad and Rouleau. *My Home, My Land*, 113.
24. *Ibid.*
25. Vargo, *Mossad: Six Landmark Missions*, 116. Klein has the same version of events; *Striking Back*, 118–121. Reeve claims that Samir, the double agent, killed Cohen while they were still in the restaurant; *One Day in September*, 178.

26. 'Israel Says that Man Slain in Madrid Was an Agent', *New York Times*, 31.01.1973.
27. That it was the photograph which gave away Cohen (and possibly Ofir) is mentioned several times. See Reeve, *One Day in September*, 178; Black and Morris, *Israel's Secret Wars*, 267; Raviv and Melman, *Every Spy a Prince*, 187.
28. Raviv and Melman, *Every Spy a Prince*, 187.
29. Reeve, *One Day in September*, 178.
30. Bergman, *Rise and Kill First*, 665.
31. Klein, *Striking Back*, 121.
32. *Monitin* 113, February 1988, cited in Black and Morris, *Israel's Secret Wars*, 274.
33. Raviv and Melman, *Every Spy a Prince*, 188.
34. Ostrovsky and Hoy, *By Way of Deception*, 188.
35. Kilowatt cable no. 7055, sent from the Italian SISDE, 'Priorité absolue', 15.02.1973, in SFA, E4320-07C, Kilowatt, 1973 (translated from French by the author).
36. Kilowatt cable no. 7056, sent from the Italian SISDE, 'Préavis d'attentat', comment: 'Priorité absolue', 15.02.1973, in SFA, E4320-07C, Kilowatt, 1973 (translated from French by the author).
37. Kilowatt cable no. 7058, sent from the Italian SISDE, 'Préavis d'attentat', 19.02.1973, in SFA, E4320-07C, Kilowatt, 1973 (translated from French by the author).
38. *Ibid.*
39. Klein, *Striking Back*, 122.
40. Sayigh, *Armed Struggle*, 355.
41. *Ibid.* For how the attack was thwarted, see also Patrick Seale, *Abu Nidal: a Gun for Hire. The Secret Life of the World's Most Notorious Terrorist* (New York: Random House, 1992), 88.
42. Kilowatt cable no. 5000, sent from MI5, 'immediate, secret, Parcel Bombs', 08.01.1973, SFA, E4320-07C, Kilowatt, 1973.
43. Kilowatt cable no. 5007, sent from MI5, 'immediate, confidential, Jordanian ambassador London', 03.03.1973, SFA, E4320-07C, Kilowatt, 1973.
44. Kilowatt cable no. 6104, sent from Mossad, 'Terrorists / Use of forged passports', comment: 'source: reliable', 12.04.1973, in SFA, E4320-07C, Kilowatt, 1973.
45. Klein, *Striking Back*, 122.
46. See 'Arms Smuggling via Mercedes Sales' in Chapter 5.
47. Vargo, *Mossad: Six Landmark Missions*, 81.
48. Klein, *Striking Back*, 123. Some accounts suggest it was a six-man terrorist squad, but most accounts say it was eight.
49. Bernhard Blumenau recounts this story on the basis of German diplomatic cables: Blumenau, *United Nations and Terrorism*, 49–52.
50. 'Guerrillas' Bravado Breaks at the End', *New York Times*, 05.03.1973.
51. *Ibid.*
52. David Carlton. *The West's Road to 9/11: Resisting, Appeasing and Encouraging Terrorism since 1970.* (London: Palgrave Macmillan, 2014), 53.

53. 'Guerrillas' Bravado Breaks at the End', *New York Times*, 05.03.1973.
54. Andrew B. Wilson. 'What Did Arafat Get for Killing US Diplomats?' *American Spectator*, 01.03.2013.
55. *Ibid.*
56. Carlton, *West's Road to 9/11*, 53.
57. Vargo, *Mossad: Six Landmark Missions*, 82.
58. Reeve, *One Day in September*, 181.
59. Vargo, *Mossad: Six Landmark Missions*, 83.
60. Klein, *Striking Back*, 124.
61. For a discussion about the relationship between Black September and PLO/ Fatah, see 'Black September Organisation' in Chapter 1.
62. Pearlman, *Palestinian National Movement*, 78–82; Chamberlin, *The Global Offensive*, 258.
63. Amos, *Palestinian Resistance*, 228.
64. Blumenau, *United Nations and Terrorism*, 50.
65. *Ibid.*
66. *Ibid.*
67. Kilowatt cable no. 1078, sent from the German BfV, 'Warnung vor Anschlägen des "Schwarzer September",' 09.03.1973, in SFA, E4320-07C, Kilowatt, 1973 (translated from German by the author).
68. *Ibid.*
69. Kilowatt cable no. 6105, sent from Mossad, 'PFLP/GC intentions to attack aircraft', comment: 'source: reliable, with access', 16.04.1973, in SFA, E4320-07C, Kilowatt, 1973.
70. Kilowatt cable no. 1056, sent from the German BfV, 'Entführung einer Lufthansamaschine am 29.10.1972', 20.11.1972, in SFA, E4320-07C, Kilowatt, 1971–1972 (translated from German by the author).
71. See 'Thwarted Surface-to-Air Missile Attacks' in Chapter 4.
72. Kilowatt cable no. 6093, sent from Mossad, 'Possible attack on El Al planes', 23.02.1973, in SFA, E4320-07C, Kilowatt, 1973.
73. Kilowatt cable no. 1074, sent from the German BfV, 'Geplante Anschläge palästinensischer Terroristen', 28.02.1973, in SFA, E4320-07C, Kilowatt, 1973 (translated from German by the author).
74. *Ibid.*
75. Kilowatt cable no. 1077, sent from the German BfV, 'Planung von Terroraktionen palästinensischer Terroristen', 06.03.1973, in SFA, E4320-07C, Kilowatt, 1973 (translated from German by the author).
76. *Ibid.*
77. Kilowatt cable no. 6094, sent from Shin Bet, 'Libya/plans for attacks on Israeli targets to be carried out by the terrorist organisations', 09.03.1973, in SFA, E4320-07C, Kilowatt, 1973.
78. *Ibid.*
79. *Ibid.*

80. Kilowatt cable no. 6095, sent from Mossad, 'Further to our Watt 6094', 12.03.1973, in SFA, E4320-07C, Kilowatt, 1973.
81. Kilowatt cable no. 6105, sent from Mossad, 'PFLP/GC intentions to attack aircraft', comment: 'source: reliable, with access', 16.04.1973, in SFA, E4320-07C, Kilowatt, 1973.
82. *Ibid.*
83. Guttmann, 'Turning Oil into Blood.'
84. There is currently no publication that mentions these events, but there is a published primary source in German on the Diplomatic Documents Switzerland (DoDis) webpage. This online-accessible report summarised what Swiss intelligence knew at the time about Palestinian terrorist circles in Europe, and it includes a mention of this Mercedes arrest. See Josef Amstutz, member of BuPo, Report intended for the Swiss Office of the Federal Attorney, 'Bericht über den Stand der Informationen der Bundesanwaltschaft über die Tätigkeiten palästinensischer Terrorgruppen und -Netzwerke in Genf, Wien und Paris', 6 June 1973, p. 21, available online: dodis.ch/39519. (This report will be mentioned again in Chapter 7, where it will be referred to as the 'BuPo Schönau report'.)
85. Kilowatt cable no. 7060, sent from the Italian SISDE, 'Automobile Mercedes suspectée de transporter des armes', 14.03.1973, in SFA, E4320-07C, Kilowatt, 1973 (translated from French by the author).
86. *Ibid.*
87. Kilowatt cable no. 4014, sent from the French DST, 'Arrestation de deux ressortissant jordaniens suspects d'être des terroristes palestiniens', comment: 'confidentiel / très urgent', 15.03.1973, in SFA, E4320-07C, Kilowatt, 1973 (translated from French by the author).
88. *Ibid.*
89. Kilowatt cable no. 4015, sent from the French DST, 'Suite notre telex watt 4014 du 15 mars', comment: 'diffusion restreinte / très urgent', 16.03.1973, in SFA, E4320-07C, Kilowatt, 1973 (translated from French by the author).
90. *Ibid.*
91. Kilowatt cable no. 1079, sent from the German BfV, 'Festnahme von zwei terrorverdächtigen Jordanier in Frankreich', comment: 'VS-vertraulich. Amtlich geheimhalten', 15.03.1973, in SFA, E4320-07C, Kilowatt, 1973 (translated from German by the author).
92. *Ibid.*
93. Kilowatt cable [no number], sent from the German BfV, 'Festnahme palästinensicher Terroristen in Frankreich', comment: 'VS-nur für den Dienstgebrauch', 16.03.1973, in SFA, E4320-07C, Kilowatt, 1973 (translated from German by the author).
94. Kilowatt cable no. 5008, sent from MI5, 'priority, secret, Omar Muhammed Talab', 16.03.1973, SFA, E4320-07C, Kilowatt, 1973.

95. Kilowatt cable no. 4017, sent from the French DST, 'Les développements de l'enquête diligente à la suite de l'arrestation à La Grave, le 14 mars 1973, des ressortissants jordaniens', comment: 'diffusion restreinte / très urgent', 20.03.1973, in SFA, E4320-07C, Kilowatt, 1973 (translated from French by the author).
96. *Ibid.*
97. *Ibid.*
98. *Ibid.*
99. *Ibid.*
100. *Ibid.*
101. Kilowatt cable no. 4018, sent from the French DST, 'Précisions complémentaires sur les activités de Omar Muhammed Talab et de Sakhr M'hamed el Khalil', comment: 'diffusion restreinte / très urgent', 21.03.1973, in SFA, E4320-07C, Kilowatt, 1973 (translated from French by the author).
102. *Ibid.*
103. *Ibid.*
104. *Ibid.*
105. Kilowatt cable no. 6099, sent from Mossad, 'Arrest of four suspects in France', 22.03.1973, in SFA, E4320-07C, Kilowatt, 1973.
106. *Ibid.*
107. *Ibid.*
108. For this assassination, see 'Updating the Murderers: The Assassination of Hadi Nakaa and Hamid Shibli' in Chapter 6.
109. Kilowatt cable no. 6099, sent from Mossad, 'Arrest of four suspects in France', 22.03.1973, in SFA, E4320-07C, Kilowatt, 1973.
110. For further details about Halloum, see 'A Terrorist Cell in Latin America and Explosive Letters' in Chapter 3.
111. Kilowatt cable [no number], sent from the German BfV, 'Festnahme von zwei terrorverdächtigen Jordaniern in Frankreich', 21.03.1973, in SFA, E4320-07C, Kilowatt, 1973 (translated from German by the author).
112. Kilowatt cable no. 1079, sent from the German BfV, 'Festnahme von zwei terrorverdächtigen Jordanier in Frankreich', comment: 'VS-vertraulich. Amtlich geheimhalten', 15.03.1973, in SFA, E4320-07C, Kilowatt, 1973 (translated from German by the author).
113. Kilowatt cable [no number], sent from the German BfV, 'Festnahme von zwei terrorverdächtigen Jordaniern in Frankreich', 21.03.1973, in SFA, E4320-07C, Kilowatt, 1973 (translated from German by the author).
114. Some agencies replied to this request but said that they had no records on these suspects; see Kilowatt cable no. 5009, sent from MI5, 'routine confidential, arrest of Jordanian terrorists in France 14 March', 23.03.1973, SFA, E4320-07C, Kilowatt, 1973.
115. Kilowatt cable no. 1082, sent from the German BfV, 'Festnahme – Mohamed Bachir Taha, geb. 1935 in Damaskus / Syrer, Reisepass Nr. 5/73', comment:

'VS-vertraulich. Amtlich geheimhalten', 23.03.1973, in SFA, E4320-07C, Kilowatt, 1973 (translated from German by the author).

116. *Ibid.*

117. Kilowatt cable no. 1085, sent from the German BfV, 'Festnahme palästinensischer Terroristen in Frankreich. Hier: Verhaftung Mohamed Bachir Taha in Berlin', comment: 'VS-vertraulich. Amtlich geheimhalten', 30.03.1973, in SFA, E4320-07C, Kilowatt, 1973 (translated from German by the author).

118. *Ibid.*

119. Kilowatt cable no. 9042, sent from the Dutch BVD, 'Daou, Antoine, born 27-11-1940 in Bichli (Lebanon)', 27.03.1973, in SFA, E4320-07C, Kilowatt, 1973.

120. *Ibid.*

121. *Ibid.*

122. Kilowatt cable no. 1084, sent from the German BfV, 'Daou, Antoine, geb. 27.11.1940 in Bichli/Libanon Inhaber des libanesischen Passes Nr. 1055', 29.03.1973, in SFA, E4320-07C, Kilowatt, 1973 (translated from German by the author).

123. Kilowatt cable no. 4020, sent from the French DST, 'Arrestation en France de deux Jordaniens soupçonnés d'activités terroristes (kilowatt nr 4014 du mars 1973)', comment: 'diffusion restreinte / urgent', 28.03.1973, in SFA, E4320-07C, Kilowatt, 1973 (translated from French by the author).

124. Kilowatt cable no. 4019, sent from the French DST, 'Refoulement de Jamil Abdelhakim et expulsion de Dianne Campbell Lefevre', comment: 'strictement confidentiel / priorité absolue', 22.03.1973, in SFA, E4320-07C, Kilowatt, 1973 (translated from French by the author).

125. *Ibid.*

126. 'La militante de Septembre noir expulsée de France serait liée aux services de renseignement britanniques', *Le Monde*, 24.03.1973.

127. Kilowatt cable no. 4022, sent from the French DST, 'Neutralisation d'un commando palestinien chargé de préparer un attentat par explosifs contre l'Ambassade de Jordanie à Paris', comment: 'mes WATTS (distribution KILOWATT) nos. 4014-4015 4019-4020 des 15, 16, 22 et 28 mars 1973', 13.04.1973, in SFA, E4320-07C, Kilowatt, 1973 (translated from French by the author).

128. *Ibid.*

129. For Black September's Jordanian targets, see 'Attacks against Jordan' in Chapter 5.

130. Kilowatt cable no. 5007, sent from MI5, 'immediate, confidential, Jordanian ambassador London', 03.03.1973, SFA, E4320-07C, Kilowatt, 1973.

131. Kilowatt cable no. 7063, sent from the Italian SISDE, 'Aéroport de Fiumicino – 19/3/1973 – Découverte de 4 mallettes contenant des armes, des explosifs et autre', 20.03.1973, in SFA, E4320-07C, Kilowatt, 1973 (translated from French by the author). For the first such aborted attack at Rome Fiumicino Airport on the night of 25/26 November 1972, see 'Suitcases with Arms in Rome' in Chapter 3.

132. *Ibid.*

133. *Ibid.*
134. Kilowatt cable no. 1092, sent from the German BfV, 'Festnahme des Mohamed Fatha, geb. 1.1.1950 in Beirut, Alias: Mohamed Kebdani, geb 1948 in Marokko', 25.05.1973, in SFA, E4320-07C, Kilowatt, 1973 (translation from German by the author).
135. *Ibid.*
136. Kilowatt cable no. 7064, sent from the Italian SISDE, 'Aéroport de Fiumicino – 19/3/1973 – Découverte de 4 mallettes contenant des armes, des explosifs et autres', comment: 'confidentiel', 21.03.1973, in SFA, E4320-07C, Kilowatt, 1973 (translated from French by the author).
137. *Ibid.*
138. Kilowatt cables no. 7065 and 7066, sent from the Italian SISDE, 'Aéroport de Fiumicino – 19/3/1973 – Découverte de quatre mallettes contenant des armes, des explosifs et autres', 23.03.1973 and 28.03.1973, in SFA, E4320-07C, Kilowatt, 1973 (translated from French by the author).
139. Kilowatt cable no. 7067, sent from the Italian SISDE, 'Aéroport de Fiumicino – 19 mars 1973 – Découverte de 4 mallettes contenant des armes, des explosifs et autre', 30.03.1973, in SFA, E4320-07C, Kilowatt, 1973 (translated from French by the author).
140. *Ibid.*
141. Kilowatt cable no. 7068, sent from the Italian SISDE, 'Aéroport de Fiumicino – 4/4/1973 – Arrestation de deux étrangers', 04.04.1973, in SFA, E4320-07C, Kilowatt, 1973 (translated from French by the author).
142. *Ibid.*
143. Kilowatt cable no. 6013, sent from Shin Bet, 'Terrorists/sabotage intentions at West European airports', 06.04.1973, in SFA, E4320-07C, Kilowatt, 1973.
144. *Ibid.*
145. Kilowatt cable no. 7069, sent from the Italian SISDE, 'Aéroport de Fiumicino – 4/4/1973 – Arrestation de deux étrangers', 04.04.1973, in SFA, E4320-07C, Kilowatt, 1973 (translated from French by the author).
146. *Ibid.*
147. Kilowatt cable no. 5014, sent from MI5, 'immediate, priority, secret, reference your telegram no watt 7068 and 7069 of 5.4.73', 06.04.1973, SFA, E4320-07C, Kilowatt, 1973.
148. *Ibid.*
149. Kilowatt cable no. 4024, sent from the French DST, 'Eventuels projets terroristes de detournement d'un bateau', comment: 'urgent, confidentiel, reference watt nr 9043', 10.04.1973, in SFA, E4320-07C, Kilowatt, 1973 (translated from French by the author).
150. Kilowatt cable no. 7072, sent from the Italian SISDE, 'Aeroporto di Fiumicino, 4.4.1973 – Arresto di due stranieri', 11.04.1973, in SFA, E4320-07C, Kilowatt, 1973 (translated from Italian by the author). For more on the shipping attack and its connection to Khair, see 'The Charges against Khair' in Chapter 5.

151. Kilowatt cable no. 7071, sent from the Italian SISDE, 'Aéroport de Fiumicino – 4/4/1973 – Arrestation de deux étrangers', 09.04.1973, in SFA, E4320-07C, Kilowatt, 1973 (translated from French by the author).

152. *Ibid.*

153. The Tarvisio arrest will be discussed further below; see 'A Parking Ticket that Kills: Using the Schönau Investigation to Track Boudia' in Chapter 7.

154. Kilowatt cable no. 7071, sent from the Italian SISDE, 'Aéroport de Fiumicino – 4/4/1973 – Arrestation de deux étrangers', 09.04.1973, in SFA, E4320-07C, Kilowatt, 1973 (translated from French by the author).

155. Cable with pictures of them and their passports: Kilowatt cable no. 7073, sent from the Italian SISDE, 'Arrestation de deux étrangers, soi-disant Iraniens, à l'Aéroport de Fiumicino/Rome le 4 avril 1973', 14.04.1973; cable with pictures of their weapons, Kilowatt cable no. 7078, sent from the Italian SISDE, 'Aéroport de Fiumicino: 4 avril 1973 – Arrestation de deux étrangers', 10.05.1973; both in SFA, E4320-07C, Kilowatt, 1973 (translated from French by the author).

156. Kilowatt cable no. 7081, sent from the Italian SISDE, 'Aéroport de Fiumicino – 4 avril 1973 – Arrestation de deux étrangers', 28.05.1973, in SFA, E4320-07C, Kilowatt, 1973 (translated from French by the author).

157. *Ibid.*

158. Kilowatt cable no. 7088, sent from the Italian SISDE, 'Aéroport de Rome/ Fiumicino – 4/4/1973, Arrestation de deux étrangers', 18.07.1973, in SFA, E4320-07C, Kilowatt, 1973 (translated from French by the author).

159. Kilowatt cable no. 7100, sent from the Italian SISDE, 'Rome: 4 avril 1973 – arrestation de deux Arabes avec des armes à l'aéroport de Fiumicino. Rome: 17 juin 1973 – explosion d'une automobile Mercedes avec deux Arabes à bord', 20.08.1973, in SFA, E4320-07C, Kilowatt, 1973 (translated from French by the author).

160. Kilowatt cable no. 7096, sent from the Italian SISDE, 'Fiumicino 4.4.73 – arrest of two foreigners', 30.07.1973, in SFA, E4320-07C, Kilowatt, 1973.

161. *Ibid.*

162. 'Arabs Kill 3 and Wound 55 in Athens Airport Lounge', *New York Times*, 06.08.1973.

163. Kilowatt cable no. 6135, sent from Mossad, 'Terrorisme arabe/L'attentat à l'aéroport d'Athens', comment: 'secret', 13.08.1973, in SFA, E4320-07C, Kilowatt, 1973 (translated from French by the author).

164. Kilowatt cable no. 1065, sent from the German BfV, 'Verdacht der Vorbereitung mehrerer Sprengstoffverbrechen sowie Mordandrohung zum Nachteil Franz-Josef Strausz', comment: 'VS-nur für den Dienstgebrauch', 24.01.1973, in SFA, E4320-07C, Kilowatt, 1973 (translated from German by the author).

165. Obviously, the embassy was in Bonn. Cologne was therefore in quotation marks in the cable. *Ibid.*

166. *Ibid.*

167. Kilowatt cable no. 6083, sent from Mossad, 'Possible attack on Franz Josef Strauss', 26.01.1973, in SFA, E4320-07C, Kilowatt, 1973.
168. *Ibid.*
169. Kilowatt cable no. 7054, sent from the Italian SISDE, 'Soupçon de préparation de divers attentats terroristes', 09.02.1973, in SFA, E4320-07C, Kilowatt, 1973.
170. Kilowatt cable no. 2039, sent from the Belgian Sureté d'État, [no title], comment: 'secret, urgent', 24.01.1973, in SFA, E4320-07C, Kilowatt, 1973.
171. *Ibid.*
172. Kilowatt cable no. 1069, sent from the German BfV, 'Planung von Terroraktionen durch Palästinenser', comment: 'geheim, amtlich geheimhalten', 12.02.1973, in SFA, E4320-07C, Kilowatt, 1973 (translated from German by the author).
173. Kilowatt cable no. 6088, sent from Mossad, 'Terror action planned by Palestinians', 13.02.1973, in SFA, E4320-07C, Kilowatt, 1973.
174. Kilowatt cable no. 6110, sent from Shin Bet, 'Theft of passport by Arabs', 09.05.1973, in SFA, E4320-07C, Kilowatt, 1973.
175. Kilowatt cable no. 6082, sent from Mossad, 'Black September – plan to attack Israeli embassy', comment: 'secret', 26.01.1973, in SFA, E4320-07C, Kilowatt, 1973.
176. *Ibid.*
177. *Ibid.*
178. Kilowatt cable no. 9040, sent from the Dutch BVD, 'Sharif abd-el Hafiz a-Shanti', comment: 'source: extremely delicate', 29.01.1973, in SFA, E4320-07C, Kilowatt, 1973.
179. *Ibid.*
180. *Ibid.*
181. Kilowatt cable no. 6085, sent from Mossad, 'Sharif abd-el Hafiz a-Shanti', 31.01.1973, in SFA, E4320-07C, Kilowatt, 1973.
182. Kilowatt cable no. 0043, sent from BuPo, 'Sharif abd-el Hafiz a-Shanti (phonetic)', 01.02.1973, in SFA, E4320-07C, Kilowatt *Sent by Switzerland*, 1971–1977.
183. *Ibid.*
184. Kilowatt cable no. 1067, sent from the German BfV, 'Sharif abd-el Hafiz a-Shanti', 02.02.1973, in SFA, E4320-07C, Kilowatt, 1973.
185. Kilowatt cable no. 5006, sent from MI5, 'routine, secret, Sharif abd-el Hafiz a-Shanti (phonetic)', 02.02.1973, SFA, E4320-07C, Kilowatt, 1973.
186. Kilowatt cable no. 6104, sent from Mossad, 'Terrorists/use of forged passports', 12.04.1973, in SFA, E4320 07C, Kilowatt, 1973.
187. *Ibid.*
188. Kilowatt cable no. 1088, sent from the German BfV, 'Missbräuchliche Benutzung von Reisespässe des afrikanischen Staates Tschad', comment: 'VS-vertraulich, amtlich geheimhalten', 19.04.1973, in SFA, E4320-07C, Kilowatt, 1973 (translated from German by the author).
189. *Ibid.*

190. Kilowatt cable no. 9041, sent from the Dutch BVD, 'Antoine Georges Layous', 31.01.1973, in SFA, E4320-07C, Kilowatt, 1973.
191. This company was the precursor to today's Abela and Co. food service management firm.
192. Kilowatt cable no. 9041, sent from the Dutch BVD, 'Antoine Georges Layous', 31.01.1973, in SFA, E4320-07C, Kilowatt, 1973.
193. Kilowatt cable no. 6089, sent from Mossad, 'Yahya Mohamed abd Jaber', comment: 'source reliable. Sub-source: with access to terrorist circles', 20.02.1973, in SFA, E4320-07C, Kilowatt, 1973.
194. *Ibid.*
195. Kilowatt cable no. 1076, sent from the German BfV, 'Verdacht der versuchten Anwerbung für einen Anschlag auf eine Maschine der El Al', 02.03.1973, in SFA, E4320-07C, Kilowatt, 1973 (translated from German by the author).
196. Kilowatt cable no. 1070, sent from the German BfV, 'Methoden bei Sabotageanschlägen', comment: 'VS-vertraulich, amtlich geheimhalten', 13.02.1973, in SFA, E4320-07C, Kilowatt, 1973 (translated from German by the author).
197. *Ibid.*
198. *Ibid.*
199. Kilowatt cable no. 6098, sent from Mossad, 'Terrorists/New possibility of smuggling weapons aboard planes', 19.03.1973, in SFA, E4320-07C, Kilowatt, 1973.
200. *Ibid.*
201. Sayigh, *Armed Struggle*, 309.

6 A 'BATTLE OF THE SPOOKS' IN PARIS, BEIRUT, NICOSIA, AND ROME

1. Klein, *Striking Back*, 127. Klein believes that the day of the assassination was 6 April, while all police reports suggest 5 April.
2. Bergman, *Rise and Kill First*, 168.
3. Reeve, *One Day in September*, 174.
4. Klein, *Striking Back*, 125.
5. Bergman, *Rise and Kill First*, 668; Reeve, *One Day in September*, 174; Klein, *Striking Back*, 126.
6. Klein, *Striking Back*, 126; Vargo, *Mossad: Six Landmark Missions*, 117; Bar-Zohar and Mishal, *Greatest Missions*, 175.
7. This attack was mentioned above; see 'Attack against the Israeli Embassy in Bangkok' in Chapter 4.
8. Bar-Zohar and Mishal, *Greatest Missions*, 175. For the 9/11-like warning, see 'Terrorist Tactics and Innovation' in Chapter 4.
9. Kilowatt cable no. 4023, sent from the French DST, 'Al-Koubaissi Basil Raoul', comment: 'diffusion restreinte, urgent', 09.04.1973, in SFA, E4320-07C, Kilowatt, 1973 (translated from French by the author).

10. Kilowatt cable no. 4026, sent from the French DST, 'Assassinat à Paris du docteur Al-Kubaissi', comment: 'confidential, très urgent', 13.04.1973, in SFA, E4320-07C, Kilowatt, 1973 (translated from French by the author).
11. *Ibid.*
12. This Swiss cable is missing from the archival records. The French cable referred to it as Kilowatt number 13, sent by the Swiss BuPo on 15 January 1972.
13. Kilowatt cable no. 4026, sent from the French DST, 'Assassinat à Paris du docteur Al-Kubaissi', comment: 'confidential, très urgent', 13.04.1973, in SFA, E4320-07C, Kilowatt, 1973 (translated from French by the author).
14. Kilowatt cable no. 5016, sent from MI5, 'routine, secret, professor al Kubaisi', 13.04.1973, in SFA, E4320-07C, Kilowatt, 1973.
15. Kilowatt cable no. 5017, sent from MI5, 'routine, secret, reference your telegram no kilowatt 4026 of 13.04.73', 16.04.1973, in SFA, E4320-07C, Kilowatt, 1973.
16. *Ibid.*
17. Kilowatt cable no. 4030, sent from the French DST, 'Concerne les mouvements et déplacements de Al-Kubaissi (Koubaissi) Basil Raoul', 17.05.1973, in SFA, E4320-07C, Kilowatt, 1973 (translated from French by the author).
18. *Ibid.*
19. Kilowatt cable no. 4034, sent from the French DST, 'Affaire Al-Koubaisi Basil, assassiné à Paris le 5.4.1973. Demande de renseignements concernant des individus ayant été en rapport avec l'intéressé', 10.07.1973, in SFA, E4320-07C, Kilowatt, 1973 (translated from French by the author).
20. Kilowatt cable no. 7089, sent from the Italian SISDE, 'Al-Koubaissi Basil, assassiné à Paris le 5.4.1973', 20.07.1973, in SFA, E4320-07C, Kilowatt, 1973 (translated from French by the author).
21. 'Le FPLP. dénonce la complicité: des autorités françaises', *Le Monde*, 09.04.1973.
22. Klein, *Striking Back*, 127.
23. The people who knew about the Club de Berne were the head of Swiss intelligence (BuPo), the minister of the interior, the attorney general, and the officers directly involved in the Kilowatt information exchanges; Guttmann, *Origins of International Counterterrorism*, 185–186.
24. See Vincent Nouzille, *Les tueurs de la République: Assassinats et opérations spéciales des services secrets* (Paris: Fayard, 2016); Damien van Puyvelde, 'French Paramilitary Actions during the Algerian War of Independence, 1956–1958', *Intelligence and National Security*, 36/6 (2021), 898–909.
25. Bergman, *Rise and Kill First*, 159.
26. Chamberlin, *The Global Offensive*, 189.
27. Black and Morris, *Israel's Secret Wars*, 275.
28. Klein, *Striking Back*, 133, 136; Reeve, *One Day in September*, 180.
29. Bergman, *Rise and Kill First*, 163.
30. 'Terror to End Terror?' *Time Magazine*, 23.04.1973, page 19 in the printed copy, page 29 in the online version accessible via their 'vault' service: https://time.com/vault/issue/1973-04-23/page/29/.

31. Bergman, *Rise and Kill First*, 163.
32. Sayigh, *Armed Struggle*, 356.
33. *Ibid.*
34. 'Terror to End Terror?' *Time Magazine*, page 20 in print, page 30 online. Black and Morris also mention that the seized documents yielded vital intelligence about Black September, Fatah, PFLP, and DFLP planned operations; see Black and Morris, *Israel's Secret Wars*, 275. The authors cite Rafik Halabi, *The West Bank Story* (New York: Harcourt, 1981), 87.
35. Bergman, *Rise and Kill First*, 167.
36. For Mohamed Abu Yussuf as sponsor of the the attack that happened in parallel to the Bangkok embassy siege, see Kilowatt cable no. 5001, sent from MI5, 'Reference to our telegram no watt 5036 of 28.12.72', comment: 'routine – secret', 09.01.1973, in SFA, E4320-07C, Kilowatt, 1973. This cable is also mentioned in 'Attack against the Israeli Embassy in Bangkok' in Chapter 4.
37. Klein, *Striking Back*, 130; Reeve, *One Day in September*, 179. Klein posits that the two were also (loosely) linked to the Munich attack.
38. Klein, *Striking Back*, 130.
39. Kilowatt cable no. 6105, sent from Mossad, 'PFLP/GC intentions to attack aircraft', comment: 'source: reliable, with access', 16.04.1973, in SFA, E4320-07C, Kilowatt, 1973.
40. *Ibid.* Paul Thomas Chamberlin discusses the American reaction to the Beirut raid, and also mentions that some Palestinians claimed there was US involvement, in Chamberlin, *The Global Offensive*, 189–190.
41. Kilowatt cable no. 6107, sent from Mossad, 'Plans for terrorist attacks during Israel's Independence Day', 30.04.1973, in SFA, E4320-07C, Kilowatt, 1973.
42. *Ibid.*
43. For such reports about Palestinians and Europeans smuggling weapons to Israel, see 'Arms Smuggling via Mercedes Sales' in Chapter 5.
44. Kilowatt cable no. 6107, sent from Mossad, 'Plans for terrorist attacks during Israel's Independence Day', 30.04.1973, in SFA, E4320-07C, Kilowatt, 1973.
45. Kilowatt cable no. 5019, sent from MI5, 'Mohammed Abdul Karim Fuheid', comment: 'priority, confidential', 07.05.1973, in SFA, E4320-07C, Kilowatt, 1973.
46. Reeve, *One Day in September*, 186.
47. *Ibid.*, 184.
48. Klein, *Striking Back*, 146; Reeve, *One Day in September*, 184.
49. Chamberlin, *The Global Offensive*, 189.
50. Dobson, *Black September*, 131. Meir's speech is also mentioned in the *Time Magazine* article, 'Terror to End Terror?', page 23 in print, page 35 online.
51. Klein, *Striking Back*, 147; Bergman, *Rise and Kill First*, 167.
52. Bergman, *Rise and Kill First*, 168; Reeve, *One Day in September*, 186. Klein mentions that one of Salameh's operatives, Moussa Abu-Zaid, was also killed in Athens on

NOTES TO PAGES 160–164

9 April. This alleged second assassination is only mentioned by Klein and could not be confirmed by another secondary source or by any primary source. Given the similarity of the two names, Moussa Abu-Zaid and Zaid Muchassi, and given that both killings were said to have happened in Athens at nearly the same time, it is conceivable that Klein thought it was two people when, in fact, it was only one person with different Arab transcriptions of their name. See Klein, *Striking Back*, 148–149.

53. Klein, *Striking Back*, 148.
54. 'A Band of Arab Guerrillas Attacks Israelis on Cyprus', *New York Times*, 10.04.1973.
55. For more detail on this Libyan-supported Palestinian group, see Guttmann, 'Turning Oil into Blood'.
56. Kilowatt cable no. 5019, sent from MI5, 'Mohammed Abdul Karim Fuheid', comment: 'priority – confidential', 07.05.1973, in SFA, E4320-07C, Kilowatt, 1973.
57. *Ibid.*
58. For an account of how the murder and subsequent arrest happened, see Paul Hofmann, 'El Al Employee in Rome Is Shot to Death by an Arab', *New York Times*, 28.04.1973.
59. Kilowatt cable no. 7075, sent from the Italian SISDE, 'Rome – 27/04/1973 – assassinat de Vittorio Olivares, employé de la Cie "El Al"', comment: 'urgent', 28.04.1973, in SFA, E4320-07C, Kilowatt, 1973 (translated from French by the author) [cable will be referred to as SISDE cable no. 7075].
60. *Ibid.* The name of the Black September killer is not anonymised because it was mentioned in other publications, for instance in Reeve, *One Day in September*, 174.
61. SISDE cable no. 7075.
62. The cable referred to Kilowatt cable no. 7032, sent from the Italian SISDE, 'Meurtre du ressortissant Jordanien Zwaiter Wael – Rome – 16 octobre 1972', 17.10.1972, in SFA, E4320-07C, Kilowatt, 1971–1972 (translated from French by the author); see Chapter 3, note 13.
63. SISDE cable no. 7075.
64. Kilowatt cable no. 7076, sent from the Italian SISDE, 'Rome – 27/04/1973 – assassinat de l'employé de la Cie "El Al" – Vittorio Olivares', 02.05.1973, in SFA, E4320-07C, Kilowatt, 1973 (translated from French by the author).
65. *Ibid.*
66. 'World News Briefs', *New York Times*, 29.04.1973.
67. *Ibid.*
68. Hofmann, 'El Al Employee in Rome Is Shot to Death by an Arab'.
69. Kilowatt cable no. 7079, sent from the Italian SISDE, 'Rome – 27/04/1973 – assassinat de Vittorio Olivares, employé de la Cie "El Al"', 15.06.1973, in SFA, E4320-07C, Kilowatt, 1973 (translated from French by the author).
70. Sayigh, *Armed Struggle*, 311.

71. Kilowatt cable no. 7074, sent from the Italian SISDE, 'Aéroport de Fiumicino 24 avril 1973 – découverte de bombes', 26.04.1973, in SFA, E4320-07C, Kilowatt, 1973 (translated from French by the author). This was the third time in a few months that weapons had been abandoned at Rome Fiumicino Airport – on 27 November 1972, then 19 March 1973, and now 24 April 1973.
72. *Ibid.*
73. Kilowatt cable no. 7080, sent from the Italian SISDE, 'Aéroport de Fiumicino / 24 avril 1973 – Découverte de bombes', 18.05.1973, in SFA, E4320-07C, Kilowatt, 1973 (translated from French by the author).
74. Kilowatt cable no. 1097, sent from the German BfV, 'Arabischer Terrorrismus', 14.06.1973, in SFA, E4320-07C, Kilowatt, 1973 (translated from German by the author).
75. Kilowatt cable [no number], sent from the German BfV, 'Aktivitäten palästinensischer Terrororganisationen', comment: 'VS-vertraulich, amtlich geheimhalten', 18.06.1973, in SFA, E4320-07C, Kilowatt, 1973 (translated from German by the author).
76. Kilowatt cable no. 1093, sent from the German BfV, 'Palestine People's Fighting Fund', 28.05.1973, in SFA, E4320-07C, Kilowatt, 1973 (translated from German by the author).
77. Kilowatt cable no. 0047, sent from BuPo, 'Palestine People's Fighting Fund', 06.06.1973, in SFA, E4320-07C, Kilowatt *Sent by Switzerland*, 1971–1977 [cable will be referred to as BuPo cable no. 0047].
78. This was also confirmed by a later cable from Italy: Kilowatt cable no. 7080, sent from the Italian SISDE, 'Palestine People's Fighting Fund', 15.05.1973, in SFA, E4320-07C, Kilowatt, 1973 (translated from French by the author).
79. BuPo cable no. 0047.
80. Kilowatt cable no. 9047, sent from the Dutch BVD, 'Palestine People's Fighting Fund', 06.06.1973, in SFA, E4320-07C, Kilowatt, 1973.
81. Kilowatt cable no. 8001, sent from SREL, 'Passage clandestine d'un Arabe palestinien non identifié à travers le Grand-Duché de Luxembourg', 04.06.1973, in SFA, E4320-07C, Kilowatt, 1973 (translated from French by the author).
82. *Ibid.*
83. Kilowatt cable no. 1096, sent from the German BfV, 'Arabischer Terrorismus', comment: 'VS – nur für den Dienstgebrauch', 07.06.1973, in SFA, E4320-07C, Kilowatt, 1973 (translated from German by the author).
84. *Ibid.*
85. Kilowatt cable no. 9048, sent from the Dutch BVD, 'M. G. A. A. [only initials given here, full name of suspect was in the cable title] born Port-Said 17.3.1930', 08.06.1973, in SFA, E4320-07C, Kilowatt, 1973.
86. Kilowatt cable no. 2041, sent from the Belgian Sureté d'État, 'Terrorisme arabe', 14.06.1973, in SFA, E4320-07C, Kilowatt, 1973 (translated from French by the author).
87. *Ibid.*

88. Kilowatt cable no. 6118, sent from Mossad, 'Arab terrorist activity', 18.06.1973, in SFA, E4320-07C, Kilowatt, 1973. For earlier alerts about stolen airline uniforms, see Chapter 3 and Chapter 5, in each chapter in the section headed 'Terrorist Tactics and Innovation'.
89. Kilowatt cable no. 2044, sent from the Belgian Sureté d'État, 'Terrorisme arabe', 16.07.1973, in SFA, E4320-07C, Kilowatt, 1973 (translated from French by the author).
90. Vargo, *Mossad: Six Landmark Missions*, 120.
91. Bergman, *Rise and Kill First*, 168.
92. Vittorio Olivares was murdered in Rome on Via XX Settembre, but the office where he worked was on Via Barberini. For Olivares' murder, see 'Black September Kills Vittorio Olivares'.
93. Klein, *Striking Back*, 149.
94. Bergman, *Rise and Kill First*, 168–169.
95. As written in an AMAN (Israeli military intelligence) annual report, cited in Bergman, *Rise and Kill First*, 168.
96. *Ibid.*
97. Kilowatt cable no. 7083, sent from the Italian SISDE, 'Rome, 17.6.1973 – explosion d'une automobile Mercedes ayant deux Arabes a bord', 18.06.1973, in SFA, E4320-07C, Kilowatt, 1973 (translated from French by the author) [hereafter cited as 'SISDE cable no. 7083'].
98. 'World News Briefs', *New York Times*, 29.04.1973.
99. SISDE cable no. 7083.
100. *Ibid.* On the same day that the Italian cable was sent, Swiss intelligence replied and informed its partners that it had no records of the two Arabs who were killed in the car explosion; Kilowatt cable no. 0049, sent from BuPo, 'Explosion d'une voiture ayant deux Arabes a bord, Rome, 17.6.1973', 18.06.1973, in SFA, E4320-07C, Kilowatt *Sent by Switzerland*, 1971–1977.
101. Kilowatt cable no. 7085, sent from the Italian SISDE, 'Rome, 17.6.1973 – explosion d'une voiture Mercedes ayant deux Arabes a bord', 26.06.1973, in SFA, E4320-07C, Kilowatt, 1973 (translated from French by the author).
102. Kilowatt cable no. 1100, sent from the German BfV, 'Explosion eines Mercedes, am 17.6.1973 in Rom', comment: 'VS-vertraulich – amtlich geheimhalten', 27.06.1973, in SFA, E4320-07C, Kilowatt, 1973 (translated from German by the author).
103. *Ibid.*
104. *Ibid.*
105. Kilowatt cable no. 7087, sent from the Italian SISDE, 'Rome, 17.6.1973 – Explosion d'une voiture Mercedes ayant deux arabes a bord', 30.07.1973, in SFA, E4320-07C, Kilowatt, 1973 (translated from French by the author).
106. The Shibli and Nakaa killing was on 17 June 1973, the Lillehammer affair on 21 July 1973, and this cable was sent on 30 July 1973 as a follow up to Shibli and Nakaa.
107. Bergman, *Rise and Kill First*, 169.

108. Kilowatt cable no. 7100, sent from the Italian SISDE, 'Rome: 4 avril 1973 – arrestation de deux Arabes avec des armes à l'aéroport de Fiumicino. Rome: 17 juin 1973 – explosion d'une automobile Mercedes avec deux Arabes à bord', 20.08.1973, in SFA, E4320-07C, Kilowatt, 1973 (translated from French by the author).
109. Kilowatt cable no. 5022, sent from MI5, 'Arab terrorism', comment: 'priority – secret', 24.05.1973, in SFA, E4320-07C, Kilowatt, 1973 [hereafter cited as 'MI5 cable no. 5022, 1973'].
110. *Ibid.*
111. *Ibid.*
112. Kilowatt cable no. 1094, sent from the German BfV, 'Arabischer Terrorismus', comment: 'VS-vertraulich – amtlich geheimhalten', 06.06.1973, in SFA, E4320-07C, Kilowatt, 1973 (translated from German by the author).
113. *Ibid.*
114. Kilowatt cable no. 1101, sent from the German BfV, 'Arabischer Terrorismus', comment: 'VS-vertraulich – amtlich geheimhalten', 28.06.1973, in SFA, E4320-07C, Kilowatt, 1973 (translated from German by the author).
115. *Ibid.*
116. For Kilowatt cooperation that revealed car dealing as terrorist cover, see 'Arms Smuggling via Mercedes Sales' in Chapter 5.
117. Kilowatt cable no. 5027, sent from MI5, 'Explosion in Arab car – Rome, 17.6.73', comment: 'priority – confidential', 19.06.1973, in SFA, E4320-07C, Kilowatt, 1973 [hereafter cited as 'MI5 cable no. 5027, 1973'].
118. MI5 cable no. 5022, 1973.
119. MI5 cable no. 5027, 1973.
120. MI5 referred here to Kilowatt cable no. 4017, sent from the French DST, 'Les développements de l'enquête diligente à la suite de l'arrestation à La Grave, le 14 mars 1973, des ressortissants jordaniens', comment: 'diffusion restreinte / très urgent', 20.03.1973, in SFA, E4320-07C, Kilowatt, 1973 (translated from French by the author) (cable also mentioned in Chapter 5, note 95).
121. MI5 cable no. 5027, 1973.
122. *Ibid.*
123. Kilowatt cable no. 9049, sent from the Dutch BVD, 'Rome, 17-6-73, explosion of an automobile, Mercedes, with two Arabs on board', 19.06.1973, in SFA, E4320-07C, Kilowatt, 1973.
124. BVD cable no. 9026; see Chapter 3, note 59. For more details about Rubhi Halloum, see 'A Terrorist Cell in Latin America and Explosive Letters' in Chapter 3.
125. Kilowatt cable no. 6130, sent from Mossad, 'Terrorists/departure of terrorist squad for Europe', comment: 'source reliable, with access to terrorist circles', 26.07.1973, in SFA, E4320-07C, Kilowatt, 1973.
126. For more details about this failed terrorist attack in which a booby-trapped record-player was smuggled aboard a plane, see 'Two Attempts at Aircraft Sabotage in Rome' in Chapter 3.

127. Kilowatt cable no. 6134, sent from Mossad, 'Departure of terrorist squad for Europe', 13.08.1973, in SFA, E4320-07C, Kilowatt, 1973.
128. Bergman, *Rise and Kill First*, 169.

7 A CAR BOMB IN PARIS, A FIRING SQUAD IN DC, A THWARTED ATTACK NEAR VIENNA

1. According to Reeve, Boudia's sex life caused such exhilaration in Mossad that they nicknamed him 'Bluebeard'; Reeve, *One Day in September*, 186.
2. Klein, *Striking Back*, 155.
3. Fred Burton and John Bruning, *Chasing Shadows: a Special Agent's Lifelong Hunt to Bring a Cold War Assassin to Justice* (New York: Palgrave Macmillan, 2011), 175.
4. Klein, *Striking Back*, 154.
5. Reeve, *One Day in September*, 187; Ostrovsky and Hoy, *By Way of Deception*, 204–205.
6. Reeve, *One Day in September*, 187.
7. For more details about this assassination, see 'Updating the Murderers: The Assassination of Mahmoud al-Hamshari' in Chapter 4.
8. Vargo, *Mossad: Six Landmark Missions*, 121; Black and Morris, *Israel's Secret Wars*, 275. See also Thomas Skelton-Robinson, 'Im Netz verheddert. Die Beziehungen des bundesdeutschen Linksterrorismus zur Volksfront für die Befreiung Palästinas (1969–1980)', in *Die RAF und der linke Terrorismus*, vol. II, edited by Wolfgang Kraushaar (Hamburg: Hamburger Edition, 2006), 828–904, 847.
9. Tinnin and Christensen, *The Hit Team*, 95–96.
10. Boudia as global terrorism coordinator and training facilitator was also mentioned by former Mossad officer Victor Ostrovsky; see Ostrovsky and Hoy, *By Way of Deception*, 202.
11. Klein, *Striking Back*, 156.
12. Bergman, *Rise and Kill First*, 169. The same informant, Sadness, revealed plans to detonate a bomb at an El Al office in Rome in June 1973, which Mossad prevented by killing Abdel Hadi Nakaa and Abdel Hamid Shibli. See 'Updating the Murderers: The Assassination of Abdel Hadi Nakaa and Abdel Hamid Shibli' in Chapter 6.
13. Reeve, *One Day in September*, 187.
14. Bergman, *Rise and Kill First*, 169; Klein, *Striking Back*, 156–157.
15. Bird, *The Good Spy*, 140. Mossad also specifically mentioned these two attacks in Kilowatt cable no. 6086, sent from Mossad, 'Preliminary investigation in Switzerland in connection with arrest of three Arabs', comment: 'ref. watt 0041 of 30 January 1973', 05.02.1973, in SFA, E4320-07C, Kilowatt, 1973.
16. Reeve, *One Day in September*, 186.
17. Klein, *Striking Back*, 156.
18. Kilowatt cable no. 6084, sent from Mossad, 'False Israeli passports in the hands of terrorists', 29.01.1973, in SFA, E4320-07C, Kilowatt, 1973.

19. *Ibid.*
20. Kilowatt cable no. 7049, sent from the Italian SISDE, 'Arabes porteurs de passeports Israéliens', 30.01.1973, in SFA, E4320-07C, Kilowatt, 1973 (translated from French by the author).
21. *Ibid.*
22. Kilowatt cable no. 7050, sent from the Italian SISDE, 'Arabes porteurs de passeports Israéliens', 03.02.1973, in SFA, E4320-07C, Kilowatt, 1973 (translated from French by the author).
23. *Ibid.*
24. For Mossad being allowed to interrogate Palestinians in Austria, see Thomas Riegler, 'Das "Spinnennetz" des internationalen Terrorismus. Der "Schwarze September" und die gescheiterte Geiselnahme von Schönau 1973', *Vierteljahrshefte für Zeitgeschichte*, September 2015, https://doi.org/10.1524/vfzg.2012.0028, 598. For Mossad being allowed to interrogate Palestinian detainees in Italy, see Ostrovsky and Hoy, *By Way of Deception*, 201.
25. Kilowatt cable no. 0041, sent from BuPo, 'Premiers résultats de l'enquête menée en Suisse en corrélation avec l'arrestation de 3 Arabes, porteurs de passeports israéliens falsifiés, à Vienne le 20 janvier 1973', 30.01.1973, in SFA, E4320-07C, Kilowatt *Sent by Switzerland*, 1971–1977 (translation from French by the author) [hereafter cited as 'BuPo cable no. 0041'].
26. *Ibid.*
27. *Ibid.*
28. *Ibid.*
29. *Ibid.* Bollier was mentioned in the online-accessible BuPo Schönau report. See also her Dodis file: dodis.ch/P51901.
30. Zohair (alternative spellings included Zohar, Zuhair and Zuheir) Abdel Kader Shibl was mentioned in the online-accessible BuPo Schönau report. See also his Dodis file: dodis.ch/P51882.
31. Catherine Erschoff was mentioned in the online-accessible BuPo Schönau report. See also her Dodis file: dodis.ch/P51904.
32. For more context about the persona and life of Daoud Barakat, see also Jonathan Kreutner, *Die Schweiz und Israel: Auf dem Weg zu einem differenzierten historischen Bewusstsein* (Zurich: Chronos, 2013), 91–152, about the establishment of a PLO observer office at the United Nations in Geneva. Barakat was a crucial figure in this process and the main official contact person for the Swiss government in matters related to the Palestinian movement. For a collection of primary documents from the Swiss Foreign Office related to Daoud Barakat and the establishment of the PLO office in Geneva, see the online database of the Diplomatic Documents Switzerland, Dodis, under the permanent link: dodis.ch/P48577.
33. In the French cable, sent a day after Boudia was killed, the same licence plate number was mentioned, and it was also noted that the car was registered to Boudia's former wife, Adria Guerrar. See DST cable no. 4032.

34. BuPo cable no. 0041. In secondary literature, it is not mentioned that Boudia had a wife and he is usually presented as a 'playboy' with many girlfriends. In this respect, intelligence files and journalistic accounts differ.
35. *Ibid.*
36. Kilowatt cable no. 44, sent from BuPo, 'Identification du soi-disant R. Bertin', 07.02.1973, in SFA, E4320-07C, Kilowatt *Sent by Switzerland*, 1971–1977.
37. Kilowatt cable no. 6086, sent from Mossad, 'Preliminary investigation in Switzerland in connection with arrest of three Arabs', comment: 'ref. watt 0041 of 30 January 1973', 05.02.1973, in SFA, E4320-07C, Kilowatt, 1973.
38. *Ibid.*
39. *Ibid.*
40. *Ibid.*
41. Kilowatt cable no. 7053, sent from the Italian SISDE, 'Arabes arrêtés à la frontière du Tarvis, en possession de faux passeports Israéliens', 07.02.1973, in SFA, E4320-07C, Kilowatt, 1973 (translated from French by the author).
42. Kilowatt cable no. 6092, sent from Mossad, 'Detention of Black September members in Vienna', comment: 'long message', 23.02.1973, in SFA, E4320-07C, Kilowatt, 1973 [hereafter cited as 'Mossad cable no. 6092'].
43. *Ibid.*
44. *Ibid.*
45. *Ibid.* This also corresponded to what the Swiss cable had said about the terrorist suspects arrested in Vienna and a fourth person in Geneva who was going to give them exact instructions; see BuPo cable no. 0041.
46. In September 1972, a few weeks after the Munich Olympics attack, the German BfV shared intelligence via Kilowatt about Black September operational methods. The German cable also stressed the 'need-to-know' approach for organising attacks; see Kilowatt cable no. 1032, sent from the German BfV, 'Leiter der Organisation Schwarzer September', 25.09.1972, in SFA, E4320-07C, Kilowatt, 1971–1972 (translated from German by the author). For a comparison of intelligence assessments of Black September methods with what is currently known from secondary literature, see Guttmann, *The Origins of International Terrorism*, 203.
47. Mossad cable no. 6092.
48. *Ibid.*
49. *Ibid.*
50. Kilowatt cable [no cable number but it was an annex to the previous cable no. 6092], sent from Mossad, 'Suite à la teneur de notre watt 6092 du 23.2.73', 23.02.1973, in SFA, E4320-07C, Kilowatt, 1973 (translated from French by the author).
51. *Ibid.*
52. *Ibid.*
53. BuPo Schönau report.
54. Kilowatt cable [no cable number, because it was a direct message from Mossad to BuPo], sent from Mossad, 'Votre telex du 6.3.1973', comment: 'Orbis Paris à

307

Police Fédérale Berne, urgent, att. Dr Amstein'; exceptionally the cable was signed personally by a member of Mossad 'cordialement votre, S. Cohen', 07.03.1973, in SFA, E4320-07C, Kilowatt, 1973 (translated from French by the author).

55. *Ibid.*
56. *Ibid.*
57. BuPo Schönau report.
58. Kilowatt cable no. 6097, sent from Shin Bet, 'Detention of Black September members in Vienna – Ali Zibag', comment: 'further to our report no. Watt 6092', 13.03.1973, in SFA, E4320-07C, Kilowatt, 1973.
59. *Ibid.*
60. *Ibid.*
61. *Ibid.*
62. For more details about Palestinian attacks against Jordan and Club de Berne warnings in this respect, see 'Attacks against Jordan' in Chapter 5.
63. Kilowatt cable no. 6101, sent from Mossad, 'Detention of Black September members in Vienna – Ali Zibag', comment: 'ref. our Watt 6092 of 23 Feb. 1973', 27.03.1973, in SFA, E4320-07C, Kilowatt, 1973.
64. Kilowatt cable no. 6100, sent from Mossad, 'Detention of Black September members in Vienna', comment: 'further to our Watt 6092 of 23 February 1973', 27.03.1973, in SFA, E4320-07C, Kilowatt, 1973.
65. Riegler, 'Das "Spinnennetz" des internationalen Terrorismus', 599. For a description of Operation Spring of Youth, see 'Operation Spring of Youth' in Chapter 6.
66. Gerald Freihofer, 'Kreisky und die PLO', *Wochenpresse*, no. 29, 1979, page 10.
67. Riegler, 'Das "Spinnennetz" des internationalen Terrorismus', 599. This is also mentioned in Dahlke, *Demokratischer Staat und transnationaler Terrorismus*, 195, who refers to Robert Kriechbaumer. *Die Ära Kreisky: Österreich 1970–1983 in der historischen Analyse, im Urteil der politischen Kontrahenten und in Karikaturen von Ironimus* (Vienna: Böhlau, 2004), 276, note 646.
68. Freihofer, 'Kreisky und die PLO', 10.
69. The account of this Schönau attack is based on Dahlke, *Demokratischer Staat und transnationaler Terrorismus*, 197–214.
70. *Ibid.*, 203.
71. *Ibid.*, 211. Dahlke refers here to the official transcript of the phone conversation between Kreisky and the Egyptian ambassador who was standing next to the terrorists' car.
72. *Ibid.*, 212.
73. Kathrin Bachleitner, 'Golda Meir and Bruno Kreisky: a Political and Personal Duel', *Israel Studies*, 23/1 (Spring 2018), 26–49, 28.
74. Fink, *West Germany and Israel*, 235, note 80.
75. Bruno Kreisky, Oliver Rathkolb, Johannes Kunz, and Margit Schmidt, *Im Strom der Politik: der Memoiren zweiter Teil* (Vienna: Kremayr and Scheriau, 2000), 322; 'Herr, öffne das Herz Österreichs', *Der Spiegel*, 41, 08.10.1973, 118.

76. Fred A. Lazin, 'Israel's Demographic Needs Versus "Freedom of Choice": the Case of Soviet Jewish Émigrés, 1967–1990', *Tel Aviver Jahrbuch für Deutsche Geschichte*, 35, 2007, 273–291.

77. Paul Thomas Chamberlin, 'Schönau and the Eagles of the Palestinian Revolution: Refugees, Guerillas, and Human Rights in the Global 1970s', *Cold War History*, 12/4 (2012), 595–614.

78. *Stern*, 7 November 1973, cited in Fink, *West Germany and Israel*, 237, note 87.

79. John Hughes-Wilson, *Intelligence Blunders* (London: Carroll and Graf, 1999), 249; 'Was the Hijacking of an Austrian Train Filled with Soviet Jews a Diversion before the Yom Kippur War?' *Israel Defence*, 18.12. 2011.

80. Kilowatt cable no. 6145, sent from Mossad, 'Terrorists / the attack on train taking Jewish emigrants from the Soviet Union to Austria', 01.10.1973, in SFA, E4320-07C, Kilowatt, 1973.

81. Dina Rezk, 'Yom Kippur War', in Dina Rezk, *The Arab World and Western Intelligence. Analysing the Middle East, 1956–1981* (Edinburgh University Press, 2017), 249–283.

82. Uri Bar-Joseph and Arie W. Kruglanski, 'Intelligence Failure and Need for Cognitive Closure: On the Psychology of the Yom Kippur Surprise', *Political Psychology*, 24/1 (2003).

83. Kilowatt cable no. 7006, sent from the Italian SISDE, 'Attacks against pipeline Trieste-Vienna. 4 August 1972', 04.08.1972; Kilowatt cable no. 7007, sent from the Italian SISDE, 'Attacks against pipeline Trieste-Vienna-Ingolstadt 4 August 1972', 07.08.1972 [hereafter cited as 'SISDE cable no. 7007']; both in SFA, E4320-07C, Kilowatt, 1971–1972.

84. Reeve, *One Day in September*, 47, 186. On 18 September 1972, Italian intelligence sent pictures of the pipeline and how it looked after the attack; Kilowatt cable no. 7023, sent from the Italian SISDE, 'Attacks against pipeline Trieste-Ingolstadt-Vienna 4.8.1972', 18.09.1972, in SFA, E4320-07C, Kilowatt, 1971–1972.

85. SISDE cable no. 7007.

86. Kilowatt cable no. 7009, sent from the Italian SISDE, 'Attacks against pipeline Trieste-Ingolstadt-Vienna. 4.8.1972', 09.08.1972, in SFA, E4320-07C, Kilowatt, 1971–1972.

87. Kilowatt cable no. 1012, sent from the German BfV, 'Irakischen Staatsangehörigen [M. a. B.], geb. 7.3.1938 in Bagdad, wohnhaft: Iserlohn, in der Langen Heeke 27', 24.08.1972, in SFA, E4320-07C, Kilowatt, 1971–1972 (translated from German by the author).

88. Kilowatt cable no. 1053, sent from the German BfV, '[M. a. B.]', comment: 'Bezug unsere Watt-nr. 1012 vom 24.8.1972', 14.11.1972, in SFA, E4320-07C, Kilowatt, 1971–1972 (translated from German by the author).

89. Kilowatt cable no. 7062, sent from the Italian SISDE, 'Attentat à l'oléoduc de Trieste – 4 aout 1972', 16.03.1973, in SFA, E4320-07C, Kilowatt, 1973 (translated from French by the author) [hereafter cited as 'SISDE cable no. 7062'].

90. Numerous newspaper articles mentioned Thérèse Lefevre. For instance, 'Une Françoise est impliquée dans l'attentat commis en 1972 contre un oléoduc à Trieste', *Le Monde*, 14.03.1973.
91. 'Les Assassinats politiques en France depuis 1972', *Le Monde*, 21.12.1974.
92. SISDE cable no. 7062.
93. *Ibid.*; Reeve, *One Day in September*, 286, note 27.
94. SISDE cable no. 7062.
95. Kilowatt cable no. 4032, sent from the French DST, 'Explosion d'une Renault R16 ayant entrainé la mort d'un militant actif pro-palestinien: Mohamed Boudia', 29.06.1973, in SFA, E4320-07C, Kilowatt, 1973 (translated from French by the author) [hereafter cited as 'DST cable no. 4032'].
96. The licence plate number and car description were identical to the details sent in the Swiss cable concerning Boudia's car; BuPo cable no. 0041 (see above, note 25).
97. DST cable no. 4032.
98. *Ibid.*
99. *Ibid.*
100. *Ibid.*
101. 'M. Boudia, militant de la cause palestinienne est tué par l'explosion de sa voiture', *Le Monde*, 29.06.1973.
102. Yossi Melman, 'Who Killed Joe Alon? Nearly 40 Years after the Murder of Israel's Air Attaché in Washington, the Case Remains Unsolved: a New Book Seeks to Shed More Light on the Affair', *Haaretz*, 01.04.2011.
103. Bernard Gwertzman, 'Israeli Attache Shot Dead at Home near Washington', *New York Times*, 02.07.1973.
104. Rami Rom, 'A 49-Year-Old Cover-up', *The Times of Israel*, 01.07.2022.
105. Burton and Bruning, *Chasing Shadows*, 214.
106. *Ibid.*
107. *Ibid.*
108. Kilowatt cable no. 6122, sent from Shin Bet, 'Terrorists / Intention to attack military attachés', comment: 'Source: with access, reliability unclear', 13.07.1973, in SFA, E4320-07C, Kilowatt, 1973.
109. *Ibid.*
110. Klein, *Striking Back*, 154.

8 LILLEHAMMER FIASCO: OFFICIAL CONDEMNATION, COVERT APPROVAL

1. The criminal records of this murder case and the transcript of the judgment can be consulted at the Eidsivating Criminal Court in Norway, case number 182/1973, 01.02.1974.
2. Black and Morris, *Israel's Secret Wars*, 276.
3. Reeve, *One Day in September*, 195.

4. *Ibid.*, 197.
5. Black and Morris, *Israel's Secret Wars*, 276.
6. Klein, *Striking Back*, 159; Bergman, *Rise and Kill First.*
7. Klein, *Striking Back*, 167.
8. Kilowatt cable no. 45, sent from BuPo, 'Kilowatt – Meldungen', comment: 'an Orbis Paris von BuPo CH', 09.05.1973, in SFA, E4320-07C, Kilowatt *Sent by Switzerland*, 1971–1977.
9. Kilowatt cable no. 6007, sent from Mossad, 'Terrorist delegation in Europe', comment: 'source with some access to terrorist circles in a European country – usually reliable', 07.12.1971; Kilowatt cable no. 6008, sent from Mossad, 'Terrorist delegation in Europe', comment: 'immediate', 09.12.1971; Kilowatt cable no. 6010, sent from Mossad, 'Terrorist delegation in Europe', comment: 'immediate', 14.12.1971; all in SFA, E4320-07C, Kilowatt, 1971–1972.
10. Kilowatt cable no. 5032, sent from MI5, 'Arab terrorism operation "Kilowatt"', comment (in French): 'A l'intention de la police fédérale', 24.12.1972; Kilowatt cable no. 5034, sent from MI5, 'Arab terrorism', comment: 'immediate – secret', 27.12.1972; both in SFA, E4320-07C, Kilowatt, 1971–1972. For more detail about the thwarted attack in Scandinavia that was meant to happen in parallel to the Bangkok attack, see 'Attack against the Israeli Embassy in Bangkok' in Chapter 4.
11. Kilowatt cable [no number], sent from the German BfV, 'Eine befreundete Stelle teilte soeben mit', 30.09.1972, in SFA, E4320-07C, Kilowatt, 1971–1972 (translated from German by the author).
12. Kilowatt cable no. 6081, sent from Mossad, 'Ahmad Misbah Omrin', comment: 'date of information: 3 January 1973', 19.01.1973, in SFA, E4320-07C, Kilowatt, 1973.
13. *Ibid.*
14. For more background about this attack of 16 August 1972, see 'Two Attempts at Aircraft Sabotage in Rome' in Chapter 3.
15. *Ibid.*
16. Kilowatt cable no. 1064, sent from the German BfV, 'Ahmad Misbah Omrin', comment: 'VS-nur für den Dienstgebrauch', 23.01.1973, in SFA, E4320-07C, Kilowatt, 1973 (translated from German by the author).
17. Kilowatt cable no. 6143, sent from Mossad, 'Intended attacks by the PFLP-GC (Jibril) in Europe', comment: 'source reliable with access to subject', 20.09.1973, in SFA, E4320-07C, Kilowatt, 1973.
18. Kilowatt cable no. 9074, sent from the Dutch BVD, 'Ahmed Musbah al-Omrin', 12.10.1973, in SFA, E4320-07C, Kilowatt, 1973.
19. Kilowatt cable no. 6087, sent from Mossad, 'PFLP / Abdalla al-Biyafi planned attacks', comments: 'source new, reliability not yet established', 07.02.1973, in SFA, E4320-07C, Kilowatt, 1973.
20. Kilowatt cable no. 6108, sent from Mossad, 'PFLP / Abdalla al-Biyafi planned attacks', comment: 'ref our watt 6087 of 7 February 1973', 27.04.1973, in SFA, E4320-07C, Kilowatt, 1973.

21. Kilowatt cable no. 5029, sent from MI5, 'Ahmed M Makhlouf', comment: 'immediate – Sweden – confidential' [because it concerned Sweden, Swedish intelligence was included in the correspondence], 22.06.1973, in SFA, E4320-07C, Kilowatt, 1973.

22. Vargo, *Mossad: Six Landmark Missions*, 124.

23. Kilowatt cable no. 6120, sent from Mossad, 'Fatah / plan to attack the Israeli ambassador in Sweden', comment: 'source reliable with access to subject', 04.07.1973, in SFA, E4320-07C, Kilowatt, 1973.

24. *Ibid.*

25. *Ibid.*

26. *Ibid.*

27. This was a reference to the arrest in London on 24 December 1972 of an Arab suspect who was on his way to Stockholm carrying weapons; see Kilowatt cable no. 5032, sent from MI5, 'Arab terrorism operation "Kilowatt"', comment (in French): 'A l'intention de la police fédérale', 24.12.1972. This case is mentioned in Chapter 4 in the context of the thwarted attack that was planned to take place simultaneously with the Black September attack in Bangkok on 28 December 1972. See 'Attack against the Israeli Embassy in Bangkok' in Chapter 4.

28. Nadia Salti Stephan interviewed Salameh for Beirut's *Monday Morning Magazine*, 5/202, 26.04–02.05.1976.

29. Tinnin and Christensen, *The Hit Team*, 50. His wife was a direct descendant of the Grand Mufti of Jerusalem, a key figure in Palestinian history and known for his efforts to prevent Jews from immigrating to Palestine in the 1930s and 1940s.

30. Bird, *The Good Spy*, chapter 'The Red Prince'.

31. Rashid Khalidi, *The Hundred Years' War on Palestine: a History of Settler Colonialism and Resistance, 1917–2017* (New York: Picador, 2021), 176.

32. Bird, *The Good Spy*, 122.

33. Kilowatt cable no. 6039, sent from Mossad, 'Black September / Plan to hijack plane', comment: 'immediate, source reliable, sub-source reliability untested', 21.07.1972, in SFA, E4320-07C, Kilowatt, 1971–1972.

34. *Ibid.*

35. *Ibid.*

36. The collection of published Swiss foreign service documents, Dodis, has a file about Daoud Barakat, in which he and the PLO representation in Geneva vehemently deny any terrorism involvement: dodis.ch/P48577.

37. Kilowatt cable no. 1032, sent from the German BfV, 'Leiter der Organisation Schwarzer September', 25.09.1972, in SFA, E4320-07C, Kilowatt, 1971–1972 (translated from German by the author). In this cable, German intelligence explained in detail how it thought Black September operated, and Salameh's cover name, Abu Hassan, was also shared.

38. Bird, *The Good Spy*, 105. Sayigh mentions Salameh as a 'Fatah senior intelligence officer'; Sayigh, *Armed Struggle*, 224.

39. Bergman, *Rise and Kill First*, 170; Bird, *The Good Spy*, 105.
40. Sayigh, *Armed Struggle*, 307.
41. *Ibid.*
42. *Ibid.*, 311. Salameh was in charge of Arafat's personal security for years.
43. Bergman, *Rise and Kill First*, 171; Black and Morris, *Israel's Secret Wars*, 269.
44. Bergman, *Rise and Kill First*, 171.
45. For a discussion based on journalistic accounts of whether Salameh was or was not involved in the Munich massacre, see Bird, *The Good Spy*, 147–150; Klein, *Striking Back*, 186–187.
46. Kilowatt cable no. 5005, sent from MI5, 'Arab terrorist activities', comment: 'reference our watt 5004 of 1.9.72', 06.09.1972, in SFA, E4320-07C, Kilowatt, 1971–1972 (this cable was also mentioned in Chapter 1, note 22).
47. *Ibid.*
48. Kilowatt cable no. 6068, sent from Mossad, 'Nazih Hilmi al-Mubasher', comments: 'source reliable, sub-source has access to terror circles', 01.12.1972, in SFA, E4320-07C, Kilowatt, 1971–1972.
49. Klein, *Striking Back*, 160.
50. Bergman specifically mentions that Mossad had only one picture of Salameh; Bergman, *Rise and Kill First*, 172.
51. General Aharon Yariv, the former head of AMAN who at the time was Golda Meir's adviser on counterterrorism, in an interview with the BBC on 23 November 1993. The *Washington Post* published this interview the next day: Hoffman, 'Israeli Confirms Assassination of Munich Massacre Plotters'.
52. Klein, *Striking Back*, 160.
53. Kilowatt cable no. 5005, sent from MI5, 'Arab terrorist activities', comment: 'reference our watt 5004 of 1.9.72', 06.09.1972, in SFA, E4320-07C, Kilowatt, 1971–1972 (this cable was also mentioned in Chapter 1, note 22, and above, note 46).
54. Bergman, *Rise and Kill First*, 171.
55. Bergman, *Rise and Kill First*, 175; Raviv and Melman, *Every Spy a Prince*, 190. Klein and Vargo mention that the car was suspicious because it raced out of Lillehammer, not because a witness noted the licence plate number: Klein, *Striking Back*, 165; Vargo, *Mossad: Six Landmark Missions*, 127. Reeve suggests that it was an observant rental agent who became suspicious and quietly called the police; Reeve, *One Day in September*, 196.
56. Klein, *Striking Back*, 165.
57. Bergman, *Rise and Kill First*, 175.
58. Klein, *Striking Back*, 167.
59. Bergman, *Rise and Kill First*, 175.
60. Reeve, *One Day in September*, 197.
61. Raviv and Melman, *Every Spy a Prince*, 190.
62. Bergman, *Rise and Kill First*, 175; Raviv and Melman, *Every Spy a Prince*, 190.
63. Vargo, *Mossad: Six Landmark Missions*, 127; Burton and Bruning, *Chasing Shadows*, 177.

64. Raviv and Melman, *Every Spy a Prince*, 190.
65. Vargo, *Mossad: Six Landmark Missions*, 128.
66. Raviv and Melman, *Every Spy a Prince*, 192.
67. Burton and Bruning, *Chasing Shadows*, 178.
68. Vargo, *Mossad: Six Landmark Missions*, 127.
69. Klein, *Striking Back*, 168.
70. Bergman, *Rise and Kill First*, 175, who cites a report by a Foreign Ministry official, Eliezer Palmor: *The Lillehammer Affair* (Jerusalem: Carmel, 2000).
71. Raviv and Melman, *Every Spy a Prince*, 191; Reeve, *One Day in September*, 197.
72. Raviv and Melman, *Every Spy a Prince*, 191.
73. Reeve, *One Day in September*, 194. For more detail about this warning, see 'Terrorist Tactics and Innovation' in Chapter 4.
74. 'The Skyjackers Strike Again', *Time Magazine*, 30.07.1973.
75. 'Ex-Red Army Member Maruoka Dies', *Japan Times*, 30.05.2011.
76. Kilowatt cable no. 9054, sent from the Dutch BVD, 'Terrorists. List with Japanese names received from American friends on 19-7-73', 20.07.1973, in SFA, E4320-07C, Kilowatt, 1973.
77. Kilowatt cable no. 9057, sent from the Dutch BVD, 'Terrorism and Japanese in connection with hijacking of JL 404 on 20-07-73', 21.07.1973, in SFA, E4320-07C, Kilowatt, 1973.
78. *Ibid.*
79. *Ibid.* There is no secondary literature about this incident and the media at the time did not publish the names of the hijackers. We do not know today whether or not Ito Kyochi was among the hijackers.
80. *Ibid.*
81. Kilowatt cable no. 7091, sent from the Italian SISDE, 'Terrorists', comment: 'ref Watt 0954 of today', 20.07.1973, in SFA, E4320-07C, Kilowatt, 1973.
82. Kilowatt cable no. 6127, sent from Mossad, 'Terrorism and Japanese [*sic*] in connection with hijacking of JL404', 24.07.1973, in SFA, E4320-07C, Kilowatt, 1973.
83. Kilowatt cable no. 6125, sent from Mossad, 'Possibility of more terrorist hijacking or sabotage operations', 23.07.1973, in SFA, E4320-07C, Kilowatt, 1973 [hereafter cited as 'Mossad cable no. 6125'].
84. For an account of Skyjack Sunday and the ensuing negotiations, see Aviva Guttmann, 'Une coalition antiterroriste sous l'égide d'un pays neutre: la réponse suisse face au terrorisme palestinien, 1969–1970', *Relations Internationales*, 163/3 (2015), 95–110.
85. Mossad cable no. 6125.
86. The cable referred to Kilowatt cable no. 6098, sent from Mossad, 'Terrorists/ New possibility of smuggling weapons aboard planes', 19.03.1973, in SFA, E4320-07C, Kilowatt, 1973. See 'Terrorist Tactics and Innovation' in Chapter 5, note 199.
87. Kilowatt cable no. 6128, sent from Mossad, 'Possibility of more terrorist hijacking or sabotage operations', 24.07.1973, in SFA, E4320-07C, Kilowatt, 1973.

88. Kilowatt cable no. 4035, sent from the French DST, [no title], comment: 'confidentiel, priorité absolue', 24.07.1973, in SFA, E4320-07C, Kilowatt, 1973 (translated from French by the author).

89. *Ibid.*

90. Kilowatt cable no. 4037, sent from the French DST, 'Détournement d'un avion de la Japan Air Lines (JAL)', comment: 'confidentiel, priorité absolue', 24.07.1973, in SFA, E4320-07C, Kilowatt, 1973 (translated from French by the author).

91. *Ibid.*

92. *Ibid.*

93. The following cables were sent via Kilowatt when the agencies tried to find out the locations of the perpetrators prior to the hijacking: Kilowatt cable no. 4038, sent from the French DST, 'Terrorisme japonais en relation avec le détournement du vol JAL 404 du 20 juillet 1973', comment: 'confidentiel, priorité absolue', 24.07.1973 (translated from French by the author); Kilowatt cable no. 9063, sent from the Dutch BVD, 'Japanese terrorism', 26.07.1973; Kilowatt cable no. 7095, sent from the Italian SISDE, 'Japanese terrorism', 25.07.1973; Kilowatt cable no. 4039, sent from the French DST, 'Terrorisme japonais en relation avec le détournement du vol JAL 404 du 20 juillet 1973', comment: 'confidentiel, priorité absolue', 25.07.1973 (translated from French by the author); Kilowatt cable no. 4041, sent from the French DST, 'Terrorisme japonais', comment: 'confidentiel, priorité absolue', 27.07.1973 (translated from French by the author); all in SFA, E4320-07C, Kilowatt, 1973.

94. Kilowatt cable no. 9067, sent from the Dutch BVD, 'Japanese terrorism', 03.08.1973, in SFA, E4320-07C, Kilowatt, 1973.

95. Kilowatt cable no. 6129, sent from Mossad, 'Hijacking of JAL airplane', 25.07.1973, in SFA, E4320-07C, Kilowatt, 1973.

96. *Ibid.*

97. Kilowatt cable no. 4042, sent from the French DST, 'Détournement d'un avion de la Japan Air Lines (JAL)', comment: 'confidentiel, urgent', 27.07.1973, in SFA, E4320-07C, Kilowatt, 1973 (translated from French by the author).

98. *Ibid.*

99. Kilowatt cable no. 4043, sent from the French DST, 'Détournement d'un avion de la Japan Air Lines (JAL)', comment: 'confidentiel, très urgent', 30.07.1973, in SFA, E4320-07C, Kilowatt, 1973 (translated from French by the author).

100. Kilowatt cable no. 4044, sent from the French DST, 'Terrorisme japonais', comment: 'confidentiel, très urgent', 30.07.1973, in SFA, E4320-07C, Kilowatt, 1973 (translated from French by the author).

101. Kilowatt cable no. 4045, sent from the French DST, 'Terrorisme japonais', comment: 'confidentiel, urgent', 01.08.1973, in SFA, E4320-07C, Kilowatt, 1973 (translated from French by the author).

102. Kilowatt cable no. 9053, sent from the Dutch BVD, 'Mohamed Bellabiod, born 22-11-1951 in Jerusalem', 16.07.1973, in SFA, E4320-07C, Kilowatt, 1973.

103. *Ibid.*

104. Kilowatt cable no. 9064, sent from the Dutch BVD, 'Bellabiod – rectified personal details, born 22-11-51 in El Harrach (Algeria), Algerian nationality', 27.07.1973, in SFA, E4320-07C, Kilowatt, 1973.

105. *Ibid.*

106. Kilowatt cable no. 1106, sent from the German BfV, 'Bellabiod Mohamed, geb. 22.11.51, in El Harrach / Alg, Alias: Ahmed Taalibi, geb. 25.1.1949 in Sale', 02.08.1973, in SFA, E4320-07C, Kilowatt, 1973 (translated from German by the author).

107. Kilowatt cable no. 9065, sent from the Dutch BVD, 'Bellabiod Mohamed', comment: 'Immediate, urgent', 27.07.1973, in SFA, E4320-07C, Kilowatt, 1973.

108. *Ibid.*

109. See 'Libyan Support for Black September Attacks' in Chapter 5.

110. Kilowatt cable no. 6123, sent from Mossad, 'Libya intends hiring local organisations for acts of terror', 18.07.1973, in SFA, E4320-07C, Kilowatt, 1973.

111. For an analysis of Club de Berne cooperation regarding Libyan state-sponsored terrorism before and after Lillehammer, see Guttmann, 'Turning Oil into Blood'.

112. See first paragraph and 'Identifying the Organisers and Accomplices of the Munich Massacre' in Chapter 2.

113. Kilowatt cable no. 5037, sent from MI5, 'Yousef Issa al-Bandak', comment: 'immediate, secret', 11.07.1973, in SFA, E4320-07C, Kilowatt, 1973.

114. Kilowatt cable no. 5038, sent from MI5, 'Bandak', comment: 'routine (BfV Germany – priority), secret', 17.07.1973, in SFA, E4320-07C, Kilowatt, 1973.

115. Kilowatt cable no. 5039, sent from MI5, 'Yousef al Bandak', comment: 'priority, secret', 18.07.1973, in SFA, E4320-07C, Kilowatt, 1973.

116. Kilowatt cable no. 1104, sent from the German BfV, 'Issa Yousef el Bandak, geb. 20.7.1924 in Bethlehem', comment: 'VS-vertraulich, amtlich geheimhalten', 24.07.1973, in SFA, E4320-07C, Kilowatt, 1973 (translated from German by the author).

117. *Ibid.*

118. Kilowatt cable no. 7097, sent from the Italian SISDE, 'Yousef al Bandak', 02.08.1973, in SFA, E4320-07C, Kilowatt, 1973.

119. *Ibid.*

120. Kilowatt cable no. 1113, sent from the German BfV, 'Issa Yousef el Bandak, geb. 20.7.1924 in Bethlehem', comment: 'VS-vertraulich, amtlich geheimhalten', 29.08.1973, in SFA, E4320-07C, Kilowatt, 1973 (translated from German by the author).

121. Kilowatt cable no. 1119, sent from the German BfV, 'Issa Yousef el Bandak, geb. 20.7.1924 in Bethlehem', comment: 'VS-vertraulich, amtlich geheimhalten', 21.09.1973; Kilowatt cable no. 1125, sent from the German BfV, 'Issa Yousef el Bandak, geb. 20.7.1924 in Bethlehem', comment: 'VS-vertraulich,

amtlich geheimhalten', 09.10.1973; both in SFA, E4320-07C, Kilowatt, 1973 (translated from German by the author).

122. Kilowatt cable no. 5013, sent from MI5, 'Letter bombs', comment: 'routine, secret', 03.04.1973, in SFA, E4320-07C, Kilowatt, 1973.

123. *Ibid.*

124. Kilowatt cable no. 5032, sent from MI5, 'Arab terrorist letter bombs', comment: 'routine, secret', 05.07.1973, in SFA, E4320-07C, Kilowatt, 1973.

125. Kilowatt cable no. 6132, sent from Mossad, 'Terrorists / letter bombs', 01.08.1973, in SFA, E4320-07C, Kilowatt, 1973.

126. *Ibid.*

127. *Ibid.*

128. Kilowatt cable no. 4049, sent from the French DST, 'Demande de renseignement sur le ressortissant irakien [MR]', comment: 'confidentiel, normal', 25.09.1973, in SFA, E4320-07C, Kilowatt, 1973 (translated from French by the author).

129. Letter from Dr Amstein to the General Secretary of the Federal Department of Justice and Police, Berne, 07.10.1981, in SFA, E4001E#1985/152#348*, *Terrorismus: Zusammenarbeit mit dem Ausland*, 1972–1982.

130. While this volume cannot discuss Club de Berne cooperation in detail over a decade, it can point to where in the archive one can find the documents attesting to the continuation of Club de Berne and Kilowatt intelligence-sharing throughout the 1970s. See SFA, E4320-07C#1994/349#806*, *Eingang* KILOWATT, 1971–1972 [this archive record was herein referred to as SFA, E4320-07C, Kilowatt, 1971–1972]; the same archival reference continues from Kilowatt 1973 to Kilowatt 1977.

CONCLUSION: A SECRET SECURITY ORDER

1. For *Le Monde* articles published after the assassination of Hamshari, see 'Le FPLP dénonce la complicité: des autorités françaises', *Le Monde*, 09.04.1973; 'Les services secrets israéliens sont-ils responsables de l'attentat commis à Paris contre M. Hamchari? La fin du "no man's land" français', *Le Monde*, 23.12.1972. For Boudia, see 'M. Boudia, militant de la cause palestinienne est tué par l'explosion de sa voiture', *Le Monde*, 29.06.1973.

2. See Nouzille, *Les tueurs de la République*; Puyvelde, 'French Paramilitary Actions during the Algerian War of Independence'.

3. See Cormac, *Disrupt and Deny*.

4. See Niccolò Petrelli, 'Through a Glass, Darkly: US–Italian Intelligence Cooperation, Covert Operations and the *Gladio* "Stay-Behind" Programme', *Diplomacy and Statecraft*, 35/1 (2024), 148–181.

5. This definition is taken from Scott, 'Secret Intelligence, Covert Action and Clandestine Diplomacy', 330.

6. Amos, *Palestinian Resistance*, 228; Chamberlin, *The Global Offensive*, 258.

7. Pearlman, *Palestinian National Movement*, 78–82.

8. Mark Ensalaco, *Middle Eastern Terrorism: From Black September to September 11* (Philadelphia: University of Pennsylvania Press, 2012), 71. See also Albert Parry, *Terrorism: From Robespierre to the Weather Underground* (Mineola, N.Y.: Dover, 2013), 463.

9. For a discussion about the difficulty of measuring the impact of a covert action, see Cormac, Walton, and van Puyvelde, 'What Constitutes Successful Covert Action?'.

10. Ostrovsky and Hoy, *By Way of Deception*, 197.

11. For arguments that Operation Wrath of God consumed too many (unnecessary) resources, see Black and Morris, *Israel's Secret Wars*, 280; Raviv and Melman, *Every Spy a Prince*, 192.

12. Kilowatt cable no. 5027, sent from MI5, [no title], comment: 'priority – secret', 12.12.1972, in SFA, E4320-07C, Kilowatt, 1971–1972.

13. Bergman, *Rise and Kill First*, 151; Christopher Dobson claims that Black September had its headquarters in Rome; Dobson, *Black September*, 136.

14. Bergman, *Rise and Kill First*, 151.

15. For one of the first most comprehensive overviews of post-9/11 European counterterrorism, see Javier Argomanz, Oldrich Bures, and Christian Kaunert, 'A Decade of EU Counter-Terrorism and Intelligence: a Critical Assessment', *Intelligence and National Security*, 30/2–3 (2015), 191–206.

16. For European examples of such alleged 'deals' with terrorist groups, see Hänni, Riegler, and Gasztold, *Terrorism in the Cold War*.

17. Kim Willsher, 'Ex-French Spy Chief Admits 1980s Pact with Palestinian Terrorists', *Guardian*, 09.08.2018. Furthermore, as mentioned in Chapter 4, Mahmoud al-Hamshari was believed to have negotiated such a deal with French authorities.

18. This alleged deal was called the 'Lodo Moro'; see Lomellini, *Il Lodo Moro*.

19. Klein, *Striking Back*, 153.

20. *Ibid.*

21. Jirát and Naegeli, 'Der geheime Club der geheimen Dienste'.

Bibliography

PRIMARY SOURCES

UNPUBLISHED PRIMARY SOURCES

Archival records from the Swiss Federal Archives (SFA) ['Schweizerisches Bundesarchiv'] in Berne about the Club de Berne general background and intelligence cooperation:

SFA, E4001E#1985/152#345*, *Terrorismus: Verschiedenes*, 1972–1982

SFA, E4001E#1985/152#348*, *Terrorismus: Zusammenarbeit mit dem Ausland*, 1972–1982

SFA, E4320C#1994/77#479*, *Terrorismus / BERNER KLUB / (5)39/5*, 1978–1989

SFA records about Kilowatt intelligence-sharing:

SFA, E4320-07C#1994/349#806*, *Eingang* KILOWATT, 1971–1972 [cited as 'SFA, E4320-07C, Kilowatt, 1971–1972']. This archival material has now been digitised and is also available online: www.recherche.bar.admin.ch/recherche/#/de/archiv/einheit/5100020.

SFA, E4320-07C#1994/349#806*, *Eingang* KILOWATT, 1973 [cited as 'SFA, E4320-07C, Kilowatt, 1973']. This archival material has now been digitised and is also available online: www.recherche.bar.admin.ch/recherche/#/de/archiv/einheit/5100021?q=Kilowatt.

SFA, E4320-07C#1994/349#812*, *Ausgang* KILOWATT, 1971–1977 [cited as 'SFA, E4320-07C, Kilowatt *Sent by Switzerland*, 1971–1977']

United States National Archives:

Access to Archival Databases (AAD), Series: Central Foreign Policy Files, created 7/1/1973–12/31/1979, documenting the period ca. 1973–12/31/1979 – Record Group 5

The criminal records of Ahmed Bouchiki's murder case and the transcript of the judgment can be consulted at:

Eidsivating Criminal Court in Norway, case number 182/1973, 01.02.1974

PUBLISHED PRIMARY SOURCES

Akten zur Auswärtigen Politik der Bundesrepublik Deutschland 1972 (Munich: Oldenbourg, 2003), https://doi.org/10.1524/9783486718157.

Diplomatic Documents of Switzerland: http://dodis.ch. Dossiers mentioned:

Würenlingen attack 1970: dodis.ch/T1389
Report about Palestinian terrorism in Geneva, Vienna, and Paris: dodis. ch/39519 [this report was referred to as 'BuPo Schönau report']
The establishment of the PLO office in Geneva: dodis.ch/P48577
Daoud Barakat: dodis.ch/P48577

Israel State Archives, *The Fortieth Anniversary of the Massacre of the Israeli Athletes in Munich*, 'Aftermath: hijacking of a Lufthansa plane and the release of the Munich terrorists cause outrage in Israel'; https://catalog.archives.gov.il/en/chapter/aftermath-hijacking-lufthansa-plane-release-munich-terrorists-lead-outrage-israel/

MEMOIRS

Brandt, Willy. *People and Politics* (Boston: Little, Brown and Company, 1978).
Iyad, Abu and Eric Rouleau. *My Home, My Land: a Narrative of the Palestinian Struggle* (New York: Times Books, 1981).
Kreisky, Bruno, Oliver Rathkolb, Johannes Kunz, and Margit Schmidt. *Im Strom der Politik: der Memoiren zweiter Teil* (Vienna: Kremayr and Scheriau, 2000).
Meir, Golda. *My Life* (New York: G. P. Putnam's Sons, 1975).

SECONDARY SOURCES

BOOKS

Amos, John W. *Palestinian Resistance: Organization of a Nationalist Movement* (New York: Pergamon, 1980).
Bar-Zohar, Michael and Eitan Haber. *Massacre in Munich: the Manhunt for the Killers behind the 1972 Olympics Massacre* (Guilford, Conn.: Lyons, 2005).
Bar-Zohar, Michael and Nissim Mishal. *Mossad: the Greatest Missions of the Israeli Secret Service* (Hopewell, N.J.: Ecco, 2014).
Ben-Rafael, Eliezer. *Israel–Palestine: a Guerrilla Conflict in International Politics* (Westport: Greenwood, 1987).
Bergman, Ronen. *Rise and Kill First: the Secret History of Israel's Targeted Assassinations* (New York: Random House, 2019).
Bird, Kai, *The Good Spy: the Life and Death of Robert Ames* (New York: Crown, 2014).
Black, Ian and Benny Morris. *Israel's Secret Wars: a History of Israel's Intelligence Services* (New York: Grove, 1991).

Blumenau, Bernhard. *The United Nations and Terrorism: Germany, Multilateralism, and Antiterrorism Efforts in the 1970s* (Basingstoke: Palgrave Macmillan, 2014).

Burton, Fred and John Bruning. *Chasing Shadows: a Special Agent's Lifelong Hunt to Bring a Cold War Assassin to Justice* (New York: Palgrave Macmillan, 2011).

Carlton, David. *The West's Road to 9/11: Resisting, Appeasing and Encouraging Terrorism since 1970* (London: Palgrave Macmillan, 2014).

Chamberlin, Paul Thomas. *The Global Offensive: the United States, the Palestine Liberation Organization, and the Making of the Post-Cold War Order* (Oxford University Press, 2012).

Chard, Daniel S. *Nixon's War at Home: the FBI, Leftist Guerrillas, and the Origins of Counterterrorism* (Chapel Hill: University of North Carolina Press, 2021).

Cline, Ray S. and Yonah Alexander. *Terrorism: the Soviet Connection* (New York: Crane Russak, 1986).

Cobban, Helena. *The Palestinian Liberation Organisation: People, Power, and Politics* (Cambridge University Press, 1984).

Cooley, John Kent. *Green March, Black September: the Story of the Palestinian Arabs* (London: Frank Cass, 1973).

Cormac, Rory. *Disrupt and Deny: Spies, Special Forces, and the Secret Pursuit of British Foreign Policy* (Oxford University Press, 2021).

Dahlke, Matthias. *Demokratischer Staat und transnationaler Terrorismus Drei Wege zur Unnachgiebigkeit in Westeuropa 1972–1975* (Munich: Oldenbourg, 2011).

De Vita, Lorena. *Israelpolitik: German–Israeli Relations, 1949–69* (Manchester University Press, 2020).

Dobson, Christopher. *Black September: Its Short, Violent History* (London: Hale, 1975).

Dolnik, Adam. *Understanding Terrorist Innovation: Technology, Tactics and Global Trends* (New York: Routledge, 2007).

Ensalaco, Mark. *Middle Eastern Terrorism: From Black September to September 11* (Philadelphia: University of Pennsylvania Press, 2012).

Fink, Carole. *West Germany and Israel: Foreign Relations, Domestic Politics, and the Cold War, 1965–1974* (Cambridge University Press, 2019).

Golan, Galia. *The Soviet Union and the Palestine Liberation Organization: an Uneasy Alliance* (New York: Praeger, 1980).

Goren, Roberta. *The Soviet Union and Terrorism* (London: George Allen and Unwin, 1984).

Guttmann, Aviva. *The Origins of International Counterterrorism: Switzerland at the Forefront of Crisis Negotiations, Multilateral Diplomacy, and Intelligence Cooperation (1969–1977)* (Leiden: Brill, 2018).

Halabi, Rafik. *The West Bank Story* (New York: Harcourt, 1981).

Hänni, Adrian, Thomas Riegler, and Przemysław Gasztold, eds., *Terrorism in the Cold War*, 2 vols. (London: I. B. Tauris, 2020–2021).

Herf, Jeffrey. *Undeclared Wars with Israel: East Germany and the West German Far Left, 1967–1989* (Cambridge University Press, 2016).

Herman, Michael. *Intelligence Power in Peace and War* (Cambridge University Press, 1996).

Hoffman, Bruce. *Inside Terrorism* (New York: Columbia University Press, 2006).

Hughes-Wilson, John. *Intelligence Blunders* (London: Carroll and Graf, 1999).

Jonas, George. *Vengeance: the True Story of an Israeli Counter-terrorist Team* (Toronto, HarperCollins, 1984).

Kellerhoff, Sven Felix. *Anschlag auf Olympia: Was 1972 in München wirklich geschah* (Darmstadt: Wissenschaftliche Buchgesellschaft, 2022).

Khalidi, Rashid. *The Hundred Years' War on Palestine: a History of Settler Colonialism and Resistance, 1917–2017* (New York: Picador, 2021).

Kimmerling, Baruch and Joel S. Migdal. *The Palestinian People: a History* (Cambridge, Mass.: Harvard University Press, 2003).

Klein, Aaron J. *Striking Back: the 1972 Munich Olympics Massacre and Israel's Deadly Response* (New York: Random House, 2005).

Kreutner, Jonathan. *Die Schweiz und Israel: Auf dem Weg zu einem differenzierten historischen Bewusstsein* (Zurich: Chronos, 2013).

Kriechbaumer, Robert. *Die Ära Kreisky: Österreich 1970–1983 in der historischen Analyse, im Urteil der politischen Kontrahenten und in Karikaturen von Ironimus* (Vienna: Böhlau, 2004).

Lachs, Samuel Tobias. *Humanism in Talmud and Midrash* (Rutherford: Fairleigh Dickinson University Press, 1993).

Lange, Brenda. *Muammar Qaddafi* (Philadelphia: Chelsea House, 2005).

Large, David Clay. *Munich 1972: Tragedy, Terror and Triumph at the Olympic Games* (New York: Rowman and Littlefield, 2012).

Law, Randall David. *Terrorism: a History* (Cambridge: Polity Press, 2018).

Leahy, Thomas. *The Intelligence War against the IRA* (Cambridge University Press, 2020).

Lomellini, Valentine. *Il Lodo Moro. Terrorismo e ragion di Stato, 1969–1986 [The Moro Agreement. Terrorism and Raison d'État]* (Bari: Laterza, 2022).

McSherry, J. Patrice. *Predatory States: Operation Condor and Covert War in Latin America* (New York: Rowman and Littlefield, 2005).

Maeke, Lutz. *DDR und PLO: Die Palästinapolitik des SED-Staates* (Berlin: De Gruyter, 2017).

Merari, Ariel and Shlomi Elad. *International Dimension of Palestinian Terrorism* (New York: Routledge, 2021; first edition 1988).

Morris, Benni. *Righteous Victims: a History of the Zionist–Arab Conflict, 1881–2001* (New York: Vintage, 2001).

Naftali, Timothy and Aleksandr Fursenko. *'One Hell of a Gamble': Khrushchev, Castro, Kennedy and the Cuban Missile Crisis, 1958–1964* (London: Norton, 1997).

Nouzille, Vincent. *Les tueurs de la République: Assassinats et opérations spéciales des services secrets* (Paris: Fayard, 2016).

O'Rourke, Lindsey A. *Covert Regime Change: America's Secret Cold War* (Ithaca: Cornell University Press, 2018).

Ostrovsky, Victor and Claire Hoy. *By Way of Deception: the Making and Unmaking of a Mossad Officer* (New York: St Martin's, 1991).

Palmor, Eliezer. *The Lillehammer Affair* (Israel: Carmel, 2000).

Parry, Albert. *Terrorism: From Robespierre to the Weather Underground* (Mineola, N.Y.: Dover, 2013).

Pearlman, Wendy. *Violence, Nonviolence, and the Palestinian National Movement* (Cambridge University Press, 2014).

Powell, Nathaniel K. *France's Wars in Chad: Military Intervention and Decolonization in Africa* (Cambridge University Press, 2021).

Poznansky, Michael. *In the Shadow of International Law: Secrecy and Regime Change in the Postwar World* (Oxford University Press, 2020).

Raviv, Dan and Yossi Melman. *Every Spy a Prince: the Complete History of Israel's Intelligence Community* (Boston: Houghton Mifflin, 1990).

Reeve, Simon. *One Day in September: the Full Story of the 1972 Munich Olympics Massacre and the Israeli Revenge Operation 'Wrath of God'* (New York: Skyhorse, 2011).

Sayigh, Yazid. *Armed Struggle and the Search for State: the Palestinian National Movement, 1949–1993* (Oxford University Press, 2011).

Schiller, Kay and Christopher Young. *The 1972 Munich Olympics and the Making of Modern Germany* (Berkeley: University of California Press, 2010).

Schmid, Alex P. and Janny de Graaf. *Violence as Communication: Insurgent Terrorism and the Western News Media* (London: Sage, 1983).

Seale, Patrick. *Abu Nidal: a Gun for Hire. The Secret Life of the World's Most Notorious Terrorist* (New York: Random House, 1992).

Smith, Michael. *New Cloak, Old Dagger: How Britain's Spies Came in from the Cold* (London: Indigo, 1996).

Taylor, Peter. *Brits: the War against the IRA* (London: Bloomsbury, 2001).

States of Terror: Democracy and Political Violence (London: Penguin, 1994).

Telepneva, Natalia. *Cold War Liberation: the Soviet Union and the Collapse of the Portuguese Empire in Africa, 1961–1975* (Chapel Hill: University of North Carolina Press, 2022).

Tinnin, David B. and Dag Christensen. *The Hit Team* (New York: Dell, 1977).

Vargo, Marc E. *Mossad: Six Landmark Missions of the Israeli Intelligence Agency, 1960–1990* (Jefferson, N.C.: McFarland, 2015).

Veilleux-Lepage, Yannick. *How Terror Evolves: the Emergence and Spread of Terrorist Techniques* (Lanham, M.D.: Rowman and Littlefield, 2020).

Walsh, James Igoe. *The International Politics of Intelligence Sharing* (New York: Columbia University Press, 2012).

BOOK CHAPTERS

Daugherty, William J. 'Covert Action: Strengths and Weakness', in *The Oxford Handbook of National Security Intelligence*, edited by Loch K. Johnson (Oxford University Press, 2010), 608–628.

Rezk, Dina. 'Yom Kippur War', in Dina Rezk, *The Arab World and Western Intelligence: Analysing the Middle East, 1956–1981* (Edinburgh University Press, 2017), 249–283.

Skelton-Robinson, Thomas. 'Im Netz verheddert. Die Beziehungen des bundes-deutschen Linksterrorismus zur Volksfront für die Befreiung Palästinas (1969–1980)', in *Die RAF und der linke Terrorismus*, vol. II, edited by Wolfgang Kraushaar (Hamburg: Hamburger Edition, 2006), 828–904.

JOURNAL ARTICLES

Argomanz, Javier, Oldrich Bures, and Christian Kaunert. 'A Decade of EU Counter-terrorism and Intelligence: a Critical Assessment', *Intelligence and National Security*, 30/2–3 (2015), 191–206.

Bachleitner, Kathrin. 'Golda Meir and Bruno Kreisky: a Political and Personal Duel', *Israel Studies*, 23/1 (Spring 2018), 26–49.

Bar-Joseph, Uri and Arie W. Kruglanski. 'Intelligence Failure and Need for Cognitive Closure: On the Psychology of the Yom Kippur Surprise', *Political Psychology*, 24/1 (2003).

Bigo, Didier. 'Shared Secrecy in a Digital Age and a Transnational World', *Intelligence and National Security*, 34/3 (2019), 379–394.

Bülow, Mathilde von. 'Franco-German Intelligence Cooperation and the Internationalization of Algeria's War of Independence (1954–62)', *Intelligence and National Security*, 28/3 (2013), 397–419.

Bures, Oldrich. 'Informal Counterterrorism Arrangements in Europe: Beauty by Variety or Duplicity by Abundance?', *Cooperation and Conflict*, 47/4 (2012), 495–518.

Canuel, Hugues. 'French Aspirations and Anglo-Saxon Suspicions: France, Signals Intelligence and the UK–USA Agreement at the Dawn of the Cold War', *Journal of Intelligence History*, 12/1 (2013), 76–92.

Chamberlin, Paul Thomas. 'Schönau and the Eagles of the Palestinian Revolution: Refugees, Guerillas, and Human Rights in the Global 1970s', *Cold War History*, 12/4 (2012), 595–614.

Clough, Chris. '*Quid Pro Quo*: the Challenges of International Strategic Intelligence Cooperation', *International Journal of Intelligence and CounterIntelligence*, 17/4 (2004), 601–613.

Cormac, Rory and Richard J. Aldrich. 'Grey is the New Black: Covert Action and Implausible Deniability', *International Affairs*, 94/3 (2018), 477–494.

Cormac, Rory, Calder Walton, and Damien van Puyvelde. 'What Constitutes Successful Covert Action? Evaluating Unacknowledged Interventionism in Foreign Affairs', *Review of International Studies*, 48/1 (2022), 111–128.

Gill, Paul, John Horgan, Samuel T. Hunter, and Lily D. Cushenbery. 'Malevolent Creativity in Terrorist Organizations', *Journal of Creative Behavior*, 47/2 (2013), 125–151.

Guttmann, Aviva. 'Combatting Terror in Europe: Euro-Israeli Counterterrorism Intelligence Cooperation in the Club de Berne (1971–1972)', *Intelligence and National Security*, 33/2 (2018), 158–175.

'Covert Diplomacy to Overcome a Crisis: West German and Israeli Intelligence after the Munich Olympics Attack', *Journal of Cold War Studies*, 25/4 (2023) 101–126.

'Mossad's Accomplices: How Israel Relied on Foreign Intelligence Agencies to Organise its Killing Campaigns', *English Historical Review* (in press).

'Secret Wires across the Mediterranean: the Club de Berne, Euro-Israeli Counterterrorism, and Swiss "Neutrality"', *International History Review*, 40/4 (2018), 814–833.

'Turning Oil into Blood: Western Intelligence, Libyan Covert Actions, and Palestinian Terrorism (1973–74)', *Journal for Strategic Studies*, 45/6–7 (2022), 993–1020.

'Une coalition antiterroriste sous l'égide d'un pays neutre: la réponse suisse face au terrorisme palestinien, 1969–1970', *Relations Internationales*, 163/3 (2015), 95–110.

'"We Have Successfully Neutralised an Attack": Historical Case Studies in Terrorism Prevention through Cooperation', *Terrorism and Political Violence* (2024), 1–17, https://doi.org/10.1080/09546553.2024.2400157.

Hass, Melinda and Keren Yarhi-Milo. 'To Disclose or Deceive? Sharing Secret Information between Aligned States', *International Security*, 45/3 (Winter 2020/2021), 122–161.

Hoffmann, Sophia. 'Circulation, not Cooperation: Towards a New Understanding of Intelligence Agencies as Transnationally Constituted Knowledge Providers', *Intelligence and National Security*, 36/6 (2021), 807–826.

Jacobs, Bart. 'Maximator: European Signals Intelligence Cooperation, from a Dutch Perspective', *Intelligence and National Security*, 35/5 (2020), 659–668.

Lander, Sir Stephen. 'International Intelligence Cooperation: an Inside Perspective', *Cambridge Review of International Affairs*, 17/3 (2004), 481–493.

Lazin, Fred A. 'Israel's Demographic Needs Versus "Freedom of Choice": the Case of Soviet Jewish Émigrés, 1967–1990', *Tel Aviver Jahrbuch für Deutsche Geschichte*, 35 (2007), 273–291.

Lefebvre, Stéphane. 'The Difficulties and Dilemmas of International Intelligence Cooperation', *International Journal of Intelligence and CounterIntelligence*, 16/4 (2003), 527–542.

Munton, Don and Karima Fredj. 'Sharing Secrets: a Game Theoretic Analysis of International Intelligence Cooperation', *International Journal of Intelligence and CounterIntelligence*, 26/4 (2013), 666–692.

Munton, Don and Miriam Matejova. 'Spies without Borders? Western Intelligence Liaison, the Tehran Hostage Affair and Iran's Islamic Revolution', *Intelligence and National Security*, 27/5 (2012), 739–760.

Oberloskamp, Eva. 'Das Olympia-Attentat 1972. Politische Lernprozesse im Umgang mit dem transnationalen Terrorismus', *Vierteljahrshefte für Zeitgeschichte*, 60/3 (2012), 321–352.

Occhipinti, John D. 'Still Moving toward a European FBI? Re-examining the Politics of EU Police Cooperation', *Intelligence and National Security*, 30/2 (2015), 234–258.

Petrelli, Niccolò. 'Through a Glass, Darkly: US–Italian Intelligence Cooperation, Covert Operations and the *Gladio* "Stay-Behind" Programme', *Diplomacy and Statecraft*, 35/1 (2024), 148–181.

Phelps, John T. 'Aerial Intrusions by Civil and Military Aircraft in Time of Peace', *Military Law Review*, 107 (1985), 255–303.

Puyvelde, Damien van. 'French Paramilitary Actions during the Algerian War of Independence, 1956–1958', *Intelligence and National Security*, 36/6 (2021), 898–909.

Ricardo Faria, João. 'Terrorist Innovations and Anti-Terrorist Policies', *Terrorism and Political Violence*, 18/1 (2006), 47–56.

Riegler, Thomas, 'Das "Spinnennetz" des internationalen Terrorismus. Der "Schwarze September" und die gescheiterte Geiselnahme von Schönau 1973', *Vierteljahrshefte für Zeitgeschichte* (September 2015).

Scott, Len. 'Secret Intelligence, Covert Action and Clandestine Diplomacy', *Intelligence and National Security*, 19/2 (2004), 322–341.

Sims, Jennifer E. 'Foreign Intelligence Liaison: Devils, Deals, and Details', *International Journal of Intelligence and CounterIntelligence*, 19/2 (2006), 195–217.

Tominaga, Erika. 'Japan's Middle East Policy, 1972–1974: Resources Diplomacy, Pro-American Policy, and New Left', *Diplomacy and Statecraft*, 28/4 (2017), 674–701.

Westerfield, H. Bradford. 'America and the World of Intelligence Liaison', *Intelligence and National Security*, 11/3 (1996), 523–560.

DISSERTATION

Fägersten, Björn. 'Sharing Secrets: Explaining International Intelligence Cooperation' (dissertation, Department of Political Science, Lund University, 2010).

NEWSPAPER ARTICLES

'A Band of Arab Guerrillas Attacks Israelis on Cyprus', *New York Times*, 10.04.1973.

'Arabs Hijack German Airliner and Gain Release of 3 Seized in Munich Killings', *New York Times*, 30.10.1972.

'Arabs Kill 3 and Wound 55 in Athens Airport Lounge', *New York Times*, 06.08.1973.

Burke, Jason. 'Bonn "faked" hijack to free killers', *Observer*, 26.03.2000.

'Ex-Red Army Member Maruoka Dies', *Japan Times*, 30.05.2011.

Freihofer, Gerald. 'Kreisky und die PLO', *Wochenpresse*, no. 29, 1979.

'Guerrillas' Bravado Breaks at the End', *New York Times*, 05.03.1973.

Gwertzman, Bernard. 'Israeli Attache Shot Dead at Home near Washington', *New York Times*, 02.07.1973.

'Herr, öffne das Herz Österreichs', *Der Spiegel*, 41, 08.10.1973.

'Hijacked Plane Lands in Havana a Second Time, 31 Hostages Free; 3 Gunmen Seized after 29 Hours', *New York Times*, 12.11.1972.

Hoffman, David. 'Israeli Confirms Assassination of Munich Massacre Plotters', *Washington Post*, 24.11.1993.

Hofmann, Paul. 'El Al Employee in Rome is Shot to Death by an Arab', *New York Times*, 28.04.1973.

'Mrs Meir to Visit Pope in First Such Call by an Israeli Premier', *New York Times*, 15.01.1973.

'Israel Says that Man Slain in Madrid Was an Agent', *New York Times*, 31.01.1973.

Jirát, Jan and Lorenz Naegeli. 'Der geheime Club der geheimen Dienste', *Wochenzeitung*, 05.03.2020 (translation into English: 'The Club de Berne: a Black Box of Growing Intelligence Cooperation', by the independent think-tank about:intel, 01.04.2020, https://aboutintel.eu/the-club-de-berne/).

'La militante de Septembre noir expulsée de France serait liée aux services de renseignement britanniques', *Le Monde*, 24.03.1973.

'Le FPLP dénonce la complicité: des autorités françaises', *Le Monde*, 09.04.1973.

'Les Assassinats politiques en France depuis 1972', *Le Monde*, 21.12.1974.

'Les services secrets israéliens sont-ils responsables de l'attentat commis à Paris contre M. Hamchari? La fin du "no man's land" français', *Le Monde*, 23.12.1972.

'M. Boudia, militant de la cause palestinienne est tué par l'explosion de sa voiture', *Le Monde*, 29.06.1973.

Marcus, Yoel. *Haaretz*, 10.06.1986.

Melman, Yossi. 'Who Killed Joe Alon? Nearly 40 Years after the Murder of Israel's Air Attaché in Washington, the Case Remains Unsolved: a New Book Seeks to Shed More Light on the Affair', *Haaretz*, 01.04.2011.

O'Loughlin, Peter. 'Arab Terrorists Flown to Cairo after Releasing Six Hostages', *Daily Telegraph*, 30.12.1972.

Rom, Rami. 'A 49-Year-Old Cover-up', *The Times of Israel*, 01.07.2022.

Rubinstein, Amnon. 'Bonn's Disgrace', *Haaretz*, 30.10.1972; cited in Yael Greenfeter, 'Israel in Shock as Munich Killers Freed', *Haaretz*, 04.11.2010.

Salti Stephan, Nadia. interview with Salameh, *Monday Morning Magazine*, 5/202, 26.04–02.05.1976.

Sattar, Majid. 'Folgen eines Anschlags. Mit einer Flugzeugentführung preßten palästinensische Terroristen im Oktober 1972 die drei überlebenden Olympia-Attentäter frei', *Frankfurter Allgemeine Zeitung*, 09.11.2006.

Sibley, John. 'Few Arab Terrorists Are Punished for Hijackings and Killings', *New York Times*, 20.12.1973.

Smith, Terence. 'Israelis Down a Libyan Airliner in the Sinai, Killing at Least 74', *New York Times*, 22.02.1973.

Taubman, Philip. 'Book on Israeli Avenger-Spy Questioned', *New York Times*, 02.05.1984.

'Terror to End Terror?', *Time Magazine*, 23.04.1973.

'The Skyjackers Strike Again', *Time Magazine*, 30.07.1973.

'Une Françoise est impliquée dans l'attentat commis en 1972 contre un oléoduc à Trieste', *Le Monde*, 14.03.1973.

'Was the Hijacking of an Austrian Train Filled with Soviet Jews a Diversion before the Yom Kippur War?', *Israel Defence*, 18.12.2011.

Whitney, Craig R. 'Israeli Embassy in Bangkok Held by Arabs 19 Hours', *New York Times*, 29.12.1972.

Willsher, Kim. 'Ex-French Spy Chief Admits 1980s Pact with Palestinian Terrorists', *Guardian*, 09.08.2018.

Wilson, Andrew B. 'What Did Arafat Get for Killing US Diplomats?', *American Spectator*, 01.03.2013.

'Women Duped into Taking Bomb to Their El Al Flight', *New York Times*, 18.08.1972.

OTHERS

'Munich', historical drama film by Steven Spielberg, 2005.

'One Day in September', documentary film by Kevin Macdonald, 1999.

Index